W9-ALJ-810

An American Chronology

JERRY BORNSTEIN

NEAL-SCHUMAN PUBLISHERS, INC.

New York   London

Published by Neal-Schuman Publishers, Inc.
100 Varick Street
New York, NY 10013

Copyright © 2000 by Jerry Bornstein

All rights reserved. Reproduction of this book, in whole or in part, without written permission of the publisher is prohibited.

Printed and bound in the United States of America.

Library of Congress Cataloging-in-Publication Data

Bornstein, Jerry.
  An American chronology / Jerry Bornstein.
     p.   cm.
  ISBN 1-55570-369-0
    1. United States—Civilization—19th century—Chronology. 2. United
States—Civilization—20th century—Chronology. I. Title.

E169.1 .B758 2000
973—dc 21   99-056396

DEDICATION

In memory of Thelma Bornstein (1924–1996)

She raised us to hate injustice, to think independently, to stand up for what we believe in, and was proud of us when we did so.

Contents

Acknowledgments

Much thanks to Patricia Schuman, to whom I first broached the idea for this book back in 1992; to Jack Neal who made many valuable suggestions on how to sculpt and organize the material; Mike Kelley, who as a good editor kept after to me to make deadlines; to my colleagues at Baruch College who supported my efforts; and a special thanks to Wanda Dobson for her help in preparing the index. And a loving thanks to Sandy, my wife and partner, who not only tolerated my staying up late night after night pounding out the manuscript, going into the library on weekends, and making a mess all over the house with clippings—some in boxes, but many just laying in stacks—but also played devil's advocate in discussing many of the lists, made suggestions, and encouraged me always.

Preface

January 28, 1986 is burnt into my memory. I was working as a research librarian at NBC News. At 11:38 A.M., my manager was on the telephone with a producer at the news special unit discussing a research request. In the background, the producer had her television set on in the office, carrying live coverage of a routine space shuttle launch. Then—suddenly—73 seconds into the launch, routine was transformed into national trauma, and the producer exclaimed, "Oh, my God! I think the shuttle just blew up!" My boss alerted all the librarians to brace for the deluge.

Within seconds the phone rang off the hook. The news desk, the specials unit, *The Today Show*, and *The Nightly News* flooded the library with research requests. A researcher from the specials unit ferried folders of printouts and clippings down to the newsroom as quickly as we could pull them together. Requests for chronological information topped the list. They urgently needed chronologies of space shuttle missions, space exploration history, and space accidents. These chronological lists became vital; they helped locate file footage, provided context and background for stories, and gave essential material to the on-air anchors to discuss during the extended coverage.

Whether an airplane fell from the sky, an earthquake shook the San Francisco Bay area, a major flood washed out miles of farmland in the Midwest, or the courts ordered a major corporation to divest in an antitrust case, it was always the same when news broke: journalists requested chronologies. When I worked on in-house background books at NBC News—whether it was the Reagan-Gorbachev summit in 1987, the Bush Inauguration, the resumption of space shuttle missions, or the Gulf War—news directors and executive producers always asked me to assemble chronologies. When I researched and wrote the text for the *NBC News/Rand McNally World News Almanac & Atlas* (1989–1992), the chronology for each country invariably proved a popular item. This made plenty of sense. Chronologies provided a point of reference for a story, served as a point of departure for further research, put the event in context, provided a basis for comparing it to other similar events, and made the story more interesting and universal. Chronology is, after all, the way most people tell stories.

As a news librarian working under intense deadline pressures, I became painfully aware that while chronologies were everywhere, paradoxically, they were often difficult to locate. Most chronology books provide a record of every event on a year-by-year, day-by-day basis. This approach may be very useful if you want to know what happened in a specific year or month, but not much use when you need a list of major railroad accidents. Other books offer chronological records for a specific subject area. In other cases, books on specific subjects often bury chronologies in the appendices. One had to thumb through books and check the list of contents to see if it offered a chronology. There was no index of chronological sources to consult, no easy way to pinpoint where to look for the chronological information.

Like a lot of other librarians who write books, it dawned on me that it would be great to have a reference book that would address my recurring research problem: easy access to chronological information. In the late 1980s I began saving chronological clippings, wire stories, references to books that had chronologies, and so on. Finally, with the new millennium, here is the first installment to fill a chronology research gap: *An American Chronology*.

An American Chronology is unique among chronology books because it is a book of lists—chronological lists organized by subject—pulling together in one volume valuable information on American history that might otherwise be scattered throughout hundreds of pages in a general year-by-year book, or dispersed in specialized texts. Its purpose is to provide convenient access to chronological information to academics, students, and journalists, as well as general readers, in a manner that is useful, accurate, and even entertaining.

Researching this book, I became alarmed by the many errors I discovered in reputable reference books. For example, one standard work on American presidents listed Ronald Reagan's tenure as president of the Screen Actors Guild (SAG) from 1947–1952. Another source listed the dates as 1947–1960. When I double-checked this discrepancy, I discovered that Reagan served as SAG president twice: once from 1947–1952, and then again in 1959–1960. In other words, both books were inaccurate. Preparing the section on presidential inaugurations, I initially found references to the weather conditions for James Madison's 1813 inaugural day listed as "unknown" or "unavailable." For *An American Chronology*, I obtained the weather conditions by consulting news reports in the *National Intelligence* of March 6, 1813 (in those days, inaugurations were held in March, not January). Even the ready-reference lists benefited from scrutiny. One almanac had more than a half dozen errors in its list of Pulitzer Prize winners.

In order to produce the most factually accurate chronologies possible, every effort was made to resolve discrepant information. I culled information from secondary and primary sources. Each fact was verified in at least two standard reference sources. Experts in the field reviewed the manuscript.

The book is organized into seven parts and contains 119 lists:

Part One, "National Highlights," presents a year-by-year general overview of American history tracing the key events in North America from prehistory to the present. The list includes the estimated arrival of the ancestors of the Native-American population, through the European period of exploration and colonization, and the founding of the Republic. It proceeds through the Civil War, the World Wars, the Cold War, and on up to the dropping of the ball in Times Square to mark the arrival of the new millennium.

Part Two, "Forming the Nation," covers key aspects in the building of the American nation, beginning with the Constitution, and continuing on with population growth and territorial expansion. It explores key contributions from the Melting Pot (including chronologies on Native Americans, African Americans, European Americans, Jewish Americans, Hispanic Americans, Asian Americans, and Gay Americans) that make

this country the most diverse in the world. It concludes with some of the great speeches that form part of our social and cultural legacy, and the landmark Supreme Court decisions that shaped our legal system.

Part Three, "The Fifty States," provides a list of when each state was admitted to the Union and key dates in the history of every state from Alabama to Wyoming, plus Washington, D.C.

Part Four, "Politics and Presidents," starts with a chronology of major national political conventions, where those who would be president are nominated. Next, it reports on major platform fights, and political firsts for women at those conventions. It continues with a chronological list of the 42 men who have occupied the highest office in the land, followed by biographical chronologies for each president, and an inaugural chronology noting what I call "the firsts, mosts, and onlys" that made each inauguration unique. This is followed by several breakout chronological lists covering presidents who won the White House without receiving a majority of the popular vote, and those who failed to win reelection or renomination. Chronological lists of runner-ups, vice presidents, and presidential impeachments follow. It ends with an expanded chronology of political and presidential assassinations and attempted assassinations in American history.

Part Five, "The Armed Forces, Wars, and Military Interventions," chronicles key dates in the histories of American military services (Army, Navy, Marines, Coast Guard, and Air Force), the role of women in the military, and America's wars and military interventions.

Part Six, "Natural Disasters and Human-Made Accidents and Incidents," covers natural and human-made calamities. It begins with major blizzards, earthquakes, fires, floods, hurricanes and tornadoes—a reminder that for all our developments in technology, we have still not tamed Mother Nature. This part continues with human-made disasters in our history including the worst American disasters, aviation crashes, hijackings, nuclear accidents, railroad accidents, space accidents, and terrorist incidents.

Part Seven, "Notably American," covers a wide gamut of American cultural phenomena, including winners of major awards and prizes. Here you will find the winners of Pulitzer Prizes, Newbery and Caldecott Medals, the Spingarn Medal, Academy Awards, Tony Awards, Emmies, Grammies, and the Miss America pageant. This part also presents an overview of television broadcast history (a particular favorite of mine), a chronology of milestones in the space program, and concludes with major professional sports championships—baseball, basketball, football, golf, hockey, horse racing, and tennis.

It wasn't possible to include everything under the sun—perhaps that will have to wait for the sequel—but this volume will offer a point of departure for researchers. This is a book of facts. The contents of many of the lists are indisputable—only one person won a particular Pulitzer Prize or Academy Award. I culled other lists of major events from other reference sources and amalgamated the information into one list based on my own viewpoint. There are an amazing number of variations of what constitutes a list of major Supreme Court decisions. Inevitably, my own point of view, as a news junkie, a professional news librarian, and an academic, whose perspectives on life, history, and politics were shaped by the turbulent Sixties, crept into some of the selections and the way I presented them. Perhaps the reader will disagree with some of my decisions on what to include or exclude from the various lists, but history is controversial and intellectual disagreement is as American as apple pie.

—Jerry Bornstein, Baruch College,
City University of New York
January 2000

PART 1

National Highlights

PREHISTORIC TO THE PRESENT

c. 38,000–18,000 BC Ancestors of American Indians migrated from Asia across the Bering Strait land bridge.

c. 10,000 BC Receding glaciers permitted southward migration from Alaska into continental North America.

c. 1000 AD Norseman Leif Ericson explored North American coast, founded Vinland, a temporary colony. Old Orabi, the oldest permanently occupied town established in what is now a Hopi reservation in Arizona.

1492 Christopher Columbus, in search of a sea route from Europe to the Far East, landed on the island of San Salvador in the Caribbean.

1497 Explorer John Cabot claimed Newfoundland for England.

1513 Spaniard Ponce de Leon explored Florida, searching for the Fountain of Youth. Vasco Nunez de Balboa explored Isthmus of Panama for Spain; sighted Pacific Ocean.

1519–1521 Hernando Cortez conquered Aztec empire in Mexico for Spain.

1519–1521 Ferdinand Magellan led first expedition to sail around the world. Magellan was killed in the Philippines; 18 crew members completed the voyage in 1522.

1524 Giovanni de Verrazano explored New York Harbor and the Hudson River for France.

1534 Frenchman Jacques Cartier explored the Gulf of St. Lawrence.

1539 Fernando de Soto conquered Florida; began exploration of southeast U.S. for Spain.

1540 Spanish explorer Francisco Coronado explored southwest North America, discovered the Grand Canyon.

1565 First permanent European colony in North America settled by Spain at St. Augustine, Florida.

1585 Sir Walter Raleigh founded first English colony in North America at what is now Roanoke Island, Virginia.

1586 Roanoke Island colonists evacuated.

1587 Roanoke Colony reestablished. Virginia Dare the first child born to English parents in America.

1591 Roanoke colonists mysteriously disappeared.

1607 Jamestown, Virginia, became the first permanent English settlement in America.

1609 Henry Hudson claimed parts of New York, New Jersey, Delaware, and Connecticut for the Netherlands.

1619 First African slaves in the English colonies arrived at Jamestown. Virginia House of Burgesses first representative legislature in New World.

1620 Pilgrims landed at Plymouth; drew up the Mayflower Compact.

1624 Dutch founded colony of New Netherlands.

1626 Dutch founded New Amsterdam on island of Manhattan.

1630 Boston founded by Puritans.

1635 Roger Williams founded colony at Providence, Rhode Island.

1636 Harvard College established, first institution of higher learning in the colonies.

1638 Sweden began colonization of Delaware (New Sweden).

1647 Massachusetts organized first public school system in the colonies.

1649 Maryland enacted first religious tolerance law in the New World.

1660 British Parliament barred colonists from exporting to any country except England.

1664 New Amsterdam captured by British; renamed New York. British seized Delaware from Sweden.

1673 Jacques Marquette and Louis Joliet explored Mississippi River.

1682 William Penn founded Philadelphia.

1692 Twenty executed for witchcraft in Salem, Massachusetts.

1693 College of William and Mary founded in Virginia.

1704 *Boston News-Letter*, the first successful newspaper in colonies, was published.

1718 French settled New Orleans.

1728 First American synagogue constructed in New York City.

1732 First Roman Catholic church in America opened in Philadelphia. Benjamin Franklin began publication of *Poor Richard's Almanack*.

1733 James Oglethorpe founded Georgia as the 13th colony. British Parliament passed the Molasses Act.

1735 John Peter Zenger acquitted in New York in a trial that established the tradition of free press in America.

1737 First public celebration of St. Patrick's Day in Boston.

1752 Benjamin Franklin conducted kite experiment, proving lightning is a form of electricity.

1754 French and Indian War began; spread to Europe as the Seven Years' War between France and England.

1759 British captured Quebec from French.

1760 Montreal fell to British; New France surrendered.

1763 Treaty of Paris formally ended Seven Years' and French and Indian Wars. British acquired Canada.

1764 British Parliament passed revenue-raising Sugar Act. James Otis protested "taxation without representation" in Boston.

1765 British Parliament passed Stamp Act and Quartering Act. Sons of Liberty organized resistance.

1766 British Parliament repealed Stamp Act.

1767 British Parliament passed Townshend Duties.

1769 Daniel Boone explored Kentucky territory.

1770 British soldiers killed five Americans at Boston Massacre.

1773 British Parliament passed Tea Act. Boston Tea Party protested tax on tea.

1774 Intolerable Acts passed by British Parliament to punish tea protests; British troops occupied Boston. First Continental Congress deliberated American response.

1775 Battles at Lexington and Concord marked beginning of American Revolution. George Washington appointed commander of the Continental Army.

1776 Declaration of Independence adopted July 4. British occupied New York City. Washington crossed Delaware and defeated British at Trenton.

1777 Articles of Confederation adopted. Continental Army camped for winter at Valley Forge.

1778 France allied with U.S., declared war on Britain.

1780 Benedict Arnold defected to British.

1781 British General Cornwallis surrendered to Washington at Yorktown, ending the American Revolutionary War. Articles of Confederation took effect.

1783 Treaty of Paris formally ended the American Revolution.

1787 Constitutional Convention deliberated in Philadelphia.

1788 Constitution ratified.

1789 Washington elected the first president. New York City declared temporary capital.

1790 Capital moved to Philadelphia. First U.S. census counted 3,929,625 Americans.

1791 Bill of Rights took effect. District of Columbia selected for site of permanent capital.

1792 Stock traders began meeting under a tree on Wall Street in New York City. Washington unanimously reelected as president.

1793 Eli Whitney invented the cotton gin. Cornerstone laid for the Capitol.

1796 Washington delivered his Farewell Address. John Adams elected president.

1798 Alien and Sedition Acts passed.

1801 Thomas Jefferson inaugurated as president.

1802 U.S. Military Academy at West Point established.

1803 Acquisition of the Louisiana Purchase nearly doubled U.S. territory.

1804 Lewis and Clark expedition departed St. Louis to explore newly acquired territory.

1807 Britain and France seized American ships. Embargo Act shut down American exports.

1808 Congress ended African slave trade.

1809 Non-Intercourse Act replaced the Embargo Act; banned trade with France and England.

1810 West Florida annexed.

1812 War of 1812 began.

1814 British burned Washington, D.C. Francis Scott Key wrote "The Star-Spangled Banner."

1815 General Andrew Jackson defeated British at the Battle of New Orleans.

1817 Erie Canal construction begun.

1818 Present design of U.S. flag adopted.

1819 Florida acquired from Spain.

1820 Missouri Compromise admitted Missouri as a slave state, Maine as a free state, settling slavery dispute.

1823	Monroe Doctrine proclaimed.
1825	Erie Canal opened.
1831	Nat Turner led bloodiest slave rebellion in Virginia.
1832	Black Hawk War in Wisconsin and Illinois. Democratic Party held first national convention. Protesting federal tariff, South Carolina threatened secession.
1834	Cyrus McCormack patented reaping machine.
1835	Seminole War in Florida.
1836	Texas declared independence from Mexico.
1839	Abner Doubleday codified baseball rules.
1844	Morse sent first telegraph message.
1845	U.S. annexed Texas. Potato famine hit Ireland resulting in massive Irish immigration to U.S. U.S. Naval Academy at Annapolis founded.
1846	Mexican War began. British ceded U.S. control of Pacific Northwest to 49th parallel.
1848	Mexican War ended; U.S. gained control of Southwest.
1849	California Gold Rush.
1850	Compromise of 1850 temporarily resolved slavery crisis.
1854	Passage of Kansas-Nebraska Act, permitting territories to decide legality of slavery, sparked widespread protest in the North.
1855	Armed struggle between pro- and anti-slavery settlers erupted in Kansas.
1856	Pottowatomie Massacre in Kansas led by John Brown.
1857	Supreme Court issued Dred Scott ruling protecting slavery.

1858	Lincoln–Douglas debates focused on slavery issue.
1859	John Brown raided Harper's Ferry, Virginia.
1860	Lincoln elected president. South Carolina first southern state to secede.
1861	Confederate attack on Fort Sumter, South Carolina, began the Civil War. Jefferson Davis elected president of Confederacy.
1862	Homestead Act passed.
1863	Emancipation Proclamation freed slaves in rebelling states. Lincoln delivered the Gettysburg Address.
1864	Ulysses S. Grant assumed command of Union army. Sherman destroyed Atlanta. Confederate army suffered crippling setback in Wilderness campaign.
1865	Confederate General Robert E. Lee surrendered to Grant at Appomattox Court House in Virginia, ending the Civil War. Lincoln assassinated by John Wilkes Booth. Thirteenth Amendment outlawed slavery.
1867	Alaska purchased from Russia. Congress superceded President Johnson's moderate reconstruction plan with a more radical plan.
1868	Johnson impeached by House of Representatives but acquitted in trial by the Senate. Fourteenth Amendment granted former slaves full citizenship.
1869	Wyoming Territory first to grant women right to vote.
1871	Great Fire destroyed most of Chicago.
1873	Panic of 1873 followed collapse of Jay Cooke's bank.
1875	Scandals wracked Grant administration.
1876	Alexander Graham Bell invented telephone. Sioux Indians defeated General George A.

Custer at Little Big Horn in Montana. Samuel J. Tilden–Rutherford B. Hayes presidential election results disputed.

1877 Special Electoral Commission awarded presidency to Hayes. Reconstruction ended; federal troops withdrew from the South. Thomas Edison invented the phonograph

1879 Thomas Edison invented the electric light.

1881 President James A. Garfield assassinated.

1882 John D. Rockefeller created Standard Oil Trust.

1883 Pendleton Act reformed civil service. Brooklyn Bridge completed.

1884 World's first skyscraper built in Chicago.

1886 American Federation of Labor organized. Statue of Liberty dedicated. Apache leader Geronimo captured.

1887 Interstate Commerce Commission established.

1889 Oklahoma Land Rush.

1890 Sherman Antitrust Act enacted. Sioux Indians massacred at Wounded Knee, South Dakota.

1891 Dr. James A. Naismith invented game of basketball, Springfield, Massachusetts. Edison invented the motion picture camera.

1894 Coxey's Army of unemployed workers marched on Washington.

1896 Supreme Court ruled racially segregated schools constitutional (*Plessy v. Ferguson*). Gold discovered in Alaska. Henry Ford produced his first car.

1898 Spanish-American War: U.S. gained Puerto Rico, Guam, Wake Island, and the Philippines; Cuba granted independence. U.S. annexed Hawaii.

1899 U.S. advocated Open Door Policy for China.

1900 American troops intervened in Boxer Rebellion in China.

1901 U.S. Steel organized. President William McKinley assassinated. Theodore Roosevelt sworn-in as president.

1903 Orville and Wilbur Wright flew first powered aircraft, Kitty Hawk, North Carolina. First feature movie, *The Great Train Robbery*, released.

1904 Roosevelt Corollary to the Monroe Doctrine warned European powers against using Latin American financial problems as a pretense to meddle in Western Hemisphere.

1905 Roosevelt mediated Treaty of Portsmouth, resolving Russo-Japanese War.

1906 San Francisco shaken by earthquake. Roosevelt awarded Nobel Peace Prize.

1907 Panic of 1907: stock market crashed resulting in a run on banks.

1908 "Gentlemen's Agreement" curtailed Japanese immigration. Model-T Ford debuted. Federal Bureau of Investigation established.

1909 National Association for the Advancement of Colored People (NAACP) founded.

1910 Boy Scouts of America founded.

1911 U.S. troops ordered to border during the Mexican Revolution. Supreme Court sustained antitrust divestitures of Standard Oil and American Tobacco. American banks took control of Nicaraguan financial matters.

1912 Titanic sank after hitting an iceberg on maiden voyage. Progressive (Bull Moose) party organized with Theodore Roosevelt as presidential candidate. Roosevelt wounded in assassination attempt. U.S. Marines dispatched to Honduras, Nicaragua, Cuba, and Santo Domingo.

1913 Income tax authorized by Sixteenth Amendment; popular election of U.S. senators by Seventeenth Amendment. Ford Motor Co. introduced assembly line production system. Federal Reserve system created.

1914 U.S. declared neutrality in World War I. Clayton Act enacted, beefing up antitrust enforcement. Mother's Day proclaimed.

1915 *Birth of a Nation*, the first full-length, mass audience movie released; film glorified Ku Klux Klan. German submarine sank *Lusitania*, killing 128 Americans. American troops sent to Haiti.

1916 U.S. troops pursued Mexican rebel Pancho Villa into Mexico after border raid. Virgin Islands purchased from Denmark. "He Kept Us Out of War" slogan helped reelect President Wilson. Louis D. Brandeis appointed first Jewish Supreme Court Justice. Jeanette Rankin (Montana) first woman elected to Congress.

1917 Ties with Germany severed after renewed submarine warfare. Zimmerman Telegram revealed German designs on Mexico. Wilson called for a world made "safe for democracy." War declared against Germany and Austro-Hungarian Empire. Race riot erupted in East St. Louis, Illinois.

1918 Wilson listed "Fourteen Points" war aims. American troops intervened with Allied forces against the Russian Revolution. Sedition Act passed by Congress. Armistice ended World War I. Versailles peace conference planned post-war peace. Influenza epidemic killed hundreds of thousands.

1919 Prohibition imposed by Eighteenth Amendment. Labor strikes spread across country. Communist Party organized in U.S. President Wilson incapacitated by a series of strokes. Senate rejected Versailles Treaty and League of Nations.

1920 Palmer Raids rounded up thousands of radicals. Sacco and Vanzetti arrested for murder. Women granted right to vote under Twentieth Amendment. Terrorist bomb blasted Wall Street, killing 30. Wilson received Nobel Peace Prize.

1921 Republican Warren G. Harding elected president, pledged "return to normalcy." Former President Taft appointed Chief Justice of Supreme Court.

1922 International treaties mandated arms race curtailment and reduced tensions in the Pacific. Congress adopted resolution for Jewish homeland in Palestine. First radio commercial broadcast.

1923 Teapot Dome oil lease scandal rocked Harding administration. Calvin Coolidge succeeded to presidency following Harding's death.

1924 Congress overrode veto, authorized bonus for World War I veterans. Immigration Act set strict quota system. Dawes Plan mapped payment schedule for war debt and reparations.

1925 Scopes Trial in Tennessee challenged right to teach evolution in schools. Ku Klux Klan demonstrated in Washington. Al Capone took control of Chicago mob.

1927 Charles Lindbergh flew, solo, nonstop from New York to Paris. Sacco and Vanzetti executed in Massachusetts. First sound motion picture, Al Jolson's *The Jazz Singer*, released.

1928 Kellogg-Briand Treaty called for outlawing war. First Mickey Mouse cartoon, "Steamboat Willie," appeared.

1929 Six gangsters slain in St. Valentine's Day Massacre in Chicago. Former Interior Secretary Albert B. Fall convicted in Teapot Dome scandal. Stock market crashed (October 29); Great Depression began.

1930 Wave of bank failures hit the country. Hawley-Smoot Tariff imposed trade barriers, worsened depression.

1931 *The Star Spangled Banner* designated as the national anthem. "Scottsboro Boys" charged with raping a white woman in Alabama. Empire State Building opened.

1932 Depression continued; stock market declined to 10 percent of 1929 value. Franklin D. Roosevelt elected president, promised "New Deal."

1933 Chicago Mayor Anton J. Cermak killed in Miami by Guiseppe Zangara during an assassination attempt aimed at president-elect Roosevelt. Roosevelt ordered "Bank Holiday." New Deal program pushed through during "Hundred Days" (March 9–June 16). Prohibition lifted. Soviet Union gained U.S. diplomatic recognition. Marines pulled out of Nicaragua.

1934 Thousands of ruined farmers from Oklahoma and Arkansas migrated to California. U.S. troops left Haiti. Outlaw John Dillinger killed by FBI.

1935 Supreme Court overturned National Industrial Recovery Act as unconstitutional. Wagner Act and Social Security Act passed. Congress of Industrial Organizations (CIO) founded. Neutrality Act adopted.

1936 U.S. maintained neutrality in Spanish Civil War. Auto workers staged sit-down strikes in Michigan. Jesse Owens collected four gold medals at Berlin Olympics.

1937 Roosevelt advocated "packing" Supreme Court. Golden Gate Bridge opened in San Francisco. Female aviator Amelia Earhart disappeared during flight over the Pacific.

1938 Roosevelt called for military build-up. House Un-American Activities Committee (HUAC) organized. Orson Welles's "Invasion from Mars" radio broadcast triggered widespread panic.

1939 U.S. declared neutrality at outbreak of World War II. Arms sales to belligerents approved.

1940 U.S. shifted from neutrality to "non-belligerency." Peacetime draft adopted. Military spending increased. Roosevelt declared U.S. "arsenal for democracy," elected to unprecedented third term.

1941 Lend-Lease program sent billions in aid to Britain. "Unlimited national emergency" declared. German, Italian, and Japanese assets frozen. Roosevelt and Winston Churchill drafted Atlantic Charter. Japan attacked Pearl Harbor. War declared against Japan, later against Germany and Italy.

1942 Economy mobilized for war. Japanese-Americans confined to internment camps. Philippines fell to Japan. U.S. victorious in naval battles at Coral Sea and Midway. American offensive launched at Guadalcanal Island. Allies invaded North Africa.

1943 Roosevelt and Churchill conferred in Casablanca, called for "unconditional surrender" of Axis powers. U.S. Marines mopped up Guadalcanal. Germans turned back Americans at Kasserine Pass, Tunisia. Allies invaded Sicily. Roosevelt and Churchill met with USSR leader Josef Stalin in Tehran, Iran. General Dwight D. Eisenhower appointed Supreme Commander of Allied Forces in Europe.

1944 Allied bombing raids on Berlin began. Allies invaded Italy, liberated Rome. D-Day allied invasion force landed at Normandy. Germans forced to retreat. Bretton Woods, New Hampshire, Conference mapped postwar financial plans. Dumbarton Oaks conference planned future United Nations organization. American forces launched drive to retake Philippines. Congress enacted GI Bill of Rights. Roosevelt elected to fourth term.

1945 Stalin, Churchill, and Roosevelt discussed postwar Europe at Yalta Conference. Allied forces maintained offensive against Germany. American air raids hit Tokyo. Harry S. Truman succeeded to presidency on Roosevelt's death. United Nations conference convened in San Francisco. Hitler committed suicide; Germany surrendered. Truman, Churchill, and Stalin conferred at Potsdam, Germany. U.S. dropped atomic bombs on Hiroshima and Nagasaki. Japan surrendered.

1946 Postwar strike wave hit American economy. Churchill warned of "Iron Curtain" across Europe in speech at Westminster College in Fulton, Missouri. Philippines gained independence.

1947 Diplomatic efforts failed to reach peace treaty

ending World War II. Truman Doctrine offered foreign aid to stem Communist subversion. Marshall Plan for postwar reconstruction in Europe unveiled. Taft-Hartley Act restricted unions. House Un-American Activities Committee probed Communism in Hollywood. Jackie Robinson broke color line in baseball.

1948 Congress approved $5.3 billion for Marshall Plan. Soviets imposed blockade on ground traffic to West Berlin; U.S. responded with airlift. Truman desegregated U.S. army, upset Dewey in presidential election.

1949 Truman promised "Fair Deal" domestic program. North Atlantic Treaty Organization (NATO) founded. Berlin blockade lifted; airlift ended. Communists took power in mainland China. Soviets tested atomic bomb.

1950 Senator Joseph R. McCarthy (R-Wis.) charged communist infiltration of U.S. government. North Korea invaded South Korea, sparking Korean War. Truman ordered U.S. troops to intervene. United Nations endorsed American action. Communist China entered war in support of North Korea. Puerto Rican nationalists failed in Truman assassination attempt.

1951 Julius and Ethel Rosenberg sentenced to death for giving Soviets atomic bomb secrets. General Douglas MacArthur relieved of Korean command for insubordination.

1952 Truman seized strike-bound steel plants. Britain, France, and U.S. signed separate peace treaty with West Germany. GI Bill of Rights expanded to include Korean War veterans. Richard M. Nixon, Republican vice presidential candidate, delivered televised "Checkers Speech," defusing "slush fund scandal." U.S. tested first hydrogen bomb. General Dwight D. Eisenhower elected president, visited troops in Korea.

1953 Julius and Ethel Rosenberg executed. Armistice ended fighting in Korea.

1954 Foreign ministers conference failed to agree on German reunification. Puerto Rican national-

ists barged into House of Representatives, shot five congressmen. Southeast Asia Treaty Organization (SEATO) organized. Senator McCarthy discredited at hearings on Communism in the Army. Supreme Court declared segregated schools unconstitutional in *Brown v. Board of Education, Topeka*. Central Intelligence Agency helped overthrow elected left-wing government in Guatemala. Senate censured Senator McCarthy.

1955 Eisenhower threatened use of atomic weapons in case of war. Treaty ended occupation of Austria. Big Four summit held in Geneva. Eisenhower suffered heart attack. AFL and CIO merged. Polio vaccine discovered. African-Americans staged anti-segregation bus boycott in Montgomery, Alabama.

1956 Soviets crushed Hungarian Revolution. U.S. criticized seizure of Suez Canal by Israel, France, and Britain. Highway Act earmarked $32 billion for national road system.

1957 Eisenhower Doctrine promised aid to Middle East nations threatened by Communism. McClellan Committee investigated Teamster union corruption. First civil rights act since Reconstruction passed by Congress. Troops sent to Little Rock, Arkansas to enforce court-ordered desegregation.

1958 Soviets launched *Sputnik*, took lead in space race. U.S. launched *Explorer I* satellite. National Aeronautics and Space Administration (NASA) created. American Marines sent to Lebanon. Atomic submarine *Nautilus* made first submerged crossing of North Pole.

1959 Castro overthrew Batista dictatorship in Cuba. U.S.-Cuba relations deteriorated. Alaska and Hawaii gained statehood. St. Lawrence Seaway completed. Landrum-Griffin Act targeted union racketeering. First U.S. ballistic missile submarine launched. TV quiz show scandal revealed.

1960 Soviets shot down American U-2 spy plane. African-American college students staged first sit-in at Woolworth's lunch counter in Greensboro, North Carolina, sparking civil rights revolution. Trade embargo imposed on Cuba following seizure of American property by Castro government. First televised presidential campaign debates between Richard M. Nixon and John F. Kennedy.

1961 Diplomatic relations severed with Cuba. Eisenhower Farewell Address warned of "military-industrial complex." Bay of Pigs invasion failed to overturn Castro regime. Alan Shepard Jr. became first American in space. Soviets erected Berlin Wall. Peace Corps and Alliance for Progress established. "Freedom Riders" challenged segregated seating on interstate buses. AMA linked smoking to heart disease.

1962 John H. Glenn Jr. became first American to orbit Earth. U.S. marshals sent to University of Mississippi to protect African-American student James H. Meredith. Cuban Missile Crisis threatened nuclear war. U.S. began military assistance to South Vietnam regime.

1963 Medicare first proposed. Limited Nuclear Test Ban Treaty concluded. Washington-Moscow hotline installed. Civil rights demonstrations staged in Birmingham, Alabama. Martin Luther King Jr. delivered "I Have A Dream" speech at massive March on Washington. President Kennedy assassinated. Lyndon Baines Johnson sworn-in as president.

1964 Johnson announced "War on Poverty." Civil rights workers Michael Schwerner, James Chaney, and Andrew Goodman murdered during Mississippi Freedom Summer project. Civil Rights Act barred discrimination in public accommodations. Tonkin Gulf Resolution passed, authorizing military escalation in Vietnam. Warren Commission found no conspiracy in Kennedy assassination. Martin Luther King Jr. awarded Nobel Peace Prize. Verrazano Narrows Bridge, world's longest suspension bridge, opened in New York City.

1965 Johnson called for "Great Society." Malcolm X assassinated. First U.S. combat troops sent to Vietnam. American forces landed in Dominican Republic. Martin Luther King Jr. led civil rights campaign in Selma, Alabama. Medicare

enacted. Congress passed Voting Rights Act. Thirty-four died in Watts riot in Los Angeles. Northeast power black-out cut electricity for 30 million people.

1966 First B-52 bombing raids ordered over North Vietnam. Supreme Court ruled suspects must be advised of their rights. Stokely Carmichael, Student Non-Violent Coordinating Committee leader, coined the phrase "Black Power." American troops in Vietnam reached 400,000.

1967 Anti-Vietnam War movement staged massive protests in spring and fall. Worst racial rioting in U.S. history erupted in Detroit; 43 died. Senator Eugene McCarthy (D-Minn.) opened anti-war presidential campaign. Thurgood Marshall named first African American Supreme Court justice.

1968 North Korea seized USS *Pueblo*. Vietnamese Communists unleashed massive Tet Offensive. Johnson announced that he would not seek re-election. Martin Luther King Jr. assassinated in Memphis, Tennessee. Student protests rocked Columbia University. Washington-Hanoi peace talks opened in Paris. Robert F. Kennedy assassinated in Los Angeles. Nuclear Non-Proliferation Treaty signed. Richard M. Nixon elected president.

1969 U.S. troop withdrawals from Vietnam began. Mary Jo Kopechne died in Chappaquiddick, Massachusetts, when Senator Edward M. Kennedy accidentally drove car off bridge. Neil Armstrong and Edwin Aldrin landed on moon. An estimated 400,000 young people flocked to the Woodstock Music Festival near Bethel, New York. Vietnam Moratorium mobilized hundreds of thousands against Vietnam War. Strategic Arms Limitation Talks (SALT) negotiations began in Helsinki, Finland.

1970 Nixon called for "Vietnamization" of war. North Vietnam bombing raids escalated. U.S. invasion of Cambodia triggered widespread protests. Four students killed by Ohio National Guard at Kent State University, Ohio. Lieutenant William Calley convicted in My Lai Massacre court-martial.

1971 American ping-pong team toured China, easing tensions with the Communist regime. Supreme Court approved school busing for integration. Forty-three died in Attica prison uprising. *New York Times* published Pentagon Papers (secret history of U.S. involvement in Vietnam). U.S. air raids escalated in Vietnam.

1972 Nixon became first president to visit China and USSR. Alabama Governor George Wallace wounded in an assassination attempt while running for president. Five men linked to Nixon reelection committee caught burglarizing Democratic Party national headquarters at Watergate complex in Washington. Nixon reelected, ordered intensified bombing of North Vietnam in December.

1973 Supreme Court legalized abortion (*Roe v. Wade*). Agreement signed ending U.S. fighting in Vietnam. North Vietnam released American POWs. White House involvement in Watergate scandal revealed. Presidential aides H.R. Haldeman, John Ehrlichman, John Dean, and Attorney General Richard Kleindienst resigned. Senate committee investigated Watergate case. Vice President Spiro Agnew resigned after pleading no contest to tax evasion charges. Arab oil embargo sent gasoline prices soaring following U.S. support to Israel in Yom Kippur War. Saturday Night Massacre: Attorney General Elliot Richardson and Assistant Attorney General William Ruckelshaus resigned rather than comply with Nixon's order to fire Watergate special prosecutor Archibald Cox. Mysterious 18.5-minute gap discovered on White House tape. Gerald R. Ford sworn in as vice president under the Twenty-fifth Amendment.

1974 Arab embargo lifted. Supreme Court ordered Nixon to turn over White House tapes to special prosecutor Leon Jaworski. House Judiciary Commitee voted three articles of impeachment against Nixon. Tape transcripts revealed Nixon ordered Watergate cover-up. President's political support collapsed. Nixon resigned in disgrace; first president to resign. Ford took office, pardoned Nixon. Ford met USSR Premier Leonid Brezhnev in Vladivostock, agreed to SALT treaty.

1975 Senate committee probed illegal CIA and FBI activities. Saigon fell to Communists. Cambodia seized USS *Mayaguez*. Ford ordered successful rescue mission. Joint Soviet-U.S. space mission linked up in space. Ford survived two assassination attempts.

1976 Supreme Court ruled death penalty constitutional. Jimmy Carter elected president.

1977 Carter pardoned Vietnam draft evaders, stressed human rights in foreign policy, signed Panama Canal treaty. Alaska oil pipeline began operations.

1978 Nationwide taxpayer's revolt touched off by California referendum on Proposition 13, cutting property taxes. Supreme Court curtailed scope of affirmative action programs. Carter mediated Camp David Accords between Egypt's Anwar Sadat and Israel's Menachem Begin.

1979 Diplomatic relations with China established. Nuclear accident at Three Mile Island, near Harrisburg, Pennsylvania. Carter and Brezhnev signed SALT II treaty in Vienna. U.S.-backed dictators in Nicaragua and Iran overthrown. Islamic militants seized U.S. embassy in Tehran, Iran, beginning 444-day hostage crisis. U.S. inflation skyrocketed as Organization of Petroleum Exporting Countries (OPEC) doubled oil prices. Russia invaded Afghanistan.

1980 Carter protested Afghanistan invasion by cutting trade, ordering boycott of Moscow Olympics, and resuming draft registration. Eight servicemen killed in botched hostage rescue mission in Iranian desert. Mount St. Helens volcano erupted in Washington State. 30 officials caught taking bribes in FBI's Abscam sting operation. Ronald Reagan elected president.

1981 Iran released hostages on Reagan's inauguration day. Reagan wounded in assassination attempt. Spacecraft *Columbia* launched in first space shuttle mission. Reagan fired 13,000 striking federal air traffic controllers. Sandra Day O'Connor appointed first female Supreme Court justice. Reagan pushed tax cut and arms buildup; dispatched military advisers to El Salvador.

1982 Antitrust suit caused breakup of AT&T. 500,000 in New York City marched for a nuclear freeze. U.S. backed Britain in Falklands War with Argentina. Unemployment soared to worst level since Great Depression.

1983 Reagan denounced USSR for shooting down a Korean airliner. U.S. Marines sent to Lebanon as part of peacekeeping force. Terrorist bomb attack killed 241 Marines in Beirut. U.S. invaded Grenada, toppled pro-Castro government. Reagan proposed Strategic Defense Initiative ("Star Wars").

1984 U.S. mining of Nicaraguan harbors condemned by World Court. Reverend Jesse Jackson launched first major presidential bid by an African-American candidate. Rep. Geraldine Ferraro (D-N.Y.) became first woman nominated as a major party vice presidential candidate. Reagan defeated Democratic presidential candidate Walter Mondale in 49 states. Marines withdrawn from Lebanon.

1985 Islamic terrorists hijacked TWA airliner in Beirut. Palestinian terrorists hijacked *Achille Lauro* cruise ship. Reagan and USSR President Mikhail Gorbachev held a summit in Geneva.

1986 Space shuttle *Challenger* exploded shortly after launch, killing six astronauts and a civilian passenger; NASA safety shortcuts blamed. Libyan forces attacked U.S. Navy vessels on maneuvers in international waters in Gulf of Sidra. Blaming Libya for terrorist attack against U.S. servicemen in Germany, Reagan ordered air raids against Libya. Reagan and Gorbachev conferred at Reykjavik, Iceland, summit.

1987 First trillion dollar budget submitted to Congress. Tower Commission faulted Reagan administration for Iran-Contra scandal. U.S. Navy ships ordered to escort Kuwaiti tankers in Persian Gulf during war between Iraq and Iran. Iraqi plane accidentally attacked USS *Stark*, killing 37 crew members. Colonel Oliver North

testified in Iran-Contra Congressional hearings. Reagan-Gorbachev third summit agreed on INF Treaty to dismantle medium range missiles.

1988 U.S. forces destroyed two Iranian oil platforms in Persian Gulf. Reagan conferred with Gorbachev at Moscow summit. USS *Vincennes* accidentally shot down Iranian passenger plane, killing 290 people. Attorney General Edwin Meese resigned amid charges of financial wrongdoing. Space shuttle missions resumed for first time since *Challenger* tragedy. George Bush elected president.

1989 *Exxon Valdez* spilled millions of gallons of oil in Prince William Sound, Alaska. Oliver North convicted in Iran-Contra scandal. Savings and loans bailout signed by President Bush. General Colin Powell named first African American to head Joint Chiefs of Staff. Earthquake shook San Francisco area. American forces invaded Panama, apprehending Panamanian dictator Manuel Noriega.

1990 President Bush signed Americans With Disabilities Act. Iraq invaded Kuwait; U.S. organized international coalition to defend other Persian Gulf nations and liberate Kuwait.

1991 Operation Desert Storm military operations defeated Iraq, liberated Kuwait. Oliver North's conviction overturned. President Bush's approval rating soared to an all-time high. Nomination of Clarence Thomas to replace Thurgood Marshall on Supreme Court challenged by allegations of sexual harassment from University of Oklahoma law professor Anita Hill.

1992 Rioting erupted in Los Angeles following acquittal of four policemen on all but one count in beating of African American, Rodney King; 52 died in violence. Bill Clinton nominated by Democrats to challenge Bush's bid for reelection. Texas billionaire H. Ross Perot complicated presidential race by waging independent candidacy, winning nearly 19 percent of popular vote.

1993 Bill Clinton inaugurated president. Terrorist

bomb at World Trade Center killed six, injured one thousand. Eight cult members died in confrontation with Bureau of Alcohol, Tobacco, and Firearms at Branch Davidian compound at Waco, Texas. Mississippi River and tributaries overflowed banks in Great Flood of 1993. White House deputy counsel Vincent Foster committed suicide under mysterious circumstances. North American Free Trade Agreement (NAFTA) approved. Whitewater scandal came to light as authorities investigated dealings of an Arkansas savings and loan linked to Clintons.

1994 Special prosecutor Ken Starr named to Whitewater scandal. U.S. lifted trade embargo against Vietnam. Aldrich Ames convicted of spying for Soviet Union, sentenced to life in prison. Four men convicted in 1993 World Trade Center bombing. O.J. Simpson charged in the murder of his former wife Nicole Brown Simpson and Ronald Goldman. Support for President Clinton's health-care reform plan evaporated; proposed legislation dropped. Conservative Republicans captured control in House of Representatives, promising "Contract with America" legislative program.

1995 Representative Newt Gingrich (R-Ga.) elected Speaker of the House. U.S.-Vietnam resumed diplomatic relations. President Clinton welcomed Sinn Fein leader Gerry Adams at White House. Timothy McVeigh charged in bombing of federal building in Oklahoma City that killed more than 168 people. U.S. space shuttle docked with Soviet space station. Senator Bob Packwood (R-Oreg.) resigned under threat of expulsion from Senate for sexual and official misconduct. *New York Times* and *Washington Post* printed Unabomber manifesto. O.J. Simpson acquitted.

1996 Congress revamped the nation's telecommunications law for the first time in more than 60 years. Unabomber suspect arrested. Republican-controlled Congress and President Clinton were locked in a long, drawn-out feud over the new budget. Atlanta Olympics were marred by pipe bomb explosion in a downtown park that killed one person and injured 100. Minimum

wage was increased for first time since 1991. TWA Flight 800 exploded off Long Island, New York, coast shortly after taking off from JFK International Airport, due to unknown causes. President Bill Clinton won re-election, defeating former Senator Bob Dole (R-Kans).

1997 O.J. Simpson found liable for deaths of former wife Nicole Brown and Ronald Goldman by civil jury. Thirty-nine members of the Heaven's Gate religious cult committed apparent suicide in California. Timothy McVeigh convicted and sentenced to death for the 1995 bombing of the Oklahoma City federal office building that killed 168 people. Congressional hearings probed abusive campaign funding practices by Clinton-Gore 1996 presidential campaign.

1998 Clinton-Lewinsky sex scandal dominated political news. Clinton became second president in U.S. history to be impeached, as House of Representatives voted on charges of lying to a grand jury and attempting to influence witnesses. Despite Clinton scandal, Democrats closed the gap in the House by picking up five seats and maintaining status quo in the Senate. House Speaker Newt Gingrich (R-Ga.) resigned from Congress. Lethal violence by school-aged children highlighted by shooting incidents in Jonesboro, Arkansas (5 dead, 10 wounded), and Springfield, Oregon (2 killed, 22 wounded, in addition to assailant's parents who were also killed). St. Louis Cardinals slugger Mark McGwire finished baseball season with 70 home runs and Sammy Sosa, of the Chicago Cubs, with 66, surpassing Roger Maris' single-season home run record of 61. Terrorist bombs exploded outside American embassies in Dar-es-Salaam, Tanzania, and Nairobi, Kenya, killing 224 (213 in Nairobi), prompting U.S. to launch retaliatory missile attacks against suspected terrorist bases in Afghanistan and the Sudan.

1999 President Clinton won acquittal in his Senate trial on two articles of impeachment voted by the House of Representatives in December 1998. U.S. forces participated in NATO air war against Yugoslavia in an effort to stop ethnic cleansing in the predominantly ethnic Albanian

Kosovo region. After the war, 6,000 American troops joined international peacekeeping forces deployed in Kosovo. Two teenage boys went on a shooting spree at Columbine High School in Littleton, Colorado, killing 12 other students and a teacher, and wounding more than 30 before committing suicide. Severe drought conditions hit much of the eastern U.S. causing widespread crop damage. Wind and flood damage caused by Hurricane Floyd reached billions of dollars from North Carolina to New England. Governor George W. Bush of Texas and Senator John McCain of Arizona emerged as leading contenders in the race for the Republican nomination for president in the 2000 election. Vice President Al Gore and former Senator Bill Bradley of New Jersey battled for the Democratic nomination. Amadou Diallo, an unarmed African immigrant, was shot and killed by police in a fusillade of 41 bullets in New York City, triggering protests against police brutality. The Dow Jones industrial average rose above 10,000 for the first time in history. First Lady Hillary Clinton unofficially began campaign for Democratic Senate nomination in New York State. Eileen M. Collins became the first woman to command a space shuttle mission. An estimated 1.5 to 2 million people gathered in New York's Times Square to welcome the new millennium.

PART 2

Forming the Nation

U.S. Constitution Chronology

1787   May – Constitutional Convention convened in Philadelphia to draft constitution for a new, stronger central government.

September 17 – 39 of 55 delegates signed Constitution.

September 28 – Congress ordered document sent to states for ratification by state conventions.

December 7 – Delaware ratified unanimously.

December 12 – Pennsylvania ratified 43–23.

December 18 – New Jersey ratified unanimously.

1788   January 2 – Georgia ratified unanimously.

January 9 – Connecticut ratified 128–40.

February 6 – Massachusetts ratified 187–168.

April 26 – Maryland ratified 63–11.

May 23 – South Carolina ratified 149–73.

June 21 – New Hampshire ratified 57–46.

June 25 – Virginia ratified 89–79.

July 26 – New York ratified 30–27.

1789   March 4 – Constitution declared in effect.

September 25 – Twelve amendments approved by Congress, submitted to states for ratification; only ten (three through twelve) ratified promptly; known as Bill of Rights (first ten amendments).[1]

November 20 – New Jersey ratified Bill of Rights.

November 21 – North Carolina ratified Constitution 194–77.

December 19 – Maryland ratified Bill of Rights.

December 22 – North Carolina ratified Bill of Rights.

1790   January 19 – South Carolina ratified Bill of Rights.

January 25 – New Hampshire ratified Bill of Rights.

January 28 – Delaware ratified Bill of Rights.

February 24 – New York ratified Bill of Rights.

March 10 – Pennsylvania ratified Bill of Rights.

May 29 – Rhode Island ratified Constitution 34–32.

---

1. Regarding the two originally proposed amendments, the first dealing with apportionment of representatives was not ratified by the necessary number of states; the second, dealing with compensation for Congressional officeholders, was approved in 1992 as the Twenty-seventh amendment.

June 7 – Rhode Island ratified Bill of Rights.

1791 January 10 – Vermont ratified Constitution; admitted to the Union March 4, 1791, as 14th state.

November 3 – Vermont ratified Bill of Rights.

December 15 – Virginia ratified Bill of Rights; Bill of Rights in effect.

1794 March 4 – Eleventh Amendment, pertaining to judicial powers, adopted by Congress, sent to states for ratification.

1795 February 7 – Ratified but declaration of ratification delayed because of difficulties in certifying results.

1798 January 8 – Eleventh Amendment declared ratified.

1803 December 9 – Twelfth Amendment, specifying method for choosing president and vice president, adopted by Congress, and submitted for ratification.

1804 June 15 – Twelfth Amendment ratified.

1865 January 31 – Thirteenth Amendment, abolishing slavery, proposed by Congress.

December 6 – Thirteenth Amendment ratified.

1866 June 13 – Fourteenth Amendment, guaranteeing citizenship rights to former slaves, proposed by Congress.

1868 July 9 – Fourteenth Amendment ratified.

July 28 – Secretary of State proclaimed Fourteenth Amendment ratified.

1869 February 26 – Fifteenth Amendment, prohibiting racial restriction of the right to vote, proposed by Congress.

1870 February 3 – Fifteenth Amendment ratified.

March 30 – Fifteenth Amendment declared ratified.

1909 July 12 – Sixteenth Amendment, authorizing income tax, proposed by Congress.

1912 May 13 – Seventeenth Amendment, mandating direct, popular election of U.S. Senators, proposed by Congress.

1913 February 3 – Sixteenth Amendment ratified.

February 25 – Proclamation declared Sixteenth Amendment ratified.

April 8 – Seventeenth Amendment ratified.

May 31 – Proclamation declared Seventeenth Amendment ratified.

1917 December 18 – Eighteenth Amendment, prohibiting sale of alcoholic beverages, proposed by Congress.

1919 January 16 – Eighteenth Amendment ratified.

January 29 – Eighteenth Amendment ratification proclaimed.

June 4 – Nineteenth Amendment, giving women right to vote, proposed by Congress.

1920 August 18 – Nineteenth Amendment ratified.

August 26 – Ratification of Nineteenth Amendment proclaimed.

1932 March 2 – Twentieth Amendment, moving presidential inauguration date forward from March 4 to January 20, proposed by Congress.

1933 January 23 – Twentieth Amendment ratified.

February 6 – Proclamation declared Twentieth Amendment ratified.

February 20 – Twenty-first Amendment, repealing Eighteenth Amendment (Prohibition), proposed by Congress.

December 5 – Twenty-first Amendment declared ratified.

1947	March 24 – Twenty-second Amendment limiting presidential service to two terms proposed by Congress.
1951	February 27 – Twenty-second Amendment ratified.
	March – Twenty-second Amendment declared ratified.
1960	June 16 – Twenty-third Amendment, granting citizens of District of Columbia right to vote for president, proposed by Congress.
1961	March 29 – Twenty-third Amendment ratified.
	April 3 – Proclamation declared Twenty-third Amendment ratification.
1962	August 27 – Twenty-fourth Amendment, banning poll tax, proposed by Congress.
1964	January 24 – Twenty-fourth Amendment declared ratified.
1965	July 6 – Twenty-fifth Amendment, dealing with presidential disability and succession, proposed by Congress.
1967	February 10 – Twenty-fifth Amendment ratified.
	February 24 – Twenty-fifth Amendment proclaimed ratified.
1971	March 23 – Twenty-sixth Amendment, lowering voting age to 18, proposed by Congress.
	July 5 – Twenty-sixth Amendment declared ratified.
1992	May 7 – Twenty-seventh Amendment, dealing with Congressional pay, ratified; amendment originally introduced September 25, 1789, as part of Bill of Rights.
	May 20 – Proclamation declared Twenty-seventh Amendment ratified.

(Sources: *Encyclopedia of Constitutional Amendments*, *Constitutional Story of the U.S.*, and *World Book*)

U.S. Census Chronology

1790	3,929,214
1800	5,308,483
1810	7,239,881
1820	9,638,453
1830	12,866,020
1840	17,069,453
1850	23,191,876
1860	31,443,321
1870	39,818,449
1880	50,155,783
1890	62,947,714
1900	75,994,575
1910	91,972,266
1920	105,710,620
1930	122,775,046
1940	131,669,275
1950	150,697,361
1960	179,323,175
1970	203,235,298
1980	226,504,825
1990	248,709,873

(Sources: *Historical Statistics of the United States* and *Statistical Abstract of the U.S.*)

Chronology of American Territorial Expansion

1775 Daniel Boone opened Wilderness Road, opening Kentucky to settlement.

1776 Thirteen colonies declared independence from England, form United States: Connecticut, Delaware, Georgia, Maryland, Massachusetts, New Hampshire, New Jersey, New York, North Carolina, Pennsylvania, Rhode Island, South Carolina, and Virginia.

1783 Treaty ending Revolutionary War doubled American territory by granting U.S. sovereignty over land from Great Lakes south to 31st parallel and west to the Mississippi River.

1785 Ordinance of 1785 established procedures for surveying and selling federal lands.

1787 Northwest Ordinance laid governmental framework for Northwest Territory.

1795 Pickney Treaty with Spain granted Americans access to Mississippi River.

1803 Louisiana Purchase again doubled American territory overnight, extending boundaries to Rocky Mountains.

1804–1806 Louis and Clark expedition explored northern part of Louisiana Territory and reached Pacific Ocean.

1818 Red River Cession in treaty with Britain gave U.S. control of parts of North Dakota, South Dakota, and Minnesota, as well as setting 49th parallel as northern boundary from Minnesota to Rockies.

1819 Florida cession by Spain gave U.S. control of Florida, parts of Alabama, Mississippi, and Louisiana.

1825 Erie Canal opened transportation to western areas in Great Lakes region.

1845 U.S. annexed Texas.

1846 Treaty with Britain extended 49th parallel as U.S. northern border from Rockies to Pacific, giving U.S. control of Washington, Oregon, Idaho, and part of Montana.

1848 Mexican cession following American victory in Mexican War extended U.S. dominion to an additional 525,000 square miles in California, and Southwest, including Nevada, Utah, Arizona, and parts of Colorado and New Mexico. Discovery of gold in California triggered Gold Rush.

1853 Gadsden Purchase acquired 29,640 square miles from Mexico, forming parts of southern Arizona and New Mexico.

1860 Pony Express sped mail from St. Joseph, Missouri, to California.

1862 Homestead Act offered free land to western settlers.

1867 Alaska purchased from Russia for $7.2 million.

1869 First transcontinental railroad completed.

1890 Settlement of western lands brought closing of frontier.

1898 Hawaii annexed. Spanish American War led to U.S. acquiring Puerto Rico, Philippines, Guam, and Wake Island.

1946 Philippines granted independence from U.S.

(Sources: *World Book* and *Americana*)

Key Contributions from the Melting Pot

Native Americans

1492 As Columbus arrived in New World, Native-American population in current U.S. area estimated at 900,000–1,500,000.

1513 Spanish explorer Juan Ponce de Leon landed in Florida.

1565 Spaniards established first European settlement in present-day U.S. at St. Augustine, Florida.

1620 Native Americans helped recently arrived settlers at Massachusetts Bay Colony survive harsh winter.

1626 Peter Minuit purchased Manhattan Island from Canarsie tribe, who had no real claim to the island. Dutch later had to deal with the island's real native inhabitants.

1637 Pequot War. Five hundred Pequot tribe killed by Connecticut colonists.

1675–1676 Wampanoag chief King Philip led Native-American coalition in war against colonists. Despite early successes, Native Americans were eventually defeated.

1680 Pueblo tribe rose against Spaniards and drove them from Pueblo territory.

1754–1763 French and Indian War. French and British forces clashed in series of wars for control of eastern North America. Each side formed alliances with various Native-American tribes.

1784 Defeated at battle of Fallen Timbers in Ohio, Native Americans were forced to cede lands in Northwest Territory to U.S. government.

1812–1815 During War of 1812 between U.S. and Great Britain, each side recruited Native American allies. After the war, U.S. punished Native Americans siding with British.

1824 Bureau of Indian Affairs established.

1830 Indian Removal Act enacted by Congress, authorized relocation of Native Americans in eastern U.S. to area west of Mississippi.

1830–1839 Trail of Tears. Ninety percent of Native Americans, living east of the Mississippi, including Cherokees, Chickasaws, Choctaws, and Alabamas forcibly removed to Indian Territory (present-day Oklahoma).

1864 Sand Creek Massacre. Three hundred Cheyennes killed by Colorado militia after armistice agreement had been reached.

1864 Navajo Long Walk. Eight thousand Navajos forced to march 350 miles to imprisonment in New Mexico until 1868.

1870s Systematic slaughter of buffalo, key food source for plains Native Americans.

1876 Battle of Little Big Horn. Sioux and Cheyenne warriors led by Sitting Bull and Crazy Horse defeated George A. Custer's Seventh Cavalry.

1879 Carlisle Indian School founded as first federally funded non-reservation boarding school for Native-American students, implementing policy of isolating students from Native-American culture and reservation life in order to assimilate them into white society.

1881 *A Century of Dishonor* by Helen Hunt Jackson was published, first major book to highlight plight of Native Americans.

1886 Apache war leader Geronimo and his band surrendered to U.S. army, ending Native-American warfare in southwest.

1889 Part of Native-American territory opened to white settlement, as 50,000 whites participated in Oklahoma Land Rush, staking claims to previously Native-American-held lands.

1890 Massacre at Wounded Knee. Three hundred Sioux, many of them women and children, were slaughtered by soldiers at Wounded Knee Creek.

1902 U.S. Commissioner of Indian Affairs banned Native-American males from wearing long hair.

1924 Native Americans became U.S. citizens.

1928 Charles Curtis, whose maternal grandmother was half Kaw, was elected Vice President of the United States.

1934 Wheeler-Howard Act enabled Native Americans to reestablish traditional culture.

1944 National Congress of American Indians organized.

1946 Native American claims commission organized.

1948 Native Americans gained right to vote in New Mexico and Arizona.

1968 Chief Joseph, leader of Nez Perce tribe's efforts to elude federal troops in 1877, was honored by 6-cent stamp issued by the U.S. Postal Service.

1973 American Indian Movement activists occupied Wounded Knee, South Dakota, in armed confrontation with federal law enforcement officials to dramatize Native Americans' plight.

1975 Two FBI agents and one Native American killed in shootout at Pine Ridge Reservation in South Dakota. American Indian Movement activist Leonard Peltier convicted of murder in 1977 trial and currently serving two life sentences, though he and supporters continue to maintain his innocence.

1975 Chief Frank Fools Crow became first Native American to perform invocation at session of the U.S. Senate. Prayer was presented in Lakotah and translated into English.

1980 Passamaquoddy and Penobscot tribes won settlement of land claims in Maine.

1982 Dr. Everett Rhoades, a Kiowa tribe member, became first Native-American director of U.S. Indian Health Service.

1984 Sine Gleska College (now University) became first tribally-controlled college on a Native-American reservation to receive accreditation on the baccalaureate level.

1987 Wilma Mankiller became first woman to hold the post of Principal Chief of the Cherokee Nation of Oklahoma. U.S. Postal Service issued a 10-cent stamp commemorating Lakota Chief Red Cloud, who had signed a peace treaty with the U.S. in 1868. U.S. Supreme Court upheld the right of federally recognized tribes to conduct gambling operations on reservations.

1988 Indian Gaming Regulatory Act established guidelines for regulating gambling on Native-American reservations.

1989 U.S. Postal Service issued 28-cent stamp honoring Sioux religious and political leader Chief Sitting Bull.

1990 National Museum of the American Indian created as part of the Smithsonian Institution. The Native American Graves Protection and Repatriation Act required federal and private museums to return human remains and sacred objects to requesting tribes. Ceremony marked 100th anniversary of Massacre at Wounded Knee, South Dakota.

1991 The Custer Battlefield National Monument was renamed the Little Bighorn Battlefield National Monument and a memorial to Native-American combatants in the historic battle was authorized.

1992 The Mashantucket Pequot Tribe dedicated the Foxwood Casino in Connecticut, largest Native-American-run gambling operation in the U.S. In all, 50 tribal-run gambling casinos were in operation across the country. Benjamin Nighthorse Campbell, a Northern Cheyenne, elected U.S. Senator from Colorado.

(Sources: *Ethnic Almanac* and *Native American Almanac*)

African Americans

1501 Spain authorized use of African slaves in New World.

1502 First African slaves brought to western hemisphere.

1565 Africans participated in founding of St. Augustine, Florida.

1619 First Africans in English North American colonies arrived at Jamestown, as indentured servants.

1626 First Africans arrived in New York City.

1641 Massachusetts became first colony to legalize slavery.

1642 Virginia adopted a fugitive slave law.

1661 Virginia gave formal legal recognition to slavery and encouraged importation of slaves.

1688 Mennonite Quakers adopted abolitionist document denouncing slavery as anti-Christian.

1700 Slave population estimated at 28,000 in American colonies.

1712 First major slave revolt occurred in New York City.

1739 A slave named Cato led first serious slave revolt in South Carolina.

1750 Slave population in the colonies estimated at 236,400.

1770 Crispus Attucks killed by British soldiers at Boston Massacre.

1775 African-American soldiers participated in Battle of Bunker Hill.

1777 Vermont abolished slavery; George Washington agreed to permit recruitment of African-American troops for Continental Army. Some 5,000 fought in Revolutionary War.

1808 Importation of slaves ended.

1820 Missouri Compromise admitted Missouri to Union as slave state, making 12 free states, 12 slave states. Slavery prohibited north of 36-30.

1822 Freed slave Denmark Vesey organized an abortive slave revolt in South Carolina. Fifty African Americans were executed for the role in the uprising.

1830–1860 Underground railway clandestinely smuggled some 49,000 slaves to freedom.

1831 Sixty whites killed in slave rebellion led by Nat Turner in Virginia.

1838 Slaveship *Amistad* diverted to Montauk, Long Island, by rebelling Africans, who are successfully defended before Supreme Court by former President John Quincy Adams.

1849 Harriet Tubman escaped from slavery. She returned 20 times to the South to guide an estimated 300 slaves to freedom.

1850 Fugitive Slave Act authorized capture of runaway slaves.

1857 Supreme Court issued Dred Scott decision holding that slave did not become free by moving to non-slave states.

1861–1865 Civil War fought.

1863 President Abraham Lincoln emancipated slaves in states in rebellion against the Union. Anti-Draft riot rocked New York, as white mobs protested draft and attacked African Americans.

1865 Thirteenth Amendment abolished slavery.

1868 Fourteenth Amendment made African Americans citizens.

1870 Fifteenth Amendment granted former slaves right to vote.

1877 Reconstruction ended in deal that resolved disputed Hayes–Tilden presidential election. Federal troops removed from South.

1881 Tennessee adopted first "Jim Crow" law, segregating railroad passengers along racial lines; other Southern states follow suit.

1896 Supreme Court ruled in *Plessy v. Ferguson* that "separate but equal" facilities were constitutional.

1910 Under leadership of W.E.B. DuBois, National Association for Advancement of Colored People was organized.

1911 National Urban League founded.

1914 Marcus Garvey founded back-to-Africa movement in Jamaica.

1917 Thirty-nine African Americans were killed in East St. Louis, Illinois, in one of U.S.'s worst race riots.

1919 Series of race riots swept the country. Thirty-eight people were killed in Chicago.

1920s Era of Harlem Renaissance.

1936 Jesse Owens wins gold medals in Berlin Olympics.

1938 Joe Louis won world heavyweight boxing title.

1942 James Farmer founded Congress of Racial Equality (CORE).

1943 Race riot by whites killed 34 people in Detroit.

1947 Jackie Robinson broke the color line in major league baseball. CORE staged first Freedom Rides in the South.

1948 President Harry S. Truman ordered desegregation of U.S. military.

1954 Supreme Court overturned "separate but equal" doctrine in *Brown v. Board of Education* (*Topeka*).

1955 Montgomery Bus Boycott. Following arrest of Rosa Parks for refusing to give up her bus seat to a white person, thousands of African Americans boycotted buses to protest segregation. Reverend Martin Luther King Jr. emerged as movement leader.

1957 Southern Christian Leadership Conference, headed by Martin Luther King Jr., founded. President Eisenhower mobilized National Guard to guarantee safety of African-American students integrating Central High School in Little Rock, Arkansas.

1960 Sit-in movement against segregated public accommodations began in Greensboro, North Carolina. Student Non-Violent Coordinating Committee (SNCC) founded.

1961 CORE staged Freedom Rides through South challenging segregated interstate transportation.

1962 Twelve thousand U.S. troops sent to restore order at University of Mississippi after rioting broke out following James Meredith's admission as graduate student.

1963 Police used firehoses and police dogs to attack civil rights demonstrators in Birmingham, Alabama. Alabama Governor George Wallace attempted to block desegregation of University of Alabama. Medgar Evers assassinated in Mississippi. Nearly 250,000 people marched on Washington in support of civil rights; Martin Luther King Jr. delivered his "I Have a Dream" speech at rally. Four little African-American girls killed in church bombing in Birmingham, Alabama.

1964 Civil Rights Act of 1964 signed by President Lyndon B. Johnson ended discrimination in public accommodations and employment. Civil rights workers Michael Schwerner, James Chaney, and Andrew Goodman were killed in Mississippi during Freedom Summer voter registration project. Ghetto riots erupted in Harlem and Bedford Stuyvesant in New York City. Martin Luther King Jr. received Nobel Peace Prize. Malcolm X left Nation of Islam and founded Organization of Afro-American Unity. Mississippi Freedom Democratic Party challenged all-white segregationist delegation from Mississippi at Democratic Convention.

1965 War on Poverty began. Malcolm X was assassinated. Civil rights marchers were attacked by police in Selma, Alabama, on "Bloody Sunday." Under protection of federalized Alabama National Guard, Martin Luther King Jr. and others led massive voting rights march from Selma to Montgomery, Alabama. Jimmie Lee Jackson, Reverend James J. Reeb and Viola Liuzzo were killed during the Selma campaign. Voting Rights Act of 1965 became law. Thirty-four persons died, 1,023 were injured, and 4,000 arrested during ghetto rioting in Watts section of Los Angeles, California.

1966 Student Non-Violent Coordinating Committee (SNCC) Chairman Stokeley Carmichael coined phrase "Black Power" during civil rights march in Mississippi. Black Panther Party was organized in Oakland, California. Martin Luther King Jr. organized open housing marches in Chicago.

1967 Muhammad Ali stripped of heavyweight boxing title after refusing induction in the U.S. military. In Newark, New Jersey, ghetto rioting 23 died, 1,200 were wounded, and 1,300 arrested over six-day period. Rioting in Detroit, Michigan, caused 43 deaths, 2,000 injuries, and 7,200 arrests. Thurgood Marshall became first African American named to the Supreme Court.

1968 Martin Luther King Jr. assassinated in Memphis, Tennessee. Rioting erupted in more than 125 cities, resulting in 46 deaths, 3,500 injuries, and 20,000 arrests. Poor People's Campaign staged series of demonstrations in Washington, D.C, to highlight problems of the poor. Kerner Commission issued report on civil disorders, warning on dangers posed by racism in American society.

1969 Chicago Black Panther leader Fred Hampton shot and killed by police.

1973 Detroit, Atlanta, Los Angeles, and other cities elected African-American mayors.

1978 Supreme Court upholds affirmative action in principle but overturns specific program at University of California medical school in Bakke decision.

1979 In *United Steelworkers of America v. Weber*, Supreme Court upholds affirmative action.

1981 Reagan administration announced opposition to racial quotas for affirmative action and busing to integrate public schools.

1983 Lt. Colonel Guion S. Buford Jr. became first African-American astronaut to travel in outer space, aboard space shuttle *Challenger*. Harold Washington elected first African-American mayor of Chicago. Martin Luther King Jr.'s birthday became national holiday.

1984 Reverend Jesse Jackson sought Democratic presidential nomination for first time.

1986 Michael Griffith murdered by racist white teenagers in Howard Beach section of Queens, New York.

1988 Jackson made impressive bid for Democratic presidential nomination, coming in second in delegate votes.

1989 David N. Dinkins elected mayor of New York City; Douglas Wilder, governor of Virginia (nation's first elected African-American governor). General Colin Powell became chair of Joint Chiefs of Staff. Rioting erupted in Overton section of Miami, Florida. Supreme Court decisions begin narrowing justification for affirmative action programs.

1991 Clarence Thomas named to Supreme Court, replacing Thurgood Marshall. Confirmation hearings marred by charges of sexual harassment lodged by Professor Anita Hill. Brutal police beating of Rodney King captured on amateur videotape in Los Angeles.

1992 Rioting broke out in Los Angeles and a dozen other major cities after all-white jury acquits police officers in Rodney King beating.

1993 Toni Morrison became first African American to win Nobel Prize in Literature.

1995 Million Man March, organized by Nation of Islam's Louis Farrakhan, called upon African-

American men to take responsibility for community and family needs. O.J. Simpson was acquitted in criminal trial on charges of double murder in trial that polarized public opinion along racial lines.

1996 Supreme Court decisions overturn congressional districts specifically drawn to assure minority representation in Congress. California referendum approves Proposition 209 banning affirmative action in government hiring programs, contracting, and college admissions. Rash of church burnings hits African-American churches in the South.

1997 Haitian immigrant Abner Louima brutally beaten and sodomized by New York City police officer Justin Volpe, triggering outcry against police brutality.

1999 African immigrant Amadou Diallo shot and killed by four white street-crime unit officers who fired 41 bullets at the unarmed Diallo who stood in the doorway of his Bronx, New York, apartment building. Massive civil disobedience demonstrations at Police Headquarters result in hundreds of arrests. The four officers win change of venue for their murder trial to upstate New York.

(Sources: *Ethnic Studies, Negro Almanac, Negro, Chronological History of the Negro in America, Black Firsts,* and *The Timetables of African American History*)

European Americans

1565 Spaniards founded St. Augustine, Florida, first European settlement in North America.

1607 First permanent English settlement established at Jamestown, Virginia.

1620 Pilgrims traveling on the *Mayflower* arrived in Massachusetts and established colony at Plymouth.

1623 Dutch West India Company founded New Netherlands.

1683 First German immigrants to North America settled in Pennsylvania.

1718 Large-scale Scots-Irish immigration to American colonies began.

1798 Federalist Party pushed Alien and Sedition Acts to crush political opponents and harass aliens.

1825 First Norwegian immigrants arrived in U.S.

1840–1850s Economic hardship and failed liberal democratic revolution led to immigration of nearly 4 million Germans.

1845–1849 Irish Potato Famine led to influx of 1.5 million Irish immigrants to U.S.

1855 Antiforeigner Know-Nothing Party reached its zenith in American politics. Castle Garden immigrant facility opened in New York.

1863 Irish working-class mobs attacked African Americans in New York City during anti-draft rioting that lasted four days.

1870s–1900 Nearly 1.5 million Scandinavians immigrated to the United States.

1880s–1920 An estimated 1 million Poles, 2.5 million eastern European Jews, 4 million Austrians, Czechs, Hungarians, and Slovaks, and 4.5 million Italians came to the U.S.

1883–1885 Economic depression contributed to increase in anti-immigrant sentiment.

1886 Following Haymarket Affair in Chicago, suspicion of foreign radicals and nativism increased sharply. Statue of Liberty dedicated.

1890 Eleven Italian Americans, accused of killing a police official, were lynched in New Orleans.

1892 Ellis Island replaced Castle Garden as entry point for European immigrants.

1901–1910 Nearly nine million immigrants entered the U.S., mostly from southern and eastern Europe.

1907 List of exclusionary categories that could be used to deny immigrants entry to U.S. was increased to included tuberculosis victims and people convicted of certain types of crimes.

1916–1919 Anti-immigrant movement advocated restrictive immigration legislation.

1919–1920 Hundreds of radical aliens were deported during the Red Scare, or Palmer Raids, period.

1921 Johnson Act established a national quota system and numerical limits on European immigration to the U.S. for the first time

1924 Johnson-Reed Act established more stringent quotas, discriminating against southern and eastern Europeans, and non-whites.

1930–1940 Immigration declined dramatically during the Great Depression.

1945 War Brides Act permitted immigration of spouse of U.S. military personnel who had married overseas.

1948 Displaced Person's Act permitted immigration of war refugees.

1952 McCarran-Walter Act continued the restrictive policies of the 1924 legislation.

1953 Refugee Relief Act further opened immigration to war refugees, including displaced Soviet citizens.

1965 Amendments to Immigration and Nationality Act decreased immigration from Europe, while increasing immigration from Caribbean, Latin America, and Asia.

1969–1985 Nearly 300,000 Russian Jews immigrated to the U.S.

1980s–1990s Influx of illegal Irish immigrants, perhaps as many as 150,000, arrived in the U.S.

(Sources: *Ethnic Studies*, *Ethnic Almanac*, *World Book*, and *Encyclopedia of Multicultural America*)

Jewish Americans

1654 Jewish immigrants from Brazil established first Jewish settlement in North America in New Amsterdam.

1730 First North American synagogue built in New York.

1775 Francis Salvador became member of South Carolina Provincial Congress, only Jewish American elected to any colonial legislature.

1776 An estimated 2,500 Jewish Americans resided in the 13 American colonies.

1781 Haym Solomon assisted in raising funds for American revolutionary cause.

1785 Virginia Statute of Religious Liberty granted religious freedom to Jewish Americans in Virginia.

1787 U.S. Constitution prohibited religious qualifications for federal office.

1791 First Amendment to Constitution guaranteed separation of church and state in United States.

1809 Jewish-American delegate Jacob Henry permitted to join House of Commons in North Carolina, despite state law barring any but Protestants from holding office.

1815 Congress of Vienna's reversal of German Jews' rights triggered growing immigration to U.S.

1826 Maryland rescinded religious tests against Jewish Americans. Jewish-American population in U.S. reached 6,000.

1845–1861 David Levy Yulee (D.-Fla.) first U.S. Senator of Jewish-American background.

1848 Following failure of Revolution of 1848, thousands of German Jews came to the U.S., increasing Jewish population in the U.S. to 150,000 by 1860.

1862 Rabbis joined Union Army as military chaplains. General Ulysses S. Grant expelled Jewish Americans from Tennessee.

1868 Fourteenth Amendment adopted, later interpreted as extending First Amendment guarantee of religious freedom to the states.

1881–1882 Jewish-American population in U.S. estimated at 250,000. "Pogroms" and anti-Jewish legislation in Russia triggered wave of immigration to U.S.

1885 Reform Jewish-Americans drafted Pittsburgh Platform, setting movement's principles.

1886 Jewish Theological Seminary founded.

1914 Louis D. Brandeis took leadership of American Zionist movement.

1915 Anti-Semitism in Georgia led to lynching of Leo Frank, a Jewish American.

1924 Immigration legislation sharply cut Jewish immigration. Jewish-American population reached 4.5 million.

1930s Spurred by Nazi propaganda, anti-Semitism in U.S. increased dramatically. Approximately 150,000 Jews fleeing Nazi persecution were allowed into the U.S.

1937 Jewish-American population peaked at 3.7 percent of national population.

1939–1945 Nazis killed six million Jews during World War II.

1948 U.S. supported partition of Palestine and establishment of Jewish state of Israel.

1967 Jewish Americans supported Israel during Six Day War.

1968 Militant leader Rabbi Meir Kahane founded Jewish Defense League.

1973 Jewish-American community supported Israel during Yom Kippur war.

1980s Many Jewish Americans were alarmed by rise of Christian Right's attempts to challenge principle of separation of church and state.

1984 Jewish-American leaders expressed alarm at anti-Semitic remarks made by African-American leader Reverend Jesse Jackson, during Jackson's campaign for Democratic party presidential campaign. Jackson apologized for remarks and sought reconciliation.

1990s Jewish-American leaders sharply criticized anti-Semitic remarks of Nation of Islam leader Louis Farrakhan.

1992 Jewish-American politicians held 33 seats in the House of Representatives and 10 in the Senate.

1994 Rabbi Menachem Mendel Schneerson, spiritual leader of the Lubavitch Hasidic group for 44 years, died at age 92. Some followers believed he was the Messiah.

(Sources: *Jewish Peoples Almanac*, *Timetables of Jewish History*, *Ethnic Almanac*, and *Ethnic Studies*)

Hispanic Americans

1493 Christopher Columbus landed on island of Boriquen (now Puerto Rico).

1508 Juan Ponce de Leon appointed governor of Puerto Rico.

1511 Taino rebellion against Spanish rule defeated in Puerto Rico.

1513 Ponce DeLeon claimed Florida for Spain; first African slaves brought to Puerto Rico.

1519 Spaniards led by Hernan Cortes arrived in Mexico.

1521 Cortes defeated Aztec Empire.

1540–1565 Spaniards introduced horses, cattle, sheep, and swine to North America.

1565 Spain founded first permanent European settlement in North America at St. Augustine, Florida.

1598 First Spanish settlement founded in present-day New Mexico.

1718 Spanish mission founded at San Antonio, Texas.

1763 Spain relinquished claim to Florida.

1769 Spanish mission founded at San Diego, California.

1810 Struggle began for Mexican independence from Spain.

1821 Mexico gained independence from Spain.

1836 American settlers in Texas declared independence from Mexico.

1845 U.S. annexed Texas, triggering Mexican-American War.

1846–1848 U.S. defeated Mexico. Treaty of Guadalupe Hidalgo ceded one-third of Mexico's territory to U.S., including most of present-day southwest U.S.

1853 Gadsden Purchase acquired additional territory from Mexico.

1859 Juan N. Cortina led rebellion against European Americans in South Texas.

1862 Mexico military forces led by Texas-Mexican Ignacio Zaragosa defeated French invasion forces at Puebla on May 5. The date is still celebrated as an important Mexican-American holiday.

1868 Puerto Rican revolutionists failed to overthrow Spanish rule.

1873 Slavery abolished in Puerto Rico.

1898 U.S. defeated Spain in Spanish-American War; Puerto Rico became U.S. territory.

1900 U.S. established government in Puerto Rico, comprised of governor and executive council appointed by U.S. president and a locally elected House of Delegates.

1910 Thousands immigrated to U.S. from Mexico to escape political turmoil of Mexican Revolution. According to U.S. Census, 1,513 Puerto Ricans were living in U.S.

1917 U.S. legislation made Puerto Ricans U.S. citizens and subject to military conscription during World War I.

1925 U.S. Border Patrol established to control Mexican border traffic.

1929 League of United Latin American Citizens organized in Harlingen, Texas.

1943 Bracero program established, permitted Mexican laborers to work temporarily in U.S.

1943 Anti-Mexican "zoot suit" rioting broke out in Los Angeles.

1947 Puerto Ricans gained right to elect their own governor.

1948 Luis Munoz Marin became first elected Puerto Rican governor.

1950 Pro-independence Puerto Rican terrorists failed in attempt to assassinate President Truman.

1952 Commonwealth of Puerto Rico established.

1954 U.S. authorities launched "Operation Wetback" aimed at deporting illegal Mexican immigrants.

1959 Fidel Castro seized power in Cuba, triggering exile migration by middle- and upper-class Cubans.

1961 U.S. severed diplomatic relations with Cuba; Cuban-exile force, backed by CIA, defeated in Bay of Pigs invasion.

1962 Commercial air flights between U.S. and Cuba ended.

1965 United Farm Workers Association, led by Cesar Chavez, organized grape strike in Delano, California. Crusade for Justice, a Chicano civil rights group led by Rodolfo "Corky" Gonzales, organized in Denver. New immigration law limited Mexican immigration to 20,000 each year. Voting rights legislation eliminated literacy tests in English as qualification for voting. U.S.-government-sponsored Cuban Refugee Airlift brought exiles from Cuba to Miami.

1967 Puerto Rican plebiscite voted to continue Commonwealth status, defeating proposals for statehood or independence.

1970 La Raza Unida party created in Texas. Herman Badillo elected to U.S. House of Representatives from Bronx, New York, first mainland Puerto Rican elected to Congress.

1973 Cuban Refugee Airlift ended.

1974 New York City Board of Education agreed to institute a program of bilingual education for Puerto Rican children in the public schools

1974 Jerry Apodaca elected governor of New Mexico.

1977 U.S. and Cuba established diplomatic interest sections in embassies of third-party countries.

1979 *Zoot Suit*, by Luis Valdez, became first Mexican-American Broadway play.

1980 125,000 Cuban refugees arrived in Florida during boatlift from Mariel, Cuba.

1981 President Reagan authorized establishment of Radio Marti to broadcast radio programs to Cuba.

1982 Toney Anaya elected New Mexico governor.

1985 Angered by Radio Marti broadcasts, Fidel Castro terminated family visits by Cuban Americans and agreement to repatriate Mariel boatlift Cubans being held in U.S. jails.

1987 Fearing deportation to Cuba, Mariel refugees imprisoned in Atlanta, Georgia, and Oakdale, Louisana, rioted.

1988 President Reagan appointed Dr. Lauro F. Cavazos as secretary of education, first Hispanic to serve in the Cabinet.

1989 Representative Ileana Ros-Lehtinen became first Cuban-born member of U.S. Congress.

1999 Emotional and highly politicized custody battle erupted over Elian Gonzalez, 6-year old Cuban boy whose mother died in ill-fated boat trip escaping from Cuba.

(Sources: *Hispanic-American Almanac*, *Ethnic Almanac*, *Ethnic Studies*, and *Facts on File*)

Asian Americans

1763 Filipino sailors jumped ship and settled in Louisiana, earning their living as fishermen.

1815 Filipino settlers fought under Jean Laffitte against the British during Battle of New Orleans in War of 1812.

1850s First Chinese immigrants, most of them from Guandong Province, began arriving on West Coast.

1862–1869 Nearly 25,000 Chinese laborers helped to build the Pacific section of the nation's first transcontinental railroad.

1868 One hundred forty-eight Japanese laborers arrived in Hawaii.

1869 Anti-Chinese riot erupted in San Francisco.

1870s Anti-Chinese immigrant movement gained strength among white population in western states.

1871 Nineteen were killed in anti-Chinese riot in Los Angeles.

1880 Number of Chinese Americans reached 105,000.

1882 Chinese Exclusion Act of 1882 stopped Chinese laborer immigration for ten years.

1885 Twenty-eight Chinese Americans were killed in anti-Chinese riot in Rock Springs, Wyoming.

1892 Chinese Exclusion Act extended for additional ten years.

1898 Philippines were ceded to U.S. after Spanish-American War. Hawaii annexed by United States. Approximately 60,000 Japanese immigrants resided in Hawaii at the time.

1902 Prohibition on Chinese immigration extended indefinitely.

1906 San Francisco ordered Asian-American students to attend segregated "Oriental School."

1907–1908 U.S. and Japanese governments reached "Gentleman's Agreement" to reduce number of Japanese immigrants to U.S.

1913 California legislature adopted bill restricting Japanese immigrants' ability to lease land.

1923–1929 Large-scale Filipino migration to Hawaii took place.

1924 Federal legislation ended Asian immigration to U.S., except for Filipinos who were considered American nationals.

1929 Anti-Filipino rioting in Exeter, California, injured 200.

1930 Filipino-American martyr Fermin Tobera killed in anti-Filipino riot in Watsonville, California.

1934 Federal legislation promised eventual independence for Philippines and restricted Filipino immigration to 50 per year.

1935 U.S. government offered free transportation for any Filipino immigrant wanting to return to Philippines.

1940 Legislation permitted naturalization of Filipino immigrants.

1941 Japan attacked Pearl Harbor on December 7; Philippines were invaded three days later.

1942 President Franklin Roosevelt authorized internment of Japanese Americans living on the West Coast.

1942–1944 Philippines occupied by Japanese forces.

1946 Japanese-American internment camps were shut down; Philippines granted independence on July 4.

1948 Legislation authorized compensation for financial losses suffered by Japanese Americans during World War II internment. Most eventually received ten cents on a dollar.

1952 McCarran-Walter Immigration Act ended total exclusion of Asian immigrants and permitted naturalization for Asian Americans.

1959 Hiram Leong Fong elected first Asian American to serve in U.S. Senate.

1965 Immigration Act of 1965 authorized 170,000 immigrants annually from Asian continent.

1970–1980 Chinese immigration to U.S. increased by 88 percent. Filipino immigration also increased dramatically.

1980 According to Census, Filipinos were second largest Asian ethnic group in America.

1981 Chinese-American sculptor Maya Lin submitted winning design for Vietnam Veterans Memorial in Washington, D.C.

1982 Chinese-American Vincent Chin beaten to death by two jobless autoworkers in Detroit who blamed Japanese for unemployment in automobile industry.

1984 Samoan-American diver Greg Louganis won gold medals in platform and springboard diving at Los Angeles Olympics.

1985 Haing S. Ngor became first Asian American to win an acting Oscar for his role in *The Killing Fields*, as Dith Pran. Astronaut Lt. Colonel Ellison Onizuka became first Asian American in space, as crew member on a space shuttle flight.

1988 U.S. government formally apologized for internment of Japanese Americans and offered a $20,000 payment for each victim. Greg Louganis again won two gold medals for diving at the Olympics in Korea.

1991 Major General John Liu Fugh became first Chinese American promoted to general rank in U.S. Army. Asian Pacific Islander population in U.S. reached 7,273,662 in 1990 census, an increase of 100 percent from 3.5 million in 1980.

1994 Margaret Cho became first Asian American to star in her own television program, *All-American Girl*.

(Sources: *Ethnic Studies*, *Ethnic Almanac*, and *Asian American Almanac*)

Gay Americans

1610 Virginia adopted first sodomy law in the American colonies, imposing death penalty.

1641 Massachusetts Bay Colony made sodomy a capital crime.

1642 Connecticut declared sodomy a capital offense.

1647 Rhode Island declared sodomy between men a capital crime.

1649 Two married women in Plymouth were charged with "lewd behavior" in bed.

1656 New Haven adopted first colonial law specifically forbidding "unnatural acts" between women.

1660 Jan Quisthout van der Linde executed for sodomy.

1668 New Jersey enacted legislation making sodomy a capital crime, but exempting children under 14 and victims of force.

1682 Quaker Pennsylvania adopted first law making sodomy a non-capital crime.

1718 Pennsylvania lawmakers changed their minds and declared sodomy a capital offense.

1778 Lieutenant Frederick Gotthold of the Continental Army was court-martialed for attempted sodomy.

1824–1826 First known American document discussing homosexuality in prison published by Louis Dwight.

1848 Several lesbian and bisexual women participated in first Women's Rights Convention in Seneca Falls, New York.

1860 Walt Whitman's *Leaves of Grass* published.

1870 *Joseph and His Friend*, first American novel to refer to gay themes, was published.

1896 In *A Florida Enchantment*, two women hug and kiss for the first time in American theater.

1897 Havelock Ellis' *Sexual Inversion* is published as first impartial treatment of homosexuality in men.

1912 Heterodoxy, a feminist luncheon club for "unorthodox women," including prominent lesbian and bisexual women, began meeting in New York to discuss political and social affairs. Discussions continued until 1940s.

1914 First printed use of the word "faggot" to refer to gay men appeared in a dictionary of criminal slang.

1920–1935 Gay and lesbian African-American writers, actors, and musicians, such as Langston Hughes, Bessie Smith, and Ethel Waters, played prominent roles in Harlem Renaissance.

1923 *God of Vengeance*, a play by Sholom Asch with lesbian content, opened on Broadway.

1924 First homosexual organization in America (Society for Human Rights) founded.

1926 *The Captive*, Broadway play with lesbian themes, triggered public controversy and was eventually shut down. The episode led to adoption of the Padlock Law, which prohibited "sex perversion" in theatrical presentations.

1927 First U.S. play with gay male theme, *The Drag*, opened in Connecticut but was forced to close before reaching Broadway.

1930 Under pressure from Catholic-led Legion of Decency, Hollywood adopted the Motion Picture Production Code, which banned homosexuality from movies and remained in force until 1960s.

1942 U.S. armed forces adopted prohibition on homosexuality in the military.

1948 Kinsey Institute study reported widespread homosexual experiences among American men.

1951 Mattachine Society, forerunner of gay rights movement, founded.

1953 Executive Order declared "sexual perversion" grounds for dismissal from federal employment. *ONE*, journal of gay and lesbian opinion, began publication. New Kinsey study reported widespread lesbian experiences among American women.

1955 Daughters of Bilitis, first lesbian organization in the U.S., was founded.

1957 American Civil Liberties Union declared support for constitutionality of sodomy and other anti-homosexual laws. Crittenden Report, conducted for U.S. Navy, concluded that homosexuals posed no security risks for the military, but Pentagon denied existence of the document for two decades.

1961 Illinois became first state to legalize consensual homosexual sex.

1964 ACLU dropped support for anti-gay laws. First gay rights demonstration occurred at Army Induction Center in New York City.

1965 Mattachine Society protested discriminatory federal hiring practices at a White House demonstration.

1967 *The Advocate*, longest continuously published gay newspaper, first appeared.

1969 Stonewall riots, the beginning of the modern gay rights movement, occurred in New York following police raid on the Stonewall Inn in Greenwich Village. Gay Liberation Front founded.

1970 First march to mark anniversary of Stonewall riots, precursor of current day Gay Pride marches, held in New York.

1971 National Organization of Women adopted position supporting lesbian rights. Connecticut repealed sodomy laws.

1972 East Lansing, Michigan, became first U.S. city prohibiting anti-gay bias in municipal employment. First American gay synagogue founded in Los Angeles.

1973 National Gay and Lesbian Task Force founded. American Psychiatric Association concluded that homosexuality was not a mental disorder. Lesbian Herstory Archives founded in New York City. American Bar Association proposed repeal of all state sodomy laws. Lambda Legal Defense and Education Fund founded.

1975 The first U.S. county to bar anti-gay discrimination was Santa Cruz County, California

1978 San Francisco's openly gay supervisor, Harvey Milk, and Mayor George Moscone murdered by Dan White.

1979 One hundred thousand marched for gay and lesbian civil rights in Washington, DC protest.

1981 U.S. military barred lesbians and gays from serving in armed forces. First published reports refer to mysterious disease afflicting gays (AIDS).

1982 Gay Related Immune Disorder (GRID) renamed Acquired Immune Deficiency Syndrome (AIDS). Gay Men's Health Crisis founded in New York to fight spread of AIDS. Alarm grows as epidemic spreads, but government officials take little action.

1983 Representative Gerry Studds publicly acknowledged that he is gay. Moral Majority founder Reverend Jerry Falwell said AIDS is "the judgment of God." International medical researchers met in Geneva to discuss AIDS epidemic.

1984 Berkeley, California, extended benefits to lesbian and gay partners of city employees. *Wall Street Journal* began using the word "gay" as adjective. Researchers in the U.S. and France independently isolate the AIDS virus. Of the 3,400 Americans diagnosed with AIDS, 1,500 are dead.

1985 Actor Rock Hudson died of AIDS. First blood tests for antibodies to AIDS virus are developed.

1986 Supreme Court upheld Georgia's sodomy law. AIDS virus officially designated as HIV.

1987 Massachusetts Representative Barney Frank announced that he is gay. Half million demonstrators marched for gay rights in Washington, D.C. ACT UP, militant action group pushing need for AIDS funding and research founded in New York. *New York Times* began using "gay" in its news reports. Of 36,000 Americans diagnosed with AIDS, 21,000 are dead. AZT became first anti-HIV drug approved by Food and Drug Administration. Names Quilt commemorating AIDS victims who have died displayed in Washington, D.C., during second gay rights march by half-million demonstrators.

1988 AIDS became the 15th leading cause of death in America.

1989 FDA approved ddI (dideoxyinosine) as anti-AIDS drug.

1990 Controversy erupted over Cincinnati Museum of Art exhibit of Robert Mapplethorpe's homoerotic photographs. AIDS deaths in America reach 100,000 mark, with approximately 1,100 deaths per month according to the Centers for Disease Control. FDA approved another anti-AIDS drug: ddC (dideoxycytidine). Americans with Disabilities Act prohibited discrimination against AIDS patients. Queer Nation, militant gay rights group, founded in New York City. CBS suspended *60 Minutes* commentator Andy Rooney for homophobic remarks.

1991 "Tongues Untied," documentary about African-American gay men broadcast on PBS.

1992 Democratic presidential candidate Bill Clinton became first nominee to refer to gays in his acceptance speech at convention. Anti-gay referenda bitterly contested in Oregon and Colorado. Oregon's measure was defeated, but Colorado's passed. Meanwhile, New Jersey, California, and Vermont adopted legislation banning anti-gay discrimination. *New York Times* stepped up coverage of gay and lesbian news as part of diversity campaign.

1993 President Clinton became first president to include a gay inaugural ball in Inauguration festivities. Clinton adopted "don't ask, don't tell" policy on gays in the military, which pleased no one. Seven hundred fifty thousand participated in March on Washington for Gay, Lesbian, and Bi Equal Rights. Hawaii Supreme Court opened possibility that same-sex marriages might by legalized in the state. Exclusion of Irish Lesbian and Gay Organization from St. Patrick's Day Parade prompted New York Mayor David Dinkins and Governor Mario Cuomo to boycott the parade. President Clinton appointed his first "AIDS czar," Kristine Gebbie, who was forced to resign a year later following criticism from AIDS activists for ineffectiveness. AIDS became leading cause of death for American males, 25–44 years of age, and 4th leading killer for women in the same age groups.

1994 Organizers cancelled Boston's St. Patrick's Day parade rather than comply with court order to permit participation of gay and lesbian group. Gay choreographer Bill T. Jones and lesbian poet Adrienne Rich received prestigious MacArthur Foundation "genius" awards. Over a million people participated in march marking 25th anniversary of Stonewall riots. Home furnishings chain IKEA aired first television commercial in the U.S. featuring an openly same-sex couple.

1995 Rhode Island adopted gay rights bill.

(Sources: *The Gay Almanac* and *The Lesbian Almanac*)

Major Speeches in U.S. History

American oratory seems to have changed in recent decades. With the predominance of television, the great speech seems to have given way to the pithy sound bite. Some of the more modern speeches included in this list may not measure up to the powerful prose of yesteryear, but are included because of their impact on American social and political history.

1644 Roger Williams–"Plea for Religious Liberty"

1735 Andrew Hamilton–"Defense of Zenger"

1741 Jonathan Edwards–"Sinners in the Hands of an Angry God"

1774 John Hancock–"Boston Massacre Oration"

1775 Patrick Henry–"Give Me Liberty or Give Me Death"

1787 Benjamin Franklin–"On the Constitution"

1788 Patrick Henry–"Against the Federal Constitution"

1788 James Madison–"For the Federal Constitution"

1801 Thomas Jefferson–"First Inaugural Address"

1833 John C. Calhoun–"On the Force Bill: Nationalism and State's Rights"

1837 Wendell Phillips–"The Murder of Lovejoy"

1837 Ralph Waldo Emerson–"The American Scholar"

1850 Frederick Douglass–"American Slavery"

1850 Henry Clay–"On the Compromise Measures"

1850 Daniel Webster–"On the Compromise Measures: the Seventh of March Speech"

1851 Sojourner Truth–"Ain't I a Woman?"

1855 Lucy Stone–"Speech to the National Woman's Rights Convention"

1858 Abraham Lincoln–"A House Divided"

1858 Stephen Douglas–"Popular Sovereignty"

1859 John Brown–"Speech to the Court"

1860 Abraham Lincoln–"Cooper Union Address"

1861 Abraham Lincoln–"First Inaugural Address"

1863 Abraham Lincoln–"Gettysburg Address"

1865 Abraham Lincoln–"Second Inaugural Address"

1873 Susan B. Anthony–"Women's Right to the Suffrage"

1884 Susan B. Anthony–"On Behalf of the Woman Suffrage Amendment"

1896 William Jennings Bryan–"Cross of Gold Speech"

1898 Albert Beveridge–"The March of the Flag"

1899 Theodore Roosevelt–"The Strenuous Life"

1900 William Jennings Bryan–"Imperialism"

1917 Woodrow Wilson–"War Message"

1918 Eugene Debs–"Statement to the Court"

1919 Woodrow Wilson–"The League of Nations"

1933 Franklin D. Roosevelt–"First Inaugural Address"

1933 Franklin D. Roosevelt–"First Fireside Chat"

1941 Franklin D. Roosevelt–"War Message"

1946 Winston Churchill–"Iron Curtain Speech"

1961 John F. Kennedy–"Inaugural Address"

1962 John F. Kennedy–"Cuban Missile Crisis Address"

1963 John F. Kennedy–"Report to the American People on Civil Rights"

1963 Martin Luther King Jr. "I Have a Dream Speech"

1964 Lyndon B. Johnson–"State of the Union" ("Great Society Speech")

1968 Lyndon B. Johnson–"Address to the Nation" (announced decision not to run for reelection)

1974 Richard M. Nixon–"Resignation Speech"

1983 Ronald Reagan–"Evil Empire Speech"

1983 Ronald Reagan–"Strategic Defense Initiative" (Star Wars).

1984 Mario Cuomo–"Keynote Address to the Democratic Convention"

1984 Jesse L. Jackson–"Address to the Democratic Convention" (Our Time Has Come).

1988 George Bush, Acceptance Speech at Republican Convention (Read My Lips)

1991 George Bush–"Address to the Nation on the Gulf War"

1995 Louis Farrakhan–"Million Man March"

1995 Reverend Billy Graham–"Mystery of Evil" (following Oklahoma City terrorist bombing)

1996 Sarah Brady–"Address to the Democratic Convention" (on gun violence in America)

(Sources: *The Many Sides of America, American Voices: Significant Speeches in American History, 1640–1945,* and *In Our Own Words: Extraordinary Speeches in American History*)

Landmark Supreme Court Decisions

1803 *Marbury v. Madison* (1 Cranch 137)–Established court's power of judicial review–power to declare laws unconstitutional.

1824 *Gibbons v. Ogden* (9 Wheaton 1)–Authority of federal government takes precedence over that of the states in regard to interstate commerce.

1857 *Dred Scott v. Sanford* (12 Howard 299)–African Americans could not be U.S. citizens and slavery could not be prohibited in U.S. territories. (These rulings were overturned by the Thirteenth and Fourteenth Amendments to the Constitution.)

1896 *Plessy v. Ferguson* (163 U.S. 537)–Separate but equal public facilities held to be constitutional. (Overturned by ruling in *Brown v. Board of Education of Topeka,* 1954.)

1919 *Schenck v. United States* (249 U.S. 47)–Government may restrict freedom of speech if a "clear and present danger" to public order is threatened.

1919 *Abrams v. United States* (250 U.S. 616)–Upheld conviction of anti-war leafleteers based on "clear and present danger" test; Holmes was joined by Brandeis in eloquent dissenting opinion defending freedom of speech.

1925 *Gitlow v. New York* (268 U.S. 652)–Extended First Amendment protections applicable to state and local governments under the provisions of the Fourteenth Amendment.

1935 Sick Chicken Case (*Schecter Poultry v. United States*) (295 U.S. 495)–National Industrial Recovery Act of 1933 declared unconstitutional.

1954 *Brown v. Board of Education of Topeka, Kansas* (347 U.S. 483)–Racially segregated schools declared unconstitutional.

1961 *Mapp v. Ohio* (367 U.S. 643)–Illegally obtained evidence barred in state courts.

1963 *Gideon v. Wainwright* (372 U.S. 335)–Accused criminals gained right to free legal counsel.

1963 *Abington Township v. Schempp* (374 U.S. 203)–Prayers in public schools held unconstitutional.

1964 *New York Times Co. v. Sullivan* (376 U.S. 254)–Public official must prove actual malice to successfully sue press organization for defamation.

1966 *Sheppard v. Maxwell* (384 U.S. 233)–Murder conviction overturned due to prejudicial pre-trial publicity.

1966 *Miranda v. Arizona* (384 U.S. 436)–Accused criminals must be informed of their legal rights.

1971 *Griggs v. Duke Power Co.* (401 U.S. 424)–Upheld right of Congress to bar employment discrimination based on race.

1972 *Furman v. Georgia* (408 U.S. 238)–Existing capital punishment laws held cruel and unusual punishment.

1973 *Roe v. Wade* (410 U.S. 113)–Women gained right to have abortion during first six months of pregnancy.

1978 *Regents of the University of California v. Bakke* (438 U.S. 265)–Affirmative action in college admissions upheld in principle, but overturned as applied at medical school in question.

1979 *United Steelworkers of America v. Weber* (443 U.S. 193)–Upheld affirmative action programs to end racial discrimination.

1986 *Thornburgh v. American College of Obstetricians and Gynecologists* (476 U.S. 747)–Reaffirmed *Roe v. Wade*, overturning Pennsylvania law designed to discourage women from seeking abortions.

1989 *Webster v. Reproductive Health Services* (492 U.S. 490)–Ruling restricted abortion rights.

1990 *Cruzan v. Director, Missouri Department of Health* (497 U.S. 261)–Court declared that a person has right to decline life-sustaining treatment and food.

1992 *Lee v. Weisman* (505 U.S. 577)–Mandatory prayer at public school graduation violates separation of church and state doctrine.

1992 *R.A.V. v. City of St. Paul* (505 U.S. 377)–Municipal ordinance prohibiting various forms of "hate speech" ruled a violation of First Amendment free speech guarantees.

1994 *Madsen v. Women's Health Center Inc.* (512 U.S. 753)–Judges may establish buffer zones outside abortion clinics to guarantee access to clinics without unduly curtailing demonstrators' free speech rights.

1996 *Romer v. Evans* (517 U.S. 620)–Amendment to Colorado State Constitution prohibiting local laws to protect homosexuals' civil rights rule violation of federal guarantees of equal protection.

1999 *Department of Commerce vs. U.S. House of Representatives* (525 U.S. 316)–Statistical sampling methods can be used to conduct the U.S. Census.

(Sources: *CQ Guide to Supreme Court, Supreme Court Compendium, World Almanac,* and *Facts on File*)

PART 3

The States

STATEHOOD CHRONOLOGY

1787 Delaware, Pennsylvania, and New Jersey

1788 Georgia, Connecticut, Massachusetts, Maryland, South Carolina, New Hampshire, Virginia, and New York

1789 North Carolina

1790 Rhode Island

1791 Vermont

1792 Kentucky

1796 Tennessee

1803 Ohio

1812 Louisiana

1816 Indiana

1817 Mississippi

1818 Illinois

1819 Alabama

1820 Maine

1821 Missouri

1836 Arkansas

1837 Michigan

1845 Florida and Texas

1846 Iowa

1848 Wisconsin

1850 California

1858 Minnesota

1859 Oregon

1861 Kansas

1863 West Virginia

1864 Nevada

1867 Nebraska

1876 Colorado

1889 North Dakota, South Dakota, Montana, and Washington

1890 Idaho and Wyoming

1896 Utah

1907 Oklahoma

1912 Arizona and New Mexico

1959 Alaska and Hawaii

(Sources: *Facts about the States* and *World Book*)

HISTORY OF THE STATES

State chronologies always run the risk of offending native state sensibilities. I don't presume to be an expert on what happened in every corner of the land since the European discovery of America. These chronologies are culled from published sources in encyclopedias, state fact books, and updated from news events in recent years. They don't list everything that happened, but they give an overview of important and unique events.

Alabama

1519 Alonzo Alvarez de Pineda first European to enter Mobile Bay.

1540 Hernando de Soto led Spanish expedition to Mobile Alabama territory; defeated Native Americans led by Chief Tuscaloosa.

1559 Spanish settlement established at Mobile Bay.

1561 Spanish colony abandoned.

1699 Pierre Le Moyne led French expedition down Mississippi River, claimed Dauphin Island region for France.

1702 First French settlement established.

1763 Treaty of Paris marking end of Seven Years' War ceded French territory east of Mississippi river to Britain; British occupied Mobile.

1780 Spain seized Mobile during American Revolutionary War.

1783 Britain ceded all territory east of Mississippi River except Florida to U.S.

1787 Georgia/Alabama border set.

1806 Jefferson College, first Alabama educational institution, founded.

1814 General Andrew Jackson defeated Native Americans at Battle of Horseshoe.

1817 Alabama Territory created.

1819 Admitted to Union as 22nd state.

1836 Forced migration of Cherokee tribe to Oklahoma territory began.

1861 Seceded from Union; joined Confederacy in Civil War.

1864 Union Admiral David Farragut defeated Confederate forces in Battle of Mobile Bay; invaded by Union forces.

1865 Union forces captured Mobile and Montgomery.

1881 Booker T. Washington founded Tuskegee Institute.

1888 First steel mill opened at Birmingham.

1931 Scottsboro Boys convicted of rape, sentenced to death.

1955 African-American seamstress Rosa Parks sparked 381-day bus boycott by refusing to give up her seat on Montgomery bus to white person.

1956 U.S. Supreme Court declared state's bus segregation laws unconstitutional.

1963 George Wallace elected governor. Wallace gained notoriety for blocking two African-American students from entering University of Alabama.

1965 Martin Luther King Jr. led Selma voting rights demonstrators in 5-day march on Montgomery.

1968 Wallace ran for president.

1972 Wallace wounded while campaigning for president in Maryland.

1982 Unemployment hit 9.8 percent. Following Wallace's moderation of his racial views, he apologizes to African Americans for his racist past, Wallace is elected to a fourth term as governor, with strong African-American support.

1992 Governor Guy Hunt and aides indicted on charges involving misuse of campaign funds.

1993 Governor Hunt convicted and removed from office.

1996 Wallace privately apologized to the two African Americans he had blocked at the schoolhouse door at University of Alabama in 1963.

1998 Wallace died of cardiac arrest, honored at funeral by African-American leaders as a repentant segregationist.

Alaska

1741 Expedition led by Danish explorer Vitus Bering, employed by Russia, landed in southeastern Alaska.

1784 Russians established first European settlement on Kodiak Island.

1867 Seward's Folly. Secretary of State William H. Seward purchased Alaska from Russians for $7.2 million.

1880 Gold discovered near present-day Juneau.

1897–1898 Klondike and Alaska gold rush brought thousands of prospectors.

1903 Border between Alaska and Canada established.

1912 Became U.S. territory.

1913 Women gained suffrage.

1942 Japanese forces landed on Aleutian Islands of Attu and Kiska.

1943 U.S. forces reclaimed Aleutian islands.

1959 Admitted to Union as 49th state.

1964 Hit by severe earthquake.

1977 Trans-Alaska oil pipeline completed.

1980 Personal income tax repealed; Congress put nearly 25 percent of state land under National Park protection.

1986 Augustine Island volcano erupted.

1989 Oil tanker *Exxon Valdez* dumped 11 million gallons of oil in Prince William Sound—worse oil spill in U.S. history.

1992 Mt. Sparr volcano erupted for first time in 39 years.

1994 Census Bureau reported Anchorage among fastest growing metropolitan areas in nation.

Arizona

1540 Expedition led by Francisco Vazquez de Coronado arrived in search of legendary Seven Cities of Cibola; Grand Canyon discovered by scouting party.

1776 Fort founded at Tucson.

1821 Became part of Mexico.

1848 Most of present-day Arizona ceded to U.S. following Mexican War.

1853 U.S. gained southern Arizona from Mexico in Gadsen Purchase.

1862 Confederate troops occupied Tucson for two months.

1863 Arizona territory created.

1881 Wyatt Earp, his two brothers, and Doc Holliday killed three adversaries in gun fight at O.K. Corral.

1886 Geronimo-led Apache warriors surrendered, ending Indian Wars.

1912 Admitted to Union as 48th state.

1919 Grand Canyon National Park established.

1936 Boulder Dam (now Hoover Dam) completed.

1981 Arizona Judge Sandra Day O'Connor appointed first female justice of U.S. Supreme Court.

1988 Governor Evan Mecham removed from office on misconduct charges.

1990s Authorities sought to deal with growing problem of pollution-caused smog affecting Grand Canyon vistas.

1991 Nine Buddhists murdered in temple.

1994 Census Bureau reported Yuma among fastest growing cities in America.

Arkansas

1541 Area explored by Hernando de Soto of Spain.

1673 French explorers Father Jacques Marquette and Louis Jolliet explored Mississippi River as far south as Arkansas River.

1682 Area claimed for France.

1803 Louisiana Purchase brought Arkansas under U.S. control.

1819 Arkansas territory created.

1836 Admitted to Union as 25th state.

1861 Seceded from Union, joined Confederacy in Civil War.

1863 Union troops occupied Little Rock.

1868 Readmitted to Union.

1891 Jim Crow legislation segregated railroads.

1906 Nation's only diamond mine opened near Murfreesboro.

1931 Hattie W. Caraway first woman elected to U.S. Senate.

1945 J. William Fulbright elected to U.S. Senate.

1957 President Eisenhower ordered federal troops and National Guard units to enforce court-ordered integration at Little Rock's Central High School.

1968 Segregationist presidential candidate, Governor George Wallace of Alabama, carried Arkansas in presidential election.

1974 J. William Fulbright left the Senate.

1983 First state to require teachers to pass basic skills exams to retain licenses.

1992 Governor Bill Clinton elected president of United States. National Safe Workplace Institute rated Arkansas the worst state in the nation for worker safety.

1995 Governor Jim Guy Tucker indicted in Whitewater scandal. Senator Fulbright died at age of 89.

1996 Tucker convicted and resigned from office.

California

1542 Juan Rodriguez Cabrillo sailed into San Diego Bay.

1579 Sir Francis Drake claimed coastal region for England.

1776 Spanish mission founded at San Francisco.

1809 Russian settlement founded near Bodega Bay.

1825 Mexico claimed California.

1841 First American settlers arrived via Oregon Trail.

1846 Americans staged "Bear Flag Rebellion"; U.S. forces captured state during Mexican War.

1848 Ceded to U.S. for $15 million payment.

1849 Gold rush began.

1850 Admitted to Union as 31st state.

1860 Pony Express delivered mail from Missouri to Sacramento.

1906 San Francisco devastated by earthquake and fire.

1937 Golden Gate Bridge opened.

1940 First freeway in America opened.

1955 Disneyland opened.

1957 New York Giants moved to San Francisco; Brooklyn Dodgers to Los Angeles.

1962 Richard M. Nixon (Republican) lost race for governor and told reporters they wouldn't have Dick Nixon to kick around anymore.

1966 Racial rioting broke out in Los Angeles' Watts district.

1967–1975 Ronald Reagan served as governor.

1964 Eight hundred students arrested during Free Speech Movement demonstrations at Berkeley.

1968 Robert F. Kennedy assassinated in Los Angeles. Californian Richard M. Nixon elected president.

1973 Thomas Bradley became first African-American mayor of Los Angeles.

1978 Voters' tax revolt led to adoption of Proposition 13, restricting property taxes.

1981 Former California governor Ronald Reagan elected president.

1989 Earthquake rocked San Francisco area.

1990 Immigrants from other countries constituted 11 percent of state's population.

1991 Stringent gasoline standards adopted in effort to reduce smog; Pete Wilson (Republican) elected governor.

1992 Rioting broke out in Los Angeles following acquittal of four white police officers in beating African-American motorist Rodney King. Fiscal crisis caused state government to issue IOUs to employees instead of checks. California became first state in the nation to elect two women senators to the U.S. Senate at the same time. Barbara Boxer (Democrat) was elected to serve out the balance of the seat vacated by Governor Pete Wilson (Republican) when he left the Senate in 1990 and appointed John Seymour to the Senate seat. Dianne Feinstein (Democrat) was elected to a full six-year term. National Safe Workplace Institute rated California number one in the nation for worker safety.

1994 Earthquake rocked Los Angeles. O.J. Simpson charged with murder of ex-wife, Nicole Brown Simpson. Orange County government declared bankruptcy.

1995 Simpson acquitted. An end to affirmative action in admissions polices at University of California institutions is set to begin in 1997.

1997 Minority enrollment at University of California dropped significantly with end of affirmative action admissions policies.

Colorado

1706 Area claimed by Spain.

1803 Eastern part of Colorado acquired by U.S. in Louisiana Purchase.

1806 Explored by Zebulon M. Pike.

1848 Following Mexican War, entire Southwest, including western Colorado, ceded to U.S.

1861 Colorado territory created.

1876 Admitted to Union as 38th state.

1914 Ludlow Massacre: 20 people, including 12 children, killed by national guardsmen attack on strikers' tent colony at Colorado Fuel & Iron Corporation.

1915 Rocky Mountain National Park established.

1958 Air Force Academy opened at Colorado Springs.

1966 North American Air Defense Command (NORAD) operation center opened at Cheyenne Mountain.

1992 Benjamin Nighthorse Campbell, a Northern Cheyenne and a Democrat, elected to U.S. Senate.

1995 Campbell switched parties, joining Republican ranks in the Senate.

1999 Massacre at Columbine High School in Littleton shocked the nation.

Connecticut

1614 Claimed by Dutch.

1632 English land grant issued.

1633 Dutch erected trading post at present-day Hartford.

1635 English settled at Saybrook.

1654 English seized Dutch fort at Hartford.

1675–1676 King Philip's War. Colonists defeated Wampanoag tribe.

1687 Colonists refused to turn Connecticut charter over to British; according to tradition charter hidden in Chart Oak tree in Hartford.

1788 Became 5th state to ratify Constitution.

1798 Eli Whitney introduced mass production techniques in manufacture of muskets in plant at Whineyville.

1806 Noah Webster published first American dictionary.

1878 First commercial telephone exchange established at New Haven.

1954 *Nautilus*, first atomic-power submarine, launched at Groton.

1974 Ella Grasso elected first woman governor elected without succeeding her husband in state's history.

1991 Bridgeport filed for bankruptcy; income tax introduced. Budget impasse prompted Governor Lowell P. Weicker Jr. (Independent) to impose five-day government shutdown.

Delaware

1609 Sailing for Dutch, explorer Henry Hudson entered Delaware Bay.

1610 Ship sent by Virginia Colony governor Lord De La Warr explored bay.

1638 Swedes established colony of New Sweden near present-day Wilmington.

1655 Dutch seized New Sweden, ruled it as part of New Netherland.

1664 British seized all of New Netherland, including Delaware.

1776 Revolutionary War naval battle fought in Delaware Bay.

1787 First state to ratify Constitution.

1800 Du Pont family migrated from France; began vast industrial holdings with construction of gunpowder plant.

1861–1865 Though a slave-holding state, remained in Union. Slaves freed in 1865 with passage of Thirteenth Amendment to Constitution.

1937 Nylon invented at Du Pont Company.

1946 Construction of Delaware Memorial Bridge authorized.

1951 Delaware Memorial Bridge opened.

1963 Delaware Turnpike opened, completing non-stop superhighway running from Boston to Washington, DC.

1971 Legislation restricts new heavy industry that might harm environment.

1983 University of Delaware marked 150th anniversary.

1987 Plagiarism scandal drove Senator Joseph Biden from campaign for Democratic presidential nomination.

1990 Due to favorable corporate laws, over 183,000 companies were incorporated in Delaware, including half of the Fortune 500.

1992 Delaware resumed executions for first time in 46 years.

Florida

1513 Claimed for Spain by explorer Ponce de Leon.

1539 Hernando de Soto led expedition landing at Tampa Bay.

1565 Spaniards founded St. Augustine, oldest city in U.S.

1586 Sir Francis Drake attacked St. Augustine but failed to capture fort.

1763 Ceded by Spain to Britain.

1783 Britain returned control to Spain.

1819–1821 U.S. acquired control from Spain.

1831 Cigar industry established in Key West.

1835 Seven-year Seminole War began.

1845 Admitted to Union as 27th state; David Lee Yulee, first U.S. senator of Jewish heritage elected.

1861 Third slave-state to secede from Union.

1868 Readmitted to Union.

1886 Cigar industry relocated to Tampa.

1888 Hit hard by yellow fever epidemic.

1898 American troops debarked from Florida ports for Spanish American War.

1928 Tamaiami Trail highway linking west and east Florida opened.

1933 Chicago Mayor Anton Joseph Cermak killed when would-be assassin failed in attack of President-elect Franklin Roosevelt.

1947 Everglades National Park established.

1958 National Aeronautics and Space Agency assumed control of Cape Canaveral; first U.S. earth satellite, *Explorer I*, launched.

1961 First U.S. manned space flight launched at Cape Canaveral.

1971 Walt Disney World founded outside Orlando.

1981 Influx of Cuban and Haitian refugees aggravated social problems.

1986 Space shuttle *Challenger* exploded just after liftoff, killing crew of seven.

1991 William Kennedy Smith tried and acquitted on rape charges.

1992 Hurricane Andrew devastated south Florida, killing 32, leaving 250,000 homeless.

1993 Severe weather with rare blizzard and tornadoes led federal government to declare disaster area.

1994 Census Bureau reported Naples one of the fastest growing cities in America. Unofficial "gay day" at Disney World attended by 20,000 people.

1999 Highly emotional and politicized custody battled erupted over Elian Gonzalez, 6-year old Cuban boy whose mother died on ill-fated boat trip fleeing Cuba.

Georgia

1540 Spanish explorer Hernando de Soto passed through Georgia.

1721 First English fort established.

1732 James Edward Oglethorpe granted charter for Georgia lands.

1733 First colonists led by Oglethorpe arrived.

1735 City of Augusta founded.

1766 Rioters in Savannah protest British Stamp Act.

1774 Declined to send delegates to first Continental Congress.

1776 Delegates signed Declaration of Independence.

1779 British forces occupied Augusta.

1781 American revolutionaries recaptured Augusta.

1819 First steamship to cross Atlantic, departed Savannah for Liverpool, England.

1861 Seceded from Union.

1864 Union General William T. Sherman captured Atlanta, marched to sea.

1865 Confederate President Jefferson Davis captured near Atlanta.

1867 Placed under military rule, following refusal to ratify Fourteenth Amendment.

1870 Readmitted to Union.

1886 John Styth Pemberton invented Coca-Cola.

1937 Atlantan Margaret Mitchell received Pulitzer Prize for *Gone With the Wind*.

1939 State legislature finally ratified Bill of Rights, 150 years after formally incorporated into Constitution.

1960 Future Governor Lester G. Maddox organized white resistance to civil rights movement's efforts to end segregation.

1968 Civil rights leader Martin Luther King Jr. buried in Atlanta, following assassination in Memphis, Tennessee.

1973 Maynard Jackson Jr. elected first African-American mayor of Atlanta.

1977 Georgian Jimmy Carter inaugurated President of United States.

1982 Wayne B. Williams convicted and sentenced for murders of 2 of 28 young African Americans murdered over two year period in Atlanta.

1994 Georgian Newt Gingrich (Republican) drafted conservative "Contract with America," led conservatives to victory in Congressional elections and became Speaker of the House.

1996 Atlanta hosted Summer Olympic Games.

1999 Gingrich resigned Congressional seat.

Hawaii

1778 British explorer Captain James Cook visited islands.

1779 Cook killed in skirmish with natives on island of Hawaii.

1796 King Kamehameha I united Hawaii.

1820 Christian missionaries arrived from New England.

1835 First permanent sugar plantation established.

1874 Hawaii King David Kalakaua visited Washington, DC, received by President Ulysses S. Grant.

1880s Pineapple industry founded with importation of pineapple plants from Jamaica.

1893 Dethroning of Queen Liliuokalani by American citizens-led revolution.

1894 Republic of Hawaii formed with Sanford B. Dole as president.

1898 Annexed by United States.

1907 "Gentlemen's Agreement" with Japan ended immigration of Japanese laborers to Hawaii.

1909 Construction began on U.S. naval base at Pearl Harbor.

1941 Japanese launched surprise attack on Pearl Harbor, marking U.S. entry into World War II.

1959 Admitted to Union as 50th state; Hiram Leong Fong, first Asian American elected to serve in U.S. Senate.

1967 First state to create office of ombudsman.

1980s: Tourist industry boomed.

1985 Illegal marijuana crop estimated at $4 billion.

1987 Japanese businesses invested heavily in Hawaiian real estate.

1991 Solemn ceremonies marked 50th anniversary of Pearl Harbor attack.

1992 Hurricane Iniki hit.

Idaho

1805 Expedition led by Meriwether Lewis and William Clark passed through Idaho area en route to Pacific Coast.

1818 U.S. and Great Britain agreed on joint control of Pacific Northwest.

1846 Treaty with Great Britain ceded Pacific Northwest below 49th parallel to U.S.

1860 Mormons founded first permanent settlement at Franklin.

1890 Admitted to Union as 43rd state.

1892 Martial law declared in northern Idaho during violence-plagued miners' strike.

1899 Martial law reimposed; federal troops dispatched against striking Western Federation of Miners.

1905 Women granted right to vote; former Governor Frank Steunenberg assassinated.

1907 Union leader William D. "Big Bill" Haywood acquitted on charges of involvement in Steunenberg murder.

1914 Moses Alexander elected first Jewish-American governor in U.S.

1942 Ten thousand Japanese Americans confined to internment camp at Hunt, Idaho.

1976 Teton Dam on Snake River collapsed, killing eleven and inflicting hundreds of millions dollars in damage.

1980 River of No Return Wilderness created as largest wilderness preserve in lower 48 states.

1986 White supremacist Aryan Nations group held World Congress at Hayden Lake.

1991 Snake River sockeye salmon declared endangered species.

1992 Three people killed during federal law enforcement siege at Ruby Ridge cabin of white supremacist Randy Weaver.

1994 Forest fires caused serious damage.

1994 Boise reported among fastest-growing metropolitan areas in nation.

1995 Wolves reintroduced in wilderness area.

Illinois

1673 French explorers Louis Jolliet and Father Jacques Marquette reached present-day Chicago.

1699 First permanent white settlement established.

1763 All French territory east of Mississippi River, except New Orleans, ceded to Great Britain.

1770s Jean Baptist Point du Sable, West Indian of African ancestry, founded permanent settlement at Chicago.

1801 Became part of Indiana Territory.

1809 Became a territory.

1818 Admitted to Union as 21st state.

1831–1832 Black Hawk War; Sauk and Fox tribes defeated.

1833 Remaining tribes ceded land.

1837 Illinois resident John Deere developed steel plow.

1844 Mormon leader Joseph Smith murdered in Carthage.

1846 Mormon leader Brigham Young led Mormons west to Utah.

1847 Cyrus McCormick began manufacture of mechanical reaper.

1858 Stephen Douglas and Abraham Lincoln held historic debates during senatorial campaign.

1860 Illinois resident Abraham Lincoln elected president.

1865 First state to ratify Thirteenth Amendment, outlawing slavery.

1871 Great Chicago Fire destroyed most of city.

1877 Knights of Labor, nation's first major labor union, founded in Illinois.

1886 Anarchists blamed for bomb that killed seven police officers at Haymarket Square rally in Chicago in favor of eight-hour day; four anarchists subsequently convicted and hanged.

1889 Jane Addams founded Hull House in Chicago to help poor residents.

1894 Federal troops suppressed Pullman Car Company railroad strike.

1915 Eight hundred twelve people killed when steamboat *Eastland* capsized in Chicago River.

1919 Racial rioting killed 22 African Americans, 16 whites.

1934 Gangster John Dillinger shot and killed at Chicago movie theater.

1942 First controlled nuclear chain reaction conducted at University of Chicago.

1955 Richard J. Daley elected mayor of Chicago for first of five consecutive terms; the world's first McDonald's hamburger restaurant opened in Des Plaines.

1959 St. Lawrence Seaway opened Chicago to ocean-going vessels.

1966 Dr. Martin Luther King Jr. organized fair housing campaign in Chicago.

1968 Police violently crush anti-Vietnam War demonstrators at Democratic Convention.

1969 Trial began for Chicago 8 defendants who organized protests at Democratic Convention.

1974 Sears Tower—then world's tallest building—completed in Chicago.

1983 Harold Washington elected first African-American mayor of Chicago.

1991 Border dispute with Kentucky resolved by Supreme Court.

1992 Carol Moseley Braun elected first female African American elected to U.S. Senate. Chicago hit by severe flooding.

1993 Midwestern flood created disaster area.

1994 Representative Dan Rostenkowski indicted in corruption scandal; lost bid for reelection.

1995 Severe heat wave caused hundreds of deaths. UAW ended 17-month long strike against Caterpillar.

Indiana

1679 Rene-Robert Cavelier, Sieur de La Salle, reached South Bend during his explorations for France.

1700s French settlement established at Vincennes.

1763 With end of French and Indian War, territory ceded to Britain.

1794 White settlement in Indiana opened up by defeat of Miamis in the Battle of Fallen Timbers, near present-day Toledo, Ohio.

1800 Indiana territory established.

1805 Indiana territory reduced in size by removal of Michigan from its jurisdiction.

1809 Indiana further reduced by creation of separate Illinois territory.

1811 Shawnee tribe defeated at Battle of Tippecanoe.

1812 Last Native-American battle fought in Indiana.

1816 Admitted to the Union as 19th state.

1901 Socialist Party founded at Indianapolis.

1911 First Indianapolis 500 auto race.

1948 Controversial Kinsey Report on American sexuality published by Indiana University researcher Alfred Kinsey.

1967 Richard D. Hatcher elected mayor of Gary, first African-American mayor in state's history.

1984 National Football League's Baltimore Colt's franchise relocated to Indianapolis.

1992 Mike Tyson tried and convicted of rape.

1995 Tyson released from prison.

Iowa

1673 French explorers Louis Jolliet and Father Jacques Marquette first Europeans in Iowa region.

1762 Ceded to Spain.

1788 French Canadian Julien Dubuque became first permanent white settler; began mining lead near present-day Dubuque.

1803 French control reestablished; ceded to U.S. in Louisiana Purchase.

1812 Incorporated into Missouri Territory.

1821 Missouri admitted to Union; Iowa left as unorganized area.

1832 Indians defeated in Black Hawk War.

1833 Permanent settlements established at Dubuque, Burlington, Fort Madison, Peru, and Bellevue.

1838 Iowa Territory created, including parts of Minnesota and Dakotas.

1846 Admitted to Union as 29th state.

1856 Train crossed first bridge across Mississippi River at Davenport.

1861–1865 Fought on Union side in Civil War.

1862 Iowa first state to establish federal land-grant college under terms of Morrill Land-Grant College Act.

1929 Iowa native Herbert Hoover inaugurated U.S. president.

1933 Prohibition repealed.

1936 University of Iowa's Writing Workshop founded.

1959 Soviet leader Nikita Khrushchev toured state, visited Roswell Garst family farm.

1965 Capital punishment abolished.

1985 Farm foreclosures reached crisis proportions.

1991 Riverboat gambling legalized. Tornadoes caused damage.

1993 Iowa was only state to have every county declared federal disaster during Midwestern floods.

1994 Flood-prone town of Chelsea slated to be moved to higher ground.

1997 McCaughey septuplets born in Des Moines.

Kansas

1541 Spanish explorer Francisco Coronado entered Kansas area.

1682 Claimed for France by explorer Rene-Robert Cavelier, Sieur de La Salle.

1762 Louisiana Territory, including Kansas, ceded by France to Spain in treaty ending Seven Years' War in Europe.

1800 Louisiana Territory returned to France

1803 Passed to U.S. control in Louisiana Purchase.

1804 Expedition led by Meriwether Lewis and William Clark passed through area.

1812 Incorporated into Missouri Territory.

1854 Kansas Territory established: pro- and anti-slavery groups flooded into territory in fight over whether Kansas would become slave or free state.

1856 Pro-slavery groups attacked free staters at town of Lawrence; free-staters led by John Brown retaliated with attack on Pottawatomie; state gained reputation as "Bleeding Kansas."

1859 Voters adopted Constitution barring slavery.

1861 Admitted to Union as 34th state.

1863 William Quantrill led Confederate guerrillas in attack on Lawrence.

1887 Susanne Medora Salter of Argonia elected nation's first woman mayor.

1890 Menninger Clinic for psychiatric research founded in Topeka.

1900 Carry Nation campaigned against saloons.

1912 Women suffrage granted.

1922 Nation's first shopping center opened in Kansas City.

1932 Republican Alfred Landon elected governor; dust storms hit southwestern part of state, beginning Midwest's Dust Bowl period.

1934 Landon only sitting Republican governor to be reelected.

1936 Landon ran as Republican candidate against Franklin D. Roosevelt in presidential race; received only eight electoral votes.

1942 Dwight D. Eisenhower, raised in Abilene, named commander of U.S. forces in Europe during World War II.

1953 Eisenhower inaugurated president of United States.

1956 Kansas turnpike opened.

1976 U.S. Senator Bob Dole nominated for vice president by Republican Party.

1991 Joan Finney elected state's first woman governor. Anti-abortion protests held in Wichita.

1993 Mississippi River flooding caused serious damage.

1994 Wichita mail delivery rated best in nation.

1996 Bob Dole defeated by President Bill Clinton in presidential election.

Kentucky

1654 Expedition led by Colonel Abraham Wood mapped much of present-day Kentucky.

1682 Rene-Robert Cavelier, Sieur de La Salle, claimed area including Kentucky for France.

1750 Cumberland Gap in Appalachian Mountains discovered.

1769 Frontiersman Daniel Boone explored wilderness.

1774 First permanent settlement established at Harrodsburg.

1775 Daniel Boone blazed Wilderness Road, founded Fort Boonesborough.

1776–1782 Boone and other frontier leaders defended settlements against British-backed Indian attacks during Revolutionary War.

1783 First Kentucky horse race held at Humble's Race Path. First whiskey distillery in Louisville established.

1786 Kentucky area separated from Virginia.

1792 Admitted to Union as 15th state.

1809 Future U.S. president Abraham Lincoln born near Hodgenville.

1828 Ministrel character "Jim Crow" created by Thomas "Daddy" Rice in Louisville.

1861 Governor refused to supply troops to Union, but state did not secede. President Lincoln guaranteed neutrality for Kentucky. Confederate forces invaded. Union forces established supply depot at Louisville. Residents fought for both sides.

1862 Confederate and Union forces clashed at Battle of Shiloh. Confederate guerrillas staged raids behind Union lines.

1864 Lincoln imposed martial law.

1875 First Kentucky Derby run.

1882 McCoy-Hatfield feud breaks out.

1890 Tobacco became state's number one crop.

1893 Mildred and Patty Hill of Louisville wrote "Happy Birthday to You."

1926 Mammoth Cave National Park created.

1937 Gold vault established at Fort Knox.

1986 Toyota opened auto plant near Lexington.

1988 Drunk driver killed 27 in church bus accident on Interstate Highway 40 miles outside Louisville

1993 Husband of former Governor Martha Layne Collins convicted of extorting bribes from contractors doing business with the state during wife's administration.

Louisiana

1541 Explored by Spaniard Hernando de Soto.

1682 Rene-Robert Cavelier, Sieur de La Salle, claimed Mississippi River valley for France.

1699 French established Louisiana colony.

1714 First permanent settlement founded at Natchitoches.

1718 New Orleans founded.

1762 Louisiana territory ceded to Spain.

1763 Acadians ("Cajuns") migrated from Canada.

1800 Returned to French control.

1803 Louisiana territory purchased by U.S.

1812 Admitted to Union as 18th state.

1815 American forces led by Andrew Jackson defeated British in Battle of New Orleans; neither side knew War of 1812 was already over.

1838 First Mardi Gras parade held in New Orleans.

1861 Seceded from Union; joined Confederacy.

1862 New Orleans captured by Union forces led by Admiral David G. Farragut.

1868 Readmitted to U.S.

1879 Dredging made New Orleans ocean port.

1896 Nation's first movie theater opened in New Orleans.

1898 Most African Americans disenfranchised by new constitution.

1928 Huey P. Long elected governor.

1935 Long assassinated.

1948 Earl Long elected governor.

1965 Hurricane Betsy killed 81 people, caused $400 million damage.

1977 Ernest N. (Dutch) Morial elected first African-American mayor of New Orleans.

1987 Cuban prisoners at federal detention facility in Oakdale rioted.

1991 Riverboat gambling legalized.

1992 Former Ku Klux Klan and American Nazi leader David Duke defeated in bid for governor's mansion running as Republican candidate. Hurricane Andrew hit the state. White homeowner shot and killed Japanese exchange student who knocked on wrong door while looking for Halloween costume party.

1993 Two-thirds of New Orleans police staged sickout.

Maine

c. 1000 Viking explorers believed to have visited coastal area.

1497–1499 John Cabot explored coastal area for England.

1524 Sailing for France, Giovanni da Verrazano explored coast.

1609 Henry Hudson explored Casco Bay.

1652 Massachusetts annexed Maine.

1763 French bid to control Maine ended with signing of Treaty of Paris.

1775 First naval battle of Revolutionary War occurred off Maine coast.

1791 Portland Head Lighthouse (oldest Atlantic coast lighthouse) began operation.

1819 Maine separated from Massachusetts.

1820 Admitted to Union as 23rd state.

1861 Maine resident Hannibal Hamlin inaugurated as Abraham Lincoln's vice president.

1870 Summer resort industry established.

1957 Edmund S. Muskie first Democrat elected to U.S. Senate from Maine.

1972 Maine Yankee Atomic Power plant opened.

1989 Kennebunkport became site of President George Bush's summer White House.

1991 Hurricane Bob caused widespread damage.

1992 Though he finished third in Maine's popular vote, independent presidential candidate Ross Perot received 30 percent of the state's popular vote.

1993 Blizzard hit Maine.

Maryland

1526 Spanish explorers visited Chesapeake Bay.

1608 Captain John Smith explored Chesapeake Bay.

1632 Cecilius Calvert, Lord Baltimore, received Maryland charter from English King Charles I.

1634 First colonists arrived.

1649 Religious toleration law enacted.

1654 William Claiborne led Puritan rebellion, seized colony, and ended toleration until 1657.

1691 Maryland became royal colony.

1729 Baltimore Town founded.

1767 Borders between Maryland, Delaware, and Pennsylvania established by Mason Dixon survey.

1772 State House completed; oldest capital building in U.S. still in use.

1774 Protesting colonists destroyed tea-loaded ship.

1784 U.S. Congress convened in Annapolis to sign 1783 Treaty of Paris ending Revolutionary War.

1788 Seventh state to ratify Constitution.

1791 Land along Potomac ceded for building of District of Columbia.

1803 First icebox invented by Thomas More in Baltimore.

1814 British attacked state during War of 1812; Francis Scott Key composed "The Star-Spangled Banner" during British bombardment of Fort McHenry.

1830 First American coal-fueled steam engine, the *Tom Thumb*, invented by Peter Cooper, began operating on Baltimore & Ohio Railroad.

1844 First telegraph line opened between Baltimore and Washington, D.C.

1850 U.S. Naval Academy opened at Annapolis.

1861 Secession rejected by legislature.

1862 23,000 casualties at Battle of Antietam (Sharpsburg)

1863 Confederate General Robert E. Lee led invading Southern forces through Maryland en route to battle at Gettysburg.

1864 New state constitution prohibited slavery.

1870 Pimlico Race Track opened.

1876 Johns Hopkins University founded.

1904 Fire damaged downtown Baltimore.

1910 State adopted nation's first workmen's compensation law for job-related injuries and death.

1952 Chesapeake Bay Bridge-Tunnel (now William Preston Lane Jr. Memorial Bridge) began operation.

1966 Republican Spiro T. Agnew elected governor.

1968 Agnew elected U.S. vice president.

1972 State hit hard by Hurricane Agnes.

1973 Agnew pleaded no contest to income tax evasion charges, resigned vice presidency.

1977 Governor Marvin Mandell convicted on mail fraud and bribery charges.

1980 Harborplace, Baltimore's revitalized waterfront area, opened.

1991 America's most liberal abortion rights bill enacted.

1992 Became first state to mandate community service as requirement for high school graduation.

1994 Workplace smoking ban enacted.

Massachusetts

c.1000 Viking explorers may have visited coastal area.

1498 John Cabot explored coast for England.

1602 English explorer Bartholomew Gosnold visited area.

1614 Captain John Smith mapped Massachusetts coast.

1620 Puritans landed at Plymouth.

1623 First Thanksgiving celebration held in July.

1630 Puritans founded city of Boston.

1636 Harvard founded as first college in colonies.

1641 Colonists adopted their first law code—the Body of Liberties.

1672 Boston Post Road complete.

1675–1676 Settlers defeated Native Americans in King Philip's War.

1691 Massachusetts Bay and Plymouth Bay Colonies united to form one colony.

1692 Nineteen people convicted and executed for witchcraft in Salem.

1764–1765 Colonists protest Sugar and Stamp Acts passed by British Parliament.

1770 British troops killed several protesting colonists in Boston Massacre.

1773 Boston Tea Party: Angry patriots, disguised as Native Americans, dumped 342 crates of British tea into Boston Harbor.

1775 First shots of Revolutionary War fired at Lexington and Concord; Battle of Bunker Hill fought.

1787 Shays' Rebellion in western Massachusetts protested poor treatment of poor farmers.

1788 Sixth state to ratify constitution.

1797 Massachusetts' native, John Adams, became second president of U.S.

1825 John Quincy Adams, son of John Adams, inaugurated nation's sixth president.

1831 William Lloyd Garrison founded anti-slavery newspaper, *The Liberator.*

1852 Became first state to require mandatory school attendance for children eight to 14 years of age.

1861–1865 State sent 160,000 men to Union Army; 30,000 to Navy.

1876 Alexander Graham Bell invented telephone in Boston.

1912 Textile strike in Lawrence focused national attention on deplorable working conditions.

1920 Republican Governor Calvin Coolidge elected U.S. vice president.

1823 President Warren G. Harding died; Coolidge became president.

1924 Coolidge reelected in landslide victory.

1927 Nicola Sacco and Bartolomeo Vanzetti executed.

1939 Massachusetts finally ratified Constitution's Bill of Rights.

1960 Massachusetts Senator John F. Kennedy elected U.S. president.

1962 Edward Kennedy elected to U.S. Senate.

1963 JFK assassinated in Dallas, Texas.

1972 Massachusetts was only state carried by Democratic candidate George McGovern in presidential election swept by Richard Nixon. After Watergate scandal breaks and Nixon's popularity plummeted, "Don't Blame Me, I'm from Massachusetts" became popular bumper sticker.

1973 Fire in Chelsea devastates 18 city blocks.

1988 Governor Michael Dukakis won Democratic Party's presidential nomination; defeated in election by Vice President George Bush.

1990 Boston's Isabella Stewart Gardner Museum hit by $100 million art theft.

1991 Nuclear Regulatory Commission ordered Yankee Rowe nuclear power plant to shut down for safety reasons. Hurricane Bob inflicted $525 million damage in Massachusetts.

1992 Ocean Liner *Queen Elizabeth II* ran aground near Cape Cod. Owners decided to shut Yankee Rowe plant permanently rather than make $25 million in repairs.

1994 Abortion clinic gunmen staged two shootings in Brookline, killing two.

1999 John F. Kennedy Jr., wife Carolyn Bessette Kennedy, and sister-in-law Lauren Bessette killed in private plane crash off Martha's Vineyard. Firemen killed fighting blaze at abandoned warehouse in Worcester.

Michigan

c. 1618–1620 French explorer Etienne Brule first European to visit Michigan.

1668 First permanent settlement founded by Father Jacques Marquette at Sault Sainte Marie.

1701 Trading post at site of present-day Detroit.

1760 Detroit captured by Rangers led by Major Robert Rogers during French and Indian War.

1763 British took possession of Michigan.

1783 U.S. gained control under Treaty of Paris, ending Revolutionary War; but British dragged out withdrawal.

1787 Michigan incorporated into Northwest Territory.

1796 British evacuated Detroit.

1805 Territory of Michigan established.

1812 British occupied Mackinac Island, captured Detroit during War of 1812.

1813 British withdrew from Detroit.

1814 War of 1812 ended; Mackinac Island returned to U.S.

1837 Admitted to Union as 26th state.

1841 University of Michigan at Ann Arbor founded.

1861–1865 Nearly 90,000 troops supplied to Union Army during Civil War.

1863 George Armstrong Custer commanded Michigan Cavalry unit that blocked General Jeb Stuart's Confederate cavalry at Gettysburg.

1900 Olds Motor Works, first U.S. auto factory, completed in Detroit.

1903 Ford Motor Company organized.

1908 Ford Model T introduced.

1914 Ford implemented $5 daily wage.

1935 United Automobile Workers union founded.

1936 Sit-down strike at General Motors plant in Flint led to union agreements at GM, later at Chrysler.

1943 Thirty-four killed in Detroit race riot.

1958 Governor G. Mennen Williams elected to unprecedented sixth term.

1967 Detroit ghetto riot left 43 dead, $50 million property damage.

1973 Coleman A. Young elected first African-American mayor of Detroit.

1974 Following President Richard M. Nixon's resignation during Watergate Scandal, Vice President Gerald R. Ford became first Michiganer to occupy White House.

1976 Ford defeated in presidential election by Jimmy Carter.

1977 Detroit's Renaissance Center opened.

1980 Chrysler Corporation saved from bankruptcy by federal bail-out plan.

1992 Became 38th state to ratify Constitutional amendment originally introduced in 1789 to bar Congress from voting itself immediate pay hike.

1993 Dr. Jack Kevorkian jailed for his role in assisted suicide, but released after suicide law declared unconstitutional.

1995 Major strike paralyzed Detroit newspapers.

1999 Detroit teachers struck, defying state strike prohibition for public sector workers. Kevorkian convicted and sentenced to 10–25 years in prison, after CBS's *60 Minutes* broadcast tape of assisted suicide.

Minnesota

1660 French explorers Pierre Esprit Radisson and Medard Chouart, Sieur de Grosseillers, visited area.

1679 Daniel Greysolon, Sieur du Luth, explored western shore of Lake Superior.

1680 Father Louis Henepin sighted and named Falls of St. Anthony on Mississippi River, at site of present-day Minneapolis.

1762–1763 Eastern part of present-day Minnesota ceded by France to Great Britain; western part to Spain.

1783 British region passed to U.S. control following Revolutionary War.

1800 Western area returned to French control.

1803 U.S. gained western part of Minnesota in Louisiana Purchase.

1818 U.S.-British agreement established northern border of western Minnesota.

1832 Henry Schoolcraft discovered source of Mississippi River at Lake Itasca.

1849 Minnesota Territory established.

1858 Admitted to Union as 32nd state.

1862 Sioux uprising put down.

1885 Novelist Sinclair Lewis, first American to win Nobel Prize for Literature, born in Sauk Centre.

1889 Mayo Clinic founded in Rochester.

1890 Iron-ore discovered in Mesabi Range.

1930 Farmer-Labor party became first third party in nation to successfully run a candidate for governor, as Floyd Olson won election.

1934 Teamsters Union won bloody Minneapolis trucking strike.

1944 Farmer-Labor party merged with Democrats.

1959 St. Lawrence Seaway opened making Duluth an Atlantic seaport.

1968 Minnesotans Vice President Hubert Humphrey and Senator Eugene McCarthy both sought Democratic presidential nomination. Humphrey nominated, but lost election to Richard M. Nixon.

1969 Minnesotan Warren E. Burger became Chief Justice of U.S. Supreme Court.

1976 Senator Walter F. Mondale elected U.S. vice president.

1984 Mondale ran unsuccessfully for president as Democratic party candidate.

1992 St. Paul anti-hate speech law voided.

1993 Sharon Sayles Belton elected first African-American mayor of Minneapolis. Severe flooding hit Minnesota. Operation Rescue targeted abortion clinics in St. Paul for demonstrations.

1995 Former Senator David Durenberger pleaded guilty and sentenced for falsifying government expense account.

1998 Former pro-wrestler Jesse "The Body" Ventura, running as Reform Party candidate, elected governor.

Mississippi

1541 Spanish explorer Hernando de Soto entered the region; discovered Mississippi River.

1542 De Soto died; buried in river.

1673 Father Jacques Marquette and Louis Jolliet explored Mississippi River.

1682 Rene-Robert Cavelier, Sieur de La Salle, claimed Mississippi River valley for France.

1699 French colony founded at Old Biloxi.

1763 Ceded to British after French and Indian War.

1775 Mississippi area, as part of British West Florida, remained loyal to Great Britain.

1779 West Florida surrendered to Spain.

1798 U.S. acquired control.

1806 "Great Cotton Era" began.

1817 Admitted to Union as 20th state.

1861 Seceded from Union.

1862 Former U.S. Senator Jefferson Davis elected president of Confederacy.

1863 Union forces seized Vicksburg.

1867 Union military rule imposed.

1868 Readmitted to Union.

1870 Hiram Revels became first African American elected to U.S. Senate during Reconstruction.

1904 Segregated streetcars mandated by law.

1927 Mississippi River floods caused more than $200 million damage.

1935 Elvis Presley born in Tupelo.

1958 African-American student Clennon King committed to mental hospital after attempt to enroll at all-white University of Mississippi.

1962 Protected by 3,000 federal troops and marshals, African-American student James Meredith enrolled at University of Mississippi.

1963 NAACP official Medgar Evers assassinated in Jackson.

1964 Civil rights workers Michael Schwerner, James Chaney, and Andrew Goodman murdered in Neshoba County during Mississippi Freedom Summer voter registration drive. Mississippi Freedom Democratic Party challenged credentials of regular party's all-white delegation at Democratic Convention at Atlantic City.

1969 Charles Evers won mayoralty election in Fayette, becoming state's first African-American mayor since Reconstruction.

1979 Hurricane Frederick caused severe damage.

1991 Kirk Fordice elected first Republican governor since Reconstruction. Drifter Leroy Evans confessed to 60 slayings, making him worst serial killer in U.S. history.

1992 Byron De La Beckwith, accused murderer of Medgar Evers, ordered extradited from Tennessee to Mississippi.

1994 De La Beckwith convicted of Evers' murder by jury of eight African Americans and four whites.

1995 Mississippi formally ratified Thirteenth Amendment, which banned slavery, the last of the 36 states in the Union at time of Civil War to do so.

Missouri

1682 Claimed for France.

1735 First permanent settlement established at Sainte Genevieve.

1762 Louisiana territory, including Missouri, ceded by France to Spain.

1764 St. Louis founded.

1799 Frontiersman Daniel Boone moved from Kentucky to Missouri.

1800 Louisiana territory returned to France.

1803 U.S. acquired control under Louisiana Purchase.

1804 Lewis and Clark expedition to explore Louisiana Purchase territory departed from St. Louis.

1812 Missouri Territory organized; severe earthquake hit New Madrid area.

1820 Missouri Compromise provided for Maine to enter Union as free state, Missouri as slave state to maintain balance.

1821 Admitted to Union as 24th state.

1831 Mormon leader Joseph Smith established religious settlement in Jackson County.

1835 Author Mark Twain (Samuel Clemens) born in Florida, Missouri.

1836 Platte Purchase added six northwestern counties to state territory.

1838 Fighting broke out between Mormons and non-Mormons.

1839 Mormons migrated to Illinois.

1854 Border fighting broke out between pro-slavery Missourians and free-staters in Kansas.

1857 U.S. Supreme Court Dred Scott decision blocked Missouri slave from gaining freedom; exacerbated national conflict over slavery.

1860 Pony Express began mail service from St. Joseph to Sacramento, California.

1861–1865 Secessionists defeated at state convention; fighting broke out between Confederate sympathizers and Union forces. St. Louis served as western headquarters of Union army.

1870 First stockyards opened in Kansas City. With 310,000 people, St. Louis was third largest U.S. city.

1882 Outlaw Jesse James killed at St. Joseph.

1904 St. Louis World's Fair boosted trade and tourism, as did Olympic Games.

1908 World's first school of journalism founded at University of Missouri.

1911 First air mail in history flown ten miles from Kinloch Park to Fairgrounds Park in St. Louis.

1931 Bagnell Dam completed, creating Lake of the Ozarks.

1944 Missourian Harry S. Truman elected U.S. vice president.

1945 On death of President Franklin D. Roosevelt, Truman became first and only Missouri resident to occupy White House.

1946 Winston S. Churchill delivered his famous "Iron Curtain" speech in Fulton.

1965 Gateway Arch completed in St. Louis.

1983 Dioxin contamination discovered at Times Beach.

1985 In the "I-70" World Series, Kansas City Royals defeated St. Louis Cardinals.

1988 St. Louis Cardinals professional football team moved to Arizona.

1990s Ozark community of Branson became major country music mecca.

1991 Emanuel Cleaver elected first African-American mayor of Kansas City.

1992 Times Beach dioxin lawsuit settled.

1993 Freeman R. Bosley Jr. elected first African-American mayor of St. Louis; state hard hit by floods.

Montana

1803 Eastern Montana acquired by U.S. in Louisiana Purchase.

1805 Lewis and Clark expedition passed through Montana.

1818 Agreement with British established Montana's northern border.

1846 Treaty with British gave U.S. control of northwestern Montana.

1862 Gold discovered.

1864 Montana Territory organized.

1876 Sioux and Cheyenne tribes defeated Seventh Cavalry Regiment led by George A. Custer at Battle of Little Bighorn.

1877 Nez Perce tribe led by Chief Joseph surrendered, ending Native-American fighting in Montana.

1881–1882 Massive slaughter of buffalo undertaken to deprive Native Americans of food source.

1883 Less than 200 buffalo remained in entire West.

1889 Admitted to Union as 41st state.

1910 Glacier National Park created.

1914 Labor violence broke out in Butte.

1916 Missoula's Jeanette Rankin became first woman elected to Congress.

1917 Miners struck following fire that killed 164 workers; federal troops intervened against strikers.

1940 Fort Peck Dam completed, providing irrigation water for farms.

1951 Oil wells began production in Williston Basin area.

1966 Yellowtail Dam on Bighorn River completed.

1976 U.S. Senator Mike Mansfield retired after 33 years in Congress; Mansfield served 15 years as Senate Majority Leader.

1984 Libby Dam hydroelectric project completed.

1991 Custer Battlefield National Monument renamed Little Bighorn Battlefield National Monument.

1994 Wildfires caused severe damage.

Nebraska

1682 Rene-Robert Cavelier, Sieur de La Salle, claimed entire Mississippi valley region for France, including Nebraska.

1739 Pierre and Paul Mallet became first Europeans to cross Nebraska.

1803 Acquired by U.S. in Louisiana Purchase.

1804 Lewis and Clark expedition passed through area.

1812 Missouri Fur Company constructed fort on Missouri River near present-day Omaha.

1843 Settlers bound for the Far West began migrating along the Oregon Trail through Nebraska.

1854 Nebraska Territory created.

1865 Construction began on Union Pacific Railroad heading west from Omaha.

1867 Admitted to Union as 37th state.

1869 University of Nebraska chartered (opened in 1871).

1874–1877 Crops ravaged by grasshoppers.

1896 Nebraskan William Jennings Bryan ran as Democratic Party candidate for president for first of three unsuccessful bids.

1905 North Platte River irrigation project began.

1917 Father E. J. Flanagan founded Boys Town, near Omaha.

1928 Omaha Community Playhouse founded; theater company gave start to careers of Henry Fonda and Marlon Brando.

1935 State farmlands devastated by dust storms.

1937 Nebraska became first state to have a unicameral legislature.

1946 Strategic Air Command based at Offutt Field, near Omaha.

1982 Initiative 300 adopted, barring corporations from purchasing farms or ranches.

1986 Republican Kay Orr elected state's first woman governor.

1991 Senator Bob Kerry began unsuccessful bid for Democratic presidential nomination.

1992 State lottery approved by voters.

1993 Severe flooding caused widespread damage.

1995 Heat wave hit the state.

Nevada

1826 Jedediah Smith led expedition through Nevada area.

1828–1830 Peter S. Ogden explored northern Nevada.

1843–1845 John C. Fremont led two expeditions through Great Basin and Sierra Nevada areas.

1846 Eighty-seven-member Donner wagon-train party trapped by heavy snow in Sierra Nevada Mountains; nearly half died.

1848 Mexico ceded Southwest, including Nevada, to U.S. after defeat in Mexican War.

1851 First permanent settlement established at present-day Genoa.

1859 Comstock Lode discovered 30 miles from Genoa, producing gold and silver.

1861 Nevada Territory organized.

1864 Admitted to Union as 36th state.

1869 Gambling legalized.

1879 Legislature sought to prohibit Chinese immigration.

1880–1890 Population dropped to 15,000.

1907 Federal troops broke miners strike at Goldfield.

1910 Gambling restricted to certain card games.

1931 Gambling restrictions lifted. State residency requirement for divorce reduced to six weeks.

1936 Boulder Dam (now called Hoover Dam) completed.

1946 Gangster "Bugsy" Siegel opened Flamingo Hotel gambling resort in Las Vegas.

1951 Above-ground nuclear weapons testing began in southern Nevada.

1962 Atmospheric nuclear testing ended; replaced by underground testing program.

1963 Supreme Court resolved dispute between Arizona, California, and Nevada for water rights to the Colorado River.

1966–1969 Howard Hughes invested heavily in Nevada, buying five Las Vegas Strip casino-hotels, airline, television station, and mining claims.

1967 Gambling laws revised to permit publicly traded companies to own casino operations.

1980 Eighty-seven people killed at MGM Grand Hotel fire in Las Vegas. Conservation laws adopted to fight pollution of Lake Tahoe.

1981 Las Vegas Hilton damaged by fire; eight killed.

1991 Sexual harassment scandal marred Navy flyer's Tailhook Association Convention in Las Vegas.

1994 Las Vegas listed as fastest growing city in nation; Nevada, the fastest growing state.

1997 Mike Tyson bit off a piece of Evander Holifield's ear during controversial heavyweight championship fight in Las Vegas.

New Hampshire

1603 Martin Pring explored mouth of Picataqua River near present-day Portsmouth.

1605 Captain John Smith explored coastal area.

1623 First settlements founded at Dover and Little Harbor (now Rye).

1640s Disputes between Quakers, Puritans, and Anglicans hampered attempts to set up government.

1641 Massachusetts took control of New Hampshire affairs.

1679 New Hampshire established as separate royal colony.

1768 Dartmouth College founded.

1776 Became first colony to declare independence from Britain, six months prior to Declaration of Independence.

1788 Ninth state to ratify Constitution.

1853 New Hampshire resident Franklin Pierce inaugurated U.S. president.

1861–1865 Fifth New Hampshire Regiment suffered more casualties than other unit in Union Army.

1909 Direct primary adopted.

1944 United Nations International Monetary conference convened at Bretton Woods.

1961 New Hampshire resident Alan B. Shepard Jr. became first American to travel in space.

1964 New Hampshire lottery began operation, first legal U.S. lottery since 1890s.

1977 Thousands protested construction of nuclear power plant at Seabrook.

1986 Concord teacher Christa McAuliffe killed in space shuttle *Challenger* disaster; Seabrook nuclear power plant completed.

New Jersey

1524 Shoreline explored by Giovanni da Verrazano.

1609 Sailing for Dutch, Henry Hudson landed at Sandy Hook, explored Hudson River.

1614 Dutch explorer Cornelius Mey explored Delaware River.

1618 Dutch trading post constructed at present-day Jersey City.

1640 Swedish settlers arrived in Cape May area.

1655 Dutch forces ended Swedish control in Delaware River area.

1664 Holland surrendered North American possessions, including New Jersey, to England.

1763 Sandy Hook lighthouse built.

1775–1781 Nearly 100 military engagements fought in New Jersey during Revolutionary War.

1776 George Washington led successful surprise attack on British forces in Battle of Trenton.

1777 British defeated at Battle of Princeton.

1781 Washington led troops across New Jersey en route to Yorktown, Virginia, for decisive battle in Revolutionary War.

1787 Third state to ratify Constitution.

1804 Aaron Burr killed Alexander Hamilton in duel in Weehawken.

1811 First steam ferry began service between Hoboken and New York.

1838 Samuel F. B. Morse demonstrated telegraph at Morristown.

1858 First dinosaur skeleton discovered in North America at Haddonfield.

1861–1865 Eighty-eight thousand New Jerseyans served in Union Army during Civil War.

1864 New Jersey voted against reelection of President Abraham Lincoln.

1870 First boardwalk constructed at Atlantic City beach.

1879 Thomas Alva Edison invented electric light bulb in lab at Menlo Park.

1884 Grover Cleveland elected president.

1910 Woodrow Wilson elected governor.

1912 Wilson elected U.S. president.

1927 Holland tunnel connecting Jersey City to New York opened.

1931 George Washington Bridge spanning Hudson River between New Jersey and upper Manhattan opened.

1932 Charles A. Lindbergh's son kidnapped in Hopewell.

1936 Bruno Richard Hauptmann executed for murder of Lindbergh baby.

1937 German dirigible *Hindenberg* exploded in flames at Lakehurst, killing 36.

1952 New Jersey Turnpike opened.

1957 Walt Whitman Bridge crossing Delaware River near Philadelphia stimulated industrial growth in New Jersey.

1967 Twenty-three killed and $10 million property damage in Newark ghetto riot.

1970 Ex-Newark Mayor Hugh Addonizio convicted on 64 counts of conspiracy to commit extortion.

1978 Casino gambling began in Atlantic City.

1987 Legality of surrogate motherhood contracts challenged by "Baby M" case.

1991 Jersey City Mayor Gerald McCann indicted on corruption charges.

1993 Republican Christine Todd Whitman became first woman governor elected in state's history.

1994 Governor Whitman granted clemency to a dog facing death sentence for attacking a little girl; Taro, a six-year-old Akita was allowed to be transferred to new owners' home in New York State.

1995–1996 New Jersey resident Steve Forbes waged unsuccessful campaign for Republican presidential nomination.

1999 New Jerseyans Forbes and former Senator Bill Bradley campaigned for presidential nomination in their respective parties.

New Mexico

1540 Francisco Vasquez de Coronado explored New Mexico in search of mythical Seven Cities of Cibola.

1598–1599 Spaniards established second-oldest European settlement in U.S., near present-day Espanola.

1610 Sante Fe founded.

1706 Albuquerque founded.

1821 Passed from Spanish to Mexican rule; Santa Fe Trail blazed from Independence, Missouri to New Mexico.

1846 During Mexican War, American forces captured Santa Fe without resistance.

1848 Mexico ceded American Southwest to U.S. at end of Mexican War.

1850 Territory of New Mexico created.

1853 Gadsen Purchase added territory in southern New Mexico.

1862 Confederate troops briefly occupied Santa Fe and Albuquerque before being defeated at Battle of Glorieta Pass.

1862–1864 Kit Carson defeated Mescalero Apache and Navajo tribes.

1868 Navajo reservation established in northwestern New Mexico/northeastern Arizona.

1876–1878 Cattle barons fought Lincoln County War. Participants included outlaw Billy the Kid.

1879 Construction of Atchison, Topeka, and Santa Fe Railroad reached New Mexico.

1881 Billy the Kid killed by Sheriff Pat Garrett.

1886 Surrender of Apache band led by Geronimo ended Native American wars.

1912 Admitted to Union as 47th state.

1916 Elephant Butte Dam and Reservoir completed; Mexican rebel Pancho Villa raided border town.

1930 Carlsbad Caverns National Park created.

1943 Atomic bomb developed at Los Alamos during World War II.

1945 First atomic bomb exploded in desert near Alamogorado.

1950 Uranium discovered in northwestern part of the state.

1967 Protesters from Alianza Federal de Mercedes (Federal Alliance of Land Grants), led by Reies Lopez Tijerina, seeking restoration of Spanish land grants, raided courthouse and clashed with law officers in Tierra Amarilla.

1970s San Juan-Chama irrigation project brought water to north-central New Mexico.

1980 Thirty-three inmates killed in prison rampage at state penitentiary near Santa Fe.

1986 Governor Toney Anaya declared state a sanctuary for refugees fleeing oppression in Central America.

1994 Census Bureau reported Las Cruces among fastest growing cities in nation.

New York

1524 Giovanni da Verrazano explored New York Bay.

1570 League of Five Nations organized by Iroquois tribes—Mohawk, Oneida, Onondaga, Cayuga, and Seneca.

1609 Henry Hudson explored Hudson River for Dutch; Samuel de Champlain explored Lake Champlain area.

1624 Dutch settlers established first permanent settlement at Fort Orange (now Albany).

1625 New Amsterdam colony founded at southern tip of Manhattan Island.

1626 Dutch colonial leader Peter Minuit purchased Manhattan Island from Native Americans for 60 guilders.

1633 First school in American colonies established in New Amsterdam.

1636 First Jewish settler arrived in New Amsterdam.

1664 New Amsterdam fell to British who renamed it New York.

1684 League of Five Nations formed alliance with British.

1690 French and Native American allies attack frontier communities.

1731 French erected fort at Crown Point.

1735 In landmark press freedom case, jury defied judge's instructions and acquitted newspaper publisher John Peter Zenger of seditious libel charges.

1762 Believed to be date of first St. Patrick's Day parade.

1764–1765 Colonists protested sugar tax and Stamp Act.

1774 New York City patriots held their own "tea party," protesting tax on tea.

1775 Ethan Allen led Green Mountain Boys in capture of Fort Ticonderoga.

1776 Provincial legislature endorsed Declaration of Independence. Washington defeated in Battle of Long Island. British occupied Manhattan. Nathan Hale executed for spying on Long Island. Washington defeated at Battle of White Plains.

1777 British defeated at Saratoga.

1779 Americans gained control of lower Hudson Valley.

1781 British defeated at Johnstown.

1783 Washington bid farewell to his officers at Fraunces Tavern in New York City.

1788 Became 11th state to ratify Constitution.

1789 Washington inaugurated first U.S. president at Federal Hall, New York City.

1797 Albany designated state capital.

1802 U.S. Military Academy founded at West Point.

1807 Robert Fulton's steamboat, *Clermont*, sailed from New York to Albany.

1814 During War of 1812 Americans defeated British in naval battle on Lake Champlain.

1817 Construction began on Erie Canal.

1821 Troy Female Seminary, first women's college in U.S., founded.

1825 Erie Canal opened.

1827 Slavery abolished.

1830 Joseph Smith of Palmyra published *Book of Mormon*.

1839 According to tradition, first baseball game played at Cooperstown.

1848 First Women's Rights convention held at Seneca Falls.

1863 New York City antidraft riots caused 1,000 casualties during Civil War.

1871 Tweed Ring of corrupt politicians broken up in New York City.

1886 Statue of Liberty dedicated.

1888 New York City paralyzed by Great Blizzard.

1901 New Yorker Theodore Roosevelt became president upon assassination of William McKinley in Buffalo.

1904 World's first subway began operations in New York City.

1917 Women gained vote in state elections.

1927 Charles A. Lindbergh departed from Roosevelt Field, New York, on his historic nonstop trans-Atlantic flight to Paris.

1929 Stock crash on Wall Street led to Great Depression.

1932 New York Governor Franklin D. Roosevelt elected U.S. president for first of four successive victories.

1939 World's Fair held in Queens.

1948 State University of New York founded.

1955 Severe damage caused by Hurricane Diane.

1959 St. Lawrence Seaway opened, linking Lake Erie and Lake Ontario ports to Atlantic Ocean.

1960 New York State Thruway (now Governor Thomas E. Dewey Thruway) completed.

1964 Second World's Fair held in Queens.

1965 Malcolm X assassinated in New York.

1967 State lottery established.

1975 New York City faced financial crisis.

1978 Most families evacuated Love Canal community in Niagara after discovery that homes were built on top of toxic waste dump.

1987 On Wall Street, Dow Jones Industrial Average plunged a record 500 points in single day.

1989 David N. Dinkins elected first African-American mayor of New York City.

1990 Eighty-seven killed in arson fire at social club in Bronx.

1991 Auto accident fatality triggered Crown Heights riots in Brooklyn.

1992 Macy's parent company filed for bankruptcy; John "Dapper Don" Gotti convicted on federal racketeering and murder charges.

1993 Terrorist bomb exploded at World Trade Center, killing six, injuring more than 1,000. Chinese refugee ship ran aground off the coast.

1997 Haitian immigrant Abner Louima's torture by police officer in Brooklyn precinct house enraged African-American community.

1999 Shooting death of unarmed West African immigrant Amadou Diallo by four plainclothes police officers who fired fusillade of 41 shots renewed debate over police brutality in New York. First Lady Hillary Clinton indicated intention to run for U.S. Senate in New York. Estimated 1.5 million people gathered in New York City's Time Square on New Year's Eve to mark arrival of the new millennium.

North Carolina

1524 Giovanni da Verrazano explored coastal area for France.

1584 English established first settlement in present-day U.S. on Roanoke Island, but most colonists returned to England in 1586 after supplies ran low.

1587 Second group of colonists settled at Roanoke; birth of Virginia Dare, first child born to English parents in New World.

1590 Supply ship returned to Roanoke but settlement had disappeared without a trace, going down in history as the "Lost Colony."

1629 King Charles I granted "Carolina" charter to Sir Robert Heath.

1712 North Carolina became a separate colony.

1718 Blackbeard the Pirate (Edward Teach) killed near Ocracoke Island.

1729 North Carolina declared royal colony.

1776 North Carolina became first colony to instruct delegates to vote for independence.

1780 Loyalists defeated at Battle of King's Mountain.

1781 British General Cornwallis defeated Americans at Battle of Guilford Courthouse.

1789 Became 12th state to ratify Constitution.

1790 U.S. government assumed jurisdiction over western North Carolina (later became Tennessee).

1792 Raleigh designated state capital.

1835 State constitution disenfranchised free African Americans.

1861 Last southern state to secede from Union.

1868 Readmitted to Union.

1890 Cigarette manufacturing became a leading industry.

1903 Orville and Wilbur Wright made first successful airplane flight at Kitty Hawk.

1920 Tobacco became state's number one crop.

1926 Great Smoky Mountains National Park established.

1942 U.S. Marine bases opened at Camp LeJeune and Cherry Point.

1958 Research Triangle Park established by Duke University, University of North Carolina at Chapel Hill, and North Carolina State.

1960 Four African-American college students staged first sit-in at Woolworth's lunch counter in Greensboro.

1971 New state constitution adopted.

1972 James E. Holshouser Jr. became first Republican elected governor since 1896. Jesse Helms became first Republican U.S. Senator since 1895.

1991 Twenty-five workers killed in fire at chicken processing plant in Hamlet.

1993 Michael Jordan's father murdered.

North Dakota

1682 Rene-Robert Cavelier, Sieur de La Salle. claimed all land drained by Mississippi River, including southwestern North Dakota, for France.

1738 Pierre Gaultier de Varennes, Sieur de La Verendrye, became first European to explore North Dakota.

1803 Acquired by U.S. in Louisiana Purchase.

1804–1806 Lewis and Clark expedition passed through North Dakota.

1851 First permanent European farm community established at Pembina.

1861 Dakota Territory organized, including present-day North Dakota and South Dakota.

1863 Homestead Act made free land available to settlers.

1876 George A. Custer led federal troops from Fort Abraham Lincoln in campaign against Sioux that ultimately ended in disaster at Little Big Horn.

1881 Sitting Bull's followers surrendered and returned to reservations.

1883 Bismarck designated capital of Dakota Territory; Theodore Roosevelt arrived in North Dakota for his health, began ranching near Medora.

1889 Admitted to Union as 39th state.

1941 International Peace Garden established at Canadian border.

1949 Theodore Roosevelt National Memorial Park created at Medora.

1951 Oil discovered near Tioga.

1960 Garrison Dam completed.

1968 Garrison Diversion Project construction began.

1989 Statehood centennial celebrated.

1990 North Dakota students ranked first in the nation on National Mathematics Test.

1993 Flooding caused massive damage.

Ohio

1655 Iroquois tribe conquered northern Ohio from Erie tribe.

1670s French explorer Rene-Robert Cavelier, Sieur de La Salle, believed to be first European to visit Ohio region.

1748 Ohio Land Company organized to colonize Ohio River Valley.

1763 French ceded Ohio to Britain.

1788 State's first permanent European settlement founded at Marietta.

1789 Construction began on Fort Washington, at site of present-day Cincinnati.

1794 General "Mad Anthony" Wayne defeated Native Americans at Battle of Fallen Timbers.

1795 Treaty of Greenville ended Native American wars in Ohio.

1800 Indiana detached from Ohio.

1803 Admitted to Union as 17th state.

1811 Steamboats appeared on Ohio River for first time.

1813 During War of 1812, Commodore Oliver H. Perry's fleet defeated British forces in Battle of Lake Erie.

1832 Ohio and Erie Canal completed.

1833 Oberlin College founded as first coeducational college in U.S.

1840 Ohioan William Henry Harrison elected U.S. president.

1861–1865 More than half the state's able-bodied men—346,326—fought in Union Army during Civil War.

1863 Confederate forces raided Ohio.

1869 Cincinnati Red Stocks became first professional baseball team in U.S.

1870 Standard Oil Company organized in Cleveland by John D. Rockefeller.

1884 First U.S. electric street railway began operation in Cleveland.

1896 First rubber auto tires manufactured in Akron by B. F. Goodrich Company.

1901 Orville and Wilbur Wright built first wind tunnel in U.S. in Dayton.

1913 Three hundred fifty people killed in severe flooding.

1914 Conservancy Act adopted to combat threat of floods.

1920 Ohioan Warren Harding elected president.

1937 Two strikers killed, 27 wounded, at Republic Steel plant in Youngstown.

1955 Ohio Turnpike opened.

1959 St. Lawrence Seaway opened, linking Lake Erie ports to oceangoing vessels.

1967 In Cleveland, Carl Stokes elected first African-American mayor of any major American city.

1970 Four unarmed students killed by National Guardsmen at Kent State University during protest against U.S. invasion of Cambodia during Vietnam War.

1971 State income tax adopted.

1972 State lottery to raise funds for education approved by voters.

1977 Shortage of natural gas caused shutdown of many schools, factories, and office buildings.

1978 Cleveland defaulted on debt payments.

1989 Baseball star Pete Rose of Cincinnati Reds banned from baseball because of gambling infractions.

1990 Cincinnati's Contemporary Arts Center directors acquitted on obscenity charges for exhibiting controversial Robert Mapplethorpe photographs.

1993 Voters approved funds for improvement and expansion of state parks.

1995 Rock and Roll Hall of Fame opened in Cleveland.

1999 Pete Rose honored by fans as member of baseball's team of the century.

Oklahoma

1541 Francisco Vasquez de Coronado passed through Oklahoma.

1682 French claimed Oklahoma as part of Louisiana territory.

1762 France ceded Louisiana territory to Spain.

1800 Spain returned Louisiana territory to France.

1803 Except for panhandle area, present-day Oklahoma acquired by U.S. in Louisiana Purchase.

1819 Oklahoma region incorporated into Arkansas Territory.

1837–1838 Cherokee tribe removed from eastern states to Oklahoma; thousands died during "Trail of Tears" trek.

1889 Oklahoma Land Rush. Part of Oklahoma opened to white settlement; state's first oil well drilled near Chelsea.

1890 Oklahoma Territory created.

1907 Admitted to Union as 46th state.

1934–1935 "Dust Bowl" conditions forced thousands of farmers to migrate to California.

1952 Oklahoma declared disaster area due to severe drought.

1959 Prohibition lifted on beer sales.

1964 National Cowboy Hall of Fame dedicated.

1973 Severe rioting erupted at state prison.

1978 Another serious drought hit the state.

1990 Became first state to impose term limits on state legislators.

1991 Oklahoma law professor Anita Hill accused Supreme Court nominee Clarence Thomas of sexual harassment during Thomas' Senate confirmation hearing. Sequoyah uranium plant closed.

1995 One hundred sixty-eight people killed by bomb explosion at Oklahoma City federal office building in worst terrorist incident in U.S. history.

1999 An F5-rated tornado (officially categorized as an "incredible tornado"), with winds over 260 miles per hour, struck south of Oklahoma City.

Oregon

1792 Navigator Robert Gray explored mouth of Columbia River.

1805–1806 Lewis and Clark expedition followed Columbia River to Pacific Ocean.

1811 First European settlement established.

1818 U.S. and Great Britain agreed Pacific Northwest would be open to citizens of both countries.

1819 Treaty with Spain fixed Oregon's southern border.

1828 Jedediah Smith explored Oregon coast.

1829 Hudson's Bay Company founded settlement on site of present-day Oregon City.

1843 American settlers in Willamette River Valley organized a provisional government; massive immigration continued over Oregon Trail through end of 1840s.

1846 Treaty established 49th parallel as Pacific Northwest boundary between U.S. and British Canada.

1848 Oregon Territory created, included Washington, northern Idaho, and western Montana until 1853.

1851 Salem designated capital.

1859 Admitted to Union as 33rd state.

1868 First salmon cannery built.

1902 Constitutional amendments authorized voter initiatives and referenda. Crater Lake National Park established.

1912 Women gained right to vote.

1937 Bonneville Dam on Columbia River completed.

1942–1945 Portland served as chief debarkation port for lend-lease goods to Soviet Union.

1953 Discrimination in public accommodations barred by law.

1955 Women guaranteed equal pay for equal work.

1966 Astoria Bridge across Columbia River opened.

1971 Oregon became first state to prohibit nonrefundable beverage containers.

1977 Use of fluorocarbon aerosol cans prohibited by law.

1981 Followers of guru Bhagwan Shree Rajneesh established community near Antelope in Wasco County; project disbanded four years later.

1990 Active volcanoes discovered in seabed off Oregon coast.

1991 Barbara Roberts became state's first woman governor.

1992 Senator Mark Hatfield rebuked by Senate ethics committee.

1994 Voters approved legalized assisted suicide. Forestlands scorched by wildfires.

1995 Senator Bob Packwood resigned amidst sexual harassment scandal

1998 High school student goes on shooting rampage, killing two and wounding 25 in Springfield.

Pennsylvania

1609 Henry Hudson explored Delaware River.

1643 First European settlement established by Swedes.

1655 Dutch seized Swedish colony.

1664 Dutch surrendered control to English.

1681 King Charles II granted Quaker William Penn proprietorship over Pennsylvania.

1682 Penn arrived in colony; arranged treaties with Native Americans.

1701 Penn issued Charter of Privileges; Philadelphia chartered.

1727 Benjamin Franklin founded association opposing slavery.

1731 Franklin organized Library Company of Philadelphia.

1755 General Braddock defeated and killed by French forces on Monongahela River.

1767 Charles Mason and Jeremiah Dixon chart boundary lines for Pennsylvania and Maryland.

1768 Colonists opposed Stamp Act and Townshend Acts.

1774 First Continental Congress convened in Philadelphia.

1776 Declaration of Independence signed in Philadelphia.

1777 Washington's forces defeated at Battle of Brandywine.

1777–1778 Liberty Bell hidden at Allentown during British occupation of Philadelphia; Washington's troops wintered at Valley Forge.

1780 Pennsylvania abolished slavery.

1787 Constitutional Convention met in Philadelphia; Pennsylvania became second state to ratify Constitution.

1800 Nation's capital moved from Philadelphia to Washington, D.C.

1812 Harrisburg designated state capital.

1859 Nation's first commercial oil well drilled at Titusville.

1863 Union victory at Battle of Gettysburg was turning point in Civil War; President Abraham Lincoln delivered historic Gettysburg Address.

1867 First practical manufacture of Bessemer steel in U.S. at Steelton.

1870 Pittsburgh became center of U.S. steel industry.

1874 Nation's first zoo opened in Philadelphia.

1889 Johnstown devastated by flood waters.

1920 World's first permanent commercial broadcasting station began operation in Pittsburgh.

1957 First nuclear powered electricity plant established at Shippingport.

1979 Serious accident releasing radiation into atmosphere occurred at Three Mile Island nuclear power plant.

1981 Three Mile Island clean-up costs put at $1 billion.

1985 Eleven killed and 61 homes destroyed by fire after police dropped incendiary bomb on fortified home of radical group MOVE in Philadelphia.

1991 Harris Wofford elected first Democratic senator from Pennsylvania in nearly thirty years.

1994 US Air crash killed 134 at Aliquippa.

Rhode Island

1511 Portuguese navigator Miguel Corte Real believed to be first European to see Rhode Island coast.

1524 Sailing for France, Giovanni da Verrazano explored Narragansett Bay.

1614 Dutch explorer Adriaen Block referred to Narrangansett Bay islands as "Roodt Eyland" (Red Island).

1636 Roger Williams, expelled from Massachusetts Colony for dissident religious and political views, founded first permanent settlement at Providence.

1638 Anne Hutchinson and others settled on Aquidneck Island.

1647 Settlements united as single colony under charter granted by England to Roger Williams.

1658 First Jews arrived in Newport.

1663 New charter granted to Rhode Island.

1693 First postal route established between Rhode Island and Boston.

1763 Rhode Island College founded (later became Brown University); Touro Synagogue first permanent synagogue built in America.

1772 Colonists protested British trade laws by burning British revenue cutter.

1774 Importation of slaves prohibited.

1776 Rhode Island became first colony to declare independence from Great Britain.

1784 Slavery abolished.

1790 Last of original 13 states to ratify Constitution.

1813 Block Island occupied by British forces during War of 1812.

1824 First recorded strike by female workers occurred in Pawtucket.

1835 First railroad train began operations between Boston and Providence.

1852 Capital punishment abolished.

1900 Providence became capital.

1920 Rhode Island did not ratify national prohibition amendment.

1946 Law guarantees women equal pay for equal work.

1976 Operation Sail marked nation's bicentennial celebration.

1977 Blizzard paralyzed state for over a week.

1981 Longest baseball game ended after 33 innings and 8 hours of play in Triple A International League.

1992 Supreme Court voided prayer at school graduation.

South Carolina

1521 Carolina coast explored by Spaniard Francisco Gordillo.

1663 Charles II granted Carolinas to eight lord proprietors.

1670 First permanent European settlement established by English at Albemarle Point.

1698 First library in U.S. established at Charles Town (now Charleston).

1712 Carolinas divided into separate colonies.

1719 Colonists overthrew British proprietors.

1729 English crown established royal colony.

1773 First public museum in U.S. organized in Charles Town (Charleston).

1777 Cherokee tribe ceded most of their land to South Carolina.

1780 After two-month siege, Charles Town fell to British during Revolutionary War. British General Cornwallis defeated Americans led by General Nathanael Green at Camden. Americans triumphed at Kings Mountain.

1781 Cornwallis defeated at Cowpens.

1782 British withdrew from Charles Town.

1782 Charles Town renamed Charleston.

1788 South Carolina 8th state to ratify Constitution.

1822 Slave rebellion put down.

1832 South Carolina nullified Tariff Act; South Carolina John C. Calhoun, nullification spokesman, resigned as U.S. vice president.

1860 First slave state to secede from Union.

1861 Confederate forces attacked Fort Sumter, beginning Civil War.

1865 Union General William T. Sherman burned Columbia.

1868 Readmitted to Union.

1876 White marauders called "Red Shirts" supporting former Confederate General Wade Hampton in gubernatorial election, intimidated African-American voters.

1877 Reconstruction ended.

1893 Hurricane killed 1,000 people.

1895 New constitution disenfranchised African-American citizens.

1921 Boll weevil devastated cotton crop.

1951 Savannah River Plant operated by U.S. Atomic Energy Commission erected to manufacture plutonium for nuclear weapons.

1964 Barry Goldwater became first Republican presidential candidate to carry South Carolina since Reconstruction.

1970 First African Americans elected to state legislature since 1902.

1974 James B. Edwards elected state's first Republican governor since 1874.

1988 Mishap at Savannah River nuclear weapons plant caused month-long shutdown.

1989 Hurricane Hugo caused more than $6 billion damage.

1991 Corruption scandals rocked state legislature.

1995 Susan Smith tried and convicted for murdering her two sons, after she first blamed an African-American car jacker.

South Dakota

1682 Rene-Robert Cavelier, Sieur de La Salle, claimed all land drained by Mississippi for France, including South Dakota.

1743 Francois La Verendrye and Louis-Joseph La Verendrye first Europeans to visit area.

1803 South Dakota became U.S. possession under Louisiana Purchase.

1804 Lewis and Clark expedition passed through South Dakota.

1815–1850 Fur trade flourished.

1861 Dakota Territory organized, including present-day North Dakota.

1874 Gold discovered in Black Hills, bringing 10,000 whites into Native-American territory over next two years.

1876 George A. Custer led Seventh Cavalry Brigade in mission to subdue Native-American bands, but unit was destroyed at Little Big Horn. Wild Bill Hickok killed in Deadwood.

1881 Sioux leader Sitting Bull returned to South Dakota from Canada, where he had hid after Little Big Horn.

1882 University of South Dakota founded.

1890 "Ghost Dance" messianic movement among Native Americans alarmed whites; Sitting Bull killed. Federal troops massacred 146 Native Americans at Wounded Knee Creek.

1941 Mount Rushmore National Memorial, featuring carved heads of Presidents Washington, Jefferson, Lincoln, and Theodore Roosevelt, completed.

1963 One hundred fifty Minuteman intercontinental ballistic missiles deployed at Wall.

1964 Oahe Dam completed.

1972 South Dakota Senator George McGovern, Democratic Party presidential candidate, failed to carry his home state in election.

1973 American Indian Movement activists seized Wounded Knee and held out for 70 days.

1980 Supreme Court ordered that South Dakota tribes receive $105 million for Black Hills land seized in 1877.

1991 Military began removal of missiles from South Dakota.

1992 According to Census Bureau, Shannon County, with 16,000 Sioux, is poorest U.S. county.

1993 Midwestern flooding caused severe damage.

Tennessee

1540 Expedition led by Hernando de Soto entered Tennessee area.

1682 Tennessee claimed for France.

1714 French trading post established near present-day Nashville.

1738 Smallpox wiped out half of Cherokee population.

1750 Cumberland Gap discovered.

1763 France surrendered all territorial claims east of Mississippi River to Great Britain.

1780 Tennesseans helped defeat British at Battle of King's Mountain in South Carolina.

1784 State of Franklin set up in three east Tennessee counties that rebelled against North Carolina.

1788 North Carolina regained control of Franklin.

1789 Tennessee region ceded to U.S. government.

1796 Admitted to Union as 16th state.

1828 Andrew Jackson elected first Tennessean to serve as U.S. president.

1835 Free African Americans disenfranchised.

1843 Nashville designated state capital.

1844 Tennessean James K. Polk elected president.

1861 Seceded from Union.

1862 Confederates suffered military defeats at Fort Henry, Fort Donelson, Battle of Shiloh and Memphis.

1865 Tennessean Vice President Andrew Johnson became president after assassination of Abraham Lincoln.

1866 First Confederate state readmitted to Union.

1871 Fisk Jubilee Singers began first concert tour.

1878 Five thousand died in Memphis during worst yellow fever epidemic in U.S. history.

1920 Tennessee's ratification of Nineteenth Amendment is decisive in extending franchise to women.

1925 John Scopes convicted for teaching evolution in Dayton school.

1926 Great Smoky National Park, straddling mountains in North Carolina and Tennessee, created.

1933 Congress created Tennessee Valley Authority (TVA).

1936 Norris Dam completed by TVA.

1956 National Guard mobilized to quell anti-integration rioting in Clinton. Senator Estes Kefauver ran unsuccessfully as Democratic candidate for vice president.

1960 Sit-ins protested lunch counter segregation in Nashville.

1968 Reverend Martin Luther King Jr. assassinated in Memphis.

1972 Opryland USA opened.

1974 Marilyn Lloyd elected first woman to represent state in Congress. Harold Ford became the state's first African-American Congressman.

1982 Knoxville World's Fair opened.

1992 Tennessean Al Gore elected vice president of the United States.

1999 Gore campaigned for Democratic nomination for president.

Texas

1519 Spaniard Alonso Alvarez de Pineda explored Texas coast.

1541 Francisco Vasquez de Coronado traveled through western Texas in search of seven "golden" cities of Cibola.

1542 Hernando de Soto explored northeastern Texas.

1682 First two Spanish missions built near present-day El Paso.

1691 Officially designated Spanish province.

1821 Mexico gained independence from Spain; Texas became part of Empire of Mexico. Stephen F. Austin led first group of European-American settlers to Texas.

1830 Mexico sought to block further American immigration.

1835 Texas Revolution began.

1836 Mexican Army, led by General Santa Anna, defeated Americans at the Alamo. General Sam Houston defeated Mexican Army, elected president of Republic of Texas.

1845 Admitted to Union as 28th state.

1846–1848 Mexican War; Mexico renounced all claims to Texas.

1853 Largest ranch in U.S.—the King ranch—established

1861 Seceded from Union. Sam Houston removed as governor after refusing to take oath of allegiance to Confederacy.

1865 Last Civil War battle fought at Palmito Hill near mouth of Rio Grande River, May 12–13; soliders didn't know war had ended April 9.

1866 Jesse Chisholm led first cattle drive from Texas to Kansas.

1900 Hurricane killed 6,000 at Galveston.

1901 Spindletop oil field discovered.

1924 Texas became second state to elect woman governor.

1930 Oil discovered in east Texas.

1934 World's first laundromat opened in Fort Worth.

1945 Texas resident Audie Murphy lauded as most decorated U.S. soldier in World War II.

1947 Ship explosion at Texas City killed 500, injured more than 3,000.

1952 Dwight D. Eisenhower, born in Denison, elected U.S. president.

1957 Five hundred killed as Hurricane Audrey struck Texas coast.

1963 President John F. Kennedy assassinated in Dallas; Texan Lyndon B. Johnson became president.

1964 Manned Spacecraft Center (now Lyndon B. Johnson Space Center) established at Houston as astronaut headquarters.

1980 Texan George H.W. Bush elected vice president.

1990 Ann Richards elected state's second woman governor.

1992 George Bush defeated by Bill Clinton in presidential race. Texas billionaire Ross Perot polled 19 percent of popular vote as independent candidate for president.

1993 Federal agents confronted members of Branch Davidian cult outside Waco; cult leader David Koresh and 90 cultists died when compound burned to ground.

1994 Texas became nation's second most populous state. Flooding caused severe damage. Forty-three killed on Texas highways in a single day (July 3, 1994).

1996 Perot made another run for president as independent.

1998 Former New York City police commissioner Lee Brown, a Democrat, elected first African-American mayor of Houston. Karla Faye Tucker became first woman executed in 135 years in Texas.

1999 Governor George W. Bush emerged as front-runner for Republican presidential nomination in 2000 election.

Utah

1776 Silvestre Velez de Escalante and Francisco Atanasio Dominguez explored Utah area.

1824–1825 Fur trapper Jim Bridger first European to see Great Salt Lake.

1843–1845 Expedition led by John C. Fremont explored and surveyed Great Salt Lake region.

1847 Arrival of first group of Mormon settlers led by Brigham Young.

1848 Following Mexican War, U.S. gained entire Southwest, including Utah.

1849 Mormon leaders founded state of Deseret with borders encompassing Utah, Nevada, Arizona, and portions of Oregon, Wyoming, Colorado, New Mexico, Idaho, and California.

1850 U.S. Congress established Utah Territory, including parts of Colorado, Wyoming, and Nevada.

1852 Polygamy announced as Mormon religious tenet.

1857 Federal troops entered Utah accompanying new federally appointed governor, sent by President James Buchanan, to replace Brigham Young. Mormons resisted.

1861 First transcontinental telegraph service completed by links at Salt Lake City.

1862 Congress prohibited polygamy.

1868 Present Utah borders established.

1869 First transcontinental railroad completed at Promontory.

1870 Women granted right to vote.

1885 Federal authorities cracked down on plural marriages.

1890 Mormon conference advises against practice of polygamy.

1895 Polygamy prohibited by Utah constitution.

1896 Admitted to Union as 45th state.

1915 Joe Hill, organizer for Industrial Workers of the World (IWW), executed for murder.

1928 Bryce Canyon National Park established.

1942–1945 During World War II, 8,000 Japanese-Americans resettled in internment camp near Delta.

1952 Uranium discovered near Moab.

1964 Flaming Gorge and Glen Canyon dams completed.

1977 Murderer Gary Gilmore executed by firing squad.

1995 Salt Lake City awarded Winter Olympics in 2002.

1996 Statehood centennial celebrated.

1999 Preparations for Winter Olympics in 2002 in Salt Lake City marred by corruption scandal involving bribes to Olympic Committee members.

Vermont

1609 Samuel de Champlain claimed for France.

1666 First French settlement built on island in Lake Champlain.

1724 First permanent English settlement established at Fort Dummer in southeast Vermont.

1752 First harvest of maple syrup and sugar by European settlers.

1763 France renounced territorial claims to Vermont.

1775 Ethan Allen and Green Mountain Boys captured Fort Ticonderoga from British at beginning of Revolutionary War.

1777 Vermont declared independence; established republic.

1785 First marble quarry in U.S. began operation.

1791 Admitted to Union as 14th state.

1802 First U.S. canal built at Bellows Falls.

1812–1814 Battles fought against British attacks during War of 1812.

1823 Champlain Canal opened water route from Vermont to New York City.

1864 Northernmost battle in Civil War fought in Vermont when 22 Confederate soldiers raided banks in St. Albans and escaped to Canada with $20,000.

1881 Vermont-born Chester A. Arthur became U.S. president.

1923 Following death of Warren G. Harding, vice president Calvin Coolidge took presidential oath of office at his parents' home in Plymouth Notch.

1927 Severe flooding killed 60 and caused extensive property damage.

1964 Lyndon Johnson became first Democratic presidential candidate to carry Vermont.

1976 Nuclear power plant in Vernon closed down for safety reasons.

1984 Madeleine M. Kunin became first woman elected Vermont governor.

1992 Flooding hit Montpelier.

Virginia

1607 First permanent European colony in New World established at Jamestown. Captain John Smith captured by Native Americans, spared by Pocahontas.

1609 Anne Burrows wed John Laydon in first European marriage in New World.

1612 John Rolfe introduced tobacco cultivation.

1619 House of Burgess began meeting as first legislative body in New World. Twenty Africans brought by Dutch trading vessel and sold as indentured servants.

1624 Became royal colony.

1629 North Carolina separated from Virginia.

1632 Maryland separated from Virginia.

1693 College of William and Mary founded.

1765 Patrick Henry protested British Stamp Act and presented Virginia Resolutions in House of Burgesses.

1775 Patrick Henry delivered "Give Me Liberty, Or Give Me Death" speech at Virginia convention. Virginian George Washington chosen military leader of Continental Army.

1776 Virginian Thomas Jefferson drafted Declaration of Independence.

1781 British surrendered at Yorktown, ending Revolutionary War.

1788 Tenth state to ratify Constitution.

1789 Washington elected U.S. president.

1792 Kentucky formed from territory in western Virginia.

1800 Jefferson elected president.

1808 Virginian James Madison elected president.

1817 Virginian James Monroe elected president.

1831 Slave rebellion led by Nat Turner.

1840 Virginia-born William Henry Harrison elected president.

1841 Following Harrison's death, another Virginian, John Tyler, succeeded to presidency.

1848 Zachary Taylor, also a Virginian, elected president.

1859 Abolitionist John Brown raided U.S. arsenal at Harpers Ferry.

1861–1865 Seceded from Union and became site of many Civil War battles.

1863 West Virginia, formed from northwestern Virginia counties, admitted to Union.

1865 Confederate General Robert E. Lee surrendered to U.S. General Ulysses S. Grant at Appomattox Court House, ending Civil War.

1870 Readmitted to the Union.

1900 Jim Crow segregation laws enacted.

1912 Woodrow Wilson became eighth Virginian-born U.S. president.

1957 Hampton Roads Bridge-Tunnel completed.

1964 Chesapeake Bay Bridge-Tunnel (now William Preston Lane Jr. Memorial Bridge), world's longest bridge-tunnel, completed. USS *Enterprise*, first atomic-powered aircraft carrier, launched at Newport News.

1972 Hurricane Agnes caused severe damage.

1989 L. Douglas Wilder became first African-American governor in U.S. history.

1993 Lorena Bobbitt arrested for cutting off her husband's penis.

1994 Bobbitt acquitted in criminal trial.

Washington

1775 Washington region claimed for Spain.

1792 Robert Gray discovered Columbia River.

1805 Lewis and Clark expedition reached Pacific Coast.

1810 Fur trading post established near present-day Spokane.

1818 British-American agreement opened Pacific Northwest to nationals of both countries.

1846 Treaty established U.S.-Canada border, putting present-day Washington in U.S.

1848 Oregon Territory organized, including Washington area.

1853 Washington Territory created, including northern Idaho and western Montana.

1858 Native American confederacy defeated by federal troops and militia; eastern Washington opened to European settlement.

1861 Territorial University (later Washington University) opened.

1889 Admitted to Union as 42nd state.

1899 Mount Ranier National Park created.

1916 William E. Boeing built airplane factory.

1941 Weyerhaeuser Corporation opened first U.S. tree farm.

1942 14,559 Japanese-Americans removed from Washington and interned in camps for duration of World War II. Grand Coulee Dam completed.

1943–1945 Hanford Engineering Works near Richland secretly produced plutonium for nuclear weapons development program.

1962 Twenty-first Century Exposition held at Seattle.

1968 North Cascades National Park created.

1974 Expo '74 World's Fair held at Spokane.

1980 Mount St. Helens volcano erupted.

1988 Logging operations curtailed by legislation protecting rare owl.

1990 Minor eruption at Mt. St. Helens causes little damage.

1999 Rioting marred World Trade Organization conference in Seattle. Millennium New Year's Celebration canceled due to threat of terrorism.

West Virginia

1669–1670 First European explorers reached the Blue Ridge Mountains

1726 First European settlement established.

1742 Coal discovered.

1748 George Washington surveyed land in western Virginia.

1774 Shawnee tribe defeated in major battle at Point Pleasant.

1859 Abolitionist John Brown led raid on arsenal at Harpers Ferry in effort to trigger slave rebellion; Brown was captured, tried, and executed.

1861	Large majority of western Virginians opposed Virginia's secession for the Union.	**1783**	Northwest Territory, including present-day Wisconsin, ceded by Great Britain to U.S.
1863	President Lincoln authorized admission of West Virginia as 35th state.	**1800–1809**	Included in Indiana Territory.

1861 Large majority of western Virginians opposed Virginia's secession for the Union.

1863 President Lincoln authorized admission of West Virginia as 35th state.

1882 Hatfield-McCoy feud broke out in Southern Appalachians.

1902 "Mother" Mary Jones led union organizing campaign among coal miners.

1920 "Matewan Massacre" in Mingo county spurred United Mine Works Union organizing efforts.

1921 First state to adopt a sales tax.

1960 John F. Kennedy defeated Hubert Humphrey in West Virginia's presidential primary; major turning point in JFK's campaign.

1973 Union reformer Arnold Miller ousted United Mine Workers Union leader Tony Boyle in union election.

1982 Unemployment hit 13.6 percent.

1983 Continuing economic difficulties led to massive state spending cuts.

1985 West Virginia had nation's highest unemployment rate.

1990 Census revealed that West Virginia suffered highest percentage loss in population during the 1980s.

Wisconsin

1634 French expedition explored Green Bay.

1673 Louis Jolliet and Father Jacques Marquette explored Wisconsin River.

1684 French post established at Green Bay.

1763 French ceded territory to British.

1783 Northwest Territory, including present-day Wisconsin, ceded by Great Britain to U.S.

1800–1809 Included in Indiana Territory.

1809–1818 Part of Illinois Territory.

1818 Became part of Michigan Territory.

1835 Wisconsin Territory created.

1848 Admitted to the Union as 30th state.

1910 Milwaukee elected socialists as congressman and mayor.

1911 First state to adopt an income tax.

1921 Green Bay Packers professional football team organized.

1924 U.S. Senator Robert La Follette carried Wisconsin in third-party presidential campaign.

1932 First state to adopt unemployment relief.

1950 U.S. Senator Joseph McCarthy began campaign against alleged Communists in government.

1977 Divorce laws liberalized.

1981 Schlitz Brewing Co. shut down its Milwaukee brewery.

1987 Parimutuel betting legalized.

1988 Henry Maier stepped down after 28 years as mayor of Milwaukee.

1992 Mutilation serial killer Jeffrey L. Dahmer found sane, convicted, and sentenced to 15 life terms.

1993 Severe flooding hit Wisconsin. State government adopted overhaul of welfare system.

1995 Dahmer murdered in prison.

Wyoming

1803 Louisiana Purchase put part of present-day Wyoming under U.S. control.

1807–1808 Explored by fur trapper John Colter.

1834 Trading post that later became Fort Laramie established.

1842 Jim Bridger and Louis Vasquez established Fort Bridger in southwest Wyoming.

1845 Annexation of Texas passed additional Wyoming territory under U.S. control.

1846 Treaty with Great Britain gave U.S. possession of more territory.

1848 End of Mexican War placed all of present-day Wyoming under U.S. control.

1868 Wyoming Territory created.

1869 Women granted right to vote.

1872 Yellowstone National Park founded.

1890 Admitted to the Union as 44th state.

1892 Johnson County War pitted gunmen hired by big cattlemen against small ranchers and homesteaders.

1897–1909 Cattlemen and sheepherders clash over use of open range.

1906 Devils Tower designated national monument.

1925 Nellie Taylor Ross became nation's first woman governor.

1929 Grand Teton National Park created.

1942–1945 Internment camp for Japanese-Americans established during World War II.

1965 Intercontinental Ballistic missiles installed at Air Force base near Cheyenne.

1986 First operational MX missiles deployed in Wyoming.

1988 Forest fires damaged Yellowstone National Park.

1995 Wolves reintroduced in Yellowstone National Park.

Washington, D.C.

1791 Site selected for federal city to serve as nation's capital.

1793 Construction of Capitol building began.

1798 Construction of White House began.

1800 Government moved from Philadelphia to Washington.

1814 British burned Washington during War of 1812.

1836 Smithsonian Institution founded.

1844 First telegraph message transmitted from Washington to Baltimore.

1861–1865 City expanded during Civil War.

1865 President Abraham Lincoln shot while attending performance at Ford's Theater.

1885 Washington Monument dedicated.

1912 Japan presented city with 3,000 cherry trees.

1922 Lincoln Memorial dedicated.

1934–1940 New Deal programs expanded government bureaucracy.

1941–1945 Government expands even more during World War II; office space erected in nearby Virginia and Maryland.

1943 Pentagon completed in Virginia.

1963 Martin Luther King Jr. delivered "I Have A Dream" speech at massive civil rights demonstration at Lincoln Memorial.

1964 Washington, D.C., residents voted in federal election for first time.

1965 Students demonstrated against Vietnam War.

1968 Rioting broke out following assassination of Martin Luther King Jr.

1970 Students protested killing of four demonstrators at Kent State University in Ohio and U.S. military incursion into Cambodia.

1975 First popularly elected mayor in 100 years inaugurated.

1981 President Ronald Reagan wounded in assassination attempt.

1982 Vietnam War Memorial dedicated.

1990 Mayor Marion Barry arrested on crack cocaine charges.

1991 Parade honored troops returning from Persian Gulf War.

1994 Barry elected mayor again.

1995 Nation of Islam's Louis Farrakhan organized Million Man March.

(Sources: *Facts About the States*, *World Book*, *Americana*, and *Facts on File*)

PART 4

Politics and Presidents

POLITICS

National Political Conventions

Year	Party	Dates	City	Nominee	Number of ballots
1831	Anti-Masonic National–	September 26–28	Baltimore	William Wirt	1
	Republican[1]	December 12–15	Baltimore	Henry Clay	1
1832	Democratic	May 21–23	Baltimore	*Andrew Jackson	1
1835	Democratic	May 20–23	Baltimore	*Martin Van Buren	1
	Whig[2]	December 14	Harrisburg, Pa.	William H. Harrison	1
1839	Whig	December 4–7	Harrisburg, Pa.	*William H. Harrison	2
1840	Democratic	May 5–6	Baltimore	Martin Van Buren	1
1844	Whig	May 1	Baltimore	Henry Clay	1
	Democratic	May 27–29	Baltimore	*James K. Polk	9
1848	Democratic	May 22–25	Baltimore	Lewis Cass	4
	Whig	June 7–9	Philadelphia	*Zachary Taylor	4
	Free Soil (Democratic)[3]	August 9–10	Buffalo	Martin Van Buren	1
1852	Democratic	June 1–5	Baltimore	*Franklin Pierce	49
	Whig	June 17–20	Baltimore	Winfield Scott	53
1856	Democratic	June 2–6	Cincinnati	*James Buchanan	17
	Republican	June 17–19	Philadelphia	John C. Fremont	2
1860	Democratic	April 23–May 3	Charleston	Deadlocked/Adjourned	57
		June 18–23	Baltimore	Stephen A. Douglas	2
	Republican	May 16–18	Chicago	*Abraham Lincoln	3
1864	Democratic	August 29–31	Chicago	George B. McClellan	1
	Republican	June 7–8	Baltimore	*Abraham Lincoln	1
1868	Democratic	July 4–9	New York	Horatio Seymour	22
	Republican	May 20–21	Chicago	*Ulysses S. Grant	1

(* indicates candidate won presidency)

Year	Party	Dates	City	Nominee	Number of ballots
1872	Democratic	July 9–10	Baltimore	Horace Greeley	1
	Republican	June 5–6	Philadelphia	*Ulysses S. Grant	1
1876	Democratic	June 27–29	St. Louis	Samuel J. Tilden	2
	Republican	June 14–16	Cincinnati	*Rutherford B. Hayes	7
1880	Democratic	June 22–24	Cincinnati	Winfield S. Hancock	2
	Republican	June 2–8	Chicago	*James A. Garfield	36
1884	Democratic	July 8–11	Chicago	*Grover Cleveland	2
	Republican	June 3–6	Chicago	James G. Blaine	4
1888	Democratic	June 5–7	St. Louis	Grover Cleveland	1
	Republican	June 19–25	Chicago	*Benjamin Harrison	8
1892	Democratic	June 21–23	Chicago	*Grover Cleveland	1
	Republican	June 7–10	Minneapolis	Benjamin Harrison	1
1896	Democratic	July 7–11	Chicago	William J. Bryan	5
	Republican	June 16–18	St. Louis	*William McKinley	1
1900	Democratic	July 4–6	Kansas City	William J. Bryan	1
	Republican	June 19–21	Philadelphia	*William McKinley	1
1904	Democratic	July 6–9	St. Louis	Alton S. Parker	1
	Republican	June 21–23	Chicago	*Theodore Roosevelt	1
1908	Democratic	July 7–19	Denver	William J. Bryan	1
	Republican	June 16–19	Chicago	*William H. Taft	1
1912	Democratic	June 25–July 2	Baltimore	*Woodrow Wilson	46
	Republican	June 18–22	Chicago	William H. Taft	1
	Progressive[4] (Bull Moose)	August 5–7	Chicago	Theodore Roosevelt	1
1916	Democratic	June 14–16	St. Louis	*Woodrow Wilson	1
	Republican	June 7–10	Chicago	Charles E. Hughes	3
1920	Democratic	June 28–July 6	San Francisco	James M. Cox	44
	Republican	June 8–12	Chicago	*Warren G. Harding	10
1924	Democratic	June 24–July 9	New York	John W. Davis	103
	Republican	June 10–12	Cleveland	*Calvin Coolidge	1
1928	Democratic	June 26–29	Houston	Alfred E. Smith	1
	Republican	June 12–15	Kansas City, Mo.	*Herbert Hoover	1
1932	Democratic	June 27–July 2	Chicago	*Franklin D. Roosevelt	4
	Republican	June 14–16	Chicago	Herbert Hoover	1
1936	Democratic	June 23–27	Philadelphia	*Franklin D. Roosevelt	Acclamation
	Republican	June 9–12	Cleveland	Alfred M. Landon	1
1940	Democratic	July 15–18	Chicago	*Franklin D. Roosevelt	1
	Republican	June 24–28	Philadelphia	Wendell L. Willkie	6
1944	Democratic	July 19–21	Chicago	*Franklin D. Roosevelt	1
	Republican	June 26–28	Chicago	Thomas E. Dewey	1
1948	Democratic	July 12–14	Philadelphia	*Harry S. Truman	1
	Republican	June 21–25	Philadelphia	Thomas E. Dewey	3
1952	Democratic	July 21–26	Chicago	Adlai E. Stevenson	3
	Republican	July 7–11	Chicago	*Dwight D. Eisenhower	1
1956	Democratic	August 13–17	Chicago	Adlai E. Stevenson	1
	Republican	August 20–23	San Francisco	*Dwight D. Eisenhower	1

(* indicates candidate won presidency)

Year	Party	Dates	City	Nominee	Number of ballots
1960	Democratic	July 11–15	Los Angeles	*John F. Kennedy	1
	Republican	July 25–28	Chicago	Richard M. Nixon	1
1964	Democratic	August 24–27	Atlantic City	*Lyndon B. Johnson	Acclamation
	Republican	July 13–16	San Francisco	Barry Goldwater	1
1968	Democratic	August 26–29	Chicago	Hubert H. Humphrey	1
	Republican	August 5–8	Miami Beach	*Richard M. Nixon	1
1972	Democratic	July 10–13	Miami	George McGovern	1
	Republican	August 21–23	Miami Beach	*Richard M. Nixon	1
1976	Democratic	July 12–15	New York	*Jimmy Carter	1
	Republican	August 16–19	Kansas City, Mo.	Gerald R. Ford	1
1980	Democratic	August 11–14	New York	Jimmy Carter	1
	Republican	July 14–17	Detroit	*Ronald Reagan	1
1984	Democratic	July 16–19	San Francisco	Walter F. Mondale	1
	Republican	August 20–23	Dallas	*Ronald Reagan	1
1988	Democratic	July 18–21	Atlanta	Michael S. Dukakis	1
	Republican	August 15–18	New Orleans	*George Bush	1
1992	Democratic	July 13–16	New York City	*Bill Clinton	1
	Republican	August 17–20	Houston	George Bush	1
1996	Democratic	August 26–29	Chicago	*Bill Clinton	1
	Republican	August 12–15	San Diego	Robert Dole	1

1. National Republican Party was absorbed into Whig Party after 1834.
2. Whig Party held no national convention for 1836 election. Harrisburg was actually a state convention: Harrison's nomination was endorsed by Anti-Masonics and other opponents of Van Buren, but Whig votes were divided among four presidential nominees.
3. Free Soil Party was formed by anti-slavery Democrats.
4. Progressive Party was formed by dissident members of Republican Party.

(Sources: *National Political Conventions 1831–1992* and *World Book*)

(* indicates candidate won presidency)

Platform Fights at National Political Conventions

Knocked out, dragged out platform fights at political conventions are a thing of the past for the Democrats and Republicans. In the last few decades, conventions have become less events for substantive decisions to be hammered out about what the party stands for and who the candidate will be and more a formal coronation of a candidate already decided in the primaries. Usually the nominee-apparent dominates the platform process. Any minority planks that are introduced are more a symbolic gesture than a manifestation of internal disagreement, which might undercut the opportunity for free television exposure for the candidate.

1860 Democratic Party convention approved by 165 to 138 platform plank leaving decision on slavery in territories to Supreme Court. Dissident Southern delegates favored position that neither state nor federal governments could outlaw slavery in territories and split party to run own candidate for president (Breckenridge).

1896 Democratic Party approved plank calling for free and unlimited coinage of silver, defeated alternative gold standard plank by 303 to 626. William Jennings Bryan delivered "Cross of Gold" speech during platform debate.

1908 Republican Party rejected substitute liberal platform proposed by minority led by Senator Robert M. LaFollette (Wisconsin). Led to eventual formation of Progressive Party.

1924 Democratic Party narrowly defeated minority plank condemning Ku Klux Klan by vote of 542-7/20 to 543-3/20.

1932 Republican Party defeated minority plank to repeal Eighteenth Amendment (Prohibition) by vote of 460-2/9 to 690-19/36.

1948 Democratic Party approved strong civil rights amendment to platform by 651-1/2 to 582-1/2, leading to split by Southern Democrats who ran Strom Thurmond for president.

1964 Republican Party rejected amendment to strengthen civil rights plank by 409 to 897.

1968 Democratic Party rejected anti-Vietnam War minority report by 1,041-1/4 to 1,567-3/4.

1972 Democratic Party rejected minority report calling for government-guaranteed income for all families by 999.34 to 1,852.86 and a women's rights plank by 1,101.37 to 1,572.80.

1980 Democratic Party platform fight focused on minority economics plank advocated by Edward M. Kennedy supporters. Plank defeated, but many points integrated into final document.

(Source: *National Political Conventions 1831–1992*)

Political Firsts for Women at Major U.S. Party Conventions

1876 First woman to address major party political convention, Sara Spencer, spoke at Republican Convention.

1892 First women alternate delegates: Therese Jenkin and Cora Carleton, both Republicans.

1900 First woman delegate – Republican Party, Frances Warren.

First woman delegate – Democratic Party; Elizabeth Cohen

First woman to second presidential nomination, Elizabeth Cohen, Democrat.

1916 First women served on Democratic convention committees.

Both parties adopted mildly-worded women's suffrage planks.

1920 First women served on Republican convention committees.

Democrats adopted rule mandating equal representation for men and women on Democratic National Committee.

1924 Republicans adopted rule giving equal representation to both genders on National Committee.

First woman to chair credentials committee, Lena Springs, Democrat.

First major-party woman nominated for vice-president, Lena Springs, Democrat.

First African-American woman delegate, Louise M. Fairweather, Republican.

First woman convention vice-chair, May Kennedy, Democrat.

First woman chair Committee on Permanent Organization, Elizabeth Price, Republican.

1928 First Republican woman to chair Credentials Committee, Mabel Walker Willebrandt.

1932 First Republican woman serving on Resolutions Committee, Martha Rober de Romeo.

First Democratic woman serving on Resolutions Committee, Jean S. Whittemore.

1936 First time equal number of men and women served as convention vice-chairs (Democratic Party).

First time equal representation on Platform Committee (Democratic).

1940 Republican Party first endorsed Equal Rights Amendment.

First woman to nominate presidential candidate, Gladys Pyle, Republican.

1944 First time women designated co-chairs for all major party committees (Democratic).

First woman convention permanent secretary, Dorothy Bush, Democrat.

First time Republicans required equal gender representation on Platform and Resolutions committees.

First time Democratic Party endorsed Equal Rights Amendment.

1948 First woman secretary Republican convention, Mrs. Dudley Hay.

1951 First time woman offered national party chair (India Edwards, Democrat); she declined.

1956 First African-American woman became member Democratic National Committee, Gladys Ford Duncan.

1960 First time rule mandated equal gender representation on all national convention committees (Republicans).

1964 First major-party woman placed in nomination for presidency, Margaret Chase Smith, Republican.

1972 First woman keynote speaker, Anne Armstrong, Republican.

First time guidelines mandated equal gender representation on all convention delegations (Democratic).

Guidelines recommended (but not required) equal gender representation on all convention delegations (Republican).

First African-American woman convention co-chair, Yvonne Brathwaite Burke, Democrat.

First major-party African-American woman to have name placed in nomination, Shirley Chisholm, Democrat.

First woman to poll significant number convention votes for vice-presidential nomination, Frances Farenthold, Democrat.

First woman to chair national party, Jean Westwood, Democrat.

1974 First woman chair of Republican Party, Mary Louise Smith.

1976 First woman national convention chair, Representative Corinne "Lindy" Boggs, Democrat.

First African-American woman keynote speaker, Representative Barbara Jordan, Democrat.

1980 Democratic Party quotas ensured women comprised 50 percent convention delegates.

First woman temporary chair of Republican convention, Senator Nancy Kassebaum.

1984 First woman vice-presidential candidate nominated, Representative Geraldine Ferraro, Democrat.

(Source: *Center for the American Woman and Politics* and *Eagleton Institute of Politics, Rutgers University*)

PRESIDENTS

Presidents of the United States

President	Born	Political Party	Served	Died
1. George Washington	February 22, 1732	None	1789–1797	December 14, 1799
2. John Adams	October 30, 1735	Federalist	1797–1801	July 4, 1826
3. Thomas Jefferson	April 13, 1743	Democratic-Republican	1801–1809	July 4, 1826
4. James Madison	March 16, 1751	Democratic-Republican	1809–1817	June 28, 1836
5. James Monroe	April 28, 1758	Democratic-Republican	1817–1825	July 4, 1831
6. John Quincy Adams	July 11, 1767	Democratic-Republican	1825–1829	February 23, 1848
7. Andrew Jackson	March 15, 1767	Democratic	1829–1837	June 8, 1845
8. Martin Van Buren	December 5, 1782	Democratic	1837–1841	July 24, 1862
9. William H. Harrison	February 9, 1773	Whig	1841	April 4, 1841
10. John Tyler	March 29, 1770	Whig	1841–1845	January 18, 1862
11. James K. Polk	November 2, 1795	Democratic	1845–1849	June 15, 1849
12. Zachary Taylor	November 24, 1784	Whig	1849–1850	July 9, 1850
13. Millard Fillmore	January 7, 1800	Whig	1850–1853	March 8, 1874
14. Franklin Pierce	November 23, 1804	Democratic	1853–1857	October 8, 1869
15. James Buchanan	April 23, 1791	Democratic	1857–1861	June 1, 1868
16. Abraham Lincoln	February 12, 1809	Republican, Union	1861–1865	April 15, 1865
17. Andrew Johnson	December 29, 1808	Union	1865–1869	July 31, 1875
18. Ulysses S. Grant	April 27, 1822	Republican	1869–1877	July 23, 1885

President	Born	Political Party	Served	Died
19. Rutherford B. Hayes	October 4, 1822	Republican	1877–1881	January 17, 1893
20. James A. Garfield	November 19, 1831	Republican	1881	September 19, 1881
21. Chester A. Arthur	October 5, 1829	Republican	1881–1885	November 18, 1886
22. Grover Cleveland	March 18, 1837	Democratic	1885–1889	June 24, 1908
23. Benjamin Harrison	August 20, 1833	Republican	1889–1893	March 13, 1901
24. Grover Cleveland	March 18, 1837	Democratic	1893–1897	June 24, 1908
25. William McKinley	January 29, 1843	Republican	1897–1901	September 14, 1901
26. Theodore Roosevelt	October 27, 1858	Republican	1901–1909	January 6, 1919
27. William H. Taft	September 15, 1857	Republican	1909–1913	March 8, 1930
28. Woodrow Wilson	December 28, 1856	Democratic	1913–1921	February 3, 1924
29. Warren G. Harding	November 2, 1865	Republican	1921–1923	August 2, 1923
30. Calvin Coolidge	July 4, 1872	Republican	1923–1929	January 5, 1933
31. Herbert C. Hoover	August 10, 1874	Republican	1929–1933	October 20, 1964
32. Franklin D. Roosevelt	January 30, 1882	Democratic	1933–1945	April 12, 1945
33. Harry S. Truman	May 8, 1884	Democratic	1945–1953	December 26, 1972
34. Dwight D. Eisenhower	October 14, 1890	Republican	1953–1961	March 28, 1969
35. John F. Kennedy	May 29, 1917	Democratic	1961–1963	November 22, 1963
36. Lyndon B. Johnson	August 27, 1908	Democratic	1963–1969	January 22, 1973
37. Richard M. Nixon	January 9, 1913	Republican	1969–1974	April 22, 1994
38. Gerald R. Ford	July 14, 1913	Republican	1974–1977	
39. Jimmy Carter	October 1, 1924	Democratic	1977–1981	
40. Ronald W. Reagan	February 6, 1911	Republican	1981–1989	
41. George H. W. Bush	June 12, 1924	Republican	1989–1993	
42. Bill Clinton	August 19, 1946	Democratic	1993–	

Biographical Chronologies of the Presidents

George Washington – First President, 1789–1797

1732 February 22 – Born, Westmoreland County, Virginia.

1754 March 15 – Commissioned lieutenant colonel in Virginia militia during French and Indian War.

1755 May 10 – Appointed to staff of Major General Edward Braddock, commander of British forces in America.

July 9 – Led survivors to safety after Braddock's Army ambushed near Turtle Creek, Pennsylvania (Braddock mortally wounded).

1759 January 6 – Married Martha Dandridge Custis.

1759–1774 Member Virginia House of Burgesses.

1774–1775 Member Continental Congress.

1775–1783 Commander Continental Army.

1776 March 20 – Captured Boston after British evacuated city March 17.

August 27 – Battle of Long Island.

October 28 – Battle of White Plains.

December 25 – Led troops in crossing of the Delaware.

December 26 – Battle of Trenton.

1777 January 3 – Battle of Princeton.

September 11 – Battle of Brandywine.

December 19 – Established winter headquarters at Valley Forge.

1781 October 19 – Defeated Gen. Cornwallis at Yorktown, Virginia.

1783 December 4 – Farewell to officers at Fraunces' Tavern, New York City.

1787 President, Constitutional Convention.

1789 February 4 – Elected president.

April 30 – Inaugurated first President of the United States.

May 1 – Attended first Inaugural Ball.

June 1 – Signed first act of Congress, establishing oaths of office for government office holders.

October 3 – Proclaimed first Thanksgiving Day (November 26, 1789) as national holiday.

1790 January 8 – Delivered first State of the Union address.

1791 December – Bill of Rights (first 10 amendments) ratified.

1792 December 5 – Reelected president.

1793 March 4 – Second inauguration.

1796 September 17 – Delivered farewell address, warned against U.S. involvement in foreign disputes.

1797 March 4 – Term ended.

1799 December 14 – Died.

John Adams – Second President, 1797–1801

1735 October 30 – Born, Braintree (now Quincy), Massachusetts.

1758 Admitted to the bar.

1764 October 25 – Married Abigail Smith.

1770 Served as defense attorney for British soldiers charged in killing of civilians in Boston Massacre.

1774–1778 Member Continental Congress.

1776 Member of committee assigned to draft Declaration of Independence.

August 2 – Signed Declaration of Independence.

1778–1779 Minister to France.

1783 Participated in negotiation of Treaty of Paris with Great Britain to end Revolutionary War.

1785–1788 Minister to Great Britain.

1789–1797 Vice President.

1796 December 7 – Elected president.

1797 March 4 – Inaugurated.

1798 June 18 – July 14 – Signed Alien and Sedition Acts (four separate laws).

July 11 – U.S. Marines established.

1800 April 24 – Library of Congress established.

November 1 – Became first president to reside in White House in District of Columbia.

December 3 – Lost bid for reelection.

1801 March 4 – Term ended.

1826 July 4 – Died, Quincy, Massachusetts.

Thomas Jefferson – Third President, 1801–1809

1743 April 13 – Born, Goochland (now Albemarle) County, Virginia.

1757 Inherited father's land- and slave-holdings.

1767 Admitted to the bar.

1769–1775 Member, Virginia House of Burgesses.

1772 January 1 – Married Martha Wayles Skelton.

1775–1776 Member, Continental Congress.

1776 Wrote first draft Declaration of Independence.

1776–1779 Member, Virginia House of Delegates.

1779–1781 Governor of Virginia.

1785–1789 Minister to France.

1790–1793 Secretary of State.

1797–1801 Vice President.

1800 December 3 – Presidential electors cast ballots, with no candidate receiving necessary majority.

1801 February 17 – Elected president by House of Representatives on 36th ballot.

February 24 – In *Marbury v. Madison* Supreme Court invalidated act of Congress as unconstitutional for first time.

March 4 – First President inaugurated in Washington, D.C.

December 8 – First President to send written State of the Union message to Congress; practice prevailed until Woodrow Wilson delivered address in person in 1913.

1803 May 2 – Louisiana territory purchased from France for about $15,000,000.

1804 May 14 – Expedition led by Meriwether Lewis and William Clark began expedition to explore Louisiana territory.

December 5 – Reelected.

1805 March 4 – Second inauguration.

1808 June 1 – Slave trade abolished.

1809 March 4 – Term ended.

1826 July 4 – Died, Charlottesville, Virginia.

James Madison – Fourth President, 1809–1817

1751 March 16 – Born, Port Conway, Virginia.

1776 Drafted Virginia's guarantee of religious freedom.

1776–1777 Member, Virginia House of Delegates.

1777–1779 Member, Governor's Council, Virginia.

1780–1783 Member, Continental Congress.

1784–1786 Member, Virginia House of Delegates.

1787 Delegate, Constitutional Convention.

1787–1788 Wrote contributions to the Federalist Papers.

1789–1797 Member, U.S. House of Representatives.

1794 September 15 – Married Polley Payne Todd.

1798–1800 Member, Virginia House of Delegates.

1801–1809 Secretary of State.

1808 December 7 – Elected president.

1809 March 4 – Inaugurated.

1812 June 18 – War declared against Great Britain.

December 2 – Reelected.

1813 March 4 – Second inauguration.

1814 August 24–25 – White House, Capitol, and other government buildings burned by British forces.

December 24 – Peace treaty signed with Britain.

1817 March 4 – Term ended.

1836 June 28 – Died, Montpelier, Virginia.

James Monroe – Fifth President, 1817–1825

1758 April 28 – Born, Westmoreland County, Virginia.

1776–1778 Served in Revolutionary Army, rising from rank of lieutenant to major; wounded at Battle of Trenton—first president injured in battle.

1783–1786 Member, Continental Congress.

1786 February 16 – Married Elizabeth Kortright.

October – Admitted to the bar.

1790–1794 Member, U.S. Senate.

1794–1796 Minister to France.

1799–1802 Governor of Virginia.

1803–1807 Minister to Great Britain.

1808 Unsuccessful candidate for president.

1811–1817 Secretary of State.

1814–1815 Secretary of War.

1817 March 4 – Inaugurated.

July 12 – Journalist Benjamin Russell coined phrase "Era of Good Feelings" to describe Monroe presidency.

1818 April 4 – Signed act establishing flag with 13 red and white stripes and white star for each state on field of blue.

1819 February 25 – Treaty with Spain gave U.S. control of Florida.

1820 December 6 – Reelected.

1821 March 5 – Second inauguration (delayed because March 4 fell on Sunday).

1823 December 2 – Monroe Doctrine proclaimed.

1831 July 4 – Died, New York City.

John Quincy Adams – Sixth President, 1825–1829

1767 July 11 – Born, Braintree (now Quincy), Massachusetts

1790 Admitted to the bar.

1794–1797 Minister to the Netherlands.

1797–1801 Minister to Prussia.

1797 July 26 – Married Louisa Catherine Johnson.

1803–1808 Member U.S. Senate.

1809–1814 Minister to Russia.

1815–1817 Minister to Great Britain.

1817–1825 Secretary of State.

1824 November 9 – Elected president; first son of a president to be elected to presidency.

1825 March 4 – Inaugurated.

1828 November 4 – Lost bid for reelection.

1829 March 4 – Term ended.

1831–1848 Member, U.S. House of Representatives.

1848 February 23 – Died, Washington, D.C.

Andrew Jackson – Seventh President, 1829–1837

1767 March 15 – Born, Waxhaw, South Carolina.

1787 Admitted to the bar.

1780–1781 Served in Revolutionary Army.

1781 April 10 – Taken prisoner of war; released by British April 25, 1781.

1791 August – Married Rachel Donelson Robards.

1796–1797 Member, U.S. House of Representatives.

1797–1798 Member, U.S. Senate.

1798–1804 Judge, Tennessee Supreme Court.

1814–1821 Major General, U.S. Army.

1815 January 8 – Defeated British in Battle of New Orleans.

1817 December 26 – Ordered to attack Seminole tribe in Florida.

1821 Governor of Florida Territory.

1823–1825 Member, U.S. Senate.

1824 November 9 – Presidential candidate. Though winning plurality in popular vote, failed to achieve majority in electoral college.

1825 February 9 – Lost presidency in election decided in House of Representatives.

1828 November 4 – Elected president.

1829 March 4 – Inaugurated. Shortly after taking office, suspended regular cabinet meetings, and instead met with unofficial advisers, dubbed the "kitchen cabinet" by critics.

1832 May 21 – Nominated for re-election at first Democratic Party national convention.

November 6 – Reelected.

1833 March 4 – Second inauguration.

1837 March 4 – Term ended.

1845 June 8 – Died, Nashville, Tennessee.

Martin Van Buren – Eighth President, 1837–1841

1782 December 5 – Born, Kinderhook, New York.

1803 Admitted to the bar.

1807 February 21 – Married Hannah Hoes.

1813–1820 Member, New York State Senate.

1816–1819 Attorney General of New York (while simultaneously retaining seat in state senate).

1821–1828 Member, U.S. Senate.

1829 Governor of New York.

1829–1831 Secretary of State.

1833–1837 Vice President.

1836 November 1 – Elected president.

1837 March 4 – Inaugurated; "Hail to the Chief" performed at inauguration for first time.

May 10 – Panic of 1837 began; depression lasted six years.

1840 November 10 – Lost bid for reelection.

1841 Mar 4 – Term ended.

1844 May 27–30 – Unsuccessful candidate for president at Democratic national convention in Baltimore.

1848 Unsuccessful presidential candidate of Free-Soil Party; first former president to run as candidate of a minor party.

1862 July 24 – Died, Kinderhook, New York.

William Henry Harrison – Ninth President, 1841

1773 February 9 – Born, Berkeley, Virginia

1791–1798 Served in U.S. Army, most of the time as aide-de-camp to General Anthony Wayne.

1795 November 25 – Married Anna Tuthill Symmes.

1801–1812 Governor of Indiana Territory.

1811 November 7 – Defeated Native Americans at Tippecanoe Creek.

1812–1813 Brigadier General, U.S. Army.

1813–1814 Major General, U.S. Army.

1816–1819 Member, U.S. House of Representatives.

1825–1829 Member, U.S. Senate.

1828–1829 Minister to Colombia.

1836 Unsuccessful candidate for president, Whig Party.

1840 November 3 – Elected president.

1841 March 4 – Inaugurated.

April 4 – First president to die in office; became ill after appearing in inauguration ceremony and parade during cold weather without wearing hat or coat.

John Tyler – Tenth President, 1841–1845

1790 March 29 – Born, Charles City County, Virginia

1809 Admitted to the bar.

1811–1816 Member, Virginia House of Delegates.

1813 March 29 – Married first wife Letitia Christian (died 1842).

1813 April – Appointed and served for a month as militia captain to defend Richmond from threatened British attack during War of 1812.

1817–1821 Member, U.S. House of Representatives.

1825–1827 Governor of Virginia.

1827–1836 Member, U.S. Senate.

1836 November 1 – Unsuccessful candidate for Vice President.

1840 November 3 – Elected vice president.

1841 Vice President.

April 6 – Inaugurated; first vice president to succeed to presidency on death of a president in office (Harrison); first president not to deliver an inaugural address.

1844 June 26 – Married second wife, Julia Gardiner.

1845 March 1 – Signed joint resolution authorizing annexation of Texas.

March 3 – First presidential veto overridden by Congress.

1861 February 4 – Chairman, Washington Peace Conference aimed at reconciling North-South differences.

February 28 – Convinced Congress would reject Peace Conference suggestions, advocated Virginia secede from the Union.

May 5 – Elected to Provisional Congress of Confederation, only U.S. president to hold office in Confederacy.

1862 January 18 – Died Richmond, Virginia

James Knox Polk – Eleventh President, 1845–1849

1795 November 2 – Born, Mecklenburg County, North Carolina.

1820 Admitted to the bar.

1823–1825 Member, Tennessee House of Representatives.

1824 January 1 – Married Sarah Childress

1825–1839 Member, U.S. House of Representatives.

1835 December 7 – Elected Speaker of the House.

1839–1841 Governor of Tennessee.

1844 May 29 – Nominated for president at Democratic Party convention on 9th ballot; first "dark horse" candidate for president.

November 5 – Elected president.

1845 March 4 – Inaugurated.

December 2 – In dispute with Great Britain, claimed Oregon as U.S. territory.

December 29 – Texas admitted as 28th state.

1846 May 13 – War declared against Mexico.

June 15 – Treaty settling Oregon dispute ratified by Senate.

1847 September 14 – Mexico City captured.

1848 February 2 – Treaty ending Mexican War signed, ratified by Senate March 10.

1849 March 4 – Term ended.

1849 June 15 – Died, Nashville, Tennessee.

Zachary Taylor – Twelfth President, 1849–1850

1784 November 24 – Born, Orange County, Virginia

1808–1848 Career military officer.

1810 June 21 – Married Margaret Mackall Smith.

1812–1815 Served in War of 1812.

1832 Served in Black Hawk War.

1837–1840 Served in Second Seminole War.

1838–1846 Brigadier General, U.S. Army.

1846–1849 Major General, U.S. Army.

1848 November 7 – Elected president.

1849 March 5 – Inaugurated; ceremony delayed because March 4 fell on Sunday.

1850 July 9 – Died in office.

Millard Fillmore – Thirteenth President, 1850–1853

1800 January 7 – Born, Cayuga County, New York.

1823 Admitted to the bar.

1826 February 5 – Married first wife, Abigail Powers (died 1853).

1829–1831 Member, New York State Assembly.

1833–1835 Member, U.S. House of Representatives.

1837–1843 Member, U.S. House of Representatives.

1848–1849 Comptroller, New York State.

1849 March 4 – Inaugurated as vice president.

1850 July 10 – Succeeded to presidency on death of Zachary Taylor.

September – Supported passage of Compromise of 1850, series of five laws designed to end slavery controversy and prevent civil war.

1852 Failed to win renomination.

1853 March 4 – End of term.

1856 November – Unsuccessful presidential candidate of American (Know-Nothing) Party; finishing third in popular vote, with 21 percent.

1858 February 10 – Married second wife, Caroline Carmichael McIntosh.

1874 March 8 – Died, Buffalo, New York.

Franklin Pierce – Fourteenth President, 1853–1857

1804 November 23 – Born, Hillsborough (now Hillsboro), New Hampshire.

1834 November 10 – Married Jane Means Appleton.

1827 Admitted to the bar.

1829–1833 Member, New Hampshire legislature.

1833–1837 Member, U.S. House of Representatives.

1837–1842 Member, U.S. Senate.

1846–1848 Served in Mexican War.

1847 Brigadier General, U.S. Army.

1852 November 2 – Elected president.

1853 March 4 – Inaugurated.

1856 June – Failed to win renomination.

1857 March 4 – Term ended.

1869 October 8 – Died, Concord, New Hampshire.

James Buchanan – Fifteenth President, 1857–1861

1791 April 23 – Born, Stony Batter, Pennsylvania.

1812 Admitted to the bar.

1815–1816 Member, Pennsylvania House of Representatives.

1821–1831 Member, U.S. House of Representatives.

1832–1834 Minister to Russia.

1834–1845 Member, U.S. Senate.

1845–1849 Secretary of State.

1853–1856 Minister to Great Britain.

1856 November 4 – Elected president.

1857 March 4 – Inaugurated.

1859 October 16 – John Brown raided Harpers Ferry, Virginia

1860 December 20 – South Carolina seceded from the Union.

1861 February 4 – Confederate States of America established.

March 4 – Term ended.

1868 June 1 – Died, Lancaster, Pennsylvania.

Abraham Lincoln – Sixteenth President, 1861–1865

1809 February 12 – Born, Hodgenville, Kentucky.

1832 Served in military during Black Hawk War but saw no combat.

1842 November 4 – Married Mary Todd.

1834–1841 Member, Illinois legislature.

1837 Admitted to the bar.

1847–1849 Member, U.S. House of Representatives.

1858 Unsuccessful candidate for Senate against Stephen Douglas.

June 17 – Delivered "House Divided" speech.

1860 November 6 – Elected president.

1861 Eleven Southern slave states seceded from the Union.

March 4 – Inaugurated.

April 12 – Confederate forces attacked, captured Fort Sumter in Charleston, South Carolina, marking beginning of Civil War.

1863 January 1 – Emancipation Proclamation freed slaves in rebelling states.

July 1–3 – Union forces led by General Meade defeated Confederate forces led by General Robert E. Lee at Gettysburg.

November 19 – Delivered Gettysburg Address.

1864 May 5–7 – Battle of the Wilderness.

September 2 – General Sherman captured Atlanta.

November 8 – Reelected.

1865 March 4 – Second inauguration.

1865 April 9 – Confederate forces surrendered at Appomattox Courthouse in Virginia.

April 14 – Assassinated by John Wilkes Booth (first presidential assassination); Lincoln died early morning hours April 15.

Andrew Johnson – Seventeenth President, 1865–1869

1808 December 29 – Born, Raleigh, North Carolina.

1827 May 17 – Married Eliza McCardle.

1835–1837 Member, Tennessee House of Representatives.

1839–1841 Member, Tennessee House of Representatives.

1841–1843 Member, Tennessee State Senate.

1843–1853 Member, U.S. House of Representatives.

1853–1857 Governor of Tennessee.

1857–1862 Member, U.S. Senate.

1862–1865 Brigadier General, U.S. Army; served as military governor of Tennessee.

1864 November – Elected vice president.

1865 April 15 – Succeeded to presidency on death of Abraham Lincoln.

December 18 – Thirteenth Amendment abolishing slavery ratified.

1866 March 29 – Alaska purchased from Russia for $7.2 million.

April 9 – Civil Rights Act granted citizenship to African Americans.

1868 May 26 – Acquitted on impeachment charges.

July 28 – Fourteenth Amendment defining national citizenship ratified.

1869 March 4 – Term ended.

1875 Member, U.S. Senate; first former president to become a senator.

July 31 – Died, Carter's Station, Tennessee.

Ulysses Simpson Grant – Eighteenth President, 1869–1877

1822 April 27 – Born, Point Pleasant, Ohio.

1843 Graduated from West Point.

1843–1854 Career military officer.

1846–1848 Served in Mexican War.

1848 August 22 – Married Julia Boggs Dent.

1861 Returned to military service.

1862–1864 Major General, U.S. Army.

1864–1866 Lieutenant General, U.S. Army.

1865 April 9 – Accepted Confederate surrender, Appomattox Courthouse, Virginia

1866 General of the Army.

1868 November 3 – Elected president.

1869 March 4 – Inaugurated.

1870 March 30 – Fifteenth Amendment guaranteeing no citizen can be denied right to vote because of race, color, or previous servitude ratified.

1872 November 5 – Reelected.

1873 March 4 – Second inauguration.

1877 March 4 – Term ended.

1885 July 23 – Died, Mount McGregor, New York.

Rutherford Birchard Hayes – Nineteenth President, 1877–1881

1822 October 4 – Born, Delaware, Ohio.

1845 Admitted to the bar.

1852 December 30 – Married Lucy Ware Webb.

1864–1865 Brigadier General, U.S. Army.

1865 Major General, U.S. Army.

1865–1867 Member, U.S. House of Representatives.

1868–1872 Governor of Ohio.

1876–1877 Governor of Ohio.

1876 November 7 – Election results indecisive; Democrat Samuel Tilden led in popular vote, but electoral votes disputed.

1877 March 2 – Special election commission awarded election to Hayes, who promised end to Reconstruction and withdrawal of occupation troops from South.

March 5 – Inaugurated.

1879 May 10 – First telephone installed at White House.

1880 February 12 – First typewriter installed at White House.

1881 March 4 – Term ended.

1893 January 17 – Died, Fremont, Ohio.

James Abram Garfield – Twentieth President, 1881

1831 November 19 – Born, Orange, Ohio.

1858 November 11 – Married Lucretia Rudolph.

1857–1861 President, Eclectic Institute, Hiram, Ohio.

1859–1861 Member, Ohio State Senate.

1862–1863 Brigadier General, U.S. Army.

1863 Major General, U.S. Army.

1863–1880 Member, U.S. House of Representatives.

1880 November 2 – Elected president.

1881 March 4 – Inaugurated; Mrs. Elizabeth Ballou Garfield first mother of president present at son's inauguration.

1881 July 2 – Mortally wounded by assassin Charles J. Guiteau.

September 19 – Died, Elberon, New Jersey.

Chester Alan Arthur – Twenty-first President, 1881–1885

1829 October 5 – Born, Fairfield, Vermont.

1854 Admitted to the bar.

1858–1862 Served in New York State militia.

1859 October 25 – Married Ellen Lewis Herndon.

1871–1878 Collector of the Port of New York.

1881 Vice President.

September 10 – Succeeded to presidency on death of James A. Garfield.

1883 January 16 – Signed Pendleton Act, creating modern civil service.

1884 Unsuccessful bid for renomination as president candidate.

1885 March 4 – Term ended.

1886 November 18 – Died, New York, New York.

Grover Cleveland – Twenty-second President, 1885–1889

1837 March 18 – Born, Caldwell, New Jersey.

1859 Admitted to the bar.

1871–1873 Sheriff of Erie County, New York.

1881–1882 Mayor of Buffalo, New York.

1883–1885 Governor of New York.

1884 November 4 – Elected president.

1885 March 4 – Inaugurated.

1886 June 2 – Married Frances Folsom; first president to wed in White House.

1887 February 4 – Interstate Commerce Act authorized federal regulation of transportation and interstate business.

1888 November 6 – Lost reelection bid to Benjamin Harrison; Cleveland won popular vote, but lost electoral vote.

1889 March 4 – Term ended.

1892 November 8 – Defeated Harrison's reelection bid, becoming first president elected to non-consecutive terms.

1893 February – Failure of Philadelphia and Reading Railroad triggered Panic of 1893; depression lasted four years.

March 4 – Second inauguration.

1897 March 4 – Term ended.

1908 June 24 – Died, Princeton, NJ.

Benjamin Harrison – Twenty-third President, 1889–1893

1833 August 20 – Born, North Bend, Ohio.

1853 Admitted to the bar.

October 20 – Married first wife Caroline Lavina Scott (died 1892).

1862–1865 Served in U.S. Army during Civil War.

1865 Brigadier General, U.S. Army.

1881–1887 Member, U.S. Senate.

1888 November 6 – Elected president; first grandson of a president elected to presidency (William Henry Harrison).

1889 March 4 – Inaugurated.

1890 July 2 – Sherman Antitrust Act illegalized restraint of trade.

1891 Electric lighting installed at White House.

1892 November 8 – Lost bid for reelection.

1893 February – Panic of 1893 began.

March 4 – Term ended.

1896 April 6 – Married second wife, Marry Scott Lord Dimmick.

1901 March 13 – Died, Indianapolis, Indiana.

Grover Cleveland – Twenty-fourth President, 1893–1897

(See Cleveland entry as Twenty-second President above.)

William McKinley – Twenty-fifth President, 1897–1901

1843 January 29 – Born, Niles, Ohio.

1861–1865 Served in U.S. Army during Civil War.

1867 Admitted to the bar.

1871 January 25 – Married Ida Saxton.

1877–1883 Member, U.S. House of Representatives.

1885–1891 Member, U.S. House of Representatives.

1892–1896 Governor of Ohio.

1896 November 3 – Elected president.

1897 March 4 – Inaugurated.

1898 February 15 – U.S. battleship *Maine* exploded in Havana harbor.

April 25 – U.S. declared war against Spain.

July 7 – Hawaii annexed.

December 10 – Cuba gained independence from Spain; Puerto Rico, Guam, and Philippines acquired by U.S.

1900 November 6 – Reelected president.

1901 March 4 – Second inauguration.

September 6 – Shot by assassin Leon Czolgosz, in Buffalo, New York.

September 14 – Died of his wounds.

Theodore Roosevelt – Twenty-sixth President, 1901–1909

1858 October 27 – Born, New York, New York.

1880 October 27 – Married first wife Alice Hathaway Lee (died 1884).

1882–1884 Member, New York State Assembly.

1886 December 2 – Married second wife Edith Kermit Carow.

1889–1895 Member of U.S. Civil Service Commission.

1895–1897 President of New York City Police Board.

1897–1898 Assistant Secretary of Navy.

1898 Organized "Rough Riders," volunteer cavalry to fight in Spanish-American War.

1899–1901 Governor of New York.

1901 Vice President.

September 14 – Succeeded to presidency on death of William McKinley.

1904 November 8 – Elected president.

December 6 – Issued Roosevelt Corollary to Monroe Doctrine, warning European powers from intervention in Western Hemisphere affairs.

1905 March 4 – Second inauguration.

1906 Won Nobel Peace Prize for negotiating Treaty of Portsmouth, settling Russo-Japanese War of 1904–1905.

1909 March 4 – Term ended.

1912 Unsuccessful presidential candidate of Progressive (Bull Moose) party.

October 4 – Wounded by would-be assassin John N. Schrank during campaign appearance in Milwaukee, Wisconsin.

November 5 – Defeated in presidential election; finished second in popular vote ahead of William Taft, Republican candidate seeking reelection.

1919 January 6 – Died, Oyster Bay, New York.

William Howard Taft – Twenty-seventh President, 1909–1913

1857 September 15 – Born, Cincinnati, Ohio.

1880 Admitted to the bar.

1886 June 19 – Married Helen Herron.

1887–1890 Judge, Ohio Superior Court.

1890–1892 U.S. Solicitor General.

1892–1900 U.S. Circuit Court Judge.

1901–1904 Governor of Philippines.

1904–1908 Secretary of War.

1908 November 3 – Elected president.

1909 March 4 – Inaugurated.

1910 April 14 – First president to open baseball season by throwing out first ball.

1912 November 5 – Lost reelection bid.

1913 February 25 – Sixteenth Amendment establishing federal income tax ratified.

March 4 – Term ended.

1913–1921 Law Professor, Yale University.

1921–1930 Chief Justice, U.S. Supreme Court; first and only president to become Chief Justice.

1930 March 8 – Died, Washington, D.C.

Woodrow Wilson – Twenty-eighth President, 1913–1921

1856 December 28[1] – Born, Staunton, Virginia

1882 Admitted to the bar.

1885 June 24 – Married first wife Ellen Louise Axson (died 1914).

1902–1910 President, Princeton University.

1911–1913 Governor of New Jersey.

1912 November 5 – Elected president.

1913 March 4 – Inaugurated.

March 15 – Held first presidential news conference.

April 8 – Broke long-standing tradition; delivered State of the Union address in person.

May 31 – Seventeenth Amendment, providing for direct election of U.S. Senators, ratified.

1914 August 4 – Proclaimed neutrality in World War I.

1915 May 7 – German submarine sinks *Lusitania*, killing 128 Americans.

December 18 – Married second wife Edith Boling Galt.

1916 November 7 – Reelected president.

1917 March 5 – Second inauguration.

April 6 – War declared against Germany.

1918 January 8 – "Fourteen Points" listed American peace terms with Germany.

May 16 – Sedition Act prohibited anti-war efforts.

November 11 – Armistice ended fighting in Europe.

December 4 – Traveled to Europe for peace conference; first president to leave country while in office.

1919 January 19 – Eighteenth Amendment, establishing Prohibition, ratified.

June 28 – Treaty of Versailles signed.

September-October – Suffered series of strokes.

1920 January-May – Red Scare raids arrested communists and anarchists.

March 19 – Senate rejected Treaty of Versailles.

August 20 – Nineteenth Amendment, enfranchising women, ratified.

November 2 – First time election results reported by radio; Harding elected.

December 20 – Awarded Nobel Peace Prize.

1921 March 4 – Term ended.

1924 February 3 – Died, Washington, D.C.

Warren Gamaliel Harding – Twenty-ninth President, 1921–1923

1865 November 2 – Born, Corsica (now Blooming Grove), Ohio.

1884–1910 Editor, Marion (Ohio) Star.

1891 July 8 – Married Florence Kling De Wolfe.

1899–1903 Ohio State Senator.

1903–1905 Lieutenant Governor of Ohio.

---

1. Most sources report December 28, 1856, as Wilson's birthday, though some report December 29.

1915–1921 Member, U.S. Senate.

1920 November 2 – Elected president.

1921 March 4 – Inaugurated; first president to drive to inaugural in automobile.

May 19 – Signed first immigration quota act.

June 10 – Legislation created federal budget bureau in treasury department.

1922 February 6 – Five Power Treaty signed, restricting naval ship construction for ten-year period.

April – Naval oil reserve at Teapot Dome, Wyoming, secretly leased by Interior department to Harry F. Sinclair.

June 14 – Became first president to speak on radio.

1923 July 27 – Suffered ptomaine poisoning after returning from trip to Alaska.

August 2 – Died in San Francisco.

Calvin Coolidge – Thirtieth President, 1923–1929

1872 July 4 – Born, Plymouth Notch, Vermont.

1897 Admitted to the bar.

1905 October 4 – Married Grace Anna Goodhue.

1907–1908 Member, Massachusetts legislature.

1910–1911 Mayor of Northampton, Massachusetts.

1912–1915 Member, Massachusetts Senate (President, 1914–1915).

1916–1918 Lieutenant Governor of Massachusetts.

1919–1920 Governor of Massachusetts.

1921–1923 Vice President.

1923 August 3 – Succeeded to presidency on death of Warren G. Harding.

1924 November 4 – Elected president.

1925 March 4 – Second inauguration.

1929 March 4 – Term ended.

1933 January 5 – Died, Northampton, Massachusetts

Herbert Clark Hoover – Thirty-first President, 1929–1933

1874 August 10 – Born, West Branch, Iowa.

1895–1913 Mining engineer.

1899 February 10 – Married Lou Henry.

1914–1919 Relief administrator in Europe.

1917–1919 U.S. Food Administrator.

1921–1928 Secretary of Commerce.

1928 November 6 – Elected president.

1929 March 4 – Inaugurated.

October 29 – Stock market crashed; Great Depression began.

1932 November 8 – Lost reelection bid.

1933 February 6 – Twentieth Amendment, changing inaugural date to January 20, ratified.

March 4 – Term ended.

1964 October 20 – Died, New York, New York.

Franklin Delano Roosevelt – Thirty-second President, 1933–1945

1882 January 30 – Born, Hyde Park, New York.

1905 March 17 – Married (Anna) Eleanor Roosevelt.

1907 Admitted to the bar.

1911–1913 Member, New York State Senate.

1913–1920 Assistant Secretary of Navy.

1920 November 2 – Unsuccessful candidate for vice president.

1929–1933 Governor of New York.

1932 July 2 – First presidential nominee to deliver acceptance speech to nominating convention.

November 8 – Elected president.

1933 February 15 – Survived assassination attempt by Giuseppe Zangara in Miami; Chicago Mayor Anton Joseph Cermak killed during Zangara attack.

March 4 – Inaugurated. Appointed Frances Perkins as Secretary of Labor, first woman cabinet member. Announced Good Neighbor Policy with Latin America.

March 9 – June 16 – "Hundred Days" session of Congress; New Deal legislation introduced.

November 16 – Recognized USSR.

December 5 – Twenty-first Amendment, repealing Prohibition, ratified.

1934 June 6 – Securities and Exchange Commission established.

June 19 – Federal Communications Commission established.

1935 July 5 – Wagner Labor Relations Act adopted.

1936 November – Reelected president.

1937 January 20 – Second inauguration.

1939 April 30 – During appearance at New York World's Fair, became first president to be televised.

September 1 – Germany invaded Poland.

September 3 – Britain and France declared war on Germany; World War II began.

September 5 – U.S. declared neutrality.

1940 November 5 – Reelected president; first and only president elected to third term.

1941 January 6 – "Four Freedoms" speech delivered.

January 20 – Third inauguration.

August 14 – With Britain's Churchill, drafted Atlantic Charter.

December 7 – Japan attacked Pearl Harbor.

December 8 – War declared against Japan.

December 11 – War declared against Germany and Italy.

1943 January 10-31 – Traveled to North Africa; conferred with Churchill. First president to leave country during wartime.

November 28-December 1 – Churchill, Roosevelt, and Stalin met in wartime summit in Tehran, Iran.

1944 June 6 – D-Day – Allied forces landed on Normandy beaches.

November 7 – Reelected to fourth term as president.

1945 January 20 – Fourth inauguration.

February 4-February 11 – Churchill, Roosevelt, and Stalin met at Yalta.

April 12 – Died in office, Warm Springs, Georgia.

Harry S. Truman – Thirty-third President, 1945–1953

1884 May 8 – Born, Lamar, Missouri.

1917–1919 Served in U.S. Army during World War I.

1919 June 28 – Married Elizabeth Virginia (Bess) Wallace.

1922–1924 Judge, Jackson County (Missouri) Court

1926–1934 Judge, Jackson County (Missouri) Court

1935–1945 Member, U.S. Senate.

1945 Vice President.

April 12 – Succeeded to presidency on death of Franklin D. Roosevelt.

May 7 – Germany surrendered.

July 17-August 2 – Potsdam Conference planned postwar Europe.

August 6 – U.S. dropped atomic bomb on Hiroshima.

August 9 – Atomic bomb dropped on Nagasaki.

August 15 – Japan surrendered.

1947 March 12 – Truman Doctrine to contain communism announced.

June 5 – Marshall Plan for economic recovery of Europe proposed.

October 5 – First presidential address telecast from White House.

1948 April 1 – Soviet Union blockaded Berlin.

April 2 – Berlin Airlift began.

November 2- Elected president.

1949 January 20 – Second inauguration.

May 12 – Berlin Blockade lifted.

August 24 – North Atlantic Treaty Organization (NATO) created.

1950 June 25 – North Korea invaded South Korea, beginning Korean War.

November 1 – Assassination attempted by Puerto Rican nationalists thwarted.

1951 February 26 – Twenty-second Amendment, limiting presidential terms, ratified.

1953 January 20 – Term ended.

1972 December 26 – Died, Kansas City, Missouri.

Dwight David Eisenhower – Thirty-fourth President, 1953–1961

1890 October 14 – Born, Denison, Texas.

1915 Graduated from West Point.

1916 July 1 – Married Marie (Mamie) Geneva Doud.

1918 Commanded army training unit during World War I; did not go overseas.

1935–1939 Major, U.S. Army; served as assistant to General MacArthur in Philippines.

1941–1942 Brigadier General, U.S. Army.

1942–1943 Major General, U.S. Army.

1942 June 25 – Appointed commander European Theatre of Operations.

November 8 – Appointed commander Allied forces in North Africa.

1943–1945 Full General, U.S. Army, and Supreme Allied Commander.

1943 July-December – Commanded invasions of Sicily and Italy.

December 24 – Appointed Supreme Commander Allied Expeditionary Force.

1944 June 6 – Directed D-Day invasion.

1945–1948 Chief of Staff, U.S. Army.

1948–1950 President, Columbia University.

1951–1952 Supreme Commander, NATO forces in Europe.

1952 November 4 – Elected president.

1953 January 20 – Inaugurated.

July 27 – Armistice ended Korean War.

1954 May 17 – Racially segregated schools declared unconstitutional by Supreme Court.

1955 January 19 – First televised presidential news conference.

September 24 – Suffered heart attack.

1956 November 6 – Reelected.

1957 January 20 – Second inauguration.

September 24 – Federal troops ordered to Little Rock, Arkansas, to protect African-American high school students attempting to integrate high school.

November 25 – Suffered mild stroke.

1959 January 3 – Alaska admitted to Union.

August 21 – Hawaii admitted to Union.

1960 May 7 – U.S. admitted U-2 plane shot down over USSR was spy-plane.

May 16 – East-West Summit collapsed because of U-2 incident.

1961 January 20 – Term ended.

1969 March 28 – Died, Washington, D.C.

John Fitzgerald Kennedy – Thirty-fifth President, 1961–1963

1917 May 29 – Born, Brookline, Massachusetts

1941–1945 Served in U.S. Navy during World War II.

1947–1953 Member, U.S. House of Representatives.

1953–1961 Member, U.S. Senate.

1953 September 12 – Married Jacqueline Lee Bouvier.

1956 Unsuccessfully sought Democratic vice presidential nomination.

1957 May 6 – Received Pulitzer Prize for *Profiles in Courage*.

1960 September 26 – First series of televised presidential debates began.

October 7- Second Nixon-Kennedy debate.

October 13 – Third Nixon-Kennedy debate.

October 21 – Fourth Nixon-Kennedy debate.

November 8 – Elected president; first Roman Catholic president; first president born in twentieth century.

1961 January 20 – Inaugurated.

January 25 – First live televised presidential news conference.

March 1 – Peace Corps established.

April 17 – Bay of Pigs Invasion ended in failure.

May 5 – Alan B. Shepard made first U.S.-manned space flight.

May 25 – Man on the moon by end of decade set as U.S. goal.

June 3-4 – Conferred with USSR leader Nikita Khrushchev in Vienna.

August 13 – Berlin Wall constructed by Communists, initiating Berlin crisis.

1962 February 20 – John Glenn made first U.S. orbital space flight.

September 30-October 10 – Federal troops sent to protect James Meredith, first African-American student admitted to University of Mississippi.

October 22-November 21 – Cuban Missile Crisis.

1963 July 25 – Nuclear Test Ban treaty agreed to by U.S., USSR, and Britain.

August 28 – March on Washington by 200,000 civil rights demonstrators.

August 30 – Hot-line communications link between Kremlin and White House installed.

November 22 – Assassinated by Lee Harvey Oswald in Dallas, Texas.

Lyndon Baines Johnson – Thirty-sixth President, 1963–1969

1908 August 27 – Born, Stonewall, Texas

1934 November 17 – Married Claudia Alta (Lady Bird) Taylor.

1937–1949 Member, U.S. House of Representatives.

1941–1942 Served in U.S. Navy as lieutenant commander (while retaining seat in House of Representatives).

1949–1961 Member, U.S. Senate (Democratic Leader 1953–1961).

1961–1963 Vice President.

1963 November 22 – Succeeded to presidency upon death of John F. Kennedy.

1964 July 2 – Signed Civil Rights Act.

August 7 – Gulf of Tonkin Resolution authorized escalation of war in Vietnam.

August 11 – War on Poverty Bill passed by Congress.

September 27 – Warren Commission concluded Lee Harvey Oswald lone assassin in killing of Kennedy.

November 3 – Elected president.

1965 January 4 – "Great Society" program enunciated in State of the Union Address.

January 20 – Inaugurated. Lady Bird Johnson first First Lady to participate in inaugural ceremony.

February 7 – Bombing of North Vietnam ordered.

March 8-9 – First U.S. combat troops arrived in Vietnam.

April 28 – U.S. troops sent to Dominican Republic.

August 6 – Signed Voting Rights Act.

October 8 – Underwent gall bladder surgery.

1967 February 10 – Twenty-fifth Amendment, providing for appointment to fill vacancy in vice presidency, ratified.

June 13 – Thurgood Marshall nominated as first African-American justice of Supreme Court.

1968 January 30 – Communists launched Tet Offensive in Vietnam.

March 31 – Johnson announced decision not to run for re-election.

April 4 – Martin Luther King Jr. assassinated in Memphis.

June 5 – Robert F. Kennedy assassinated in California.

October 31 – U.S. bombing halted in North Vietnam.

1969 January 20 – Term ended.

1973 January 22 – Died, San Antonio, Texas.

Richard Milhous Nixon – Thirty-seventh President, 1969–1974

1913 January 9 – Born, Yorba Linda, California.

1937 Admitted to the bar.

1940 June 21 – Married Thelma Catherine (Pat) Ryan.

1942–1946 Served in U.S. Navy during World War II.

1947–1951 Member, U.S. House of Representatives.

1951–1953 Member, U.S. Senate.

1952 September 23 – Delivered "Checkers Speech," as vice presidential candidate, defusing "slush fund" scandal.

1953–1961 Vice President.

1958 May – Attacked by anti-American demonstrators while touring Caracas, Venezuela.

1959 July 24 – Impromptu debate with USSR Premier Krushchev while visiting U.S. Exhibition in Moscow (known as "kitchen debate" because occurred in model kitchen at Exhibition).

1960 November 8. Unsuccessful candidate for president.

1962 November 6 – Unsuccessful candidate for California governor.

1963–1968 Practiced law in New York.

1968 November 5 – Elected president.

1969 January 20 – Inaugurated.

July 20 – Neil Armstrong and Edwin Aldrin became first men to walk on moon.

1970 May 4 – National Guard killed four students at Kent Sate University, Ohio, during antiwar demonstration against spread of war to Cambodia. Campus unrest swept nation.

1971 June 30 – Twenty-sixth Amendment, lowering voting age to 18, ratified.

August 15 – Imposed wage/price controls to curb inflation.

October 25 – Communist China admitted to UN; Nationalist China removed.

1972 February 21 – First president to visit Beijing.

May 22 – First president to visit Moscow.

April 15 – Bombing of Hanoi and Haiphong ordered.

June 17 – Break-in by Republican operatives at Democratic Party Headquarters at Watergate complex in Washington (beginning of Watergate Scandal).

November 7 – Reelected president.

1973 January 20 – Second inauguration.

January 22 – Supreme Court ruling in *Roe v. Wade* legalized abortion.

January 28 – Ceasefire in Vietnam.

February 22 – China and U.S. agreed to establish diplomatic liaison offices in each country.

April 30 – Watergate resignations announced. Attorney General Richard G. Kleindienst and White House aides H.R. Haldeman and John D. Ehrlichman resigned. John Dean, counsel to president, dismissed.

May 18 – Archibald Cox appointed Watergate special prosecutor.

July 16 – Alexander P. Butterfield, former White House appointments secretary, revealed existence of secret White House tapes.

October 10 – Vice President Spiro Agnew resigned after pleading no contest to tax evasion charges.

October 12 – Gerald R. Ford became first appointed vice president.

October 19-21 – Arab nations imposed oil embargo against U.S. in retaliation for support to Israel.

October 20 – "Saturday Night Massacre." Attorney General Elliot L. Richardson resigned rather than fire special prosecutor Cox, as ordered by President; Assistant Attorney General William Ruckelshaus also refused to comply and resigned.

November 5 – Leon Jaworski appointed new special prosecutor.

November 26 – Seven White House tapes turned over to Judge Sirica.

1974   March 1 – Seven presidential aides indicted in Watergate scandal.

May 9 – House Judiciary Committee opened impeachment hearings.

July 27-30 – House Judiciary Committee voted articles of impeachment against President.

August 5 – White House transcripts from June 23, 1972, released; revealed President ordered FBI to terminate Watergate probe.

August 9 – Nixon first president to resign from office.

September 8 – Pardoned by President Ford.

1976   July 8 – Disbarred in New York because of obstruction of justice in Watergate scandal.

1994   April 22 – Died, New York, New York.

Gerald Rudolph Ford – Thirty-eighth President, 1974–1977

1913   July 14 – Born, Omaha, Nebraska.

1941   Admitted to the bar.

1942–1946   Served in U.S. Navy.

1948   October 15 – Married Elizabeth (Betty) Bloomer Warren.

1949–1973   Member, U.S. House of Representatives (Republican Leader. 1965–1973).

1973–1974   Vice President.

1974   August 9 – Succeeded to presidency upon resignation of Richard M. Nixon.

September 8 – Pardoned former president Nixon.

September 16 – Clemency granted Vietnam-era draft evaders and military deserters.

November 23-24 – Held summit with USSR leader Leonid Brezhnev on curtailing offensive nuclear weapons.

December 19 – Nelson A. Rockefeller sworn in as vice president.

1975   April 30 – Saigon fell to Communists.

May 15 – U.S.S. *Mayaguez* Incident.

December 9 – Federal bail-out loan for New York City authorized.

1976 July 4 – U.S. marked bicentennial.

September 5 – Escaped assassination attempt by Lynette "Squeaky" Fromme.

September 22 – Escaped second assassination attempt by Sara Jane Moore.

November 2 – Lost election.

1977 January 20 – Term ended.

James Earl Carter – Thirty-ninth President, 1977–1981

1924 October 1 – Born, Plains, Georgia.

1946 July 7 – Married Rosalynn Smith.

1946 Graduated U.S. Naval Academy.

1946–1953 Served in U.S. Navy.

1954–1963 Managed family farm and peanut brokerage, Plains, Georgia.

1963–1967 Member, Georgia State Senate.

1971–1975 Governor of Georgia.

1976 November 2 – Elected president.

1977 January 20 – Inaugurated.

January 21 – Pardoned Vietnam draft evaders.

March 5 – First presidential call-in broadcast.

1978 June 16 – Signed Panama Canal Treaties in Panama City.

September – Camp David Accords; Carter-brokered agreement between Israel's Menachem Begin and Egypt's Anwar Sadat that provided basis for peace settlement between the two Middle East nations.

1979 January 1 – Full diplomatic relations established with China for first time since 1949.

March 26 – Israel and Egypt signed formal peace treaty in Washington.

October 1 – Panama took formal control of Canal Zone.

November 4 – Americans taken hostage at U.S. embassy in Tehran.

December 27 – USSR invaded Afghanistan.

1980 April 25 – Failed hostage rescue attempt in Iran.

November 4 – Lost reelection bid.

1981 January 20 – Term ended.

Ronald Wilson Reagan – Fortieth President, 1981–1989

1911 February 6 – Born, Tampico, Illinois.

1932–1937 Worked as sportscaster.

1937 Film career began; appeared in *Love Is On the Air*.

1942–1945 Served in U.S. Army reserve during World War II.

1940 January 24 – Married first wife Jane Wyman (divorced 1949).

1947–1952 President, Screen Actors Guild.

1952 March 4 – Married second wife Nancy Davis.

1959–1960 President, Screen Actors Guild.

1962 Changed from Democratic to Republic party.

1962–1965 Hosted television show *Death Valley Days*.

1967–1975 Governor of California.

1968 Unsuccessful candidate for Republican presidential nomination.

1972 Unsuccessful candidate for Republican presidential nomination.

1976 Unsuccessful candidate for Republican presidential nomination.

1980 November 4 – Elected president.

1981 January 20 – Inaugurated; American hostages in Iran released.

March 30 – Wounded in assassination attempt by John Hinckley Jr.

July 7 – Appointed Sandra Day O'Connor first woman member of Supreme Court.

August 5 – Striking federal air traffic controllers fired en masse.

1983 October 23 – Truck bombing killed 243 American peacekeepers stationed in Lebanon.

October 25 – U.S. invaded Grenada.

1984 November 6 – Reelected president.

1986 January 28 – Space shuttle *Challenger* exploded shortly after launch.

April 5 – American warplanes bombed Libya in retaliation for terrorist attack against American servicemen at Berlin disco.

November 3 – Iran Contra Scandal broke.

1987 October 19 – Stock market crashes.

December 8 – U.S. and USSR signed Intermediate-Range Nuclear Forces Treaty, dismantling medium-range missiles.

1989 January 20 – Term ended.

George Herbert Walker Bush – Forty-first President, 1989–1993

1924 June 12 – Born, Milton, Massachusetts.

1942–1945 Served in U.S. Navy during World War II.

1945 January 6 – Married Barbara Pierce.

1948–1966 Oil industry businessman.

1964 July 13-16 – Goldwater delegate from Texas at Republican convention.

November 3 – Unsuccessful candidate for U.S. Senate.

1967–1971 Member, U.S. House of Representatives.

1970 November 5 – Unsuccessful candidate for U.S. Senate.

1971–1973 Ambassador to United Nations.

1973–1974 Chairman, Republican National Committee.

1974–1975 Liaison, People's Republic of China.

1976–1977 Director, Central Intelligence Agency.

1981–1989 Vice President

1985 July 3 – Became first acting president of the United States when, under provisions of Twenty-fifth Amendment, President Reagan temporarily transferred presidential authority to Bush for 7 hours and 54 minutes during the time he was under anesthesia for cancer surgery.

1988 November 8 – Elected president.

1989 January 20 – Inaugurated.

March 9 – Senate rejected nomination of Senator John G. Tower for Secretary of Defense.

March 24 – In Prince William Sound, Alaska, tanker *Exxon Valdez* caused largest oil spill in American history.

November 12 – Berlin Wall crumbled.

December 3 – Summit with Soviet leader Gorbachev on board ship near Malta.

December 20 – U.S troops invaded Panama; apprehended General Manuel Noriega and installed new government.

1990 August 2 – Iraq invaded Kuwait.

1991 January 17 – Operation Desert Storm began; American-led UN coalition forces launched military effort to liberate Kuwait from Iraqi-occupation.

February 24-27 – Coalition ground war defeated Iraq.

February 28 – Operation Desert Storm hostilities ended.

March 1 – Public opinion polls reported unprecedented 91-percent approval rating.

August 19 – Attempted coup by Soviet hardliners turned back by pro-democracy forces led by Boris Yeltsin.

December 25 – USSR dissolved.

1992 February 1 – Met with Yeltsin at Camp David; declared Cold War over.

November 3 – Lost bid for reelection.

December 4 – Authorized dispatch of U.S. troops to famine-stricken Somalia.

December 24 – Pardoned six officials for Iran Contra Scandal misdeeds.

1993 January 20 – Term ended.

William Jefferson "Bill" Clinton – Forty-second President, 1993–

1946 August 19 – Born, Hope, Arkansas.

1967 Staff member for Senator J. William Fulbright.

1968–1970 Rhodes Scholar, Oxford University, England.

1973–1976 Law Professor, University of Arkansas.

1975 October 11 – Married Hillary Diane Rodham.

1977–1979 Attorney General of Arkansas.

1979–1981 Governor of Arkansas.

1983–1992 Governor of Arkansas.

1992 November 3 – Elected president.

1993 January 20 – Inaugurated.

February 4 – Signed Family and Medical Leave Act.

April 19 – Eight cult members died in confrontation with Bureau of Alcohol, Tobacco, and Firearms at Branch Davidian compound at Waco, Texas.

September 13 – U.S.-sponsored negotiations reached peace agreement between Palestinian Liberation Organization (PLO) and Israel. PLO's Yasir Arafat and Israeli Prime Minister Yitzhak Rabin joined hands in historical handshake in White House ceremony.

October – Clinton proposed revamping of medical care insurance, but plan was later dropped after severe Congressional criticism.

November 17 – North American Free Trade Agreement (NAFTA) approved.

1994 January 5 – Special prosecutor appointed to investigate Whitewater scandal.

September 19 – American troops dispatched to Haiti to assure peaceful return to power of democratically elected president Jean-Baptiste Aristide, who had been overthrown in 1991 by military leaders.

November 9 – Republicans won control in both Houses of Congress.

1995 January 28 – Diplomatic relations with Vietnam restored.

March 9 – Clinton welcomed Sinn Fein leader Gerry Adams at White House.

April 19 – Terrorist bomb destroyed federal office building in Oklahoma City, killing 168 in worst terrorist attack in U.S. history.

November 1 – U.S.-brokered peace agreement reached at Dayton, Ohio, marking end of hostilities in Bosnia.

December 2 – American peacekeeping troops dispatched to Bosnia and Herzegovina.

1996 February 1 – Signed Telecommunications Act.

March 12 – Helms-Burton law tightened sanctions against Cuba.

August 22 – Signed legislation revamping welfare system.

November 5 – Reelected president.

1997 Ongoing investigation of abusive campaign fundraising activities by Democrats.

April 27–29 – Volunteerism Summit in Philadelphia attended by Clinton and three former presidents.

May 2 – Unemployment fell to 24-year low.

June 12 – Appointed special Presidential Commission to examine problems of race in America.

August 11 – Exercised line item veto for first time.

October 27 – Stock market suffered largest single-day decline in history.

1998 January 21 – Clinton/Lewinsky sex scandal became public knowledge.

February 2 – For first time in nearly 30 years, a federal budget with a projected surplus ($9.5 billion) was announced.

February 19 – Trade deficit hit ten-year high.

March 26 – Clinton became first American president to visit South Africa.

June 25 – Supreme Court ruled 1996 Line Item Veto Act unconstitutional.

November 3 – Republicans lost ground in the House of Representatives, as Democrats gained five seats.

December 16 – U.S. and British air forces attacked Iraq in dispute over UN weapons inspections. Many legislators charged attack was politically motivated, as impeachment vote is postponed.

December 19 – Clinton impeached on two charges of perjury before grand jury and obstruction of justice.

1999 January 7 – Impeachment trial convened in Senate, with Chief Justice William Rehnquist presiding.

February 12 – Clinton acquitted on perjury (45 guilty, 55 not guilty) and obstruction of justice (50 guilty, 50 not guilty—67 votes needed for conviction).

March 24 – U.S. began bombing raids against Yugoslavia as part of NATO campaign against ethnic cleansing against ethnic Albanians in Kosovo province.

(Sources: *World Book*, *Facts on File*, and *The Presidents: A Reference History*)

Presidential Inaugurations

1789 April 30 – George Washington inaugurated in Senate Chamber, Federal Hall, New York City, then nation's capital. Weather: cloudy, intermittent sunshine.

– First inauguration held outdoors

– First president to say "So help me God" and kiss Bible after taking oath.

– First inaugural ball held May 7, one week after ceremony.

1793 March 4 – Washington's second inauguration held in Senate Chamber of Congress Hall in temporary capital of Philadelphia, Pennsylvania. Weather: clear.

– Shortest Inaugural Address; only 135 words.

1797 March 4 – John Adams inaugurated at Congress Hall in Philadelphia. Weather: unknown.

– Only president other than Washington to be inaugurated in Philadelphia.

– First president to take oath administered by Chief Justice of Supreme Court (Oliver Ellsworth).

1801 March 4 – Thomas Jefferson inaugurated in Senate Chamber at Capitol building in Washington, D.C. Weather: clear.

– First to be inaugurated in Washington, D.C.

– First time outgoing president did not attend successor's inaugural. (Crushed by defeated reelection bid, Adams left Washington the night before Jefferson's inauguration.)

– First time president chosen by House of Representatives, due to electoral vote tie between Jefferson and Aaron Burr with 73 electoral votes; Adams had 65.

– First and only time new president walked to and from inauguration.

– First time text of Inaugural Address leaked to press in advance.

– First time widower elected president.

1805 March 4 – Jefferson's second inauguration held in Senate Chamber. Weather: sunny.

– First time president and vice president elected separately in accordance with Twelfth Amendment. (Previously vice president was presiden-

tial candidate with second-highest electoral vote total.)

– First inaugural parade down Pennsylvania Avenue en route to Capitol.

1809 March 4 – James Madison inaugurated in Chamber of House of Representatives. Weather: brisk, sunny.

– First time oath administered some place other than Senate Chamber in Washington, D.C.

– First time wife (Dolley) witnessed husband's inauguration.

– First president to wear only American-made clothing to inauguration.

– First formal inaugural ball in Washington.

– First time Marine Band played at inaugural ball.

– First president to serve previously as congressman.

1813 March 4 – Madison's second inauguration held in Chamber of House of Representatives. Weather: sunny.

– First inauguration while nation at war.

1817 Mar 4 – James Monroe's first inauguration held on platform erected at east portico of Capitol building. Weather: clear, unusually warm for March.

– First outdoor inauguration in Washington, D.C.

– First and only time president-elect and vice president-elect rode to inauguration together.

– First president to serve previously as U.S. Senator.

1821 March 5 – Monroe's second inauguration held in the Hall of the House Chamber. Weather: rain, sleet, snow, slush; 28 degrees.

– First time inauguration delayed (March 4 fell on Sunday.)

– First time Marine Band performed at inauguration.

1825 John Quincy Adams inaugurated in the Hall of the House of Representatives. Weather: rain.

– First time outgoing president accompanied successor to inauguration.

– First president not to take oath on a Bible; held his hand volume of laws.

– First president sworn-in wearing long trousers.

– Only president to be son of previous president.

– First time popular vote for president tabulated.

1829 March 4 – Andrew Jackson inaugurated on east portico of Capitol. Weather: clear, mild, sunny; springlike.

– First inauguration held at White House.

– Second time outgoing president refused to attend successor's inauguration.

– First president not descended from aristocratic family.

1833 March 4 – Jackson's second inauguration held at Chamber of House of Representatives. Weather: snowy.

– First time city of Washington, D.C., had official inauguration role (mayor formally greeted president at Capitol).

1837 March 4 – Martin Van Buren inaugurated on east portico of White House. Weather: clear, bright, sunny.

– First time outgoing and incoming president rode together in same carriage to Capitol for ceremonies.

– First time two inaugural balls held.

– First president born under U.S. flag.

– First time floats included in inaugural parade.

– First time inaugural programs printed and distributed to crowd.

– Last time vice president elected immediately to succeed his president (until George Bush succeeded Ronald Reagan in 1988).

1841 March 4 – William Henry Harrison inaugurated on east portico of Capitol. Weather: Cold, strong, chilling wind.

– First president-elect to arrive in Washington, D.C., by railroad.

– First official planning of inaugural parade.

– Longest inaugural address—8,445 words.

– Broke precedent by beginning address, taking oath, then resuming address.

– First and only president to contract fatal illness at inauguration (refusing to wear hat or coat during ceremony in frigid weather, Harrison caught cold, developed pneumonia, and died April 4).

1841 April 6 – John Tyler became first vice president to succeed to presidency on death of a president. Oath administered by Chief Justice at Indian Queen Hotel, Washington, D.C.

1845 March 4 – James Knox Polk inaugurated on east portico of Capitol. Weather: heavy rain.

– First "dark horse" candidate elected president.

– First inauguration covered by telegraph.

– First time "Hail to the Chief" played at inauguration.

– First time inaugural ball turned a profit; $1,000 subsequently donated to two orphanages.

– First president to serve previously as Speaker of the House.

– Known as the "rainy inauguration."

1849 March 5 – Zachary Taylor inaugurated on east portico of Capitol on March 5, because March 4 fell on Sunday. Weather: cloudy, snowed later in day.

– First time Pennsylvania Avenue lighted by gas for inauguration.

– First election in which all voters went to polls on first Tuesday in November.

1850 July 9 – Millard Fillmore took oath in Hall of Representatives.

– Second vice president to succeed to presidency on death of president.

1854 March 4 – Franklin Pierce inaugurated on east portico of Capitol. Weather: snow.

– First president born in nineteenth century (November 23, 1804).

– Only president to "affirm" rather than "swear" oath of office. (Objection to swearing based on religious grounds [Matthew 5:34-7].)

– Only elected president to seek but not win renomination.

– Only president to deliver inaugural address without referring to notes.

– First newspaper illustration of inauguration carried in Frank Leslie's *Illustrated Weekly*.

1857 March 4 – James Buchanan inaugurated on east portico of Capitol. Weather: clear.

– First bachelor to be inaugurated; only one to remain bachelor.

– First inaugural parade using large floats.

– First inauguration photographed.

1861 March 4 – Abraham Lincoln inaugurated on east portico of Capitol. Weather: cloudy, cleared in afternoon.

– First president to wear beard.

– First time military troops used as guard, not ceremonial purposes.

– First inauguration extensively photographed.

– Five former presidents alive at time of inauguration: Van Buren, Tyler, Fillmore, Pierce, and Buchanan.

1865 March 4 – Lincoln's second inauguration held on east portico of Capitol. Weather: rain.

– First time African-American civic associations and troops participated in inauguration (as part of presidential escort).

1865 April 15 – Andrew Johnson took oath of office at Kirkwood House hotel in Washington, D.C., following assassination of Lincoln.

– First time Chief Justice administered oath to vice president on death of president (previous occasions oath administered by Chief Justice of Washington Circuit Court).

– First president not to have early military or legal background.

1869 March 4 – Ulysses S. Grant inaugurated on east portico of Capitol. Weather: rain, muddy underfoot.

– First Civil War hero elected president.

– Most extensive military participation in inaugural parade (eight divisions).

– First president whose parents both alive when inaugurated (also true of John F. Kennedy).

1873 March 4 – Grant's second inauguration held on east portico of White House: Weather: clear, very cold; second coldest in history.

– First time congressional committee called for president and escorted him to Capitol.

– First time governors of the states, as a body, present at inauguration.

– Weather so cold several West Point cadets lost consciousness during parade; valves on musicians' instruments froze at inaugural ball and ice cream and champagne froze solid.

1877 March 5 – Rutherford B. Hayes inaugurated in public ceremony at east portico of Capitol. (Ceremony delayed because March 4 was a Sunday.) Earlier private swearing-in ceremony held March 3 in White House Red Room. Weather: rainy, cloudy.

– First president to take oath in White House.

– First president to repeat oath twice for same term (private and public ceremonies).

1881 March 4 – James A. Garfield inaugurated on east portico of Capitol. Weather: snow, rain, driving wind.

– First time president-elect's mother accompanied son to inaugural ceremony.

– First president to review inaugural parade from specially constructed stand in front of White House.

– First left-handed president.

– First time Pennsylvania Avenue paved.

– First time special seating erected along parade route.

– No wine or liquor served at inaugural ball.

1881 September 20 – Chester A. Arthur took oath at his home at 123 Lexington Avenue, New York City, following death of President Garfield on September 19. Oath administered by New York State Supreme Court justice. Oath repeated September 22 in Vice President's room at Capitol.

– First time president inaugurated at own private residence.

1885 March 4 – Grover Cleveland inaugurated on east portico of Capitol. Weather: clear.

– First Democratic president elected since Civil War.

– First president elected after Civil War not to have served in the war.

– Took oath on his mother's Bible.

– Second bachelor inaugurated president; first married in White House (June 2, 1886).

1889 March 4 – Benjamin H. Harrison inaugurated on east portico of Capitol. Weather: rain.

– First grandson of a president to be inaugurated president.

1893 March 4 – Grover Cleveland inaugurated for second time on east portico of Capitol. Weather: snow, temperature in 20s.

– First president reelected to non-consecutive term.

1897 March 4 – William McKinley inaugurated on east portico of Capitol. Weather: clear.

– Last of Civil War presidents.

– First inauguration for which motion picture film available.

1901 March 4 – McKinley inaugurated for second time on east portico of Capitol. Weather: rain

– First time House of Representatives joined with Senate to plan inaugural arrangements.

1901 September 14 – Theodore Roosevelt took oath of office at residence of Ansley Wilcox, Buffalo, New York, following death of President McKinley.

– Youngest man to take oath of office.

– First president to win Nobel Peace Prize.

1905 March 4 – Roosevelt's second inauguration held on east portico of Capitol. Weather: bright, sunny.

– First president to deliver address bareheaded.

– Inaugural parade viewed by 200,000 spectators.

1909 March 4 – William H. Taft inaugurated in Senate Chamber. Weather: snowy, nine inches fell evening of March 3; windy, cold.

– Ceremony moved indoors due to weather conditions.

– First time wife rode with president in procession from Capitol to White House.

1913 March 4 – Woodrow Wilson inaugurated on east portico of Capitol. Weather: cloudy in morning, but sun broke through in time for ceremony.

– Second Democratic president since Civil War.

– First president with doctoral degree.

– First president who was previously university president.

1917 March 5 – Wilson's second inauguration delayed because March 4 fell on Sunday; oath administered in private ceremony on March 4. Weather: clear, but chilling wind.

– First time oath administered on Sunday.

– First time women marched in inaugural parade.

– First president inaugurated over new granite steps at east portico of Capitol.

1921 March 4 – Warren G. Harding inaugurated on east portico of Capitol. Weather: clear.

– First president elected after women received right to vote.

– First president to ride to and from ceremony in automobile.

– First inauguration receiving radio news coverage.

– First time loudspeakers used at inauguration.

1923 August 3 – Calvin Coolidge took oath of office at family home in Plymouth, Vermont, at 2:47A.M., following death of President Harding. Oath administered by Coolidge's father, local justice of the peace. Oath repeated August 21 at Willard Hotel, Washington, D.C.

– First president sworn in by father.

1925 March 4 – Coolidge's second inauguration held on east portico of Capitol; oath administered by Chief Justice William H. Taft, former president. Weather: cloudy, sun broke through as oath administered.

– First inauguration broadcast nationally on radio (25 stations).

– First and only time former president (Taft) administered oath.

1929 March 4 – Herbert Clark Hoover inaugurated on east portico of Capitol. Weather: rain.

– First president born in Iowa.

– Dirigible *Los Angeles*, four blimps, and 30 airplanes flew over Washington, D.C., as part of celebration.

1933 March 4 – Franklin D. Roosevelt inaugurated on east portico of Capitol. Weather: cloudy, chilly.

– First time Electoral College members invited to inauguration.

– First president whose mother could have voted for him.

1937 January 20 – Roosevelt's second inauguration held on east portico of Capitol. Weather: rain;

1.77 inches of rain fell; heaviest inaugural downpour.

– First inauguration held January 20 in accordance with Twentieth Amendment.

– First time mother witnessed second inauguration.

1941 January 20 – Roosevelt's third inauguration held on east portico of Capitol. Weather: clear, cold.

– First and only third inauguration for a president.

– First and only time mother witnessed son's third inauguration.

1945 January 20 – Roosevelt's fourth inauguration held on south portico of White House. Weather: cloudy, snow on ground from early morning snowfall; sunny in afternoon.

– First and only fourth inauguration.

1945 April 12 – Harry S. Truman took oath in Cabinet Room at White House following Roosevelt's death.

– First president born in Missouri.

1949 January 20 – Truman inaugurated for a second term on east portico of Capitol. Weather: clear.

– First time Jewish rabbi participated in inauguration.

– First televised inauguration (estimated 10 million viewers).

1953 January 20 – Dwight D. Eisenhower inaugurated on east portico of Capitol. Weather: sunny, mild.

– First inauguration seen live on West Coast television.

– First time homburg hats worn by official party rather than black top hats.

– First time president recited personal prayer rather than kiss Bible following oath taking.

– First president inaugurated under constitutional term limitation (two-term limit designated by Twenty-second Amendment).

1957 January 21 – Eisenhower's second inauguration held on east portico of Capitol January 21, because January 20 fell on Sunday. (Private swearing in held on 20th in White House East Room.) Weather: cloudy.

– First inaugural appearance by cadets from new Air Force Academy.

1961 January 20 – John F. Kennedy inaugurated on platform erected at east front of Capitol. Weather: snowed night before; clear, wind, chilly.

– First president born in twentieth century.

– First Roman Catholic elected president.

– First time both parents of president-elect witnessed son's inauguration.

– First time inauguration held over steps of new, extended east front of Capitol.

– First inauguration broadcast in color (over NBC television).

– Inauguration distinguished by Robert Frost reading poem.

– First time five inaugural balls.

– First time Speaker of the House administered oath to vice president.

– Army flame-throwers cleared Pennsylvania Avenue of snow from earlier storm.

1963 November 2 – Lyndon B. Johnson took oath aboard *Air Force One* at Love Field, Dallas, Texas, upon death of President Kennedy.

– First time oath administered aboard airplane.

– First time woman (U.S. District Judge Sarah T. Hughes) administered oath.

1965 January 20 – Johnson inaugurated for full term on east portico of Capitol. Weather: near freezing temperatures.

– First time president's wife participated in ceremony by holding Bible while oath administered.

1969 January 20 – Richard M. Nixon inaugurated on east portico of Capitol. Weather: overcast; rain held off until parade ended.

– One-hundred ninety-two Medal of Honor recipients present at ceremony.

– Fifteen thousand police, troops, and guardsmen deployed along parade route.

1973 January 20 – Nixon inaugurated for second time on east portico of Capitol. Weather: temperatures in 40s; stiff breeze.

– Thirteenth president sworn in for second term.

– Inauguration marred by anti-Vietnam War demonstrations.

1974 August 9 – Gerald R. Ford took oath in East Room of White House following resignation of President Nixon because of Watergate Scandal.

– First president to hold top two national posts without being elected to either (had been appointed vice president following resignation of Spiro Agnew).

– First president to pardon another president.

– First vice president to succeed to presidency because of resignation of sitting president.

1977 January 20 – Jimmy Carter inaugurated on platform erected on east portico of Capitol. Weather: subfreezing temperatures.

– First president to walk, with wife Rosalynn, mile-and-a-half from Capitol to White House.

– First president to be born in a hospital.

– First to view parade from solar heated reviewing stand.

– First president from Georgia.

– First president to graduate from U.S. Naval Academy.

– First president sworn in using his nickname.

1981 January 20 – Ronald W. Reagan inaugurated at West Front of Capitol, symbolic of president's western roots. Weather: unusually warm; 56 degrees.

– Oldest president ever inaugurated.

– First time inauguration held at West Front of Capitol.

– Most expensive inauguration in history to date.

– First president born in Illinois.

– First president to have been divorced.

– First president to have been actor.

– First president to have been union leader (Screen Actors Guild).

1985 January 21 – Reagan inaugurated for second term in public ceremony in Capitol Rotunda on January 21 because 20th fell on Sunday. Private ceremony held on 20th in White House Grand Foyer. Weather: subfreezing, coldest inauguration on record.

– Due to weather, outdoor events cancelled, switched indoors.

1989 January 20 – George H. W. Bush inaugurated on west portico of Capitol. Weather: windy, temperature in low 50s.

– Second time west portico used as inaugural site.

– First extensive use of metal detectors at inauguration; all ticketed spectators attending swearing-in ceremony required to pass through metal detector gates.

1993 January 20 – Bill Clinton inaugurated on west portico of Capitol. Weather: mild, temperature in 40s.

– First president born after World War II.

– Third shortest inaugural address.

– Maya Angelou read poem specifically written for inauguration (first poetry reading at inauguration since Frost read at Kennedy's in 1961).

– Inaugural parade included gay and lesbian group.

– First time inaugural morning prayer service held at predominantly African-American church.

– Eleven inaugural balls held, including one for gays and lesbians.

1997 January 20 – Bill Clinton inaugurated for second term on West Portico of Capitol. Weather: near freezing temperatures, breezy.

– Thirty-three million dollars spent on inaugural activities.

– Arkansas poet Miller Williams read his poem "Of History and Hope."

– Fourteen inaugural balls held.

(Sources: *The Inaugural Story, 1789–1969*, *Inaugural Cavalcade*, *Facts on Files*, and *Washington Post*)

Non-Majority Presidents

Seventeen times candidates who failed to win a majority in the popular vote were elected president of the United States, either because they won in the Electoral College or were awarded the election by the House of Representatives. Three presidents actually lost in the popular vote: John Quincy Adams (1824), Rutherford B. Hayes (1876), and Benjamin Harrison (1888).

	Candidate	Percentage	Electoral
1824	Jackson	41.34	99
	*Adams	30.92	84
	Clay	12.99	37
	Crawford	11.17	41

(Election decided by House of Representatives)

	Candidate	Percentage	Electoral
1844	*Polk	49.54	170
	Clay	48.08	105
	Birney	2.30	–
1848	*Taylor	47.28	163
	Cass	42.49	127
	Van Buren	10.12	–
1856	*Buchanan	45.28	174
	Fremont	33.11	114
	Fillmore	21.53	8
1860	*Lincoln	39.82	180
	Douglas	29.46	12
	Breckenridge	18.09	72
	Bell	12.61	3
1876	Tilden	50.97	184
	*Hayes	47.95	165
	Cooper	0.97	–

(Twenty disputed electoral votes from Florida, Louisiana, South Carolina, and Oregon were awarded to Hayes by a special Electoral Commission on March 2, 1877, giving him a total of 185.)

(* indicates candidate who was elected.)

	Candidate	Percentage	Electoral		Candidate	Percentage	Electoral
1880	*Garfield	48.27	214		Benson	3.18	–
	Hancock	48.25	155		Others	1.46	–
	Weaver	3.32	–	**1948**	*Truman	49.52	303
	Others	0.15	–		Dewey	45.12	189
1884	*Cleveland	48.50	219		Thurmond	2.40	39
	Blaine	48.25	182		Wallace	2.38	–
	Butler	1.74	–	**1960**	*Kennedy	49.72	303
	St. John	1.47	–		Nixon	49.55	219
1888	Cleveland	48.62	168		Others	0.72	–
	*Harrison	47.82	233	**1968**	*Nixon	43.42	301
	Fisk	2.19	–		Humphrey	42.72	191
	Streeter	1.29	–		Wallace	13.53	46
1892	*Cleveland	46.05	277		Others	0.33	–
	Harrison	42.96	145	**1992**	*Clinton	42.95	370
	Weaver	8.50	–		Bush	37.40	168
	Others	2.25	–		Perot	18.36	–
1912	*Wilson	41.84	435	**1996**	*Clinton	49.3	379
	Roosevelt	27.39	88		Dole	40.7	159
	Taft	23.18	8		Perot	8.4	–
	Debs	5.99	–				
1916	*Wilson	49.24	277				
	Hughes	46.11	254				

(Sources: *Presidential Elections Since 1789, The Presidents (Graff) World Almanac & Book of Facts; World Book*, and *Facts on File*)

(* indicates candidate who was elected.)

(* indicates candidate who was elected.)

Failed Presidential Reelection Attempts

1800 John Adams lost to Thomas Jefferson.

1828 John Quincy Adams lost to Andrew Jackson.

1840 Martin Van Buren lost to William Henry Harrison.

1856 Millard Fillmore lost to James Buchanan.

1888 Grover Cleveland lost to Benjamin Harrison.

1892 Benjamin Harrison lost to Grover Cleveland.

1912 Theodore Roosevelt (and William H. Taft) lost to Woodrow Wilson.

(not an attempt at re-election to a consecutive term by Roosevelt)

1932 Herbert Clark Hoover lost to Franklin Delano Roosevelt.

1976 Gerald R. Ford lost to Jimmy Carter.

1980 Jimmy Carter lost to Ronald Reagan.

1992 George H.W. Bush lost to Bill Clinton.

(Sources: *Book of Presidents*, *Facts on File*, and *Presidential Elections Since 1789*)

Presidents Denied Renomination

1844 John Tyler lost Whig Party nomination to Henry Clay. (Martin Van Buren, who had lost reelection attempt in 1840, unsuccessfully sought Democratic party nomination in 1844, and ran unsuccessfully as Free Soil party candidate for president in 1848)

1852 Millard Fillmore lost Whig Party nomination to Winfield Scott.

1856 Franklin Pierce lost Democratic Party nomination to James Buchanan.[1]

1868 Andrew Johnson lost Democratic Party nomination to Horatio Seymour.

1884 Chester A. Arthur lost Republic Party nomination to James G. Blaine.

(Sources: *Book of Presidents*, *Facts on File*, and *Presidential Elections Since 1789*)

Presidential Runner-Ups

Election Year	Winner	Runner-up
1789	George Washington	John Adams
1792	George Washington	John Adams
1796	John Adams	Thomas Jefferson
1800	Thomas Jefferson	Aaron Burr
1804	Thomas Jefferson	Charles C. Pinckney
1808	James Madison	Charles C. Pinckney
1812	James Madison	De Witt Clinton
1816	James Monroe	Rufus King
1820	James Monroe	no opposition
1824	John Quincy Adams	Andrew Jackson
1828	Andrew Jackson	John Quincy Adams
1832	Andrew Jackson	Henry Clay
1836	Martin Van Buren	William H. Harrison
1840	William H. Harrison	Martin Van Buren

1. Pierce was only elected president who failed to win renomination; others had succeeded to presidency on death of a president.

Election Year	Winner	Runner-up
1844	James K. Polk	Henry Clay
1848	Zachary Taylor	Lewis Cass
1852	Franklin Pierce	Winfield Scott
1856	James Buchanan	John C. Fremont
1860	Abraham Lincoln	Stephen A. Douglas
1864	Abraham Lincoln	George B. McClellan
1868	Ulysses S. Grant	Horatio Seymour
1872	Ulysses S. Grant	Horace Greeley
1876	Rutherford B. Hayes	Samuel J. Tilden
1880	James A. Garfield	Winfield S. Hancock
1884	Grover Cleveland	James G. Blaine
1888	Benjamin Harrison	Grover Cleveland
1892	Grover Cleveland	Benjamin Harrison
1896	William McKinley	William J. Bryan
1900	William McKinley	William J. Bryan
1904	Theodore Roosevelt	Alton B. Parker
1908	William H. Taft	William J. Bryan
1912	Woodrow Wilson	Theodore Roosevelt
1916	Woodrow Wilson	Charles E. Hughes
1920	Warren G. Harding	James M. Cox
1924	Calvin Coolidge	John W. Davis
1928	Herbert C. Hoover	Alfred E. Smith
1932	Franklin D. Roosevelt	Herbert Hoover
1936	Franklin D. Roosevelt	Alfred M. Landon

Election Year	Winner	Runner-up
1940	Franklin D. Roosevelt	Wendell L. Willkie
1944	Franklin D. Roosevelt	Thomas E. Dewey
1948	Harry S. Truman	Thomas E. Dewey
1952	Dwight D. Eisenhower	Adlai E. Stevenson
1956	Dwight D. Eisenhower	Adlai E. Stevenson
1960	John F. Kennedy	Richard M. Nixon
1964	Lyndon B. Johnson	Barry M. Goldwater
1968	Richard M. Nixon	Hubert H. Humphrey
1972	Richard M. Nixon	George S. McGovern
1976	Jimmy Carter	Gerald R. Ford
1980	Ronald W. Reagan	Jimmy Carter
1984	Ronald W. Reagan	Walter F. Mondale
1988	George H. W. Bush	Michael S. Dukakis
1992	Bill Clinton	George H.W. Bush
1996	Bill Clinton	Bob Dole

(Sources: *World Book, Presidential Elections Since 1789*, and *Book of Presidents*)

Vice Presidents of the United States

Vice President	Years Served	President
* John Adams	1789–1797	Washington
* Thomas Jefferson	1797–1801	Adams
Aaron Burr	1801–1805	Jefferson

@ Succeeded to presidency on death of president.
* Later elected president.
+Succeeded to presidency on resignation of president.

Vice President	Years Served	President	Vice President	Years Served	President
George Clinton	1805–1809	Jefferson	Charles W. Fairbanks	1905–1909	T. Roosevelt
George Clinton	1809–1812	Madison	James S. Sherman	1909–1912	Taft
Eldridge Gerry	1813–1814	Madison	Thomas R. Marshall	1913–1921	Wilson
Daniel D. Tompkins	1817–1825	Monroe	@*Calvin Coolidge	1921–1923	Harding
John C. Calhoun	1825–1829	J. Q. Adams	Charles C. Dawes	1925–1929	Coolidge
John C. Calhoun	1829–1832	Jackson	Charles Curtis	1929–1933	Hoover
* Martin Van Buren	1833–1837	Jackson	John N. Garner	1933–1941	F.D. Roosevelt
Richard M. Johnson	1837–1841	Van Buren	Henry A. Wallace	1941–1945	F.D. Roosevelt
@ John Tyler	1841	W. H. Harrison	@*Harry S. Truman	1945	F.D. Roosevelt
George M. Dallas	1845–1849	Polk	Alben W. Barkley	1949–1953	Truman
@ Millard Fillmore	1849–1850	Taylor	* Richard M. Nixon	1953–1961	Eisenhower
William R. King	1853	Pierce	@*Lyndon B. Johnson	1961–1963	Kennedy
John C. Breckinridge	1857–1861	Buchanan	Hubert H. Humphrey	1965–1969	Johnson
Hannibal Hamlin	1861–1865	Lincoln	Spiro T. Agnew	1969–1973	Nixon
@ Andrew Johnson	1865	Lincoln	+ Gerald R. Ford	1973–1974	Nixon
Schuyler Colfax	1865–1873	Grant	Nelson A. Rockefeller	1974–1977	Ford
Henry Wilson	1873–1875	Grant	Walter F. Mondale	1977–1981	Carter
William A. Wheeler	1877–1881	Hayes	* George H.W. Bush	1981–1989	Reagan
@ Chester A. Arthur	1881	Garfield	Dan Quayle	1989–1993	Bush
Thomas A. Hendricks	1885	Cleveland	Al Gore	1993–	Clinton
Levi P. Morton	1889–1893	B. Harrison			
Adlai E. Stevenson	1893–1897	Cleveland			
Garret A. Hobart	1897–1901	McKinley			
@*Theodore Roosevelt	1901	McKinley			

(Sources: *Presidential Elections Since 1789*, *World Book*, *Presidential Also-Rans and Running Mates, 1788–1980*, and *The Presidents, First Ladies, and Vice Presidents*)

@ Succeeded to presidency on death of president.
* Later elected president.
+Succeeded to presidency on resignation of president.

Presidential Impeachments

Key Dates in Andrew Johnson Impeachment

February 1866–March 1867 Strained relations between Congress and President Johnson developed over disagreements on Reconstruction policies.

August 12, 1867 Johnson suspended Secretary of War Edwin M. Stanton, but Senate failed to endorse suspension.

January 1868 Johnson formally dismissed Stanton, which opponents charged constituted violation of Tenure of Office Act.

February 24 House of Representatives voted to impeach president.

March 2 and 3 House adopted 11 articles of impeachment.

March 5 Senate convened as court of impeachment, with Chief Justice Salmon P. Chase presiding.

March 13 Impeachment trial began in Senate.

May 16 Johnson acquitted on article 11, 35-19 (one vote short of 36 needed for conviction).

May 26 Johnson acquitted on two additional articles, 35–19; trial thereafter adjourned with Johnson remaining in office.

(Sources: *World Book* and *Book of Presidents*)

Key Dates in Bill Clinton Impeachment

1994 January 12 – President Clinton called for appointment of independent counsel to investigate charges against him in Whitewater land deal scandal.

January 20 – Robert B. Fiske named to investigate Whitewater scandal.

May 6 – Paula Jones filed sexual harassment suit against Clinton for alleged incident in 1991 when Clinton was Arkansas governor.

August 5 – Kenneth Starr appointed to take over Whitewater probe.

1997 May 27 – Supreme Court ordered Jones' lawsuit to proceed while Clinton was still in office.

December 5 – Monica Lewinsky named as potential witness in Jones' case.

December 19 – Lewinsky subpoenaed for deposition in Jones' case, and to turn over gifts she received from Clinton.

1998 January 7 – Lewinsky signed affidavit denying sexual relationship with Clinton.

January 12 – Lewinsky colleague and friend, Linda Tripp, provided independent prosecutor with tape conversations in which Lewinsky acknowledged sexual relationship with Clinton, and said president asked her to lie about it.

January 17 – In Jones' case, under oath, Clinton denied sexual relationship with Lewinsky.

January 21 – Media reported Starr's office began probe of perjury and subordination of perjury by president.

January 26 – In television press conference, Clinton denied sexual relationship with Lewinsky, or that he ever asked anyone to lie.

March 15 – Former White House aide, Kathleen Willey, appeared on CBS *60 Minutes* and accused Clinton of sexual harassment.

April 1 – Jones' lawsuit dismissed.

August 6 – Under grant of immunity, Lewinsky testified before federal grand jury.

August 17 – Clinton testified for four hours before grand jury via closed circuit television.

Later, he addressed the nation on television admitting, "relationship with Ms. Lewinsky that was not appropriate," but denied perjury and attacked independent prosecutor Starr.

August 21 – Lewinsky appeared before grand jury for second time.

September 3 – Senator Joseph Lieberman, a Clinton ally, in Senate speech, assailed Clinton's behavior as "immoral."

September 4 – Speaking in Dublin, Clinton used the word "sorry" in regard to Lewinsky affair for first time.

September 9 – Starr informed House leaders he found credible grounds for impeachment of the president and delivered report and 36 boxes of supporting material to the Hill.

September 12 – White House issued 42-page response to Starr's report.

September 18 – House Judiciary Committee voted to release to public Clinton's August 17 grand jury videotaped testimony.

September 21 – Clinton videotape broadcast on U.S. television.

October 8 – House voted impeachment inquiry.

November 13 – Clinton and Jones settled out of court. She received $850,000 to drop lawsuit.

November 17 – Lewinsky/Tripp taped conversations aired on television.

November 19 – House Judiciary Committee opened impeachment hearings.

November 27 – In response to 81 written questions from House Judiciary Committee Chair Henry Hyde, Clinton denied his testimony before grand jury was false and misleading. His tone angered many Congressmen.

December 12-13 – Four articles of impeachment approved in committee in party line vote.

December 13 – Hyde called upon Clinton to resign; President refused.

December 16 – U.S. and British air forces attacked Iraq in dispute over UN weapons inspections. Many legislators charged attack was politically motivated, as impeachment vote is postponed.

December 18 – Debate on impeachment articles began on House floor.

December 19 – Clinton impeached on two charges of perjury before grand jury and obstruction of justice. Other impeachment articles rejected.

1999 January 7 – Impeachment trial convened in Senate, with Chief Justice William Rehnquist presiding.

January 14–21 Senate heard opening presentations from House prosecutors and Clinton defenders.

January 27 – Senate rejected motion to dismiss charges against Clinton and voted to continue trial.

February 1–3 – Lewinsky, Clinton friend Vernon Jordan, and White House aide Sidney Blumenthal deposed by House prosecutors and presidential lawyers.

February 4 – Senate rejected calling live witnesses; authorized presentation of videotaped excerpts from testimony.

February 6 – Videotaped clips presented.

February 8 – House prosecutors and presidential lawyers presented closing arguments.

February 9 – Senate voted against open deliberations on impeachment verdict.

February 10–11 – Closed-door deliberations proceeded.

February 12 – Clinton acquitted on perjury (45 guilty, 55 not guilty) and obstruction of justice 50 guilty, 50 not guilty (67 votes needed for conviction).

(Sources: *Associated Press* and *Facts On File*)

Political and Presidential Assassinations and Attempted Assassinations

Presidential Assassinations

April 14, 1865   Abraham Lincoln shot by John Wilkes Booth, actor and Confederate sympathizer; died April 15. Booth shot and killed April 26, 1865.

July 2, 1881   James A. Garfield shot by Charles Julius Guiteau, disappointed office-seeker; survived 81 days; died of blood poisoning in Elberon, New Jersey, while recuperating. Guiteau tried, convicted, and hanged June 30, 1882.

September 6 ,1901   William McKinley shot by anarchist Leon Czolgosz while attending Pan American Exposition in Buffalo, New York; died September 14, 1901. Czolgosz tried, convicted and electrocuted October 29, 1901.

November 22, 1963   John F. Kennedy shot in Dallas, Texas, by gunman Lee Harvey Oswald; died an hour later. Oswald arrested and murdered in police custody by Jack Ruby, local nightclub owner.

Political Assassinations and Attempted Assassinations in American History

January 30, 1835   President Andrew Jackson attacked by Richard Lawrence, mentally disturbed house painter, who fired two pistols—both which misfired—at Jackson during funeral services at Capitol rotunda.

February 11, 1861   Plot to assassinate president-elect Abraham Lincoln thwarted by detective assigned to protect Lincoln.

April 14, 1865   President Abraham Lincoln shot and fatally wounded by actor John Wilkes Booth, Confederate sympathizer, at Ford's Theatre in Washington, D.C.; died next day.

July 2, 1881   President James Garfield shot by mentally deranged office-seeker, Charles Guiteau, in Washington, D.C.; died September 19, 1881 in New Jersey.

September 6, 1901   President William McKinley shot by Leon Czolgosz, an anarchist, while attending Pan-American Exposition in Buffalo, New York; died eight days later.

October 14, 1912   Former President Theodore Roosevelt, running for third term as candidate of Progressive (Bull Moose) Party, shot by John Schrank in Milwaukee, Wisconsin. Despite wound, Roosevelt delivered scheduled campaign speech before seeking medical attention.

February 15, 1933   Chicago Mayor Anton Cermak shot in Miami during attempted assassination of President-elect Franklin D. Roosevelt by Joseph Zangara. Cermak succumbed to wounds March 6.

September 8, 1935   Louisiana Senator Huey P. Long shot and killed by Dr. Carl Austin Weiss in Baton Rouge.

November 1, 1950   Two Puerto Rican nationalists attempted assassination of President Harry S. Truman. Assailants Griselio Torresola and Oscar Collazo killed one presidential guard, wounded two others. Torresola killed in the shootout, Collazo wounded.

June 12, 1963   Civil rights leader Medgar Evers murdered in Jackson, Mississippi.

November 22, 1963   President John F. Kennedy assassinated while riding in motorcade in Dallas, Texas. Accused assassin, Lee Harvey Oswald, murdered by Jack Ruby during prisoner transfer as millions watched on television.

February 21, 1965 African-American nationalist leader Malcolm X fatally shot at public meeting at Audubon Ballroom in New York City.

April 4, 1968 Civil rights leader Martin Luther King Jr. shot by sniper James Earl Ray in Memphis, Tennessee. Ray received 99-year sentence.

June 5, 1968 After winning California presidential primary, New York Senator Robert F. Kennedy, brother of John F. Kennedy, shot by Sirhan Sirhan, Jordanian immigrant, at Hotel Ambassador in Los Angeles. Sirhan sentenced to life in prison.

May 15, 1972 Alabama Governor George C. Wallace seriously wounded and paralyzed for life while campaigning for Democratic presidential nomination in Laurel, Maryland. Gunman Arthur H. Bremer sentenced to 53 years in prison.

September 5, 1975 Lynette Alice ("Squeaky") Fromme, follower of convicted murderer Charles Manson, pointed gun at President Gerald R. Ford in a crowd near California State Capitol in Sacramento. Secret service agent blocked gun from firing. Fromme tried, convicted, and sentenced to life imprisonment November 26, 1975.

September 22, 1975 Sara Jane Moore, political activist and paid FBI informer, fired shot at President Gerald R. Ford as he left St. Francis Hotel in San Francisco, California. Bullet missed president but slightly wounded a bystander. Moore disarmed by former Marine Oliver Sipple and police officers. Moore pleaded

guilty to attempted assassination; sentenced December 16, 1975 to life imprisonment. Escaped from prison February 5, 1979; recaptured four hours later.

May 29, 1980 Unknown sniper critically injured civil rights leader Vernon E. Jordan Jr. of National Urban League in Fort Wayne, Indiana.

March 30, 1981 President Ronald Reagan shot and wounded by John W. Hinckley Jr. in Washington, D.C. Presidential Press Secretary James S. Brady and two security officers also wounded. Hinckley committed to mental institution.

December 16, 1989 Federal Judge Robert Vance killed by mail bomb in Birmingham, Alabama, suburb in what police described as racially motivated murder.

December 18, 1989 Robert Robinson, local political official and one-time lawyer for NAACP in Savannah, Georgia, killed by letter bomb in another racially motivated attack.

November 5, 1990 Rabbi Meir Kahane, extremist Israeli politician and founder of Jewish Defense League, shot and killed after delivering speech at a New York hotel. Alleged gunman El Sayyid A. Nosair, Egyptian-born U.S. citizen, wounded while attempting to escape, though later acquitted in murder trial.

October 29, 1994 Francisco Duran shot at tourist resembling President Bill Clinton outside White House; later convicted of attempted assassination.

(Sources: *American Assassins: The Darker Side of Politics*; *Assassinations and Executions: An Encyclopedia of Political Violence*; and *The Presidents (Graff)*)

PART 5

The Armed Forces, Wars, and Military Interventions

THE ARMED FORCES

U.S. Army

1775 Continental Congress established Continental Army under command of General George Washington to fight Revolutionary War against Britain.

1789 Congress created Department of War.

1802 U.S. Military Academy at West Point opened.

1812–1815 Army of 38,000 troops fought against British in War of 1812.

1845–1847 During Mexican War, Army fought outside U.S. boundaries, used steamships as troop transports, and established military government over occupied territory for first time.

1861–1865 Army troop strength peaked at one million during Civil War.

1863 Congress enacted first military conscription in U.S. history.

1898 Health and sanitation problems plagued American forces in Philippines and Cuba during Spanish-American war. Disease caused more American deaths than combat.

1903 Army adopted general staff system.

1907 Aeronautical division established within Army Signal Corps.

1914 Army engineers completed construction of Panama Canal.

1917 U.S. declared war on Germany in World War I, dispatching nearly two million soldiers to Europe.

1941–1945 During World War II, Army strength peaked at 8,270,000 soldiers.

1942 Women's Auxiliary Corps established. It became a part of the Army the following year as the Women's Army Corps.

1944 Army forces participated in D-Day Normandy invasion, largest amphibious assault in history.

1945 Atomic bombs, developed by scientists working under Army supervision, were dropped on Hiroshima and Nagasaki, Japan, during World War II.

1958 Army launched *Explorer I* satellite into orbit.

1965 First U.S. combat forces dispatched to Vietnam.

1973 American forces withdrawn from Vietnam following signing of cease-fire agreement.

1973 Military draft established; all-volunteer army established.

1976 Women admitted to U.S. Military Academy for first time.

1978 Women's Army Corps dissolved.

1991 Army forces led Allied land attack against Iraqi troops in Persian Gulf War.

1996 Investigation launched into charges of sexual abuse of female recruits by non-commissioned officers at Army training camps.

1999 Army personnel participated in international peacekeeping force in Kosovo.

U.S. Navy

1779 *Bonhomme Richard*, commanded by John Paul Jones, defeated British vessel *Serapis*. Jones coined phrase "I have not yet begun to fight" during this Revolutionary War battle.

1794 U.S. Navy established in law.

1812 *The Constitution*, commanded by Isaac Hull, defeated British ship *Guerrier* in War of 1812.

1813 Fatally wounded *Chesapeake* commander James Lawrence uttered historic watchword "Don't give up the ship" in battle with British forces. Forces led by Oliver Hazard Perry defeated British in Battle of Lake Erie.

1845 U.S. Naval Academy founded at Annapolis, Maryland. (Previously, midshipmen were trained aboard ship.)

1862 The Union's *Monitor* and Confederacy's *Merrimack* confronted each other in first battle of ironclad ships.

1864 Union fleet sailed into Confederacy's Mobile Bay. Commander David Farragut said, "Damn the torpedoes! Full speed ahead."

1898 Battleship *Maine* blown up in Havana harbor. U.S. fleet defeated Spanish in Battle of Manila Bay.

1941 German submarine sank U.S. destroyer *Reuben James* in Atlantic two months before war officially declared. Navy vessels devastated by surprise Japanese air raid against naval base at Pearl Harbor, Hawaii.

1942 Navy blocked Japanese at Midway Island.

1944 Pacific fleet demolished Japanese naval forces at Leyte Gulf in biggest sea battle in history.

1954 *Nautilus*, world's first nuclear submarine, commissioned.

1958 Cruising beneath frozen waters, *Nautilus* became first ship to reach North Pole.

1963 Nuclear-powered submarine USS *Thresher* sank in North Atlantic with 129 crewmen aboard.

1964–1973 U.S. Naval forces operated in Vietnam war via air strikes from aircraft carriers and offshore bombardments of enemy positions by cruisers, destroyers, and battleship *New Jersey*.

1991 During Persian Gulf War, Navy airplane strikes and battleship bombardments targeted Iraqi forces. Charges of sexual abuse of 87 women during Navy aviators Tailhook Convention in Las Vegas led to disciplinary charges against participants and investigation of sexual harassment in the Navy.

1999 Navy forces played important role in U.S. participation in Kosovo war.

U.S. Marine Corps

1775 Continental Congress created two battalions of marines.

1776 Marines landed in the Bahamas during Revolutionary War.

1798 Marine Corps reorganized as separate military service.

1805 Marines defeated Barbary pirates on shores of Tripoli, making Mediterranean safe from piracy.

1834 Marines placed under authority of the Navy secretary.

1847 During Mexican War, Marines occupied Mexico City, including government buildings ("Halls of Montezuma").

1913 Aviation section created within Marine Corps.

1918 Marines fought at Belleau Wood to block German advance on Paris, France, during World War I.

1942 Marines launched first American offensive during World War II at Guadalcanal.

1945 During World War II, Marines captured island of Iwo Jima from Japanese forces in one of bloodiest Marine battles in history.

1950 In major amphibious operation, Marines landed at Inchon in Korean War.

1952 Marine commandant was added to Joint Chiefs of Staff.

1958 Marine regiment dispatched to Lebanon to help prevent overthrow of government.

1965 Marine units sent to Dominican Republic.

1965–1973 An estimated 450,000 Marines served in Vietnam combat.

1982–1984 Marines served in peacekeeping force in Lebanon.

1991 Ninety-four thousand Marines served in Persian Gulf War.

1999 Marine units participated in U.S. contingent in international peacekeeping force in Kosovo.

U.S. Coast Guard

1790 Coast Guard created with fleet of ten cutters as Revenue Cutter Service, under auspices of Treasury Department, to patrol coastal waters to combat smuggling and piracy.

1798–1800 Cooperated with newly created Navy in combating against French privateers.

1831 Revenue Cutter Service began winter-time rescue patrols to assist distressed ships.

1848 Congress funded construction of life-saving stations staffed by volunteers to aid seafarers.

1871 U.S. Life-Saving Service established under supervision of Revenue Cutter Service.

1878 Life-Saving Service became independent agency within Treasury Department.

1910 U.S. Coast Guard Academy established at New London, Connecticut. (Previously, cadets were trained aboard ship.)

1915 Life-Saving and Revenue Cutter Services were merged in formation of U.S. Coast Guard.

1917 During World War I, Coast Guard personnel were integrated into U.S. Navy service convoying transport ships.

1918 Coast Guard vessel *Tampa* exploded during convoy escort duty, killing 111 Coastguardsmen and 4 Navy men. Authorities suspected that German U-boat torpedo was responsible.

1939 Federal Lighthouse Service became part of Coast Guard.

1941–1945 During World War II, Coast Guard personnel served as branch of the Navy.

1957 Coast Guard cutters became first ships to sail through the northwest passage.

1965–1972 Coast Guard vessels patrolled South Vietnamese coastal waters.

1967 Department of Transportation assumed authority over Coast Guard.

1976 Women admitted to Coast Guard Academy for the first time.

1989 Coast Guard oversaw cleanup of *Exxon Valdez* oil spill in Alaska.

U.S. Air Force

1861-1865 Observation balloons used against Confederate forces during Civil War.

1898 Observation balloons used during Spanish-American War.

1907 Aeronautical Division established by U.S. Army in the Office of the Chief Signal Officer.

1909 U.S. Army purchased first airplane.

1917 U.S. entered World War I and immediately began training combat pilots.

1918 American pilots entered combat in Europe. During the war, U.S. fliers destroyed more than 750 enemy aircraft and 70 balloons.

1926 U.S. Army Air Corps created.

1941 Army Air Forces established by Congress.

1941–1945 During World War II, AAF peaked at 2,411,000 servicemen and 80,000 planes, dropped 1.8 million metric tons of bombs, destroyed 40,000 enemy aircraft, and lost 23,000 of its own planes (almost half in non-combat situations). Nearly 90,000 airmen died.

1945 Atomic bombs were dropped on Hiroshima and Nagasaki, Japan.

1947 United States Air Force established as independent military branch, on equal footing with Navy and Army. Experimental rocket-powered plane piloted by Captain Charles Yeager broke sound barrier.

1948 Berlin Airlift operations began following Soviet blockade of land routes to Allied sectors in occupied Berlin.

1950–1953 Air Force jets engaged in combat operations during Korean War, shooting down 900 enemy aircraft and losing 139 planes.

1957 Air Force tested first intercontinental ballistic missile.

1959 First class graduated from U.S. Air Force Academy.

1961–1973 American planes dropped more conventional bombs during Vietnam War than both sides had dropped during World War II.

1971 Jeanne M. Holm became first Air Force woman promoted to rank of general.

1976 Women admitted to Air Force Academy.

1986 Air Force planes attacked Libya.

1991 During Persian Gulf War, Air Force planes flew more than 37,000 combat missions and lost only 14 planes. "Stealth" bombers were used for first time in extensive combat.

1999 U.S. Air Force planes played crucial role in Kosovo war.

Women in the Military

1777–1783 Women served as nurses, spies, and camp followers during the Revolutionary War. Lucy Brewer, disguised as a man, served in the U.S. Navy during the War of 1812 for three years.

1861-1865 A number of women, disguised as men, served in the Union Army, including Sarah Edwards and Loreta Velasquez. Many women served as nurses in military hospitals caring for the wounded, including Louisa May Alcott and Clara Barton. Mary Edwards Walker, a physician, served as a surgeon in the Army, often participating in missions behind enemy lines. Captured by Confederate forces in 1864, she later became the first woman to receive the Congressional Medal of Honor.

1917 U.S. Navy enlisted 12,000 women to perform clerical jobs so that men might be freed up for combat assignments. Army nurses granted some officer privileges. Julia Stimson, superintendent of Army nurses, became first female major.

1942 During World War II, women were admitted to the Army's Women's Auxiliary Corps (WAC), the Navy's Women Accepted for Voluntary Emergency Service (WAVES), and the Women's Air Service Pilots (WASPs).

1945 By the end of World War II, 90,000 women served in the WACs. Army-Navy Nurse Act established permanent commissions for military nurses. First woman officer commissioned in regular army. Women's Armed Services Integration Act passed by Congress. First woman doctor commissioned in regular Navy.

1953 Staff Sergeant Barbara O. Barnwell became first woman to receive U.S. Navy-Marine Corps Medal for Heroism. First woman doctor granted commission in regular Army.

1970 Anna Mae Hays and Elizabeth Hoisington became first women promoted to rank of brigadier generals in U.S. Army. First female ROTC student granted a military commission. Jeanne Holm of the U.S. Air Force named first American female major general. Arlene B. Duerk appointed first Navy female admiral. Navy pilot training program opened to women. Fran McKee became first female line officer promoted to admiral in U.S. Navy. Female cadets admitted to Army, Navy, Air Force, and Coast Guard academies.

1978 Margaret A. Brewer named first female brigadier general in Marine Corps. U.S. Army barred women from 23 combat-related jobs.

1988 Brigadier General Gail Reals named first Marine Corps base commander. Kristin Baker named first female captain of West Point Corps of Cadets.

1991 During Persian Gulf War, women were assigned to combat zone duty for first time, providing communications and intelligence services, maintaining equipment, and supplying and transporting troops. Memorial for 10,000 U.S. women killed in Vietnam won federal approval. Twenty-six women were sexually assaulted and harassed at U.S. Navy Tailhook Convention in Las Vegas.

1995 Cadet Rebecca E. Marier, ranked number one in her class, became first woman valedictorian at West Point graduation.

African Americans in the Military

1770 Crispus Attucks killed by British soliders at Boston Massacre.

1775 African American soldiers participated in Battle of Bunker Hill

1776 1781 Black soldiers and spies serve in American revolutionary army.

1778 Seven hundred black troops fight under George Washington's command in battle at Monmouth Court House. Washington approves recruitment of 300 former slaves for rebel forces fighting in Rhode Island.

1779 Black slave, Pompey, played pivot role in Gen. Anthony Wayne's capture of Stony Point Fort , NY during Revolutionary War.

1812–1815 Free blacks and slaves fought for U.S. military during War of 1812.

1861–1865 A quarter of million blacks served in Union army during Civil War; 38,000 were killed.

1862 Congress authorized enlistment of freed blacks in Union forces, at half pay of white soldiers. First South Carolina volunteers is first all-black regiment organized in Union army.

1863 Sgt. William H. Carney won Congressional Medal of Honor for his role in 54th Massachusetts Volunteers regiment attack on Fort Wagner in Charlestone, S.C.

1867 All-black regular army units established by Congressional order. Know as "Buffalo Soldiers." these units were involved in Indian fighting in the West, and 11 of them received the Congressional Medal of Honor.

1877 Henry O. Flipper became first African American to graduate from West Point.

1898 Twenty-five black soldiers participated in the U.S. assault at San Juan Hill in Cuba during Spanish-American War.

1917–1918 Three hundred thousand African Americans fought in American forces during World War I; 1,400 served as officers.

1940 Benjamin O. Davis, Sr. became first black general in U.S. Army.

1941 Tuskegee Training program for black pilots established.

1944 First black naval officers received commissions.

1945 Tuskegee Airmen (332 Fighter Group) flew raid over Berlin.

1948 President Harry Truman order desegregation of U.S. military.

1951 During Korean War, Private William Thompson posthumously received Congressional Medal of Honor; last all-black army unit deactivated. 1971

1971 Samuel Lee Gravely, Jr. became first black admiral in U.S. Navy.

1975 Daniel "Chappie" James became first African American four-star general in U.S. Air Force.

1982 Roscoe Robinson, Jr. became first African American four-star general in U.S. Army

1989 Gen. Colin Powell became first African American to serve as Chairman of Joint Chiefs of Staff.

(Sources: *Timetables of African-American History, Black Firsts, Notable Black Americans*)

Wars and Military Interventions

American Wars Chronology

Years	War	U.S. Deaths	War Costs (000s)
1775–1783	Revolutionary War	25,324*	$101,000
1812–1815	War of 1812	2,260	$90,000
1846–1848	Mexican War	13,283	$71,000
1861–1865	Civil War		
	Union	360,222	$3,183,000
	Confederacy	260,000*	$2,000,000
1898	Spanish-American War	2,446	$283,200
1917–1918	World War I	116,516	$18,676,000
1941–1945	World War II	405,399	$263,259,000
1950–1953	Korean War	54,246	$67,386,000
1960–1975	Vietnam War	58,000*	$150,000,000*
1991	Persian Gulf War	305	$61,000,000

* Estimated

Revolutionary War

1775 April 19 – Minutemen battled British troops at Lexington and Concord; Revolutionary War began.

June 15 – George Washington named commander of Continental Army.

June 17 – British drove Americans back in Battle of Bunker Hill.

1776 March 17 – British withdrew from Boston.

July 4 – Congress adopted Declaration of Independence.

August 2 – Most Congress members signed Declaration in Philadelphia.

August 27 – British defeated revolutionary forces on Long Island.

September 15 – British took control of New York City.

December 26 – Washington led successful surprise attack against Hessian mercenaries at Trenton.

1777 January 3 – Washington triumphed in Battle of Princeton.

August 16 – Revolutionaries inflicted crushing defeat on Hessians at Bennington.

September 11 – British defeated Americans at Battle of Brandywine (Pennsylvania).

September 19 – Rebel forces led by Gates blocked Burgoyne's army in First Battle of Freeman's Farm (New York).

September 26 – British occupied Philadelphia.

October 4 – Washington defeated at Germantown, Pennsylvania.

October 7 – British defeated at Second Battle of Freeman's Farm.

October 17 – Burgoyne surrendered at Saratoga, New York.

December 19 – Washington retreated to winter quarters at Valley Forge.

1778 February 6 – U.S. forged alliance with France.

June 28 – Battle of Monmouth (New Jersey) ended in stalemate.

December 29 – British occupied Savannah.

1779 June 21 – Spain declared war against Britain.

September 23 – U.S. naval vessel *Bonhomme Richard*, commanded by John Paul Jones, defeated British ship *Serapis*.

1780 May 12 – British captured Charleston.

August 16 – Americans defeated at Camden, South Carolina.

October 7 – American frontiersmen attacked pro-British loyalists at King's Mountain, South Carolina.

1781 January 17 – Americans triumphed at Cowpens, South Carolina.

March 15 – British abandoned North Carolina after Cornwallis clashed with American forces led by Greene at Guilford Courthouse, North Carolina.

September 5 – French fleet severely weakened British naval forces in battle in Chesapeake Bay.

October 6–19 – British General Cornwallis surrendered to Washington at Yorktown, Virginia.

1782 November 30 – Preliminary peace agreement reached with Britain in Paris.

1783 September 3 – Final peace treaty signed in Paris officially ending Revolutionary War; United States granted control of all territory between Canada and Florida, Atlantic Ocean and the Mississippi River.

War of 1812

1812 June 18 – United States declared war on Great Britain.

October 13 – British forces triumphed at Battle of Queenston Heights in Canada.

1813 April 27 – Americans captured York (now Toronto) and later burned public buildings.

September 10 – U.S. naval forces commanded by Oliver Hazard Perry defeated British in Battle of Lake Erie.

October 5 – Americans won Battle of Thames River in Canada.

1814 August 24 – British forces raided Washington, D.C.; burned White House and Capitol building.

1814 September 11 – Americans won Battle of Lake Champlain.

December 24 – British and U.S. representatives signed peace treaty in Ghent, Belgium.

1815 January 8 – American forces commanded by Andrew Jackson defeated British at Battle of New Orleans; news of peace treaty did not reach New Orleans until after battle.

Mexican War

1845 Fall – Mexican government refused to consider American offer of $25 million for purchase of California and New Mexico and acceptance of Rio Grande River as border.

1846 April – General Zachary Taylor and American troops reached Rio Grande.

April 25 – Mexican soldiers attacked and defeated small U.S. cavalry contingent north of Rio Grande.

May 8 – Taylor's troops drove back Mexicans at Battle of Palo Alto.

May 9 – Mexicans also lost at Battle of Resaca de la Palma.

May 13 – War declared on Mexico.

May 18 – Taylor crossed Rio Grande and occupied Matamoros.

June – American settlers led by John C. Fremont revolted against Mexican authorities.

July – American naval forces captured Monterey and occupied San Francisco area.

August – U.S. captured New Mexico.

September 24 – Taylor captured Mexican city of Monterrey

December 6 – Battle of San Pasqual fought near San Diego, California.

December 25 – U.S. forces triumphed at Battle of El Brazito.

1847 January – Naval and army forces won Battle of San Gabriel near Los Angeles, completing conquest of California.

February 22–23 – Taylor's badly outnumbered forces successfully held off Mexican attack against narrow mount pass and established American dominance in northeastern Mexico.

February 28 – U.S. won Battle of Sacramento, outside city of Chihuahua.

March 1 – American forces occupied Chihuahua.

March 9 – General Winfield Scott landed with 10,000 troops at Veracruz.

March 29 – Scott captured Veracruz.

April 8 – Scott began advance on Mexico City.

April 17–18 – Scott's troops stormed mountain pass at Cerro Gordo, forcing larger Mexican force to flee and opening way to Mexico City.

August 19 – Mexicans defeated at Contreras.

August 20 – Mexicans lost a Churubusco.

September 12–13 – Scott's forces attack Chapultepec, fortified hill guarding entrance to Mexico City.

September 14 – U.S. troops entered Mexico City.

1848 February 2 – Treaty signed at village of Guadalupe Hidalgo, near Mexico City; in return for $15 million, Mexico ceded 525,000 square miles to U.S.

Civil War

1861 April 12 – Confederate forces attacked Fort Sumter in Charleston, South Carolina.

April 15 – President Lincoln issued call for troops to put down rebellion.

April 19 – Lincoln ordered blockade of South.

May 21 – Confederates designated Richmond, Virginia, as capital.

July 21 – Northern forces routed at First Battle of Bull Run (Manassas, Va.).

1862 February 6 – Northern troops captured Fort Henry.

February 16 – Northern troops commanded by General Ulysses S. Grant captured Fort Donelson, Tennessee.

March 9 – First battle of ironclad ships, between Union's *Monitor* and Confederacy's *Merr-imack*, ended in draw.

April 6–7 – Union forces won Battle of Shiloh (Tennessee); both sides suffered heavy losses.

April 16 – Confederacy imposed conscription.

April 18–25 Union forces commanded by Farragut captured New Orleans.

May 4 – McClellan-led Union forces took Yorktown, Virginia, marched on Richmond.

June 6 – Union forces occupied Memphis.

June 25–July 1 – Confederate forces led by General Robert E. Lee saved Richmond in Battles of the Seven Days.

August 27–30 – Southern forces triumphant in Second Battle of Bull Run.

September 17 – Union forces victorious in Battle of Antietam (Sharpsburg, Maryland); Southern troops retreated in disorder.

September 22 – Lincoln issued preliminary Emancipation Proclamation.

October 8 – Confederate army forced to abandon Kentucky after defeat in Battle of Perryville.

December 13 – Union troops suffered devastating setback at Battle of Fredericksburg (Virginia).

December 21–January 2, 1863 – Confederates retreated after defeat in Battle of Stones River (Murfreesboro, Tennessee).

1863 January 1 – Lincoln issued Emancipation Proclamation, freed slaves in secessionist states.

March 3 – North imposed military draft.

May 1–4 – Northern forces defeated at Battle of Chancellorsville (Virginia); Southern General Stonewall Jackson killed.

May 1–19 – Grant-led Union forces defeated Southern forces, laid siege to Vicksburg.

July 1–3 – Southern defeat in Battle of Gettysburg (Pennsylvania) marked turning point in war.

July 4 – Vicksburg fell to Grant's forces.

September 19–20 – Confederates won Battle of Chickamauga (Georgia).

November 19 – Lincoln delivered Gettysburg Address.

November 23–25 – Union forces won Battle of Chattanooga, gaining control of Tennessee.

1864 March 9 – Grant named commander of Northern armies.

May 5–6 – Despite heavy losses in Battle of Wilderness, Grant continued to pressure Lee's army.

May 8–19 – Grant and Lee confronted each other again in Battle of Spotsylvania Court House (Virginia).

June 1–3 – Grant suffered heavy losses in Battle of Cold Harbor (Virginia).

June 20 – Grant's troops began nearly ten-month siege of Petersburg, Virginia

July 11–12 – Confederate attempt to reach Washington, D.C., turned back.

August 5 – Farragut won Battle of Mobile Bay (Alabama), closing major Southern port.

September 2 – Sherman-led Union troops captured Atlanta.

Sept 19.–October 19 – Sheridan's troops rampaged through Shenandoah Valley.

November 8 – Lincoln reelected president.

November 15 – Sherman began march through Georgia to sea.

November 30 – Confederate forces suffered heavy casualties in Battle of Franklin (Tennessee).

December 15–16 – Confederates suffered decisive defeat in Battle of Nashville (Tennessee), effectively ending resistance in West.

December 21 – Sherman's Union troops occupied Savannah, Georgia.

1865 January 31 – Thirteenth Amendment, abolishing slavery, proposed by Congress.

February 6 – Lee appointed chief general of Southern forces.

April 2 – Southern forces gave up Richmond and St. Petersburg.

April 9 – Lee surrendered to Grant at Appomattox Court House (Virginia).

April 14 – Lincoln shot by assassin John Wilkes Booth.

April 15 – Lincoln died; Vice President Andrew Johnson succeeded to presidency.

April 26 – Johnston's Southern troops surrendered to Sherman.

May 4 – Confederate troops in Mississippi and Alabama surrendered.

May 11 – Confederate President Jefferson Davis captured.

May 26 – Last Southern troops surrendered.

Spanish-American War

1895 Revolutionary struggle broke out for Cuban independence from Spain, received sympathetic press coverage in U.S.

1897 U.S. President McKinley pressured Spain to grant limited self-rule for Cuba, triggering riots by pro-Spanish Cubans.

1898 January 25 – U.S. battleship *Maine* arrived in Havana harbor to protect Americans from rioters.

February 15 – *Maine* rocked by explosion; 260 killed; Spain blamed.

March – McKinley sent three notes demanding full Cuban independence.

April 19 – U.S. Congress passed resolution asserting Cuban independence, authorizing military force to secure Spanish withdrawal.

April 25 – U.S. declared state of war existed with Spain since April 21.

May 1 – Commodore George Dewey led squadron of six ships in attack on Manila Bay in Philippines; destroyed Spanish fleet and blockaded harbor.

May 28 – U.S. naval forces blockaded Spanish fleet in Santiago de Cuba harbor.

June 22 – Fifteen thousand American troops landed near Santiago.

July 1 – American forces successfully attacked Spanish positions at El Caney, Kettle Hill, and San Juan Hill suffering 1,600 casualties; Lt. Colonel Theodore Roosevelt and Rough Riders regiment won fame for charge at Kettle Hill.

July 3 – Spanish fleet attempted to run blockade but all vessels were sunk or beached by pursuing American ships.

July 17 – Santiago surrendered.

July 25 – U.S. invasion of Puerto Rico met only token resistance.

August 13 – American troops occupied Philippines.

December 10 – Treaty of Paris granted Cuba independence, ceded Guam, Puerto Rico, and Philippines to U.S.

1899   February 6 – Treaty ratified in U.S. Senate by one-vote margin.

World War I

United States entry into World War I didn't come until 1917. This chronology traces the international events leading up to the outbreak of war in Europe in 1914, as well as the war itself, to provide a fuller context for understanding American involvement.

1914   June 28 – Austro-Hungarian Archduke Franz Ferdinand assassinated in Sarajevo by Serb nationalist.

July 6 – Germany confirmed support for Austro-Hungarian ally.

July 23 – Austria-Hungary issued ultimatum to Serbia.

July 24 – Serbia appealed to Russia for support.

July 28 – Austria-Hungary declared war on Serbia.

July 29 – Belgrade bombarded by Austria.

July 31 – Russia mobilized forces. Germany issued ultimata to Russia and France.

August 1 – Germany declared war on Russia.

August 2 – German forces entered Luxembourg.

August 3 – Germany declared war on France.

August 4 – Germany invaded Belgium. Great Britain declared war on Germany.

August 5 – Austria-Hungary declared war on Russia.

August 10 – France declared war on Austria-Hungary.

August 12 – Britain declared war on Austria-Hungary; Austria-Hungary invaded Serbia.

August 14 – French invaded Lorraine region of Germany.

August 15 – Russia invaded East Prussia.

August 10 – Austria-Hungary invaded Russia.

August 23 – Japan declared war on Germany.

September 6–9 – Allies blocked German advance in France at First Battle of the Marne.

September 28 – Germany opened offensive in Poland.

October 29 – Turkey attacked Russian positions in Black Sea; joined Central Powers.

November – Western Front locked into trench warfare.

November 16 – Turkey declared Holy War (Jihad) against British Empire.

December – Eastern Front locked into trench warfare.

1915 January 31 – First large-scale use of gas warfare at Bolimov, northern Galicia.

February 4 Germany announced submarine campaign.

March 22 – First zeppelin raid against Paris.

April 8 – Turkey began forced deportations of Armenians.

April 22 – First successful gas attack used by Germans in offensive at Ypres.

Apr 25 – Allied forces landed on Gallipoli Peninsula, Turkey.

May 7 – German submarine sank passenger ship *Luisitania*, killing 1,198 passengers, 128 of them Americans.

May 23 – Italy declared war on Austria-Hungary.

May 31 – First zeppelin raid on London.

August 4 – Germany occupied Warsaw.

August 27 – Germany limited action by submarines.

September 5 – Tsar Nicholas II took charge as commander-in-chief of Russian forces.

September 15 – Anti-war socialists conferred in Zimmerwald, Switzerland.

December 15 – German military attaches expelled from U.S.

1916 January 29 – First "tank" tested in Britain.

February 21 – Battle of Verdun began.

March 16 – Germany began second unrestricted submarine campaign.

April 20 – Under U.S. pressure, Germany rescinded unlimited submarine warfare.

May 31–June 1 – British and German naval forces fought Battle of Jutland, North Sea.

June 5 – Arab revolt against Ottoman Empire proclaimed near Medina.

June 8 – Arab rebels took Mecca.

July 1 – Allies initiated Battle of the Somme.

November 5 – Lawrence joined Arab army.

1917 January 22 – U.S. President Wilson delivered "peace without victory" speech to Congress.

February 1 – Germany began new unrestricted submarine campaign.

February 3 – U.S. severed diplomatic ties with Germany.

March 1 – U.S. revealed Zimmerman note, detailing German designs on Mexico.

March 15 – Tsar Nicholas II abdicated.

March 16 – Russian provisional government maintained war effort.

April 6 – United States declared war on Germany.

June 24 – First American troops arrived in France.

November 5 – Bolshevik-led revolution overthrew provisional government in Russia; promised end to war.

November 6–9 – Allies held summit meeting at Rapallo, Italy.

December 9 – British took Jerusalem. White rebellion against Russian revolution revealed.

December 16 – Russian Communist government signed armistice with Germany; fighting ceased on Eastern Front.

1918 January 8 – U.S. President Woodrow Wilson announced Fourteen Points as basis for peace settlement.

March 3 – Russia signed Treaty of Brest Litovsk, formally ending Russian involvement in war.

March 21 – Germany launched first of final three offensives on Western Front.

March 26 – British "Whippet" tanks used for first time in France.

September 26 – Allies began final offensive.

October 30 – Mutiny in German High Seas Fleet began.

November 3 – Austria-Hungary signed armistice agreement with Allies; Germany navy mutiny spread.

November 7 – King of Bavaria fled to exile.

November 8 – Socialist republic proclaimed in Bavaria; King of Wurttemberg and Duke of Brunswick abdicated.

November 9 – Kaiser Wilhelm II abdicated; Socialist Party took power in Berlin.

November 11 – Armistice took effect; Hungarian republic declared.

November 21 – German High Seas Fleet surrendered.

November 25 – German troops in East Africa surrendered.

November 26 – Germany withdrew from Belgium.

December 1 – Yugoslavia founded.

1919 January 12 – Paris Peace Conference convened.

January 15 – German revolutionary leaders Rosa Luxemburg and Karl Liebknecht murdered in Berlin.

July 7 – Germany ratified Treaty of Versailles.

November 19 – U.S. Senate rejected Treaty of Versailles.

1920 January 20 – Paris Peace Conference ended.

(Sources: *World Book, Americana, Dictionary of First World War, The European Powers in the First World War: An Encyclopedia*)

World War II

The U.S. didn't enter World War II until the Japanese attack on Pearl Harbor in December 1941. However, in order to provide a context for appreciating American involvement in the war, this chronology begins with the outbreak of hostilities in Europe in 1939.

1939 September 1 – Germany invaded Poland.

September 3 – France and Britain declared war on Germany.

1940   April 9 – Germany invaded Denmark and Norway.

May 10 – German forces invaded Belgium and Netherlands.

June 10 – Italy declared war against Britain and France.

June 22 – France signed armistice with Germany.

July 10 – Battle of Britain began—first battle for control of air.

October 16 – Selective Service (draft) registration began in the U.S.

1941   January 6 – President Roosevelt stated the Four Freedoms messages and asked Congress to authorize Lend Lease program.

March 1 – Bulgaria joined the Axis powers.

March 30 – German Afrika Korps under General Erwin Rommel initiated offensive against British in Libya.

April 6 – Germany invaded Greece and Yugoslavia.

May 27 – German battleship *Bismarck* sunk by British forces.

June 14 – U.S. government froze Axis assets in the U.S.

June 22 – German troops invaded Soviet Union.

July 7 – U.S. forces occupied Iceland.

July 25 – U.S. froze Japanese and Chinese assets.

August 9-12 – Roosevelt and British Prime Minister Churchill hold secret talks in Newfoundland.

September 8 – German forces began siege of Leningrad (lasted until January 1944).

October 30 – Roosevelt offered Soviet Union $1 billion in credits to aid war effort.

November 26 – U.S. imposed oil embargo against Japan.

November 27 – Japanese emissaries met with President Roosevelt and Secretary of State Cordell Hull to avoid war.

December 7 – Japan attacked Pearl Harbor.

December 8 – United States, Great Britain, and Canada declared war on Japan; Japan attacked Hong Kong, Guam and Wake Island, and Thailand.

December 10 – Japan invaded Philippines.

December 19 – Hitler assumed direct control of German army.

December 25 – Hong Kong fell to Japanese.

1942   Jan 1. – In Washington, 26 nations signed the Declaration of the United Nations, based on the Atlantic Charter.

February 1 – German-controlled government established in Norway, headed by Vidkun Quisling.

February 15 – Singapore fell to Japan, with 85,000 British troops captured

February 18 – German U-boats attacked Aruba and Trinidad.

February 26-28 – Japanese naval forces defeated Allies in Battle of Java Sea.

March 1 – U.S. forces sank their first U-boat off Newfoundland.

April 9 – Seventy-five thousand U.S. and Filipino forces surrendered to Japan on Bataan Peninsula, Philippines.

April 18 – Lt. Colonel James H. Doolittle led U.S. bombers in daring air raid over Tokyo.

April 24 – Selective Service registration for American males from age 45 to 64 began.

May 4–8 – Allies successfully blocked Japanese attack in Battle of Coral Sea.

May 6 – Last American holdouts near Bataan on Corregidor Island surrendered in Philippines.

June 4–6 – Japanese defeated in Battle of Midway.

June 11 – U.S. and Soviet Union signed mutual aid treaty.

June 21 – Rommel's forces defeated British and Australian forces and captured Tobruk.

August 7 – American Marines landed at Guadalcanal.

August 25 – Hitler ordered assault on Stalingrad.

October 1 – German forces bogged down at Stalingrad.

October 23–24 – British forces attacked enemy at El Alamein in Egypt.

November 8 – Allied forces landed in North Africa, at Algeria and Morocco.

November 12 – Drafting of 18- and 19-year-old men approved by Congress.

November 19 – Soviets went on offensive at Stalingrad.

December 1 – British Parliament member reported deaths of estimated 2,000,000 Jews at Nazi hands.

December 2 – Research scientists in U.S. achieved first nuclear chain reaction as part of efforts to develop atomic bomb.

1943 January 14 – Roosevelt and Churchill began ten-day conference at Casablanca.

January 22 – Japanese defeated at Sanananda in New Guinea.

February 2 – Germans surrendered at Stalingrad.

February 4 – Shoe rationing began in U.S.

February 9 – Organized Japanese resistance on Guadalcanal ended.

May 13 – Axis forces in North Africa surrendered.

July 10 – Allies invaded Sicily.

July 25 – Italian dictator Benito Mussolini overthrown by coup.

August 1–2 – PT-109, commanded by Lieutenant John F. Kennedy, sunk in Solomon Islands.

September 8 – Italy surrendered to Allies.

September 9 – Allies landed at Salerno, Italy.

September 10 – German forces seized Rome.

October 1 – British forces occupied Naples.

November 20 – American troops invaded Tarawa.

November 23 – Roosevelt, Churchill, and Soviet leader Joseph Stalin conferred in Teheran, in first Big Three summit.

1944 January 22 – American troops landed at Anzio, south of Rome, but hesitate and fail to capture the city.

May 18 – Allies captured Cassino.

June 6 – D-Day invasion at Normandy beaches began liberation of France from Nazi control.

June 13 – First German Buzz bombs hit England.

June 19 – Japanese defeated in naval battle in Philippine Sea.

July 18 – Japanese Prime Minister Tojo resigned.

July 20 – Assassination plot against Hitler ended in failure.

August 4 – Allies occupied Florence, Italy.

August 19 – French uprising against Nazis began in Paris.

August 25 – Paris liberated.

September 3 – Brussels liberated.

October 20 – Allied invasion began to liberate Philippines.

October 23 – Allies recognized provisional French government, headed by General Charles De Gaulle.

October 23-26 – Japanese navy defeated in Battle of Leyte Gulf, Philippines.

December 16 – Germany launched counterattack in Battle of the Bulge.

1945   January 3 – Allied offensive launch in the Ardennes.

January 16 – Hitler moved to underground bunker in Berlin, where he remained for the duration of war.

January 17 – Soviets captured Warsaw.

January 28 – Burma Road opened.

February 4-16 – Allied leaders met at Yalta Conference.

February 19 – American Marines invaded Iwo Jima.

March 7 – Cologne fell to Allies.

March 16 – Iwo Jima fell to Americans.

March 23 – U.S. Third Army crossed the Rhine.

April 1 – Allies invaded Okinawa.

April 9 – Allies began final offensive in Italy.

April 12 – Roosevelt died at Warm Springs, Georgia.

April 23 – Soviet troops entered Berlin.

April 28 – Mussolini executed by Italian guerrillas.

April 30 – Hitler committed suicide.

May 2 – Berlin fell to Soviet forces.

May 7 – Germany surrendered unconditionally, ending war in Europe.

August 6 – Americans dropped atomic bomb on Hiroshima.

August 8 – Soviet Union entered war against Japan.

August 9 – Second atomic bomb dropped on Nagasaki.

August 14 – Japan agreed to surrender unconditionally.

September 2 – Formal signing ceremony of Japanese surrender held aboard battleship USS *Missouri* in Tokyo Bay.

(Sources: *World Book*, *Americana*, *Britannica*, *World War II Almanac*, and *World War II: The Encyclopedia of the War Years*)

Korean War

1950   June 25 – Communist North Korea invaded South Korea.

June 27 – U.S. President Truman ordered American air and naval forces to assist South Korean defense; United Nations called for aid to South Korea.

June 28 – Seoul fell to North Korean forces.

June 29 – Truman agreed with journalist's description of Korean conflict as "police action."

June 30 – Truman committed U.S. ground forces to South Korea.

July 8 – General Douglas MacArthur named chief commander United Nations force Korea.

August 18 – First tank-to-tank fighting in Korea.

September 15 – Allied forces landed behind enemy lines at Inchon in surprise move.

September 27 – UN forces recaptured Seoul.

October 19 – North Korean capital Pyongyang captured.

October 25 – China entered war on North Korea's side.

November 1 – First jet-to-jet fighting in military history.

November 25 – Chinese troops began combat.

November 26 – UN forces retreated after Chinese attack.

December 16 – Truman declared State of National Emergency.

December 31 – Chinese began new offensive, forcing further UN retreat.

1951 January 4 – Seoul fell to Communists again.

February 13 – General MacArthur criticized UN/U.S. military policy.

March 7 – MacArthur again criticized military policy.

March 14 – UN forces retook Seoul.

April 11 -Truman relieved MacArthur of command; named General Matthew B. Ridgeway as replacement.

April 19 – MacArthur delivered "Old Soldiers Never Die" speech to joint session of Congress.

July 10 – Truce talks began, but fighting continued.

1952 April 28 – Communists rejected proposal for voluntary repatriation of prisoners of war.

May 12 – General Mark Clark named new UN Commander.

July – August – Heavy UN air strikes nearly destroyed Pyongyang.

November 4 – Dwight D. Eisenhower elected U.S. president.

December 2-5 – Eisenhower toured Korea, fulfilling campaign promise to visit war zone.

1953 March 7 – July 7 – Battle of Pork Chop Hill.

March 28 – Agreement reached on exchange of sick and wounded prisoners.

April 26 – Truce talks resumed

July 27 – Armistice agreement halted fighting in Korea.

Vietnam War

1954 March 12–May 7 – French forces defeated at Battle of Dien Bien Phu.

July 20 – Geneva agreement partitioned Vietnam along 17th parallel pending national referendum.

1955 July 16 – South Vietnamese President Ngo Dinh Diem rejected national election mandated by Geneva Accords.

1957 Communists began political struggle to overturn Diem regime in South Vietnam.

1959 January – North Vietnam Communists adopted "armed struggle" strategy to depose Diem regime.

May – North Vietnamese Group 559 began enlargement of Ho Chi Minh Trail to transport supplies to guerrillas in South Vietnam.

July 8 – Military advisers Major Dale Buis and Master Sergeant Chester Ovnard first Americans killed in Vietnam during a Viet Cong attack.

December 31 – Estimated 760 U.S. servicemen stationed in Vietnam.

1960 December 20 – Communists organized National Liberation Front, the political arm of Viet Cong.

December 31 – Estimated 900 U.S. military personnel in Vietnam.

1961 January 28 – Newly inaugurated U.S. President John F. Kennedy approved Vietnam counterinsurgency plan setting political reform and military reorganization as precondition for expanded U.S. assistance.

May 9–15 – U.S. Vice President Lyndon B. Johnson visited Southeast Asia, called for strong action in Vietnam.

December 15 – President Kennedy renewed pledge to maintain South Vietnamese independence.

December 31 – U.S. military personnel in South Vietnam reached 3,205.

1962 February 14 – Kennedy warned U.S. military advisers would return fire if fired upon.

March 22 – U.S. began participation in Vietnam strategic hamlet (rural pacification) program.

December 31 – American military personnel in Vietnam now numbered 11,300.

1963 May-August – Buddhists staged anti-government demonstrations; seven monks self-immolated to protest Diem's policies.

August 21 – Diem ordered military attack against Buddhist pagodas.

August 22 – Henry Cabot Lodge named U.S. Ambassador to Vietnam.

November 1 – Military coup overthrew Diem.

November 2 – Diem and brother Ngo Dinh Nhu assassinated.

November 22 – President Kennedy assassinated; Johnson sworn in as president.

December 31 – U.S. forces in Vietnam numbered 16,300.

1964 January – Lieutenant General William Westmoreland appointed commander American forces in Vietnam.

June 23 – Maxwell Taylor named new U.S. Ambassador.

June 30 – New terminology of "search and destroy" and "clearing operations" adopted by U.S. military.

August 2 – U.S. destroyer *Maddox* reported alleged attack by North Vietnamese patrol boats in international waters in Tonkin Gulf.

August 4 – U.S. destroyer *Turner Joy* reported similar attacks. (Later, these reports acknowledged as erroneous.)

August 7 – U.S. Congress passed Tonkin Gulf Resolution authorizing President to employ "all necessary means" to "prevent further aggression."

December 31 – U.S. personnel level in Vietnam numbered 23,300.

1965 March 2 – U.S. began Operation Rolling Thunder—air strikes against North Vietnamese targets.

March 8-9 – First American ground troops landed in Vietnam, at Da Nang.

March 25 – Faculty at University of Michigan staged first anti-war teach-in.

April 6 – Johnson authorized offensive operations by U.S. ground forces.

April 7 – Johnson offered North Vietnam foreign aid in exchange for peace in a speech at Johns Hopkins University.

April 15 – Students for Democratic Society organized anti-war demonstration in Washington, D.C.

July 8 – Henry Cabot Lodge reappointed Ambassador to South Vietnam.

October 15-16 – Anti-war protests in 40 U.S. cities.

December 25 – Johnson suspended Operation Rolling Thunder bombing raids to induce North Vietnam to negotiate.

December 31 – U.S. service personnel in Vietnam numbered 184,300.

1966 January 19 – President Johnson requested appropriation of additional $12.8 billion for Vietnam war.

January 31- Operation Rolling Thunder bombing raids resumed.

February 4 – Senate Foreign Relations Committee began televised hearings on the war.

June 29 – Johnson ordered bombing of oil installations in Haiphong and Hanoi, North Vietnam.

September 23 – U.S. announced use of defoliants to destroy communist groundcover.

October 26 – President Johnson visited U.S. troops in Vietnam.

December 31 – U.S. military personnel in Vietnam numbered 385,300.

1967 February 22 – Largest operation in Vietnam to date, Operation Junction City began by twenty-two U.S. and four South Vietnamese battalions.

April 15 – One hundred thousand protest war in New York City; twenty thousand in San Francisco.

May 1 – Ellsworth Bunker replaced Lodge as ambassador.

September 2 – Nguyen Van Thieu elected South Vietnamese President.

September 29 – Johnson offered to stop bombing if halt would lead to prompt negotiations.

October – For first time, public opinion polls showed more Americans opposed than supported war.

October 21 – Fifty thousand protesters staged "March on Pentagon."

December 31 – U.S. service personnel in Vietnam numbered 485,600.

1968 January 3 – Senator Eugene McCarthy (D-Minn.) announced anti-war candidacy for Democratic presidential nomination.

January 21 – North Vietnamese troops besieged U.S. base at Khe Sanh.

January 30 – Viet Cong and North Vietnamese unleashed massive Tet Offensive in three-fourths of South Vietnam's provincial capitals.

January 31 – Viet Cong attack on U.S. embassy blocked; Viet Cong and North Vietnamese captured Hue.

February 1–25 – Communists massacred 2,800 civilians at Hue.

February 10–17 – U.S. casualties hit all-time high in Vietnam: 543 killed, 2,547 wounded.

February 20 – Senate Foreign Relations Committee opened hearings on events surrounding passage of Tonkin Gulf Resolution.

February 25 – Americans recaptured Hue.

March 1 – Clark Clifford replaced Robert McNamara as U.S. Secretary of Defense.

March 12 – McCarthy's surprisingly strong 42-percent vote in New Hampshire primary indicated depth of disaffection with Vietnam War.

March 16 – Senator Robert F. Kennedy (D-N.Y.) announced candidacy for Democratic presidential nomination.

March 31 – Johnson announced de-escalation of war; withdrew as presidential candidate.

March – Vietnamese civilians in My Lai village massacred by U.S. military unit.

April 26 – Two hundred thousand protested war in New York City demonstration.

May 3 – Paris peace talks set.

June 6 – Robert Kennedy assassinated.

July 1 – General Creighton Abrams replaced Westmoreland as commander of U.S. forces in Vietnam.

August 28 – Anti-war protests and police riot marred Democratic convention in Chicago.

October 31 – Johnson ended bombing of North Vietnam.

November 5 – Richard Nixon elected president.

December 31 – U.S. service personnel in Vietnam numbered 536,100.

1969 March 18 – U.S. Air Force began secret bombing raids in Cambodian border region.

March – U.S. announced "Vietnamization" policy.

April 30 – U.S. personnel levels in Vietnam peaked at 543,400.

May – Battle of "Hamburger Hill" (Ap Bia).

June 8 – President Nixon announced withdrawal of 25,000 U.S. troops.

September 3 – North Vietnamese leader Ho Chi Minh died.

October 15 – Millions participated in National Moratorium anti-war demonstrations across country.

November 15 – Two hundred fifty thousand demonstrate in Washington, D.C., against Vietnam War.

November 16 – My Lai massacre revealed.

December 1 – Selective Service held draft lottery—first since 1942.

December 31- U.S. troop levels in Vietnam at 475,200.

1970 February 20 – Secret peace talks began in Paris.

March 16–22 – Anti-draft demonstrations held across U.S.

March 18 – In Cambodia, neutralist Prince Norodom Sihanouk overthrown by General Lon Nol.

April 4 – Pro-war demonstration held in Washington, D.C.

April 30 – Nixon announced Cambodian "incursion."

May 4 – Four student demonstrators killed at Kent State University in Ohio by Ohio National Guard Troops.

June 30 – Ground operations in Cambodia ended.

December 22 – U.S. Congress prohibited U.S. military forces in Cambodia or Laos.

December 31 – U.S. military personnel in Vietnam declined to 334,600.

1971 March 29 – U.S. Army court martial found Lieutenant William L. Calley Jr. guilty of premeditated murder at My Lai massacre.

June 13 – *New York Times* began publishing "Pentagon Papers."

June 30 – Supreme Court upheld *New York Times*' right to publish "Pentagon Papers."

November 12 – President Nixon announced U.S. ground forces henceforth limited to defensive actions.

December 31 – U.S. military strength in Vietnam dropped to 156,800.

1972 September 26–27 – National Security Adviser Henry Kissinger held private talks with North Vietnamese representatives.

November 20–21 – Kissinger met privately with Le Duc Tho of North Vietnam in Paris.

December 13 – Paris peace talks deadlocked.

December 18–29 – U.S. conducted "Christmas Bombing" of Hanoi and Haiphong.

December 31 – U.S. military strength in Vietnam declined to 24,200.

1973 January 8–12 – More secret talks held between Kissinger and Le Duc Tho.

January 15 – Nixon ordered halt to offensive actions against North Vietnam.

January 27 – Peace agreement signed in Paris.

March 29 – U.S. ground troops withdrawn from Vietnam; 590 U.S. prisoners of war released by Communists.

December 30 – U.S. military presence in Vietnam limited to 50.

1974 August 9 – Nixon resigned presidency in aftermath of Watergate scandal; Gerald R. Ford sworn in as president.

September 16 – Ford offered clemency to Vietnam War-era draft evaders and military deserters.

1975 January 8 – North Vietnamese Politburo ordered "liberation" of South Vietnam.

March 26 – Hue fell to North Vietnamese.

March 30 – Da Nang fell to North Vietnamese.

April 29 – Corporal Charles McMahon Jr., USMC, and Lance Corporal Darwin Judge, USMC, last U.S. military personnel killed in Vietnam.

April 29-30 – All U.S. personnel and selected Vietnamese evacuated from Saigon.

April 30 – Saigon fell to Communists; Vietnam War ended.

Persian Gulf War

1990 July 17 – Iraq accused Kuwait of building military posts on Iraqi territory and stealing $2.4 billion worth of Iraqi oil.

July 25 – U.S. Ambassador April Glaspie gave Saddam Hussein mixed signals on border dispute; said U.S. would take sides in dispute between Arab brothers.

August 1 – Iraq-Kuwait negotiations collapse in Saudi Arabia.

August 2 – Iraq invaded Kuwait.

August 3 – U.S. President George Bush ordered American naval forces to Persian Gulf; UN

Security Council condemned invasion; in unprecedented development, Soviet Union issued joint statement with U.S. condemning invasion.

August 6 – UN Security Council imposed economic sanctions against Iraq.

August 8 – Iraq annexed Kuwait.

August 9 – American forces, including ground troops, arrived in Saudi Arabia; UN Security Council nullifies Iraqi annexation of Kuwait.

August 10–12 – Arab nations agreed to join Coalition force led by U.S.

August 15 – Iraq offered settlement of dispute with Iran.

August 16 – Iraq rounded up Americans stranded in Iraq and Kuwait.

August 17 – U.S. Navy began blockade of shipping to Iraq.

August 22 – President Bush called up 40,000 reservists.

September 1 – One hundred thousand U.S. military personnel in Gulf region or on way.

September 9 – President Bush and Soviet President Mikhail Gorbachev held summit in Helsinki, Finland; declared support for economic sanctions, warned of further actions.

October 23 – U.S. reported 700-800 stranded Americans held as "human shield" hostages by Iraq.

November 11 – Bush charged Saddam outdid Hitler in "committing outrageous acts of barbarism."

November 29 – UN Security Council authorized military action unless Iraq withdraws from Kuwait by January 15 deadline.

December 6 – Saddam announced release of foreign hostages.

1991 January 6 – Hussein declared Iraqi readiness for "mother of all battles."

January 17 – International Coalition began bombing Iraqi targets.

February 24 – Coalition forces began ground attack.

February 27 – Kuwait City liberated.

February 28 – Coalition ceased military attacks.

April 6 – Iraq accepted formal cease-fire agreement.

April 11 – UN Security Council declared end to Persian Gulf War.

Major U.S. Military Interventions

1898–1902 Cuba: U.S. military controlled Cuba following Spanish-American War.

1903 Panama: After Colombia refused U.S. permission to build canal across Isthmus of Panama, President Theodore Roosevelt dispatched warships to block Colombia from stopping Panama's secession; after independence, Panama then allowed U.S. to build canal.

1906–1909 Cuba: American troops reoccupied Cuba after rebellion against government.

1912–1917 Cuba: U.S. forces returned again in 1912 and 1917 following uprisings by workers and African-Cubans.

1914–1917 Mexico: When factional fighting during Mexican revolution threatened U.S. business interests, President Woodrow Wilson authorized military expeditions against Vera Cruz and several border areas, as well as hot pursuit of Mexican guerrilla bands attacking U.S. border towns.

1915–1934 U.S. Marines occupied Haiti.

1916–1924 Dominican Republic: Occupied by American forces to quell political disorder; U.S. military administration paved way for Rafael Trujillo to take power, and establish a repressive dictatorship.

1926–1933 Nicaragua: American invasion and occupation bolstered rule of conservative Nicaraguan leaders linked to U.S. business interests; paved way for Somozo family to establish dictatorship after U.S. withdrawal.

July-August, 1946 Italy: President Truman deployed American naval units in Trieste to block feared Yugoslav-Soviet attack.

August 1946 Turkey: Truman deployed naval carrier force to counter Soviet threat to Turkish control of Bosporus Straits.

September 1946 Greece: U.S. aircraft carrier deployed off Greece during threatened Communist coup.

January 1948 Italy: Marine reinforcements dispatched to Mediterranean as warning to forestall Yugoslav moves against 5,000 American troops in Trieste.

July 1948 Palestine: Marine consular guard dispatched to protect U.S. consular general in Jerusalem during Arab-Israeli war; two Marines wounded.

April 1948-November 1949 China: U.S. Marines sent to Nanking and Shanghai to protect U.S. Embassy and assist evacuation following Communist takeover in China.

1954 Guatemala: CIA organized and financed a successful invasion from Honduras by right-wing Guatemalan military officers, toppling elected leftist government of Jacob Arbenz Guzman.

November 1956 Egypt: Marine battalion evacuated 1,500 Americans from Alexandria during Suez crisis.

February 1957 Indonesia: Marines placed on standby to protect Americans during Indonesian revolt.

July 1957 Taiwan: Four U.S. aircraft carriers deployed to defend Taiwan during Communist shelling of Quemoy.

March 1958 Indonesia: Marines' helicopter squadron deployed with 7th Fleet off Indonesian coast to protect American citizens.

July-October 1958 Lebanon: At request of beleaguered Lebanese government, President Eisenhower sent 14,000 troops to intervene in civil war.

July 1959-May 1975 Vietnam: American forces support anti-Communist government in South Vietnam, first as trainers, then advisers, later as combatants.

November 1959-February 1960 Cuba: Marine Ground Task Force sent to Cuba to protect American citizens during Cuban revolution.

April 1961 Cuba: U.S.-supported Cuban exiles launched unsuccessful invasion of Cuba at Bay of Pigs.

November 1961 Dominican Republic: Naval forces deployed off coast in show of force to discourage Trujillo family from trying to regain power.

May-July 1962 Thailand: Five thousand Marines dispatched to Thailand for nine weeks to help block Communist threat.

October-December 1962 Cuba: Following Soviet missile deployment in Cuba, 180 U.S. naval vessels and nuclear-armed B-52 bombers established quarantine around Cuba. Soviets agreed to withdraw missiles.

May 1963 Haiti: In show of force, U.S. Marines deployed off Haitian coast following anti-Duvalier government protests and threat of Dominican intervention.

November 1964 Congo: American aircraft transported Belgian paratroopers in rescue mission to free American and other civilian hostages held by rebels.

May 1964-January 1973 Laos: American jets attacked Communists' Pathet Lao positions.

April 1965 Dominican Republic: President Johnson sent 21,500 U.S. troops to block suspected pro-Communists from taking power.

June 1967 Syria: President Johnson deployed 6th Fleet off Syrian coast as show of force to warn Soviets against interfering in Arab-Israeli war.

July-December 1967 President Johnson dispatched transport planes to assist Congolese President Mobutu in struggle against Katangese rebels.

April-June 1970 Cambodia: U.S. ground forces invaded Cambodia to destroy Vietnamese Communist sanctuaries.

May 1975 Cambodia: President Ford sent Navy, Marine, and Air Force units to rescue U.S. merchant vessel *Mayaguez* and crew held by Cambodian Communists.

April 1980 Iran: Rescue mission to free American hostages held in Tehran aborted as eight men died in helicopter collision in Iranian desert.

August 1981 Libya: Navy fighters shot down two Libyan jets over Gulf of Sidra, 60 miles off Libyan coast.

October 1983 Lebanon: Two hundred forty-one U.S. Marines deployed as peacekeepers in Lebnon killed in terrorist attack at Beirut airport.

October 1983 Grenada: U.S. forces and troops from eastern Caribbean nations invaded Grenada, toppled pro-Communist government.

December 1983 Lebanon: American jets attacked Syrian positions in Lebanon.

March 1986 Libya: U.S. 6th Fleet crossed Libya's self-declared "line of death" in Gulf of Sidra, provoking missile attacks against American

planes. American forces retaliated with largest air strikes since Vietnam War.

1987 Persian Gulf: U.S. naval forces provided protection to civilian shipping in Persian Gulf during Iraq-Iran War; Iraqi missile accidentally hit USS *Stark*, killing 37 American personnel.

1989 Panama: American forces invaded Panama, deposed and apprehended Panamanian dictator Manual Noriega on drug trafficking charges, dispersed Noriega's forces, and installed democratically elected government.

1990–1991 Persian Gulf: Following Iraqi invasion and occupation of neighboring Kuwait, American-led coalition, under United Nations auspices, liberated Kuwait.

1992 Somalia: Under UN authorization, American-led coalition dispatched troops to famine-stricken Somalia to provide security for international food relief workers and supplies.

1993 American forces occupied Haiti as military rulers transferred power to constitutionally elected President Bertrand Aristide, who had been deposed by military coup in 1991.

1993 Yugoslavia: American peacekeeping force sent to former Yugoslavian republic of Macedonia in an effort to prevent spread of civil war in neighboring Bosnia and Herzegovina.

1995–1996 Bosnia and Herzegovina: Twenty thousand U.S. troops dispatched to Bosnia and Herzegovina as part of international peacekeeping force, under NATO auspices as part of U.S.-brokered peace agreement negotiated at Dayton, Ohio, peace conference.

(Sources: *World Book, Americana, Colliers, Encyclopedia of Korean War, Vietnam War Almanac, World War II Almanac, Dictionary of First World War, Oxford Companion to World War II, Encyclopedia of Vietnam War, Vietnam War Almanac, Facts on File,* and *World Almanac*)

PART 6

Natural Disasters and Human-Made Accidents and Incidents

NATURAL DISASTERS

Blizzards

A blizzard is more than just a lot of snow. The National Weather Service defines a blizzard as a severe storm with heavy snowfall, at least 35 mile-per-hour winds, with blowing snow reducing visibility to less than one quarter of a mile for three hours.

1888 March 11–14 – 400 died in major blizzard hitting Eastern U.S.

1940 November 11–12 – Blizzard struck Northeast and Midwest U.S., killing 144.

1947 December 26 – New York City and north Atlantic states hit by massive snowstorm; 55 lives lost.

1958 February 15–16 – 171 deaths attributed to blizzard in Northeastern U.S.

1967 December 12–20 – Blizzard struck Southwest U.S., killing 51.

1993 March 13–14 – 200 lives lost in blizzard in Eastern U.S.

1996 January 7–8 – 100 lives lost in blizzard in Eastern U.S.

1998 February 4–6 – 10 deaths attributed to blizzard in Kentucky and West Virginia.

(Sources: *Disasters*, *World Book*, *World Almanac*, and *NYPL Book of Chronologies*)

Earthquakes

1811 December 16 – New Madrid, Missouri, hit by series of strong quakes (possibly as high as 8.8 on Richter scale) continuing until February 1812. Death toll unknown in sparsely settled area.

1886 August 31 – Charleston, South Carolina, hit by 6.6. Richter scale quake; 60 lives lost.

1906 April 18 – Earthquake registering 8.3 on the Richter scale hit San Francisco, California, destroying four square mile area; 500 killed.

1918 October 11 – Mona Passage, Puerto Rico, rocked by 7.5 Richter scale quake; 116 killed.

1933 March 10 – Long Beach, California, experienced 6.2 Richter scale quake; 115 lives lost.

1964 March 27 – Strongest earthquake to hit North America (8.5 on Richter scale) shook Anchorage, Alaska; killed 118.

1971 February 9 – Earthquake registering 6.6 on the Richter scale shook San Fernando Valley, California; 65 lives lost.

1989 October 17 – San Francisco Bay area hit by a 7.1 quake, disrupting World Series games in Oakland; 62 lives lost.

1992 June 28 – Earthquake registering 7.5 on the Richter scale shook Southern California; one killed.

1994 January 17 – Earthquake registering 6.8 on the Richter scale hit Northridge, California; 61 lives lost.

(Sources: *Disasters*, *World Book*, *World Almanac*, and *NYPL Book of Chronologies*)

Fires

1835 December 16 – Fire destroyed 674 buildings in New York City.

1871 October 8 – Great Chicago Fire destroyed 17,000 buildings, caused $196 million damage, and killed 250 people.

October 8 – Peshtigo, Wisconsin, forest fire killed 1,200, destroyed two billion trees.

1872 November 9 – Fire destroyed 800 buildings in Boston.

1876 December 5 – Theater fire killed 295 in Brooklyn, New York.

1894 September 1 – Minnesota forest fire killed 413.

1900 June 30 – Fire on Hoboken, New Jersey, docks killed 326.

1902 September 20 – Birmingham, Alabama, church fire killed 115.

1903 December 30 – Fire at Iroquois Theater, Chicago, Illinois, killed 602.

1906 April 18 – San Francisco Earthquake caused three-day fire; 25,000 buildings destroyed, 500 lives lost.

1908 January 13 – Fire at Rhoads Theater, Boyertown, Pennsylvania, killed 170.

March 4 – School fire in Collinwood, Ohio, killed 176.

1911 March 25 – Fire at Triangle Shirtwaist factory killed 146 workers in Greenwich Village, New York.

1918 October 12 – Minnesota forest fire killed 400.

1929 May 15 – Clinic fire in Cleveland, Ohio, killed 125.

1930 April 21 – Fire at Columbus, Ohio, prison killed 320.

1940 April 23 – Fire at dance hall in Natchez, Mississippi, killed 198.

1942 November 28 – Cocoanut Grove nightclub fire in Boston, Massachusetts, killed 491.

1944 July 6 – Ringling Circus fire in Hartford, Connecticut, killed 168.

1946 December 7 – Atlanta hotel fire killed 119.

1977 May 28 – Nightclub fire in Southgate, Kentucky, killed 164.

1986 December 31 – Dupont Plaza Hotel fire in Puerto Rico killed 96.

1990 March 25 – Arson at Bronx, New York, social club killed 87 people.

1991 September 3 – 25 workers killed in fire at chicken-processing plant in Hamlet, North Carolina.

1993 April 19 – 72 died in fire at Branch Davidian cult during standoff with federal authorities in Waco, Texas.

(Sources: *Disasters*, *World Book*, *World Almanac*, *NYPL Book of Chronologies*, and *Encyclopedia of New York City*)

Floods

1889 May 31 – 2,209 lives lost in Johnstown, Pennsylvania, flood.

1900 September 8 – 6,000 killed in Galveston, Texas, flood.

1903 June 15 – 325 died in flooding in Heppner, Oregon.

1913 March 25-27 – More than 730 lives lost in flood in Ohio and Indiana.

1915 August 17 – 250 lives lost in Galveston, Texas, flood.

1928 March 13 – 450 died after dam collapsed in Saugus, California.

September 13 – 2,000 killed in flood at Lake Okeechobee, Florida.

1937 January 22 – Flooding in Mississippi and Ohio River Valleys killed 250.

1969 August 20–22 – More than 180 killed in western Virginia.

1972 February 26 – 118 killed at Buffalo Creek, West Virginia.

June 9 – 236 killed in Rapid City, South Dakota.

1976 June 5 – 11 killed following Teton Dam collapse in Idaho.

July 31 – 139 died in Big Thompson Canyon, Colorado, flooding.

1977 July 19–20 – 68 fatalities due to flooding in Johnstown, Pennsylvania.

November 6 – 39 killed by flooding in Toccoa, Georgia.

1980 February 13–22 – 26 killed by flooding in Southern California and Arizona.

1990 June 14 – 23 lives lost in Shadyside, Ohio, flooding.

1993 July-August – Flood of the Century, affecting Mississippi River and tributaries, devastated Midwest U.S., killed 48.

1994 July – 32 died in Georgia and Alabama flooding.

1996 December – January 1997 – 29 killed in Norwestern floods.

1997 March – 35 died in Ohio River Valley flooding.

1998 August 24 – 16 lives lost in flooding from southern Texas to Mexico.

(Sources: *Disasters*, *World Book*, *World Almanac*, and *NYPL Book of Chronologies*)

Hurricanes

With sustained winds of at least 73 miles per hour, and accompanying heavy rainfall, hurricanes generally originate in the tropical waters of the Atlantic Ocean and Caribbean Sea and head north and northwest, threatening the islands of the Caribbean, Central America, the southern U.S. from Texas to Florida, and on up the eastern coastal region as far north as New England. Since these fearsome storms are undeterred by national boundaries and Americans are accustomed to weather reports tracking the paths of hurricanes, this list includes storms that struck our neighbors in Central America and the Caribbean as well as those that made landfall in the U.S.

1775 September 2–9 – Hurricane killed 4,170 from North Carolina to Nova Scotia.

1856 August 11 – Hurricane hit Last Island, Georgia, killing 400.

1893 August 28 – Hurricane hit Savannah, Georgia; Charleston, South Carolina; and Sea Islands, South Carolina; killing 1,000.

1900 August 27–September 15 – Hurricane killed 6,000 in Galveston, Texas, and Texas Gulf Coast area.

1909 Sept 10–21 – 350 killed by hurricane in Louisiana and Mississippi.

1915 September 29 – 500 killed by hurricane in Louisiana.

1926 September 11–22 – Hurricane caused 243 deaths in Florida and Alabama.

October 20 – 600 killed by hurricane in Cuba.

1928 September 6–20 – 1,836 lives lost to hurricane in southern Florida.

1930 September 3 – Hurricane struck Dominican Republic, killing 2,000.

1954 October 5–18 – Hurricane Hazel killed 347 in Haiti and Eastern U.S.

1955 August 7–21 – Hurricane Diane claimed 400 lives in Eastern U.S.

September 19 – Hurricane Hilda killed 200 in Mexico.

September 22–28 – 500 died in Caribbean area due to Hurricane Janet.

1957 June 25–30 – 390 lives lost to Hurricane Audrey in Gulf Coast states from Alabama to Texas.

1961 October 31 – Hurricane Hattie killed 400 in British Honduras.

1963 October 4–8 – 6,000 lives lost to Hurricane Flora in Caribbean.

1966 September 24–30 – 293 killed in Caribbean, Florida, and Mexico by Hurricane Inez.

1969 August 17–18 – 256 killed in Mississippi and Louisiana by Hurricane Camille.

1974 September 19–20 – Hurricane Fifi killed 2,000 in Honduras.

1979 August 30–September 7 – 1,100 lives lost to Hurricane David in Caribbean and Eastern U.S.

1980 August 4–11 – 272 lives claimed by Hurricane Allen in Caribbean and Texas.

1988 September 10–17 – 260 killed by Hurricane Gilbert in Caribbean and Gulf of Mexico region.

1989 September 16–22 – 504 lives lost to Hurricane Hugo in Caribbean and Southeastern U.S.

1998 September 21–23 – Hurricane Georges killed more than 600 in Caribbean, Florida Keys, and U.S. Gulf Coast.

October 26–31 – Hurricane Mitch hit Central America, killing more than 7,600, mostly in Honduras and Nicaragua, and leaving a million homeless.

1999 September 4–17 – Hurricane Floyd killed more than 65 in the Bahamas and Eastern U.S.

(Sources: *Disasters, World Book, World Almanac, NYPL Book of Chronologies,* and *Facts on File*)

Tornadoes

1925 March 18 – 695 deaths caused by tornado in Missouri, Illinois, and Indiana.

1932 March 21 – Series of tornadoes in Alabama killed 268.

1936 April 5 – 455 died from tornadoes in Mississippi and Georgia.

1936 April 6 – Tornado killed 203 people at Gainesville, Georgia.

1944 June 23 – 150 died due to tornadoes in Ohio, Pennsylvania, West Virginia, and Maryland.

1945 April 12 – Tornado killed 102 in Oklahoma and Arkansas.

1947 April 9 – 169 died from tornadoes in Texas, Oklahoma, and Kansas.

1952 March 21 – Series of tornadoes killed 208 in Arkansas, Missouri, and Tennessee.

1953 May 11 – 114 killed by tornadoes at Waco, Texas.

1953 June 8 – 142 died from tornadoes in Michigan and Ohio.

1955 May 25 – 115 lives lost due to tornadoes in Kansas, Missouri, Oklahoma, and Texas.

1965 April 11 – 271 deaths attributed to tornadoes in Indiana, Illinois, Ohio, Michigan, and Wisconsin.

1971 February 21 – 110 killed by tornadoes in Mississippi Delta area.

1974 April 3-4 – 315 lives lost to tornadoes in Alabama, Georgia, Tennessee, Kentucky, and Ohio.

1999 May 3 – 76 huge tornadoes hit Oklahoma, Kansas, Nebraska, Texas, and South Dakota, including a rare F5-rated storm (officially designated an "incredible tornado," winds from 260 to 318 miles per hour). 47 deaths, 700 injuries, and 2,000 destroyed homes resulted.

(Sources: *Disasters*, *World Book*, *World Almanac*, and *NYPL Book of Chronologies*)

ACCIDENTS AND INCIDENTS

Worst U.S. Disasters

1811 December 16 – New Madrid, Missouri: Series of three largest earthquakes in U.S. history, estimated at 8.6, 8.4, and 8.8 on Richter scale.

1865 April 27 – Boiler on Mississippi River steamboat *Sultana* exploded; 1,547 killed.

1871 October 8 – Great Chicago Fire destroyed 17,000 buildings, caused $196 million damage, and killed 250 people.

1871 October 8 – Peshtigo, Wisconsin, forest fire killed 1,200, destroyed 2 billion trees.

1888 March 11-14 – Blizzard of 1888 dumped as much as five feet of snow on northeast; 400 died.

1889 May 31 – Johnstown, Pennsylvania, flood killed 2,209.

1900 August 27-September 15 – Galveston, Texas: Hurricane winds and tidal wave killed 6,000.

1906 April 18 – San Francisco, California, earthquake and fire killed more than 500.

1907 December 6 – Monogha, West Virginia, coal mine explosion took 361 lives.

1918 Nationwide influenza epidemic killed 500,000.

1918 July 9 – Nashville, Tennessee, train collision killed 101.

1925 March 18 – Great Tri-State Tornado killed 695 in Missouri, Illinois, and Indiana.

1928 March 13 – Santa Paula, California, dam collapse killed 450.

1963 April 10 – Atomic powered submarine, USS *Thresher*, sank in North Atlantic, killing 129 crew members.

1979 March 28 – Partial core meltdown at nuclear power plant at Three Mile Island in Middletown, Pennsylvania, caused by equipment malfunction and human error. Considered worst nuclear accident in U.S. history.

May 25 – Chicago, Illinois: American Airlines flight crashed, 272 passengers and 3 people on the ground died. Worst U.S. aviation disaster in history.

1985 December 12 – Charter plane returning American servicemen from Middle East crashed; 256 killed.

1989 March 24 – Prince William Sound, Alaska: *Exxon Valdez* oil tanker spills ten million gallons of oil; worst oil spill in U.S. history.

1995 April 19 – Terrorist bomb exploded at Federal Building in Oklahoma City, killing 168. Worst terrorist attack in U.S. history.

1996 May 11 – ValuJet airliner crashed in Florida Everglades near Miami, killing 110.

July 17 – TWA Flight 800 mysteriously exploded off Long Island, New York, coast a few minutes after take-off from John F. Kennedy International airport; 230 passengers killed.

1999 May 3 – 76 huge tornadoes hit Oklahoma, Kansas, Nebraska, Texas, and South Dakota, including a rare F5-rated storm (officially designated an "incredible tornado," winds from 260 to 318 miles per hour). 47 deaths, 700 injuries, and 2,000 destroyed homes resulted.

(Sources: *Disasters*, *World Book*, *World Almanac*, and *NYPL Book of Chronologies*)

American Aviation Disasters

A rather broad definition of "American Aviation Disasters" was employed in compiling this list. American companies like Boeing and McDonnell-Douglas (now merged into one company) manufactured most of the world's passenger airplane stock and trained the airline personnel who fly them. Therefore a Dutch DC-8 (a McDonnell-Douglas aircraft) crashing in Mecca with Moslem pilgrims aboard, or a Japanese Boeing 707 slamming into Mount Fuji—though not American-owned—both have a definite American connection. Likewise, foreign aviation mishaps involving a substantial number of American passengers have also been included.

1907 September 17 – Lieutenant Thomas E. Self-ridge, first aviation fatality; killed in crash while flying with Orville Wright.

1947 May 30 – Eastern Airlines' DC-4 crashed in Maryland; 53 killed.

1955 November 1 – Bomb planted aboard United Air Lines' DC-6B exploded; 44 killed.

1956 June 30 – Mid-air collision between TWA jet and DC-7 over Grand Canyon killed 128.

1959 February 3 – Airliner crashed in East River in New York City, killing 66.

1960 December 16 – United Airlines' DC-8 and TWA jet collided in air over Staten Island, New York; 136 died.

1961 February 15 – Sabena's Boeing 707 crash near Brussels, Belgium, killed 73, including entire U.S. figure skating team.

1962 March 1 – American Airlines' Boeing 707 crashed in Jamaica Bay, New York City, killed 95.

March 4 – British Airways' DC-7 crashed in Cameroon; 111 died.

1963 November 29 – TWA plane crashed in Montreal with 118 fatalities.

1965 February 8 – Eastern Airlines' DC-7B crashed into Atlantic Ocean shortly after taking off from Kennedy Airport.

1966 March 5 – British Airways' Boeing 707 crashed into Mount Fuji in Japan; 124 dead.

1966 December 24 – Binh Thai, South Vietnam: Chartered military jet crash killed 129.

1967 April 20 – Swiss airliner crashed in Cyprus, killed 126.

1969 March 16 – DC-9 crashed near La Coruba, Venezuela, after gunman shot pilot; 155 killed.

1970 July 5 – Air Canada's DC-8 crashed near Toronto; 109 killed.

1971 July 30 – Japanese Boeing 727 and F-86 fighter plane collided in midair over Morioka, Japan; 162 died.

1972 March 15 – Danish plane accident in Oman killed 112.

May 5 – Alitalia's DC-8 crashed near Palermo, Sicily; 115 lives lost.

October 13 – USSR airliner crashed while landing at Kranaya Polyana, USSR; 176 lives lost.

December 3 – Spanish chartered Convair 990A carrying West German tourists crashed after takeoff from Tenife, Canary Islands; 155 killed.

1973 January 22 – 176 Moslem pilgrims and crew died while returning from Mecca when a Boeing 707 crashed near Kano, Nigeria.

1974 March 3 – 346 died in a Turkish DC-10 crash after takeoff near Paris, France.

December 4 – Dutch DC-8 carrying Moslem pilgrims to Mecca crashed while landing at Colombo, Sri Lanka, killing 191.

1975 April 4 – 172, mostly Vietnamese children, died when U.S. Air Force Galaxy C-5A crashed on takeoff near Saigon.

August 3 – Chartered Boeing 707 crashed near Agadir, Morocco; 188 killed.

1976 September 10 – Yugoslav DC-9 and British Airways' Trident collided in midair near Zagreb, Yugoslavia, killed 176.

1977 March 27 – KLM and Pan American Boeing 747s collided on runway, killing 582; worst death toll in aviation disaster.

1978 January 1- Air India 747 exploded after taking off from Bombay; 213 died.

September 25 – Pacific Southwest airliner collided in midair with Cessna, killing 144, including all 135 aboard airliner, 2 in Cessna, and 7 on ground.

November 15 – Chartered Icelandic DC-8 carrying Moslem pilgrims from Mecca crashed during landing approach; 183 killed.

1979 November 26 – 156 Moslem pilgrims died when a Pakistani International Airlines' 707 crashed on takeoff from Jidda, Saudi Arabia.

1980 August 19 – Burning Saudi Arabian aircraft landed safely at Riyadh but all 301 aboard died when unable to escape plane.

1981 December 1 – Yugoslav DC-9 Super 80 crashed on landing approach in Corsica. killing 178.

1982 July 9 – 153 died in Pan American plane crash after take off in Kenner, Louisiana.

1983 August 30 – Korean Airline Flight 007 (Boeing 747) strayed off course, entering USSR air space, and was shot down by Soviet fighter plane; 269 killed.

November 26 – Columbia Avianca's Boeing 747 crashed near Madrid, Spain airport, killing 183.

1985 June 23 – Air India's Boeing 747 exploded midair off coast of Ireland; 329 killed.

1986 August 12 – Japan Air Lines' Boeing 747 crashed into mountain near Tokyo; 520 killed in worst ever single-aircraft accident.

December 12 – A Chartered Arrow Air DC-8 bringing U.S. soldiers home for Christmas crashed on taking off at Gander, Newfoundland; 256 died.

1987 August 16 – 156 died when a Northwest Airlines' McDonnell Douglas MD-30 crashed in ball of flames. Only a 4-year old girl survived.

November 26 – South African Boeing 747 crashed in rough seas near Mauritius; 160 killed.

November 29 – Bomb planted by North Korean agents exploded aboard a Korean Air Lines' Boeing 747 near Burma; 115 killed.

1988 July 3 – USS *Vincennes* mistakenly shot down an Iranian Air A300 Airbus, killing 290.

December 21 – Terrorist bomb exploded aboard a Pan American Boeing 747 over Lockerbie, Scotland; killing 270—259 aboard plane and 11 on ground.

1989 June 7 – Suriname Airways' DC-8 crashed in jungle on landing approach; 168 killed.

July 19 – United Airlines' DC-10 crash-landed in Sioux City, Iowa; 110 passengers were killed, but thanks to heroic efforts of pilot Alfred Haynes, 185 survived.

1991 July 11 – Canadian-charter DC-8 carrying Moslem pilgrims returning from Mecca crashed after takeoff at Jidda, Saudi Arabia; 261 died.

1994 April 26 – China Airlines' A-300 Airbus crashed landed and exploded on runway at Nagoya, Japan; 271 killed.

1996 May 11 – ValuJet airliner crashed in Florida Everglades near Miami, killing 110.

July 17 – TWA Flight 800 mysteriously exploded off Long Island, New York, coast a few minutes after takeoff from John F. Kennedy International airport; 230 passengers killed.

November 12 – In worst midair collision in aviation history, Saudi Arabian Airlines' 747 collided with Kazakhstan Airlines' cargo plane near New Delhi, India, killing 349.

1997 February 16 – China Airlines' aircraft crashed on approach at Taipei, Taiwan; 203 killed.

1998 September 2 – Swissair's MD-11 crashed off Halifax, Nova Scotia; 229 lives lost.

1999 October 21 – Egypt Air's Boeing 767 crashed into the Atlantic off Nantucket Island, killing 217 passengers and crew.

(Sources: *Disasters*, *World Book*, *World Almanac*, *NYPL Book of Chronologies*, *New York Times*, and *Facts on File*)

Aviation Hijackings

The world's first recorded aviation hijacking occurred on a domestic flight in Peru in 1931.

November 1958 First hijacking on U.S. territory: Cubana Airlines' Viscount plane seized by five men; crashed en route to Havana; 17 of 20 on board died.

May 1961 First American plane hijacked: National Airlines' plane diverted to Cuba from Florida.

September 6, 1970 Palestinian terrorists forced three hijacked planes (TWA, Swissair, and British Airways) to land in Jordan and Egypt; planes blown up on ground; passengers and crew held hostage, exchanged for Palestinian prisoners in Europe.

September 1974 Heaviest loss of life in hijacking incident: hijacker released two hand grenades aboard Air Vietnam plane leaving Danang; all 70 aboard killed.

August 1980 Largest number of hijackers in single incident: 168 Cuban refugees broke through airline terminal fence, seized Braniff jet in Lima, Peru; demanded to be flown to Miami; group surrendered after American officials agreed to expedite applications to emigrate to U.S.

June 1985 Longest hijacking incident: June 14 two Lebanese Shi'ite Moslem terrorists hijacked TWA airliner out of Athens, Greece, with 153 aboard; 16 days later, June 30, hijacking ended at Beirut airport; one hostage killed, 39 released.

September 1986 Four Palestinians seized a Pan Am Boeing 747 airliner with 400 passengers in Karachi; 22 died in battle when Pakistani forces stormed plane.

(Sources: *Almanac of Modern Terrorism*, *Global Patterns of Terrorism*, and *NBC News*)

Nuclear Accidents

The United States has never suffered a nuclear accident as serious as the 1986 disaster at the Chernobyl nuclear power plant near Kiev, USSR (now Ukraine), but the American nuclear industry has had its share of mishaps over the years.

1961 January 3 – Three workers at experimental reactor at government facility near Idaho Falls, Idaho, died from exposure to radiation.

1966 October 5 – Partial core meltdown caused by cooling system failure occurred at Enrico Fermi breeder reactor near Detroit, Michigan. Radiation contained.

1975 March 22 – Fire at Brown's Ferry reactor in Decatur, Alabama, caused $100 million damage.

1979 March 28 – Partial core meltdown at Three Mile Island in Middletown, Pennsylvania, caused by equipment malfunction and human error. Considered worst nuclear accident in U.S. history.

1981 February 11 – Eight employees contaminated by radioactive coolant at Sequoyah 1 nuclear plant operated by Tennessee Valley Authority (TVA) in Tennessee.

(Sources: *Disasters*, *World Book*, *World Almanac*, and *NYPL Book of Chronologies*)

Railroad Accidents

1831 June 17 – Boiler on *The Best Friend of Charleston*, first American passenger train locomotive, exploded, killing fireman; first American killed in railway accident.

1833 November 8 – World's first train wreck and passenger fatalities occurred when Camden & Amboy train carrying 24 passengers derailed. Two killed; all others injured, including former president John Quincy Adams and Cornelius Vanderbilt, passengers on train.

1853 May 6 – New Haven Railroad train ran through open drawbridge, plunged into Norwalk River; 46 killed.

1876 December 29 – Lake Shore train plunged into Ashtabula River when bridge collapsed near Ashtabula, Ohio; 92 died.

1887 August 10 – Toledo, Peoria, and Western Railroad train crashed when burning trestle collapsed near Chatsworth, Illinois; 81 killed, 372 injured.

1904 August 7 – Derailment during flash flood in Eden, Colorado, killed 96.

1910 March 1 – Avalanche swept two trains into canyon in Wellington, Washington; 96 killed.

1918 November 1 – Subway train derailment in New York City killed 92.

1950 November 22 – Rear-end collision between two Long Island Railroad trains in Richmond Hill, New York, killed 79.

1951 February 6 – Pennsylvania Railroad train crashed near Woodbridge, New Jersey; 85 killed.

1972 October 30 – Morning rush-hour collision between two commuter trains in Chicago killed 45, injured more than 200.

1993 September 22 – Train wreck at Big Bayou Conot, Alabama, killed 47.

1999 March 15 – 11 died in wreck in Bourbonnais, Illinois.

(Sources: *Disasters*, *World Book*, *World Almanac*, and *NYPL Book of Chronologies*)

Space Accidents

Efforts to conquer space were so dominated for three decades by the Cold War rivalry between the United States and the Soviet Union that it is difficult to think of a "space" in purely American terms. This list of space accidents includes both the American and Russian space programs.

1967 January 27 – Fire aboard *Apollo I* space capsule on launch pad killed astronauts Virgil I. Grissom, Edward H. White, and Roger Chaffee.

April 23–24 – Cosmonaut Vladimir M. Komarov killed in crash on return to earth from space mission.

1971 June 6-30 – Cosmonauts Georgi T. Dolrovotsky, Vladislav N. Volkov, and Viktor I. Patsayev died on re-entry into earth's atmosphere, apparently because of loss of pressurization.

1980 March 18 – Rocket exploded during refueling on launch pad at Plesetsk Space Center, USSR, killing 50 people.

1986 January 28 – All seven crew members aboard *Challenger* space shuttle died when spacecraft exploded 73 seconds after liftoff at Cape Kennedy, Florida. Crew members were Christa McAuliffe, Francis R. Scobee, Michael J. Smith, Judith A. Resnick, Ronald E. McNair, Ellison S. Onizuka, and Gregory B. Jarvis.

(Sources: *Disasters*, *World Book*, *World Almanac,* and *NYPL Book of Chronologies*)

Terrorist Incidents

This list includes not only terrorist incidents that occurred in the United States but also incidents that occurred on foreign soil that targeted American officials, military personnel, or ordinary citizens.

1970 September 6 – Palestinian terrorists simultaneously hijacked three jetliners (including a TWA plane), two to Jordan and one to Egypt. All three planes were blown up on the ground.

1973 March 1 – Palestinian terrorists occupied Saudi Arabian embassy in Sudan and killed Belgian and American ambassadors.

1976 June 27 – Palestinians hijacked Air France jet to Entebbe, Uganda. At least nine Americans were among the 258 passengers taken hostage. Israeli commandos staged daring rescue operation July 3. Three hostages were killed.

1983 April 18 – Islamic fundamentalist suicide bomber attacked U.S. Embassy in Beirut, Lebanon; 63 killed, including 16 Americans.

October 23 – Suicide bomber attacked headquarters of U.S. Marines participating in multinational peacekeeping force at Beirut Airport, Lebanon; 241 U.S. servicemen killed. Similar attack killed 58 French paratroopers.

1984 September 20 – Car bomb exploded near American Embassy Annex in East Beirut, killing 23.

1985 June 14 – Hizballah terrorists hijacked TWA Flight 847 and held 39 Americans hostage for 17 days.

October 7 – Palestinian terrorists hijacked Italian cruise ship *Achille Lauro*, one American passenger was murdered.

November 23 – Egyptian airliner hijacked by Palestinians to Malta. Sixty people died during rescue attempt by Egyptian commandos November 24.

December 27 – Palestinians staged grenade and machine gun attacks at Rome and Vienna airports, killing 16 and wounding 60.

1986 April 5 – Bombing attributed to Libyan agents at a West Berlin disco frequented by U.S. servicemen killed 3 and wounded 200.

1988 December 21 – Bomb exploded aboard Pan American Flight 103 over Lockerbie, Scotland, killing 259 on plane and 11 on the ground. American and British investigators eventually accused two Libyans of responsibility.

1993 February 26 – Bombing at World Trade Center in New York City killed 6, injured more than

1,000. Followers of Egyptian fundamentalist Sheik Omar Abdul Rahman convicted.

1995 April 19 – Terrorist bomb exploded at Federal Building in Oklahoma City, killing 168. Worst terrorist attack in U.S. history.

November 13 – Terrorist bomb in parking lot near U.S.-run military training center in Riyadh, Saudi Arabia, killed 7 and injured 60.

1996 June 25 – Truck bomb exploded near U.S. military housing facility in Dhahran, Saudi Arabia, killing 19 and wounding 400.

(Sources: *Almanac of Modern Terrorism*, *Patterns of Global Terrorism*, and *NBC News*)

PART 7

Notably American

PRIZE WINNERS

Pulitzer Prizes

Endowed by a bequest from Joseph Pulitzer (1847–1911) to Columbia University, Pulitzer Prizes are awarded each year in journalism, letters, and music.

Meritorious Public Service

1918 *New York Times*

1919 *Milwaukee Journal*

1920 Not awarded

1921 *Boston Post*

1922 *New York World*

1923 *Memphis Commercial Appeal*

1924 *New York World*

1925 Not awarded

1926 *Enquirer-Sun* (Columbus, Georgia)

1927 *Canton* (Ohio) *Daily News*

1928 *Indianapolis Times*

1929 *New York Evening World*

1930 Not awarded

1931 *Atlanta Constitution*

1932 *Indianapolis News*

1933 *New York World-Telegram*

1934 *Medford* (Oregon) *Mail-Tribune*

1935 *Sacramento Bee*

1936 *Cedar Rapids* (Iowa) *Gazette*

1937 *St. Louis Post-Dispatch*

1938 *Bismarck* (North Dakota) *Tribune*

1939 *Miami Daily News*

1940 *Waterbury* (Connecticut) *Republican and American*

1941 *St. Louis Post-Dispatch*

1942 *Los Angeles Times*

1943 *Omaha World Herald*

1944 *New York Times*

1945 *Detroit Free Press*

1946 *Scranton* (Pennsylvania) *Times*

1947 *Baltimore Sun*

1948 *St. Louis Post-Dispatch*

1949 *Nebraska State Journal*

1950 *Chicago Daily News*; *St. Louis Post-Dispatch*

1951 *Miami Herald* and *Brooklyn Eagle*

1952 *St. Louis Post-Dispatch*

1953 *Whiteville* (North Carolina) *News Reporter*; *Tabor City* (North Carolina) *Tribune*

1954 *Newsday* (Long Island, New York)

1955 *Columbus* (Georgia) *Ledger* and *Sunday Ledger-Enquirer*

1956 *Watsonville* (California) *Register-Pajaronian*

1957 *Chicago Daily News*

1958 *Arkansas Gazette* (Little Rock, Arkansas)

1959 *Utica* (New York) *Observer-Dispatch* and *Utica Daily Press*

1960 *Los Angeles Times*

1961 *Amarillo* (Texas) *Globe-Times*

1962 *Panama City* (Florida) *News-Herald*

1963 *Chicago Daily News*

1964 *St. Petersburg* (Florida) *Times*

1965 *Hutchinson* (Kansas) *News*

1966 *Boston Globe*

1967 *Louisville Courier-Journal*; *Milwaukee Journal*

1968 *Riverside* (California) *Press-Enterprise*

1969 *Los Angeles Times*

1970 *Newsday* (Long Island, New York)

1971 *Winston Salem* (North Carolina) *Journal & Sentinel*

1972 *New York Times*

1973 *Washington Post*

1974 *Newsday* (Long Island, New York)

1975 *Boston Globe*

1976 *Anchorage Daily News*

1977 *Lufkin* (Texas) *News*

1978 *Philadelphia Inquirer*

1979 *Point Reyes* (California) *Light*

1980 Gannett News Service

1981 *Charlotte Observer*

1982 *Detroit News*

1983 *Jackson* (Mississippi) *Clarion-Ledger*

1984 *Los Angeles Times*

1985 *Ft. Worth* (Texas) *Star-Telegram*

1986 *Denver Post*

1987 *Pittsburgh Press*

1988 *Charlotte Observer*

1989 *Anchorage Daily News*

1990 *Philadelphia Inquirer*, Gilbert M. Gaul; *Washington* (North Carolina) *Daily News*

1991 *Des Moines Register*, Jane Schorer

1992 *Sacramento Bee*, Tom Knudson

1993 *Miami Herald*

1994 *Akron Beacon Journal*

1995 *The Virgin Islands Daily News* (St. Thomas)

1996 *News and Observer* (Raleigh, North Carolina)

1997 *New Orleans Times-Picayune*

1998 *Grand Forks* (North Dakota) *Herald*

1999 *Washington Post*

Reporting

Initially, reporting awards did not differentiate between local, national, and international reporting. National and international reporting later became separate categories.

1917 Herbert Bayard Swope, *New York World*

1918 Harold A. Littledale, *New York Evening Post*

1919 Not awarded

1920 John J. Leary Jr., *New York World*

1921 Louis Seibold, *New York World*

1922 Kirke L. Simpson, Associated Press

1923 Alva Johnston, *New York Times*

1924 Magner White, *San Diego Sun*

1925 James W. Mulroy and Alvin H. Goldstein, *Chicago Daily News*

1926 William Burke Miller, *Louisville Courier-Journal*

1927 John T. Rogers, *St. Louis Post-Dispatch*

1929 Paul Y. Anderson, *St. Louis Post-Dispatch*

1930 Russell D. Owens, *New York Times*

1931 A.B. MacDonald, *Kansas City* (Missouri) *Star*

1932 W.C. Richards, D.D. Martin, J.S. Pooler, F.D. Webb, and J.N.W. Sloan, *Detroit Free Press*

1933 Francis A. Jamieson, Associated Press

1934 Royce Brier, *San Francisco Chronicle*

1935 William H. Taylor, *New York Herald Tribune*

1936 Lauren D. Lyman, *New York Times*

1937 John J. O'Neill, *New York Herald Tribune*; William L. Laurence, *New York Times*; Howard W. Blakeslee, AP; Gobind Behari Lal, Universal Service; and David Dietz, Scripps-Howard Newspapers

1938 Raymond Sprigle, *Pittsburgh Post-Gazette*

1939 Thomas L. Stokes, Scripps-Howard Newspaper Alliance

1940 S. Burton Heath, *New York World-Telegram*

1941 Westbrook Pegler, *New York World-Telegram*

1942 Stanton Delaplane, *San Francisco Chronicle*

1943 George Weller, *Chicago Daily News*

1944 Paul Schoenstein, *New York Journal-American*

1945 Jack S. McDowell, *San Francisco Call-Bulletin*

1946 William L. Laurence, *New York Times*

1947 Frederick Woltman, *New York World-Telegram*

1948 George E. Goodwin, *Atlanta Journal*

1949 Malcolm Johnson, *New York Sun*

1950 Meyer Berger, *New York Times*

1951 Edward S. Montgomery, *San Francisco Examiner*

1952 George de Carvalho, *San Francisco Chronicle*

(1) General or Spot; (2) Special or Investigative

1953 (1) *Providence* (Rhode Island) *Journal and Evening Bulletin*; (2) Edward J. Mowery, *New York World-Telegram & Sun*

1954 (1) Vicksburg (Mississippi) *Sunday Post-Herald*; (2) Alvin Scott McCoy, *Kansas City* (Missouri) *Star*

1955 (1) Mrs. Caro Brown, *Alice* (Texas) *Daily Echo*; (2) Roland K. Towery, *Cuero* (Texas) *Record*

1956 (1) Lee Hills, *Detroit Free Press*; (2) Arthur Daley, *New York Times*

1957 (1) *Salt Lake Tribune* (Utah); (2) Wallace Turner and William Lambert, *Portland Oregonian*

1958 (1) *Fargo* (North Dakota) *Forum*; (2) George Beveridge, *Washington Evening Star*

1959 (1) Mary Lou Werner, *Washington Evening Star*; (2) John Harold Brislin, *Scranton* (Pennsylvania) *Tribune* and *The Scrantonian*

1960 (1) Jack Nelson, *Atlanta Constitution*; (2) Miriam Ottenberg, *Washington Evening Star*

1961 (1) Sanche de Gramont, *New York Herald Tribune*; (2) Edgar May, *Buffalo Evening News*

1962 (1) Robert D. Mullins, *Deseret News* (Utah); (2) George Bliss, *Chicago Tribune*

1963 (1) Shared by Sylvan Fox, William Longgood, and Anthony Shannon, *New York World-Telegram & Sun*; (2) Oscar Griffin Jr., *Pecos* (Texas) *Independent and Enterprise*

1964 (1) Norman C. Miller, *Wall Street Journal*; (2) Shared by James V. Magee, Albert V. Gaudiosi, and Frederick A. Meyer, *Philadelphia Bulletin*

1965 (1) Melvin H. Ruder, *Hungry Horse News* (Columbia Falls, Montana); (2) Gene Goltz, *Houston Post*

1966 (1) *Los Angeles Times* staff; (2) John A. Frasca, *Tampa Tribune*

1967 (1) Robert V. Cox, *Chambersburg* (Pennsylvania) *Public Opinion*; (2) Gene Miller, *Miami Herald*

1968 (1) *Detroit Free Press* staff; (2) J. Anthony Lukas, *New York Times*

1969 (1) John Fetterman, *Louisville Courier-Journal and Times*; (2) Shared by Albert L. Delugach, *St. Louis Globe Democrat*, and Denny Walsh, *Life*

1970 (1) Thomas Fitzpatrick, *Chicago Sun-Times*; (2) Harold Eugene Martin, *Montgomery Advertiser & Alabama Journal*

1971 (1) *Akron Beacon Journal* staff; (2) William Hugh Jones, *Chicago Tribune*

1972 (1) Richard Cooper and John Machacek, *Rochester Times-Union*; (2) Timothy Leland, Gerard M. O'Neill, Stephen A. Kurkjian, and Anne De Santis, *Boston Globe*

1973 (1) *Chicago Tribune*; (2) Sun Newspapers of Omaha

1974 (1) Hugh F. Hough, Arthur M. Petacque, *Chicago Sun Times*; (2) William Sherman, *New York Daily News*

1975 (1) *Xenia* (Ohio) *Daily Gazette*; (2) *Indianapolis Star*

1976 (1) Gene Miller, *Miami Herald*; (2) *Chicago Tribune*

1977 (1) Margo Huston, *Milwaukee Journal*; (2) Acel Moore and Wendell Rawls Jr., *Philadelphia Inquirer*

1978 (1) Richard Whitt, *Louisville Courier-Journal*; (2) Anthony R. Dolan, *Stamford* (Connecticut) *Advocate*

1979 (1) *San Diego* (California) *Evening Tribune*; (2) Gilbert M. Gaul and Elliot G. Jaspin, *Pottsville* (Pennsylvania) *Republican*

1980 (1) *Philadelphia Inquirer*; (2) Stephen A.

Kurkjian, Alexander B. Hawes Jr., Nils Bruzelius, Joan Vennochi, and Robert M. Porterfield, *Boston Globe*

1981 (1) *Longview* (Washington) *Daily News* staff; (2) Clark Hallas and Robert B. Lowe, *Arizona Daily Star*

1982 (1) *Kansas City Star* and *Kansas City Times*; (2) Paul Henderson, *Seattle Times*

1983 (1) *Fort Wayne* (Indiana) *News-Sentinel*; (2) Loretta Tofani, *Washington Post*

1984 (1) *Newsday* (New York); (2) *Boston Globe*

1985 (1) Thomas Turcol, *Virginian-Pilot and Ledger-Star* (Norfolk, Virginia); (2) Shared by William K. Marimow, *Philadelphia Inquirer*, and Lucy Morgan and Jack Reed, *St. Petersburg* (Florida) *Times*

1986 (1) Edna Buchanan, *Miami Herald*; (2) Jeffrey A. Marx and Michael M. York, *Lexington* (Kentucky) *Herald-Leader*

1987 (1) *Akron Beacon Journal*; (2) Shared by Daniel R. Biddle, H.G. Bissinger, and Fredric N. Tulsky, *Philadelphia Inquirer*, and John Woestendiek, *Philadelphia Inquirer*

1988 (1) *Alabama Journal*; *Lawrence* (Massachusetts) *Eagle-Tribune*; (2) Walt Boudanich, *Wall Street Journal*

1989 (1) *Louisville Courier-Journal*; (2) Bill Dedman, *Atlanta Journal and Constitution*

1990 (1) *San Jose Mercury News*; (2) Lon Kilzer and Chris Ison, *Star Tribune* (Minneapolis-St. Paul, Minnesota)

1991 (1) *Miami Herald*; (2) Joseph T. Hallinan and Susan M. Headden, *Indianapolis Star*

1992 (1) *Newsday* (New York); (2) Lorraine Adams and Dan Malone, *Dallas Morning News*

1993 (1) *Los Angeles Times*; (2) Jeff Brazil and Steve Berry, *Orlando Sentinel*

1994 (1) *New York Times* staff; (2) *Providence Journal-Bulletin* staff

1995 (1) *Los Angeles Times* staff; (2) Brian Donovan and Stephanie Saul, *Newsday*

1996 (1) Robert D. McFadden, *New York Times*; (2) *Orange County Register* (California)

1997 (1) *Newsday* (New York) staff; (2) Eric Nalder, Deborah Nelson and Alex Tizon, *Seattle Times*

1998 (1) *Los Angeles Times* staff; (2) Gary Cohn and Will Englund, *Baltimore Sun*

1999 (1) *Hartford Courant* staff (2) *Miami Herald* staff

Criticism or Commentary

(1) Criticism; (2) Commentary

1970 (1) Ada Louise Huxtable, *New York Times*; (2) Marquis W. Childs, *St. Louis Post-Dispatch*

1971 (1) Harold C. Schonberg, *New York Times*; (2) William A. Caldwell, *The Record* (Hackensack, New Jersey)

1972 (1) Frank Peters Jr., *St. Louis Post-Dispatch*; (2) Mike Royko, *Chicago Daily News*

1973 (1) Ronald Powers, *Chicago Sun Times*; (2) David S. Broder, *Washington Post*

1974 (1) Emily Genauer, *Newsday* (New York); (2) Edwin A. Roberts Jr., *National Observer*

1975 (1) Roger Ebert, *Chicago Sun Times*; (2) Mary McGrory, *Washington Star*

1976 (1) Alan M. Kriegsman, *Washington Post*; (2) Walter W. (Red) Smith, *New York Times*

1977 (1) William McPherson, *Washington Post*; (2) George F. Will, *Washington Post* Writers Group

1978 (1) Walter Kerr, *New York Times*; (2) William Safire, *New York Times*

1979 (1) Paul Gapp, *Chicago Tribune*; (2) Russell Baker, *New York Times*

1980 (1) William A. Henry III, *Boston Globe*; (2) Ellen Goodman, *Boston Globe*

1981 (1) Jonathan Yardley, *Washington Star*; (2) Dave Anderson, *New York Times*

1982 (1) Martin Bernheimer, *Los Angeles Times*; (2) Art Buchwald, *Los Angeles Times* Syndicate

1983 (1) Manuela Hoelterhoff, *Wall Street Journal*; (2) Claude Sitton, *Raleigh* (North Carolina) *News & Observer*

1984 (1) Paul Goldberger, *New York Times*; (2) Vermont Royster, *Wall Street Journal*

1985 (1) Howard Rosenberg, *Los Angeles Times*; (2) Murray Kempton, *Newsday* (New York)

1986 (1) Donald J. Henahan, *New York Times*; (2) Jimmy Breslin, *New York Daily News*

1987 (1) Richard Eder, *Los Angeles Times*; (2) Charles Krauthammer, *Washington Post*

1988 (1) Tom Shales, *Washington Post*; (2) Dave Barry, *Miami Herald*

1989 (1) Michael Skube, *Raleigh News and Observer* (North Carolina); (2) Clarence Page, *Chicago Tribune*

1990 (1) Allan Temko, *San Francisco Chronicle*; (2) Jim Murray, *Los Angeles Times*

1991 (1) David Shaw, *Los Angeles Times*; (2) Jim Hoagland, *Washington Post*

1992 (1) No award; (2) Anna Quindlen, *New York Times*

1993 (1) Michael Dirda, *Washington Post*; (2) Liz Balmaseda *Miami Herald*

1994 (1) Lloyd Schwartz, *Boston Phoenix*; (2) William Raspberry, *Washington Post*

1995 (1) Margo Jefferson, *New York Times*; (2) Jim Dwyer, *Newsday* (New York)

1996 (1) Robert Campbell, *Boston Globe*; (2) E. R. Shipp, *Daily News* (New York)

1997 (1) Tim Page, *Washington Post*; (2) Eileen McNamara, *Boston Globe*

1998 (1) Michiko Kakutani, *New York Times*; (2) Mike McAlary, *New York Daily News*

1999 (1) Blair Kamin, *Chicago Tribune*; (2) Maureen Dowd, *New York Times*

National Reporting

1942 Louis Stark, *New York Times*

1943 Not awarded

1944 Dewey L. Fleming, *Baltimore Sun*

1945 James B. Reston, *New York Times*

1946 Edward A. Harris, *St. Louis Post-Dispatch*

1947 Edward T. Folliard, *Washington Post*

1948 Bert Andrews, *New York Herald Tribune*; Nat S. Finney, *Minneapolis Tribune*

1949 Charles P. Trusell, *New York Times*

1950 Edwin O. Guthman, *Seattle Times*

1951 Not awarded

1952 Anthony Leviero, *New York Times*

1953 Don Whitehead, Associated Press

1954 Richard Wilson, *Des Moines Register*

1955 Anthony Lewis, *Washington Daily News*

1956 Charles L. Bartlett, *Chattanooga Times*

1957 James Reston, *New York Times*

1958 Relman Morin, Associated Press; Clark Mollenhoff, *Des Moines Register & Tribute*

1959 Howard Van Smith, *Miami News*

1960 Vance Trimble, Scripps-Howard, Washington, DC

1961 Edward R. Cony, *Wall Street Journal*

1962 Nathan G. Caldwell and Geene S. Graham, *Nashville Tennessean*

1963 Anthony Lewis, *New York Times*

1964 Merriman Smith, United Press International

1965 Louis M. Kohlmeier, *Wall Street Journal*

1966 Haynes Johnson, *Washington Evening Star*

1967 Monroe Karmin and Stanley Penn, *Wall Street Journal*

1968 Howard James, *Christian Science Monitor*; Nathan K. Kotz, *Des Moines Register*

1969 Robert Cahn, *Christian Science Monitor*

1970 William J. Eaton, *Chicago Daily News*

1971 Lucinda Franks and Thomas Powers, UPI

1972 Jack Anderson, United Feature Syndicate

1973 Robert Boyd and Clark Hoyt, Knight Newspapers

1974 James R. Polk, *Washington Star-News*; Jack White, *Providence Journal-Bulletin*

1975 Donald L. Barlett and James B. Steele, *Philadelphia Inquirer*

1976 James Risser, *Des Moines Register*

1977 Walter Mears, Associated Press

1978 Gaylord D. Shaw, *Los Angeles Times*

1979 James Risser, *Des Moines Register*

1980 Charles Stafford and Bette Swenson Orsini, *St. Petersburg Times*

1981 John M. Crewdson, *New York Times*

1982 Rick Atkinson, *Kansas City Times*

1983 Staff, *Boston Globe*

1984 John Noble Wilford, *New York Times*

1985 Thomas J. Knudson, *Des Moines Register*

1986 Craig Flournoy and George Rodrigue, *Dallas Morning News*; Arthur Howe, *Philadelphia Inquirer*

1987 *Miami Herald*; *New York Times*

1988 Tim Weiner, *Philadelphia Inquirer*

1989 Donald L. Barlett and James B. Steel, *Philadelphia Inquirer*

1990 Ross Anderson, Bill Dietrich, Mary Ann Gwinn, and Eric Nalder, *Seattle Times*

1991 Marji Lundstrom and Rochelle Sharpe, Gannett News Service

1992 Jeff Taylor and Mike McGraw, *Kansas City Star*

1993 David Maraniss, *Washington Post*

1994 Eileen Welsome, *Albuquerque Tribune*

1995 Tony Horwitz, *Wall Street Journal*

1996 Alix M. Freedman, *Wall Street Journal*

1997 *Wall Street Journal*

1998 Russell Carollo and Jeff Newsmith, *Dayton Daily News*

1999 *New York Times* staff, especially Jeff Gerth

International Reporting

1942 Laurence Edmund Allen, Associated Press

1943 Ira Wolfert, North American Newspaper Alliance

1944 Daniel DeLuce, Associated Press

1945 Mark S. Watson, *Baltimore Sun*

1946 Homer W. Bigart, *New York Herald Tribune*

1947 Eddy Gilmore, Associated Press

1948 Paul W. Ward, *Baltimore Sun*

1949 Price Day, *Baltimore Sun*

1950 Edmund Stevens, *Christian Science Monitor*

1951 Keyes Beech and Fred Sparks, *Chicago Daily News*; Homer Bigart and Marguerite Higgins, *New York Herald Tribune*; Relman Morin and Don Whitehead, Associated Press

1952 John M. Hightower, Associated Press

1953 Austin C. Wehrwein, *Milwaukee Journal*

1954 Jim G. Lucas, Scripps-Howard Newspapers

1955 Harrison Salisbury, *New York Times*

1956 William Randolph Hearst Jr. and Frank Conniff, Hearst Newspapers; Kingsbury Smith, INS

1957 Russell Jones, United Press

1958 *New York Times*

1959 Joseph Martin and Philip Santora, *New York Daily News*

1960 A.M. Rosenthal, *New York Times*

1961 Lynn Heinzerling, Associated Press

1962 Walter Lippmann, *New York Herald Tribune* Syndicate

1963 Hal Hendrix, *Miami News*

1964 Malcolm W. Browne, Associated Press; David Halberstam, *New York Times*

1965 J. A. Livingston, *Philadelphia Bulletin*

1966 Peter Arnett, Associated Press

1967 R. John Hughes, *Christian Science Monitor*

1968 Alfred Friendly, *Washington Post*

1969 William Tuohy, *Los Angeles Times*

1970 Seymour M. Hersh, Dispatch News Service

1971 Jimmie Lee Hoagland, *Washington Post*

1972 Peter R. Kann *Wall Street Journal*

1973 Max Frankel, *New York Times*

1975 William Mullen and Ovie Carter, *Chicago Tribune*

1976 Sydney H. Schanberg, *New York Times*

1977 Not awarded

1978 Henry Kamm, *New York Times*

1979 Richard Ben, *Philadelphia Inquirer*

1980 Joel Brinkley and Jay Mather, *Louisville Courier-Journal*

1981 Shirley Christian, *Miami Herald*

1982 John Darnton, *New York Times*

1983 Thomas L Friedman, *New York Times*; Loren Jenkins, *Washington Post*

1984 Karen Elliot House, *Wall Street Journal*

1985 Josh Friedman, Dennis Bell and Ozier Muhammad, *Newsday* (New York)

1986 Lewis M. Simons, Pete Carey and Katherine Ellison, *San Jose Mercury News*

1987 Michael Parks, *Los Angeles Times*

1988 Thomas L. Friedman, *New York Times*

1989 Glenn Frankel, *Washington Post*; Bill Keller, *New York Times*

1990 Nicholas D. Kirstof and Sheryl Wu Dunn, *New York Times*

1991 Caryle Murphy, *Washington Post*; Serge Schmemann, *New York Times*

1992 Patrick J. Sloyan, *Newsday* (New York)

1993 John F. Burns, *New York Times*; Roy Gutman, *Newsday* (New York)

1994 *Dallas Morning News* team

1995 Mark Fritz, Associated Press

1996 David Rohde, *Christian Science Monitor*

1997 John F. Burns

1998 *New York Times* staff

1999 *Wall Street Journal* staff

Correspondence

This category for foreign and Washington correspondents was merged with national and international reporting in 1948.

1929 Paul Scott Mowrer, *Chicago Daily News*

1930 Leland Stowe, *New York Herald Tribune*

1931 H.R. Knickerbocker, *Philadelphia Public Ledger* and *New York Evening Post*

1932 Walter Duranty, *New York Times*; Charles G. Ross, *St. Louis Post-Dispatch*

1933 Edgar Ansel Mowrer, *Chicago Daily News*

1934 Frederick T. Birchall, *New York Times*

1935 Arthur Krock, *New York Times*

1936 Wilfred C. Barber, *Chicago Tribune*

1937 Anne O'Hare McCormick, *New York Times*

1938 Arthur Krock, *New York Times*

1939 Louis P. Lochner, Associated Press

1940 Otto D. Tolischus, *New York Times*

1941 Bronze plaque to commemorate work of American correspondents on war fronts

1942 Carlos P. Romulo, *Philippines Herald*

1943 Hanson W. Baldwin, *New York Times*

1944 Ernest Taylor Pyle, Scripps-Howard Newspaper Alliance

1945 Harold V. (Hal) Boyle, Associated Press

1946 Arnaldo Cortesi, *New York Times*

1947 Brooks Atkinson, *New York Times*

Editorial Writing

1917 New York *Tribune*

1918 *Louisville* (Kentucky) *Courier-Journal*

1920 Harvey E. Newbranch, *Omaha Evening World-Herald*

1921 Not awarded

1922 Frank M. O'Brien, *New York Herald*

1923 William Allen White, *Emporia Gazette*

1924 Frank Buxton, *Boston Herald*; Special Prize: Frank I. Cobb, *New York World*

1925 Robert Lathan, *Charleston* (South Carolina) *News and Courier*

1926 Edward M. Kingsbury, *New York Times*

1927 F. Lauriston Bullard, *Boston Herald*

1928 Grover C. Hall, *Montgomery Advertiser*

1929 Louis Isaac Jaffe, *Norfolk Virginian-Pilot*

1930 Not awarded

1931 Chas. Ryckman, *Fremont* (Nebraska) *Tribune*

1932 Not awarded

1933 *Kansas City Star*

1934 E. P. Chase, *Atlantic* (Iowa) *News Telegraph*

1936 Felix Morley, *Washington Post*; George B. Parker, Scripps-Howard Newspapers

1937 John W. Owens, *Baltimore Sun*

1938 W.W. Waymack, *Des Moines Register and Tribune*

1939 Ronald G. Callvert, *Portland Oregonian*

1940 Bart Howard, *St. Louis Post-Dispatch*

1941 Reuben Maury, *New York Daily News*

1942 Geoffrey Parsons, *New York Herald Tribune*

1943 Forrest W. Seymour, *Des Moines Register and Tribune*

1944 Henry J. Haskell, *Kansas City Star*

1945 George W. Potter, *Providence* (Rhode Island) *Journal-Bulletin*

1946 Hodding Carter, *Greenville* (Mississippi) *Delta Democrat-Times*

1947 William H. Grimes, *Wall Street Journal*

1948 Virginius Dabney, *Richmond* (Virginia) *Times-Dispatch*

1949 John H. Crider, *Boston Herald*; Herbert Elliston, *Washington Post*

1950 Carl M. Saunders, *Jackson* (Mississippi) *Citizen-Patriot*

1951 William H. Fitzpatrick, *New Orleans States*

1952 Louis LaCoss, *St. Louis Globe Democrat*

1953 Vermont C. Royster, *Wall Street Journal*

1954 Don Murray, *Boston Herald*

1955 Royce Howes, *Detroit Free Press*

1956 Lauren K. Soth, *Des Moines Register and Tribune*

1957 Buford Boone, *Tuscaloosa* (Alabama) *News*

1958 Harry S. Ashmore, *Arkansas Gazette*

1959 Ralph McGill, *Atlanta Constitution*

1960 Lenoir Chambers, *Norfolk Virginian-Pilot*

1961 William J. Dorvillier, *San Juan* (Puerto Rico) *Star*

1962 Thomas M. Storke, *Santa Barbara News-Press*

1963 Ira B. Harkey Jr., *Pascagoula* (Mississippi) *Chronicle*

1964 Hazel Brannon Smith, *Lexington* (Mississippi) *Advertiser*

1965 John R. Harrison, *Gainesville* (Florida) *Sun*

1966 Robert Lasch, *St. Louis Post-Dispatch*

1967 Eugene C. Patterson, *Atlanta Constitution*

1968 John S. Knight, Knight Newspapers

1969 Paul Greenberg, *Pine Bluff* (Arkansas) *Commercial*

1970 Philip L. Geyelin, *Washington Post*

1971 Horance G. Davis Jr., *Gainesville* (Florida) *Sun*

1972 John Strohmeyer, *Bethlehem* (Pennsylvania) *Globe-Times*

1973 Roger B. Linscott, *Berkshire Eagle* (Pittsfield, Massachusetts)

1974 F. Gilman Spencer, *Trenton* (New Jersey) *Trentonian*

1975 John D. Maurice, *Charleston* (West Virginia) *Daily Mail*

1976 Philip Kerby, *Los Angeles Times*

1977 Warren L. Lerude, Foster Church, and Norman F. Cardoza, *Reno* (Nevada) *Evening Gazette* and *Nevada State Journal*

1978 Meg Greenfield, *Washington Post*

1979 Edwin M. Yoder, *Washington Star*

1980 Robert L. Bartley, *Wall Street Journal*

1981 Not awarded

1982 Jack Rosenthal, *New York Times*

1983 Editorial board, *Miami Herald*

1984 Albert Scardino, *Georgia Gazette*

1985 Richard Aregood, *Philadelphia Daily News*

1986 Jack Fuller, *Chicago Tribune*

1987 Jonathan Freedman, *Tribune* (San Diego)

1988 Jane Healy, *Orlando Sentinel*

1989 Lois Wille, *Chicago Tribune*

1990 Thomas J. Hylton, *Pottstown* (Pennsylvania) *Mercury*

1991 Ron Casey, Harold Jackson, and Joey Kennedy, *Birmingham News*

1992 Mana Henson, *Lexington* (Kentucky) *Herald-Leader*

1993 Not awarded

1994 R. Bruce Dold, *Chicago Tribune*

1995 Jeffrey Good, *St. Petersburg Times*

1996 Robert B. Semple Jr., *New York Times*

1997 Michael G. Gartner, *Daily Tribune* (Ames, Iowa)

1998 Bernard L. Stein, *Riverdale* (New York) *Times*

1999 Editorial board, *New York Daily News*

Editorial Cartooning

1922 Rollin Kirby, *New York World*

1923 Not awarded

1924 Jay N. Darling, *Des Moines Register*

1925 Rollin Kirby, *New York World*

1926 D. R. Fitzpatrick, *St. Louis Post-Dispatch*

1927 Nelson Harding, *Brooklyn Eagle*

1928 Nelson Harding, *Brooklyn Eagle*

1929 Rollin Kirby, *New York World*

1930 Charles Macauley, *Brooklyn Eagle*

1931 Edmund Duffy, *Baltimore Sun*

1932 John T. McCutcheon, *Chicago Tribune*

1933 H. M. Talburt, *Washington Daily News*

1934 Edmund Duffy, *Baltimore Sun*

1935 Ross A. Lewis, *Milwaukee Journal*

1937 C. D. Batchelor, *New York Daily News*

1938 Vaughn Shoemaker Chicaqo *Daily News*

1939 Charles G. Werner, *Daily Oklahoman*

1940 Edmund Duffy, *Baltimore Sun*

1941 Jacob Burck, *Chicago Times*

1942 Herbert L. Block, Newspaper Enterprise Association

1943 Jay N. Darling, *Des Moines Register*

1944 Clifford K. Berryman, *Washington Star*

1945 Bill Mauldin, United Feature Syndicate

1946 Bruce Alexander Russell, *Los Angeles Times*

1947 Vaughn Shoemaker, *Chicago Daily News*

1948 Reuben L. (Rube) Goldberg, *New York Sun*

1949 Lute Pease, *Newark* (New Jersey) *Evening News*

1950 James T. Berryman, *Washington Star*

1951 Reginald W. Manning, *Arizona Republic*

1952 Fred L. Packer, *New York Mirror*

1953 Edward D. Kuekes, *Cleveland Plain Dealer*

1954 Herbert L. Block, *Washington Post & Times-Herald*

1955 Daniel R. Fitzpatrick, *St. Louis Post-Dispatch*

1956 Robert York, *Louisville Times*

1957 Tom Little, *Nashville Tennessean*

1958 Bruce M. Shanks, *Buffalo Evening News*

1959 Bill Mauldin, *St. Louis Post-Dispatch*

1961 Carey Orr, *Chicago Tribune*

1962 Edmund S. Valtman, *Hartford Times*

1963 Frank Miller, *Des Moines Register*

1964 Paul Conrad, *Denver Post*

1965 Not awarded

1966 Don Wright, *Miami News*

1967 Patrick B. Oliphant, *Denver Post*

1968 Eugene Gray Payne, *Charlotte Observer*

1969 John Fischetti, *Chicago Daily News*

1970 Thomas F. Darcy, *Newsday* (New York)

1971 Paul Conrad, *Los Angeles Times*

1972 Jeffrey K. MacNelly, *Richmond News-Leader*

1973 Not awarded

1974 Paul Szep, *Boston Globe*

1975 Garry Trudeau, Universal Press Syndicate

1976 Tony Auth, *Philadelphia Inquirer*

1977 Paul Szep, *Boston Globe*

1978 Jeffrey K. MacNelly, *Richmond News Leader*

1979 Herbert L. Block, *Washington Post*

1980 Don Wright, *Miami News*

1981 Mike Peters, *Dayton* (Ohio) *Daily News*

1982 Ben Sargent, *Austin American-Statesman*

1983 Richard Lochner, *Chicago Tribune*

1984 Paul Conrad, *Los Angeles Times*

1985 Jeffrey K. MacNelly, *Chicago Tribune*	**1948** Frank Cushing, *Boston Traveler*
1986 Jules Feiffer, *Village Voice* (New York)	**1949** Nathaniel Fein, *New York Herald Tribune*
1987 Berke Breathed, *Washington Post*	**1950** Bill Crouch, *Oakland Tribune*
1988 Doug Marlette, *Atlanta Constitution, Charlotte Observer*	**1951** Max Desfor, Associated Press
1989 Jack Higgins, *Chicago Sun Times*	**1952** John Robinson and Don Ultang, *Des Moines Register* and *Tribune*
1990 Tom Toles, *Buffalo News*	**1953** William M. Gallagher, *Flint* (Michigan) *Journal*
1991 Jim Borgman, *Cincinnati Enquirer*	**1954** Mrs. Walter M. Schau, amateur
1992 Signe Wilkinson, *Philadelphia Daily News*	**1955** John L. Gaunt Jr., *Los Angeles Times*
1993 Stephen R. Benson, *Arizona Republic*	**1956** *New York Daily News*
1994 Michael P. Ramirez, *Commercial Appeal* (Memphis, Tennessee)	**1957** Harry A. Trask, *Boston Traveler*
1995 Mike Luckovich, *Atlanta Constitution*	**1958** William C. Beall, *Washington Daily News*
1996 Jim Morin, *Miami Herald*	**1959** William Seaman, *Minneapolis Star*
1997 Walt Handelsman, *New Orleans Times-Picayune*	**1960** Andrew Lopez, UPI
1998 Stephen P. Breen, *Asbury Park Press* (Neptune, New Jersey)	**1961** Yasushi Nagao, *Mainichi Newspapers* (Tokyo)
1999 David Horsey, *Seattle Post-Intelligence*	**1962** Paul Vathis, Associated Press
	1963 Hector Rondon, *La Republica* (Caracas, Venezuela)

Spot News Photography

1942 Milton Brooks, *Detroit News*	**1964** Robert H. Jackson, *Dallas Times-Herald*
1943 Frank Noel, Associated Press	**1965** Horst Faas, Associated Press
1944 Frank Filan, Associated Press; Earl L. Bunker, *Omaha World-Herald*	**1966** Kyoichi Sawada, United Press International
1945 Joe Rosenthal, Associated Press	**1967** Jack R. Thornell, Associated Press
1946 Not awarded	**1968** Rocco Morabito, *Jacksonville Journal*
1947 Arnold Hardy, amateur, Atlanta, Georgia	**1969** Edward Adams, Associated Press
	1970 Steve Starr, Associated Press

1971 John Paul Filo, *Valley Daily News & Daily Dispatch* (Tarentum and New Kensington, Pennsylvania)

1972 Horst Faas and Michel Laurent, Associated Press

1973 Huynh Cong Ut, Associated Press

1974 Anthony K. Roberts, Associated Press

1975 Gerald H. Gay, *Seattle Times*

1976 Stanley Forman, *Boston Herald American*

1977 Neal Ulevich, Associated Press; Stanley Forman, *Boston Herald American*

1978 John H. Blair, United Press International

1979 Thomas J. Kelly III, *Pottstown* (Pennsylvania) *Mercury*

1980 United Press International

1981 Larry C. Price, *Ft. Worth Star-Telegram*

1982 Ron Edmonds, Associated Press

1983 Bill Foley, Associated Press

1984 Stan Grossfeld, *Boston Globe*

1985 *The Register* (Santa Ana, California)

1986 Carol Guzy and Michel duCille, *Miami Herald*

1987 Kim Komenich, *San Francisco Examiner*

1988 Scott Shaw, *Odessa* (Texas) *American*

1989 Ron Olshwanger, *St. Louis Post-Dispatch*

1990 *Oakland Tribune* photo staff

1991 Greg Mannovich, Associated Press

1992 Associated Press staff

1993 Ken Geiger and William Snyder, *Dallas Morning News*

1994 Paul Watson, *Toronto Star*

1995 Carol Guzy, *Washington Post*

1996 Charles Porter IV, freelancer

1997 Annie Wells, *Santa Rosa* (California) *Press Democrat*

1998 Martha Rial, *Pittsburgh Post-Gazette*

1999 Associated Press

Feature Photography

1968 Toshio Sakai, UPI

1969 Moneta Sleet Jr., *Ebony*

1970 Dallas Kinney, *Palm Beach Post*

1971 Jack Dykinga, *Chicago Sun-Times*

1972 Dave Kennerly, UPI

1973 Brian Lanker, *Topeka Capitol-Journal*

1974 Slava Veder, Associated Press

1975 Matthew Lewis, *Washington Post*

1976 *Louisville Courier-Journal* and *Louisville Times*

1977 Robin Hood, *Chattanooga News-Free Press*

1978 Ross Baughman, Associated Press

1979 Staff photographers, *Boston Herald American*

1980 Erwin H. Hagler, *Dallas Times-Herald*

1981 Taro M. Yamasaki, *Detroit Free Press*

1982 John H. White, *Chicago Sun Times*

1983 James B. Dickman, *Dallas Times-Herald*

1984 Anthony Suad, *Denver Post*

1985 Stan Grossfeld, *Boston Globe*; Larry C. Price, *Philadelphia Inquirer*

1986 Tom Gralish, *Philadelphia Inquirer*

1987 David Peterson, *Des Moines Register*

1988 Michel duCille, *Miami Herald*

1989 Manny Crisostomo, *Detroit Free Press*

1990 David C. Turnley, *Detroit Free Press*

1991 William Snyder, *Dallas Morning News*

1992 John Kaplan, Block Newspapers (*Herald*, Monterey, California, and *Pittsburgh Post*)

1993 Associated Press staff

1994 Kevin Carter, *New York Times*

1995 Associated Press staff

1996 Stephanie Welsh, freelancer

1997 Alexander Zemlianichenko, AP

1998 Clarence Williams, *Los Angeles Times*

1999 Associated Press

Special Citation

1930 William O. Dapping, *Auburn* (New York) *Citizen*

1938 *Edmonton* (Alberta, Canada) *Journal*, bronze plaque

1941 *New York Times*

1944 Byron Price and Mrs. William Allen White

1945 Press cartographers for war maps

1947 Columbia University and the Graduate School of Journalism, and *St. Louis Post-Dispatch*

1948 Dr. Frank Diehl Fackenthal

1951 Cyrus L. Sulzberger, *New York Times*

1952 Max Kase, *New York Journal-American, Kansas City Star*

1953 Lester Markel, *New York Times*

1958 Walter Lippmann, *New York Herald Tribune*

1964 Gannett Newspapers

1973 James T. Flexner (for biography of George Washington)

1976 John Hohenberg (for services to American journalism)

1978 Richard Lee Strout, *Christian Science Monitor* and *New Repubic*

1987 Joseph Pulitzer Jr.

1996 Herb Caen, *San Francisco Chronicle*

Feature Writing

1979 Jon D. Franklin, *Baltimore Evening Sun*

1980 Madeleine Blais, *Miami Herald Tropic Magazine*; Janet Cooke, *Washington Post*

1981 Teresa Carpenter, *Village Voice* (New York)

1982 Saul Pett, Associated Press

1984 Peter M. Rinearson, *Seattle Times*

1985 Alice Steinbach, *Baltimore Sun*

1986 John Camp, *St. Paul Pioneer Press & Dispatch*

1987 Steve Twomey, *Philadelphia Inquirer*

1988 Jacqui Banaszynski, *St. Paul Pioneer Press Dispatch*

1989 David Zucchino, *Philadelphia Inquirer*

1990 Dave Curtin, *Colorado Springs Gazette Telegraph*

1991 Sheryl James, *St. Petersburg Times*

1992 Howell Raines, *New York Times*

1993 George Lardner Jr., *Washington Post*

1994 Isabel Wilkerson, *New York Times*

1995 Ron Suskind, *Wall Street Journal*

1996 Rick Bragg, *New York Times*

1997 Lisa Pollak, *Baltimore Sun*

1998 Clarence Williams, *Los Angeles Times*

1999 Associated Press

Explanatory Journalism

1985 Jon Franklin, *Baltimore Evening Sun*

1986 *New York Times* staff

1987 Jeff Lyon and Peter Gorner, *Chicago Tribune*

1988 Daniel Hertzberg and James B. Stewart, *Wall Street Journal*

1989 David Hanners, William Snyder and Karen Blessen, *Dallas Morning News*

1990 David A. Vise and Steve Coll, *Washington Post*

1991 Susan C. Faludi, *Wall Street Journal*

1992 Robert S. Capers and Eric Lipton, *Hartford* (Connecticut) *Courant*

1993 Mike Toner, *Atlanta Journal-Constitution*

1994 Ronald Kotulak, *Chicago Tribune*

1995 Leon Dash and Lucian Perkins, *Washington Post*

1996 Laurie Garrett, *Newsday* (New York)

1997 Michael Vitez, Ron Cortes, and April Saul, *Philadelphia Inquirer*

1998 Paul Salopek, *Chicago Tribune*

1999 Richard Read, *Oregonian* (Portland, Oregon)

Specialized Reporting (1985–1990) (discontinued category)

1985 Randall Savage, Jackie Crosby, *Macon* (Georgia) *Telegraph and News*

1986 Andrew Schneider and Mary Pat Flaherty, *Pittsburgh Press*

1987 Alex S. Jones, *New York Times*

1988 Walt Bogdanich, *Wall Street Journal*

1989 Edward Humes, *Orange County* (California) *Register*

1990 Tamar Stieber, *Albuquerque Journal*

Beat Reporting

1991 Natalie Angier, *New York Times*

1992 Deborah Blum, *Sacramento Bee*

1993 Paul Ingrassia and Joseph B. White, *Wall Street Journal*

1994 Eric Freedman and Jim Mitzelfeld, *Detroit News*

1995 David Shribman, *Boston Globe*

1996 Bob Keeler, *Newsday* (New York)

1997 Byron Acohido, *Seattle Times*

1998 Linda Greenhouse, *New York Times*

1999 Chuck Philips and Michael A. Hiltzik, *Los Angeles Times*

Letters

FICTION

1917 Not awarded

1918 Ernest Poole, *His Family*

1919 Booth Tarkington, *The Magnificent Ambersons*

1920 Not awarded

1921 Edith Wharton, *The Age of Innocence*

1922 Booth Tarkington, *Alice Adams*

1923 Willa Cather, *One of Ours*

1924 Margaret Wilson, *The Able McLaughlins*

1925 Edna Ferber, *So Big*

1926 Sinclair Lewis, *Arrowsmith* (prize refused)

1927 Louis Bromfield, *Early Autumn*

1928 Thornton Wilder, *Bridge of San Luis Rey*

1929 Julia M. Peterkin, *Scarlet Sister Mary*

1930 Oliver LaFarge, *Laughing Boy*

1931 Margaret Ayer Barnes, *Years of Grace*

1932 Pearl S. Buck, *The Good Earth*

1933 T. S. Stribling, *The Store*

1934 Caroline Miller, *Lamb in His Bosom*

1935 Josephine W. Johnson, *Now in November*

1936 Harold L. Davis, *Honey in the Horn*

1937 Margaret Mitchell, *Gone With the Wind*

1938 John P. Marquand, *The Late George Apley*

1939 Marjorie Kinnan Rawlings, *The Yearling*

1940 John Steinbeck, *The Grapes of Wrath*

1941 Not awarded

1942 Ellen Glasgow, *In This Our Life*

1943: Upton Sinclair, *Dragon's Teeth*

1944 Martin Flavin, *Journey in the Dark*

1945 John Hersey, *A Bell for Adano*

1946 Not awarded

1947 Robert Penn Warren, *All the King's Men*

1948 James A. Michener, *Tales of the South Pacific*

1949 James Gould Cozzens, *Guard of Honor*

1950 A. B. Guthrie Jr., *The Way West*

1951 Conrad Richter, *The Town*

1952 Herman Wouk, *The Caine Mutiny*

1953 Ernest Hemingway, *The Old Man and the Sea*

1954 Not awarded

1955 William Faulkner, *A Fable*

1956 MacKinlay Kantor, *Andersonville*

1957 Not awarded

1958 James Agee, *A Death in the Family*

1959 Robert Lewis Taylor, *The Travels of Jaimie McPheeters*

1960	Allen Drury, *Advise and Consent*	**1985**	Alison Lurie, *Foreign Affairs*
1961	Harper Lee, *To Kill a Mockingbird*	**1986**	Larry McMurtry, *Lonesome Dove*
1962	Edwin O'Connor, *The Edge of Sadness*	**1987**	Peter Taylor, *A Summons to Memphis*
1963	William Faulkner, *The Reivers*	**1988**	Toni Morrison, *Beloved*
1964	Not awarded	**1989**	Anne Tyler, *Breathing Lessons*
1965	Shirley Ann Grau, *The Keepers of the House*	**1990**	Oscar Hijuelos, *The Mambo Kings Play Songs of Love*
1966	Katherine Anne Porter, *Collected Stories of Katherine Anne Porter*	**1991**	John Updike, *Rabbit at Rest*
1967	Bernard Malamud, *The Fixer*	**1992**	Jane Smiley, *A Thousand Acres*
1968	William Styron, *The Confessions of Nat Turner*	**1993**	Robert Olen Butler, *A Good Scent From a Strange Mountain*
1969	N. Scott Momaday, *House Made of Dawn*	**1994**	E. Annie Proulx, *The Shipping News*
1970	Jean Stafford, *Collected Stories*	**1995**	Carol Shields, *The Stone Diaries*
1971	Not awarded	**1996**	Richard Ford, *Independence Day*
1972	Wallace Stegner, *Angle of Repose*	**1997**	Steven Millhauser, *Martin Dressler: The Tale of an American Dreamer*
1973	Eudora Welty, *The Optimist's Daughter*	**1998**	Philip Roth, *American Pastoral*
1974	Not awarded	**1999**	Michael Cunningham, *The Hours*
1975	Michael Shaara, *The Killer Angels*		
1976	Saul Bellow, *Humboldt's Gift*		

Drama

1977	Not awarded
1978	James Alan McPherson, *Elbow Room*
1979	John Cheever, *The Stories of John Cheever*
1980	Norman Mailer, *The Executioner's Song*
1981	John Kennedy Toole, *A Confederacy of Dunces*
1982	John Updike, *Rabbit Is Rich*
1983	Alice Walker, *The Color Purple*
1984	William Kennedy, *Ironweed*

1918	Jesse Lynch Williams, *Why Marry?*
1919	Not awarded
1920	Eugene o'Neill, *Beyond the Horizon*
1921	Zona Gale, *Miss Lulu Bett*
1922	Eugene O'Neill, *Anna Christie*
1923	Owen Davis, *Icebound*
1924	Hatcher Hughes, *Hell-Bent for Heaven*

1925 Sidney Howard, *They Knew What They Wanted*

1926 George Kelly, *Craig's Wife*

1927 Paul Green, *In Abraham's Bosom*

1928 Eugene O'Neill, *Strange Interlude*

1929 Elmer Rice, *Street Scene*

1930 Marc Connelly, *The Green Pastures*

1931 Susan Glaspell, *Alison's House*

1932 George S. Kaufman, Morrie Ryskind, and Ira Gershwin, *Of Thee I Sing*

1933 Maxwell Anderson, *Both Your Houses*

1934 Sidney Kingsley, *Men in White*

1935 Zoe Akins, *The Old Maid*

1936 Robert E. Sherwood, *Idiot's Delight*

1937 George S. Kaufman and Moss Hart, *You Can't Take It With You*

1938 Thornton Wilder, *Our Town*

1939 Robert E. Sherwood, *Abe Lincoln in Illinois*

1940 William Saroyan, *The Time of Your Life* (award declined)

1941 Robert E. Sherwood, *There Shall Be No Night*

1942 Not awarded

1943 Thornton Wilder, *The Skin of Our Teeth*

1944 Not awarded

1945 Mary Chase, *Harvey*

1946 Russel Crouse and Howard Lindsay, *State of the Union*

1947 Not awarded

1948 Tennessee Williams, *A Streetcar Named Desire*

1949 Arthur Miller, *Death of a Salesman*

1950 Richard Rodgers, Oscar Hammerstein II, and Joshua Logan, *South Pacific*

1951 Not awarded

1952 Joseph Kramm, *The Shrike*

1953 William Inge, *Picnic*

1954 John Patrick, *Teahouse of the August Moon*

1955 Tennessee Williams, *Cat on a Hot Tin Roof*

1956 Frances Goodrich and Albert Hackett, *The Diary of Anne Frank*

1957 Eugene O'Neill, *Long Day's Journey Into Night*

1958 Ketti Frings, *Look Homeward, Angel*

1959 Archibald MacLeish, *J. B.*

1960 George Abbott, Jerome Weidman, Sheldon Harnick, and Jerry Bock, *Fiorello*

1961 Tad Mosel, *All the Way Home*

1962 Frank Loesser and Abe Burrows, *How to Succeed in Business Without Really Trying*

1963 Not awarded

1964 Not awarded

1965 Frank D. Gilroy, *The Subject Was Roses*

1966 Not awarded

1967 Edward Albee, *A Delicate Balance*

1969 Howard Sackler, *The Great White Hope*

1970 Charles Gordone, *No Place to Be Somebody*

1971 Paul Zindel, *The Effect of Gamma Rays on Man-in-the-Moon Marigolds*

1972 Not awarded

1973 Jason Miller, *That Championship Season*

1974 Not awarded

1975 Edward Albee, *Seascape*

1976 Michael Bennett, James Kirkwood, Nicholas Dante, Marvin Hamlisch, and Edward Kleban, *A Chorus Line*

1977 Michael Cristofer, *The Shadow Box*

1978 Donald L. Coburn, *The Gin Game*

1979 Sam Shepard, *Buried Child*

1980 Lanford Wilson, *Talley's Folly*

1981 Beth Henley, *Crimes of the Heart*

1982 Charles Fuller, *A Soldier's Play*

1983 Marsha Norman, *'night, Mother*

1984 David Mamet, *Glengarry Glen Ross*

1985 Stephen Sondheim and James Lapine, *Sunday in the Park With George*

1986 Not awarded

1987 August Wilson, *Fences*

1988 Alfred Uhry, *Driving Miss Daisy*

1989 Wendy Wasserstein, *The Heidi Chronicles*

1990 August Wilson, *The Piano Lesson*

1991 Neil Simon, *Lost in Yonkers*

1992 Robert Schenkkan, *The Kentucky Cycle*

1993 Tony Kushner, *Angels in America: Millennium Approaches*

1994 Edward Albee, *Three Tall Women*

1995 Horton Foote, *The Young Man From Atlanta*

1996 Jonathan Larson, *Rent*

1997 Not awarded

1998 Paula Vogel, *How I Learned to Drive*

1999 Margaret Edson, *Wit*

History

1917 J. J. Jusserand, *With Americans of Past and Present Days*

1918 James Ford Rhodes, *History of the Civil War*

1919 Not awarded

1920 Justin H. Smith, *The War With Mexico*

1921 William Sowden Sims, *The Victory at Sea*

1922 James Truslow Adams, *The Founding of New England*

1923 Charles Warren, *The Supreme Court in United States History*

1924 Charles Howard McIlwain, *The American Revolution: A Constitutional Interpretation*

1925 Frederick L. Paxton, *A History of the American Frontier*

1926 Edward Channing, *A History of the U.S.*

1927 Samuel Flagg Bemis, *Pinckney's Treaty*

1928 Vernon Louis Parrington, *Main Currents in American Thought*

1929 Fred A. Shannon, *The Organization and Administration of the Union Army, 1861–65*

1930 Claude H. Van Tyne, *The War of Independence*

1931 Bernadette E. Schmitt, *The Coming of the War, 1914*

1932 General John J. Pershing, *My Experiences in the World War*

1933 Frederick J. Turner, *The Significance of Sections in American History*

1934 Herbert Agar, *The People's Choice*

1935 Charles McLean Andrews, *The Colonial Period of American History*

1936 Andrew C. McLaughlin, *The Constitutional History of the United States*

1937 Van Wyck Brooks, *The Flowering of New England*

1938 Paul Herman Buck, *The Road to Reunion 1865–1900*

1939 Frank Luther Mott, *A History of American Magazines*

1940 Carl Sandburg, *Abraham Lincoln: The War Years*

1941 Marcus Lee Hansen, *The Atlantic Migration, 1607–1860*

1942 Margaret Leech, *Reveille in Washington*

1943 Esther Forbes, *Paul Revere and the World He Lived In*

1944 Merle Curti, *The Growth of American Thought*

1945 Stephen Bonsai, *Unfinished Business*

1946 Arthur M. Schlesinger Jr., *The Age of Jackson*

1947 James Phinney Baxter III, *Scientists Against Time*

1948 Bernard De Voto, *Across the Wide Missouri*

1949 Roy F. Nichols, *The Disruption of American Democracy*

1950 O. W. Larkin, *Art and Life in America*

1951 R. Carlyle Buley, *The Old Northwest: Pioneer Period, 1815–1840*

1952 Oscar Handlin, *The Uprooted*

1953 George Dangerfield, *The Era of Good Feelings*

1954 Bruce Catton, *A Stillness at Appomattox*

1955 Paul Horgan, *Great River: The Rio Grande in North American History*

1956 Richard Hofstadter, *The Age of Reform*

1957 George F. Kennan, *Russia Leaves the War*

1958 Bray Hammond, *Banks and Politics in America—From the Revolution to the Civil War*

1959 Leonard D. White and Jean Schneider, *The Republican Era: 1869–1901*

1960 Margaret Leech, *In the Days of McKinley*

1961 Herbert Feis, *Between War and Peace: The Potsdam Conference*

1962 Lawrence H. Gibson, *The Triumphant Empire: Thunderclouds Gather in the West*

1963 Constance McLaughlin Green, *Washington: Village and Capital, 1800–1878*

1964 Sumner Chilton Powell, *Puritan Village: The Formation of a New England Town*

1965 Irwin Unger, *The Greenback Era*

1966 Perry Miller, *Life of the Mind in America*

1967 William H. Goetzmann, *Exploration and Empire: The Explorer and Scientist in the Winning of the American West*

1968 Bernard Bailyn, *The Ideological Origins of the American Revolution*

1969 Leonard W. Levy, *Origin of the Fifth Amendment*

1970 Dean Acheson, *Present at the Creation: My Years in the State Department*

1971 James McGregor Burns, *Roosevelt: The Soldier of Freedom*

1972 Carl N. Degler, *Neither Black nor White*

1973 Michael Kammen, *People of Paradox: An Inquiry Concerning the Origins of American Civilization*

1974 Daniel J. Boorstin, *The Americans: The Democratic Experience*

1975 Dumas Malone, *Jefferson and His Time*

1976 Paul Horgan, *Lamy of Santa Fe*

1977 David M. Potter, *The Impending Crisis*

1978 Alfred D. Chandler Jr., *The Visible Hand: The Managerial Revolution in American Business*

1979 Don E. Fehrenbacher, *The Dred Scott Case: Its Significance in American Law and Politics*

1980 Leon F. Litwack, *Been in the Storm So Long*

1981 Lawrence A. Cremin, *American Education: The National Experience, 1783–1876*

1982 C. Vann Woodward, ed., *Mary Chestnut's Civil War*

1983 Rhys L. Issac, *The Transformation of Virginia, 1740–1790*

1984 Not awarded

1985 Thomas K. McCraw, *Prophets of Regulation*

1986 Walter A. McDougall, *. . . The Heavens and the Earth*

1987 Bernard Bailyn, *Voyagers to the West*

1988 Robert V. Bruce, *The Launching of Modern American Science, 1846–1876*

1989 Taylor Branch, *Parting the Waters: America in the King Years, 1954–63; and James M. McPherson, Battle Cry of Freedom: The Civil War Era*

1990 Stanley Karnow, *In Our Image: America's Empire in the Philippines*

1991 Laurel Thatcher Ulrich, *A Midwife's Tale: The Life of Martha Ballard, Based On Her Diary, 1785–1812*

1992 Mark E. Neely Jr., *The Fate of Liberty: Abraham Lincoln and Civil Liberties*

1993 Gordon S. Wood, *The Radicalism of the American Revolution*

1994 Not awarded

1995 Doris Kearns Goodwin, *No Ordinary Time: Franklin and Eleanor Roosevelt: The Home Front in World War II*

1996 Alan Taylor, *William Cooper's Town: Power and Persuasion on the Frontier of the Early American Republic*

1997 Jack N. Rakove, *Original Meanings: Politics & Ideas in the Making of the Constitution*

1998 Edward J. Larson, *Summer for the Gods: The Scopes Trial and America's Continuing Debate Over Science and Religion*

1999 Mike Wallace and Edwin G. Burrows, *Gotham: A History of New York to 1898*

Biography or Autobiography

For distinguished biography or autobiography by an American author.

1917 Laura E. Richards and Maude Howe Elliott, assisted by Florence Howe Hall, *Julia Ward Howe*

1918 William Cabell Bruce, *Benjamin Franklin, Self-Revealed*

1919 Henry Adams, *The Education of Henry Adams*

1920 Albert J. Beveridge, *The Life of John Marshall*

1921 Edward Bok, *The Americanization of Edward Bok*

1922 Hamlin Garland, *A Daughter of the Middle Border*

1923 Burton J. Hendrick, *The Life and Letters of Walter H. Page*

1924 Michael Pupin, *From Immigrant to Inventor*

1925 M. A. DeWolfe Howe, *Barrett Wendell and His Letters*

1926 Harvey Cushing, *Life of Sir William Osler*

1927 Emory Holloway, *Whitman: An Interpretation in Narrative*

1928 Charles Edward Russell, *The American Orchestra and Theodore Thomas*

1929 Burton J. Hendrick, *The Training of an American: The Earlier Life and Letters of Walter H. Page*

1930 Marquis James, *The Raven* (Sam Houston)

1931 Henry James, *Charles W. Eliot*

1932 Henry F. Pringle, *Theodore Roosevelt*

1933 Allan Nevins, *Grover Cleveland*

1934 Tyler Dennett, *John Hay*

1935 Douglas Southall Freeman, *R. E. Lee*

1936 Ralph Barton Perry, *The Thought and Character of William James*

1937 Allan Nevins, *Hamilton Fish: The Inner History of the Grant Administration*

1938 Odell Shepard, *Pedlar's Progress*; and Marquis James, *Andrew Jackson*

1939 Carl Van Doren, *Benjamin Franklin*

1940 Ray Stannard Baker, *Woodrow Wilson, Life and Letters*

1941 Ola Elizabeth Winslow, *Jonathan Edwards*

1942 Forrest Wilson, *Crusader in Crinoline*

1943 Samuel Eliot Morison, *Admiral of the Ocean Sea* (Columbus)

1944 Carleton Mabee, *The American Leonardo: The Life of Samuel F. B. Morse*

1945 Russell Blaine Nye, *George Bancroft; Brahmin Rebel*

1946 Linny Marsh Wolfe, *Son of the Wilderness*

1947 William Allen White, *The Autobiography of William Allen White*

1948 Margaret Clapp, *Forgotten First Citizen: John Bigelow*

1949 Robert E. Sherwood, *Roosevelt and Hopkins*

1950 Samuel Flagg Bemis, *John Quincy Adams and the Foundations of American Foreign Policy*

1951 Margaret Louise Colt, *John C. Calhoun: American Portrait*

1952 Merlo J. Pusey, *Charles Evans Hughes*

1953 David J. Mays, *Edmund Pendleton, 1721–1803*

1954 Charles A. Lindbergh, *The Spirit of St. Louis*

1955 William S. White, *The Taft Story*

1956 Talbot F. Hamlin, *Benjamin Henry Latrobe*

1957 John F. Kennedy, *Profiles in Courage*

1958 Douglas Southall Freeman (died 1953), *George Washington, Vols. I–VI; John Alexander Carroll and Mary Wells Ashworth, Vol. VII*

1959 Arthur Walworth, *Woodrow Wilson: American Prophet*

1960 Samuel Eliot Morison, *John Paul Jones*

1961 David Donald, *Charles Sumner and the Coming of the Civil War*

1962 Not awarded

1963 Leon Edel, *Henry James: Vol. II, The Conquest of London, 1870–1881; Vol. III, The Middle Years, 1881–1895*

1964 Walter Jackson Bate, *John Keats*

1965 Ernest Samuels, *Henry Adams*

1966 Arthur M. Schlesinger Jr., *A Thousand Days*

1967 Justin Kaplan, *Mr. Clemens and Mark Twain*

1968 George F. Kennan, *Memoirs (1925–1950)*

1969 B. L. Reid, *The Man From New York: John Quinn and His Friends*

1970 T. Harry Williams, *Huey Long*

1971 Lawrence Thompson, *Robert Frost: The Years of Triumph, 1915–1938*

1972 Joseph P. Lash, *Eleanor and Franklin*

1973 W. A. Swanberg, *Luce and His Empire*

1974 Louis Sheaffer, *O'Neill, Son and Artist*

1975 Robert A. Caro, *The Power Broker: Robert Moses and the Fall of New York*

1976 R.W.B. Lewis, *Edith Wharton: A Biography*

1977 John E. Mack, *A Prince of Our Disorder: The Life of T.E. Lawrence*

1978 Walter Jackson Bate, *Samuel Johnson*

1979 Leonard Baker, *Days of Sorrow and Pain: Leo Baeck and the Berlin Jews*

1980 Edmund Morris, *The Rise of Theodore Roosevelt*

1981 Robert K. Massie, *Peter the Great: His Life and World*

1982 William S. McFeely, *Grant: A Biography*

1983 Russell Baker, *Growing Up*

1984 Louis R. Harlan, *Booker T. Washington*

1985 Kenneth Silverman, *The Life and Times of Cotton Mather*

1986 Elizabeth Frank, *Louise Bogan: A Portrait*

1987 David J. Garrow, *Bearing the Cross: Martin Luther King Jr. and the Southern Christian Leadership Conference*

1988 David Herbert Donald, *Look Homeward: A Life of Thomas Wolfe*

1989 Richard Ellmann, *Oscar Wilde*

1990 Sebastian de Grazia, *Machiavelli in Hell*

1991 Steven Naifeh and Gregory White Smith, *Jackson Pollock: An American Saga*

1992 Lewis B. Puller Jr., *Fortunate Son: The Healing of a Vietnam Vet*

1993 David McCullough, *Truman*

1994 David Levering Lewis, *W.E.B. DuBois: Biography of a Race, 1868–1919*

1995 Joan D. Hedrick, *Harriet Beecher Stowe: A Life*

1996 Jack Miles, *God: A Biography*

1997 Frank McCourt, *Angela's Ashes*

1998 Katharine Graham, *Personal History*

1999 A. Scott Berg, *Lindbergh*

American Poetry

1918 Sara Teasdale, *Love Songs*

1919 Margaret Widemer, *Old Road to Paradise;* Carl Sandburg, *Corn Huskers*

1921 Not awarded

1922 Edwin Arlington Robinson, *Collected Poems*

1923 Edna St. Vincent Millay, *The Ballad of the Harp Weaver; A Few Figs From Thistles; Eight Sonnets in American Poetry, 1922; A Miscellany*

1924 Robert Frost, *New Hampshire: A Poem With Notes and Grace Notes*

1925 Edwin Arlington Robinson, *The Man Who Died Twice*

1926 Amy Lowell, *What's O'Clock*

1927 Leonora Speyer, *Fiddler's Farewell*

1928 Edwin Arlington Robinson, *Tristram*

1929 Stephen Vincent Benet, *John Brown's Body*

1930 Conrad Aiken, *Selected Poems*

1931 Robert Frost, *Collected Poems*

1932 George Dillon, *The Flowering Stone*

1933 Archibald MacLeish, *Conquistador*

1934 Robert Hillyer, *Collected Verse*

1935 Audrey Wurdemann, *Bright Ambush*

1936 Robert P. Tristram Coffin, *Strange Holiness*

1937 Robert Frost, *A Further Range*

1938 Marya Zaturenska, *Cold Morning Sky*

1939 John Gould Fletcher, *Selected Poems*

1940 Mark Van Doren, *Collected Poems*

1941 Leonard Bacon, *Sunderland Capture*

1942 William Rose Benet, *The Dust Which Is God*

1943 Robert Frost, *A Witness Tree*

1944 Stephen Vincent Benet, *Western Star*

1945 Karl Shapiro, *V-Letter and Other Poems*

1946 Not awarded

1947 Robert Lowell, *Lord Weary's Castle*

1948 W. H. Auden, *The Age of Anxiety*

1949 Peter Viereck, *Terror and Decorum*

1950 Gwendolyn Brooks, *Annie Allen*

1951 Carl Sandburg, *Complete Poems*

1952 Marianne Moore, *Collected Poems*

1953 Archibald MacLeish, *Collected Poems*

1954 Theodore Roethke, *The Waking*

1955 Wallace Stevens, *Collected Poems*

1956 Elizabeth Bishop, Poems, *North and South*

1957 Richard Wilbur, *Things of This World*

1958 Robert Penn Warren, *Promises: Poems 1954–1956*

1959 Stanley Kunitz, *Selected Poems 1928–1958'*

1960 W. D. Snodgrass, *Heart's Needle*

1961 Phyllis McGinley, *Times Three: Selected Verse from Three Decades*

1962 Alan Dugan, *Poems*

1963 William Carlos Williams, *Pictures From Breughel*

1964 Louis Simpson, *At the End of the Open Road*

1965 John Berryman, *77 Dream Songs*

1966 Richard Eberhart, *Selected Poems*

1967 Anne Sexton, *Live or Die*

1968 Anthony Hecht, *The Hard Hours*

1969 George Oppen, *Of Being Numerous*

1970 Richard Howard, *Untitled Subjects*

1971 William S. Merwin, *The Carrier of Ladders*

1972 James Wright, *Collected Poems*

1973 Maxine Winokur Kumin, *Up Country*

1975 Gary Snyder, *Turtle Island*

1976 John Ashbery, *Self-Portrait in a Convex Mirror*

1977 James Merrill, *Divine Comedies*

1978 Howard Nemerov, *Collected Poems*

1979 Robert Penn Warren, *Now and Then: Poems 1976–1978*

1980 Donald Justice, *Selected Poems*

1981 James Schuyler, *The Morning of the Poem*

1982 Sylvia Plath, *The Collected Poems*

1983 Galway Kinnell, *Selected Poems*

1984 Mary Oliver, *American Primitive*

1985 Carolyn Kizer, *Yin*

1986 Henry Taylor, *The Flying Change*

1987 Rita Dove, *Thomas and Beulah*

1988 William Meredith, *Partial Accounts: New and Selected Poems*

1989 Richard Wilbur, *New and Collected Poems*

1990 Charles Simic, *The World Doesn't End*

1991 Mona Van Duyn, *Near Changes*

1992 James Tate, *Selected Poems*

1993 Louise Gluck, *The Wild Iris*

1994 Yusef Komunyakaa, *Neon Vernacular*

1995 Philip Levine, *The Simple Truth*

1996 Jorie Graham, *The Dream of the Unified Field*

1997 Lisel Mueller, *Alive Together: New & Selected Poems*

1998 Charles Wright, *Black Zodiac*

1999 Mark Strand, *Blizzard of One*

General Nonfiction

1962 Theodore H. White, *The Making of the President 1960*

1963 Barbara W. Tuchman, *The Guns of August*

1964 Richard Hofstadter, *Anti-Intellectualism in American Life*

1965 Howard Mumford Jones, *O Strange New World*

1966 Edwin Way Teale, *Wandering Through Winter*

1967 David Brion Davis, *The Problem of Slavery in Western Culture*

1968 Will and Ariel Durant, *Rousseau and Revolution*

1969 Norman Mailer, The Armies of the Night; Rene Jules Dubos, *So Human an Animal: How We Are Shaped by Surroundings and Events*

1970 Eric H. Erikson, *Gandhi's Truth*

1971 John Toland, *The Rising Sun*

1972 Barbara W. Tuchman, *Stilwell and the American Experience in China, 1911–1945*

1973 Frances Fitzgerald, *Fire in the Lake: The Vietnamese and the Americans in Vietnam*; Robert Coles, *Children of Crisis, Volumes II & III*

1974 Ernest Becker, *The Denial of Death*

1975 Annie Dillard, *Pilgrim at Tinker Creek*

1976 Robert N. Butler, *Why Survive? Being Old in America*

1977 William W. Warner, *Beautiful Swimmers*

1978 Carl Sagan, *The Dragons of Eden*

1979 Edward O. Wilson, *On Human Nature*

1980 Douglas R. Hofstadter, *Godel, Escher, Bach: An Eternal Golden Braid*

1981 Carl E. Schorske, *Fin-de-Siecle Vienna: Politics and Culture*

1982 Tracy Kidder, *The Soul of a New Machine*

1983 Susan Sheehan, *Is There No Place on Earth for Me?*

1984 Paul Starr, *Social Transformation of American Medicine*

1985 Studs Terkel, *The Good War*

1986 Joseph Lelyveld, *Move Your Shadow;* J. Anthony Lukas, *Common Ground*

1987 David K. Shipler, *Arab and Jew*

1988 Richard Rhodes, *The Making of the Atomic Bomb*

1989 Neil Sheehan, *A Bright Shining Lie: John Paul Vann and America in Vietnam*

1990 Dale Maharidge and Michael Williamson, *And Their Children After Them*

1991 Bert Holldobler and Edward O. Wilson, *The Ants*

1992 Daniel Yergin, *The Prize: The Epic Quest for Oil*

1993 Garry Wills, *Lincoln at Gettysburg*

1994 David Remnick, *Lenin's Tomb: The Last Days of the Soviet Empire*

1995 Jonathan Weiner, *The Beak of the Finch: A Story of Evolution in Our Time*

1996 Tina Rosenberg, *The Haunted Land: Facing Europe's Ghosts After Communism*

1997 Richard Kluger, *Ashes to Ashes: America's Hundred-Year Cigarette War, the Public Health & the Unabashed Triumph of Philip Morris*

1998 Jared Diamond, *Guns, Germs, and Steel: the Fates of Human Societies*

1999 John McPhee, *Annals of the Former World*

1944 Richard Rodgers and Oscar Hammerstein II, for musical, *Oklahoma!*

1957 Kenneth Roberts (for historical novels)

1960 Garrett Mattingly (for *The Armada*)

1961 American Heritage *Picture History of the Civil War*

1973 James Thomas Flexner (for *George Washington, Vols. I–IV*)

1977 Alex Haley (for *Roots*)

1978 E. B. White

1984 Theodore Geisel (*Dr. Seuss*)

1985 William Schuman (composer, educational leader)

1992 Art Spiegleman (for *Maus*)

Music

1943 William Schuman, "Secular Cantata No. 2, A Free Song"

1944 Howard Hanson, "Symphony No. 4, op. 34"

1945 Aaron Copland, "Appalachian Spring"

1946 Leo Sowerby, "The Canticle of the Sun"

1947 Charles E. Ives, "Symphony No. 3"

1948 Walter Piston, "Symphony No. 3"

1949 Virgil Thomson, "Louisiana Story"

1950 Gian-Carlo Menotti, "The Consul"

1951 Douglas Moore, "Giants in the Earth"

1952 Gail Kubik, "Symphony Concertante"

1953 Not awarded

1954 Quincy Porter, "Concerto for Two Pianos and Orchestra"

1955 Gian-Carlo Menotti, "The Saint of Bleecker Street"

1956 Ernest Toch, "Symphony No. 3"

1957 Norman Dello Joio, "Meditations on Ecclesiastes"

1958 Samuel Barber, "Vanessa"

1959 John La Montaine, "Concerto for Piano and Orchestra"

1960 Elliott Carter, "Second String Quartet"

1961 Walter Piston, "Symphony No. 7"

1962 Robert Ward, "The Crucible"

1963 Samuel Barber, "Piano Concerto No. 1"

1964 Not awarded

1965 Not awarded

1966 Leslie Bassett, "Variations for Orchestra"

1967 Leon Kirchner, "Quartet No. 3"

1968 George Crumb, "Echoes of Time and The River"

1969 Karel Husa, "String Quartet No. 3"

1970 Charles W. Wuorinen, "Time's Encomium"

1971 Mario Davidovsky, "Synchronisms No. 6"

1972 Jacob Druckman, "Windows"

1973 Elliott Carter, "String Quartet No. 3"

1974 Donald Martino, "Notturno"; (Special Citation) Roger Sessions

1975 Dominick Argento, "From the Diary of Virginia Woolf"

1976 Ned Rorem, "Air Music"

1977 Richard Wernick, "Visions of Terror and Wonder"

1978 Michael Colgrass, "Deja Vu for Percussion and Orchestra"

1979 Joseph Schwantner, "Aftertones of Infinity"

1980 David Del Tredici, "In Memory of a Summer Day"

1981 Not awarded

1982 Roger Sessions, "Concerto for Orchestra"; (Special Citation) Milton Babbitt

1983 Ellen T. Zwilich, "Three Movements for Orchestra"

1984 Bernard Rands, "Canti del Sole"

1985 Stephen Albert, "Symphony, River Run"

1986 George Perle, "Wind Quintet IV"

1987 John Harbison, "The Flight Into Egypt"

1988 William Bolcom, "12 New Etudes for Piano"

1989 Roger Reynolds, "Whispers Out of Time"

1990 Mel Powell, "Duplicates: A Concerto for Two Pianos and Orchestra"

1991 Shulamit Ran, "Symphony"

1992 Wayne Peterson, "The Face of the Night, The Heart of the Dark"

1993 Christopher Rouse, "Trombone Concerto"

1994 Gunther Schuller, "Of Reminiscences and Reflections"

1995 Morton Gould, "String Music"

1996 George Walker, "Lilacs"

1997 Wynton Marsalis, "Blood on the Fields"

1998 Aaron Jay Kernis, "String Quartet No. 2"

1999 Melinda Wagner, "Concerto for Flute, Strings and Percussion"

Newbery Medal

Awarded annually by the Association for Library Service to Children, a division of the American Library Association, for most distinguished contribution to American children's literature.

1922 *The Story of Mankind*, Hendrik Willem van Loon

1923 *The Voyages of Dr. Doolittle*, Hugh Lofting

1924 *The Dark Frigate*, Charles Boardman Hawes

1925 *Tales From Silver Lands*, Charles Joseph Finger

1926 *Shen of the Sea*, Arthur Bowie Chrisman

1927 *Smoky, the Cowhorse*, Will James

1928 *Gay-Neck*, Dhan Gopal Mukerji

1929 *The Trumpeter of Krakow*, Eric P. Kelly

1930 *Hitty, Her First Hundred Years*, Rachel Field

1931 *The Cat Who Went to Heaven*, Elizabeth Coatsworth

1932 *Waterless Mountain*, Laura Adams Armer

1933 *Young Fu of the Upper Yangtze*, Elizabeth Foreman Lewis

1934 *Invincible Louisa*, Cornelia Lynde Meigs

1935 *Dobry!* Monica Shannon

1936 *Caddie Woodlawn*, Carol Ryrie Brink

1937 *Roller Skates*, Ruth Sawyer

1938 *The White Stag*, Kate Seredy

1939 *Thimble Summer*, Elizabeth Enright

1940 *Daniel Boone*, James Daugherty

1941 *Call It Courage*, Armstrong Sperry

1942 *The Matchlock Gun*, Walter D. Edmonds

1943 *Adam of the Road*, Elizabeth Janet Gray

1944 *Johnny Tremain*, Esther Forbes

1945 *Rabbit Hill*, Robert Lawson

1946 *Strawberry Girl*, Lois Lenski

1947 *Miss Hickory*, Carolyn S. Bailey

1948 *Twenty-One Balloons*, William Pene Du Bois

1949 *King of the Wind*, Marguerite Henry

1950 *The Door in the Wall*, Marguerite de Angeli

1951 *Amos Fortune, Free Man*, Elizabeth Yates

1952 *Ginger Pye*, Eleanor Estes

1953 *Secret of the Andes*, Ann Nolan Clark

1954 *. . . And Now Miguel*, Joseph Krumgold

1955 *The Wheel on the School*, Meindert DeJong

1956 *Carry On, Mr. Bowditch*, Jean Lee Latham

1957 *Miracles on Maple Hill*, Virginia Sorensen

1958 *Rifles for Watie*, Harold Keith

1959 *The Witch of Blackbird Pond*, Elizabeth George Speare

1960 *Onion John*, Joseph Krumgold

1961 *Island of the Blue Dolphins*, Scott O'Dell

1962 *The Bronze Bow*, Elizabeth George Speare

1963 *A Wrinkle in Time*, Madeleine L'Engle

1964 *It's Like This, Cat*, Emily Cheney Neville

1965 *Shadow of a Bull*, Maja Wojciechowska

1966 *I, Juan de Pareja*, Elizabeth Borton de Trevino

1967 *Up a Road Slowly*, Irene Hunt

1968 *From the Mixed-Up Files of Mrs. Basil E. Frankweiler*, E. L. Konigsburg

1969 *The High King*, Lloyd Alexander

1970 *Sounder*, William H. Armstrong

1971 *The Summer of the Swans*, Betsy Byars

1972 *Mrs. Frisby and the Rats of NIMH*, Robert C. O'Brien

1973 *Julie of the Wolves*, Jean George

1974 *The Slave Dancer*, Paula Fox

1975 *M. C. Higgins the Great*, Virginia Hamilton

1976 *Grey King*, Susan Cooper

1977 *Roll of Thunder, Hear My Cry*, Mildred D. Taylor

1978 *Bridge to Terabithia*, Katherine Paterson

1979 *The Westing Game*, Ellen Raskin

1980 *A Gathering of Days*, Joan Blos

1981 *Jacob Have I Loved*, Katherine Paterson

1982 *A Visit to William Blake's Inn: Poems for Innocent and Experienced Travelers*, Nancy Willard

1983 *Dicey's Song*, Cynthia Voigt

1984 *Dear Mr. Henshaw*, Beverly Cleary

1985 *The Hero and the Crown*, Robin McKinley

1986 *Sarah, Plain and Tall*, Patricia MacLachlan

1987 *The Whipping Boy*, Sid Fleischman

1988 *Lincoln: A Photobiography*, Russell Freedman

1989 *Joyful Noise: Poems for Two Voices*, Paul Fleischman

1990 *Number the Stars*, Lois Lowry

1991 *Maniac Magee*, Jerry Spinelli

1992 *Shiloh*, Phyllis Reynolds Naylor

1993 *Missing May*, Cynthia Rylant

1994 *The Giver*, Lois Lowry

1995 *Walk Two Moons*, Sharon Creech

1996 *The Midwife's Apprentice*, Karen Cushman

1997 *The View from Saturday*, E.L. Konigsburg

1998 *Out of the Dust*, Karen Hesse

1999 *Holes*, Louis Sachar

Caldecott Medal

Awarded by the Association for Library Service to Children to honor the illustrator of the best children's picture book each year.

1938 *Animals of the Bible*, Dorothy P. Lathrop

1939 *Mel Li*, Thomas Handforth

1940 *Abraham Lincoln*, Ingri and Edgar Parin d'Aulaire

1941 *They Were Strong and Good*, Robert Lawson

1942 *Make Way for Ducklings*, Robert McCloskey

1943 *The Little House*, Virginia Lee Burton

1944 *Many Moons*, Louis Slobodkin

1945 *Prayer for a Child*, Elizabeth Orton Jones

1946 *The Rooster Crows*, Maude and Miska Petersharn

1947 *The Little Island*, Leonard Weisgard

1948 *White Snow, Bright Snow,* Roger Duvoisin

1949 *The Big Snow*, Berta and Elmer Hader

1950 *Song of the Swallows*, Leo Politi

1951 *The Egg Tree*, Katherine Milhous

1952 *Finders Keepers,* Nicolas Mordvinoff

1953 *The Biggest Bear*, Lynd Ward

1954 *Madeline's Rescue*, Ludwig Bemelmans

1955 *Cinderella, or the Little Glass Slipper*, Marcia Brown

1956 *Frog Went A-Courtin*, Feodor Rojankovsky

1957 *A Tree Is Nice*, Marc Simont

1958 *Time of Wonder*, Robert McCloskey

1959 *Chanticleer and the Fox*, Barbara Cooney

1960 *Nine Days to Christmas*, Marie Hall Ets

1961 *Baboushka and the Three Kings*, Nicolas Sidjakov

1962 *Once a Mouse*, Marcia Brown

1963 *The Snowy Day*, Ezra Jack Keats

1964 *Where the Wild Things Are*, Maurice Sendak

1965 *May I Bring a Friend?*, Beni Montressor

1966	*Always Room for One More*, Nonny Hogrogian
1967	*Sam, Bang, and Moonshine*, Evaline Ness
1968	*Drummer Hoff*, Ed Emberley
1969	*The Fool of the World and the Flying Ship*, Uri Shulevitz
1970	*Sylvester and the Magic Pebble*, William Steig
1971	*A Story A Story*, Gail E. Haley
1972	*One Fine Day*, Nonny Hogrogian
1973	*The Funny Little Woman*, Blair Lent
1974	*Duffy and the Devil*, Margot Zemach
1975	*Arrow to the Sun*, Gerald McDermott
1976	*Why Mosquitoes Buzz in People's Ears*, Leo and Diane Dillon
1977	*Ashanti to Zulu: African Traditions*, Leo and Diane Dillon
1978	*Noah's Ark*, Peter Spier
1979	*The Girl Who Loved Wild Horses*, Paul Goble
1980	*Ox-Cart Man*, Barbara Cooney
1981	*Fables*, Arnold Lobel
1982	*Jumanji*, Chris Van Allsburg
1983	*Shadow*, Marcia Brown
1984	*The Glorious Flight: Across the Channel with Louis Bleriol*, Alice and Martin Provensen
1985	*Saint George and the Dragon*, Trina Schart Hyman
1986	*The Polar Express*, Chris Van Allsburg
1987	*Hey, Al*, Richard Egielski

1988	*Owl Moon*, John Schoenherr
1989	*Song and Dance Man*, Stephen Grammell
1990	*Lon Po Po: A Red-Riding Hood Story From China*, Ed Young
1991	*Black and White*, David Macaulay
1992	*Tuesday*, David Wiesner
1993	*Mirette on the High Wire*, Emily Arnold McCully
1994	*Grandfather's Journey*, Allen Say
1995	*Smoky Night*, David Diaz
1996	*Officer Buckle and Gloria*, Peggy Rathmann
1997	*Golem*, David Wisniewski
1998	*Rapunzet*, Paul O. Zelinsky
1999	*Snowflake Bentley*, Mary Azarian

The Spingarn Medal

Awarded annually since 1914 by the National Association for the Advancement of Colored People for the highest achievement by an African American.

1915	Ernest E. Just
1916	Charles Young
1917	Harry T. Burleigh
1918	William S. Braithwaite
1919	Archibald H. Grimke
1920	W. E. B. Du Bois
1921	Charles S. Gilpin
1922	Mary B. Talbert
1923	George W. Carver

1924	Roland Hayes	1949	Ralph J. Bunche
1925	James W. Johnson	1950	Charles H. Houston
1926	Carter G. Woodson	1951	Mabel K. Staupers
1927	Anthony Overton	1952	Harry T. Moore
1928	Charles W. Chesnutt	1953	Paul R. Williams
1929	Mordecai W. Johnson	1954	Theodore K. Lawless
1930	Henry A. Hunt	1955	Carl Murphy
1931	Richard B. Harrison	1956	Jack R. Robinson
1932	Robert R. Moton	1957	Martin Luther King Jr.
1933	Max Yergan	1958	Mrs. Daisy Bates and the Little Rock Nine
1934	William T. B. Williams	1959	Edward Kennedy (Duke) Ellington
1935	Mary McLeod Bethune	1960	Langston Hughes
1936	John Hope	1961	Kenneth B. Clark
1937	Walter White	1962	Robert C. Weaver
1938	no award	1963	Medgar W. Evers
1939	Marian Anderson	1964	Roy Wilkins
1940	Louis T. Wright	1965	Leontyne Price
1941	Richard Wright	1966	John H. Johnson
1942	A. Philip Randolph	1967	Edward W. Brooke
1943	William H. Hastie	1968	Sammy Davis Jr.
1944	Charles Drew	1969	Clarence M. Mitchell Jr.
1945	Paul Robeson	1970	Jacob Lawrence
1946	Thurgood Marshall	1971	Leon H. Sullivan
1947	Dr. Percy L. Julian	1972	Gordon Parks
1948	Channing H. Tobias	1973	Wilson C. Riles

1974	Damon Keith	**1999**	Earl G. Graves Sr.

1974 Damon Keith

1975 Henry (Hank) Aaron

1976 Alvin Ailey

1977 Alex Haley

1978 Andrew Young

1979 Mrs. Rosa L. Parks

1980 Dr. Rayford W. Logan

1981 Coleman Young

1982 Dr. Benjamin E. Mays

1983 Lena Horne

1984 Thomas Bradley

1985 Bill Cosby

1986 Dr. Benjamin L. Hooks

1987 Percy E. Sutton

1988 Frederick D. Patterson

1989 Jesse Jackson

1990 L. Douglas Wilder

1991 General Colin L. Powell

1992 Barbara Jordan

1993 Dorothy I. Height

1994 Maya Angelou

1995 John Hope Franklin

1996 A. Leon Higginbotham

1997 Carl T. Rowan

1998 Myrlie Evers-Williams

1999 Earl G. Graves Sr.

Academy Awards (Oscars)

The motion picture industry honors the best achievements in cinematic production and performance each year with the presentation of the Oscar statuette. This list includes only the major awards.

1928 Picture: *Wings*

Actor: Emil Jannings, *The Way of All Flesh*

Actress: Janet Gaynor, *Seventh Heaven*

Director: Frank Borzage, *Seventh Heaven*; Lewis Milestone, *Two Arabian Knights*

1929 Picture: *Broadway Melody*

Actor: Warner Baxter, *In Old Arizona*

Actress: Mary Pickford, *Coquette*

Director: Frank Lloyd, *The Divine Lady*

1930 Picture: *All Quiet on the Western Front*

Actor: George Arliss, *Disraeli*

Actress: Norma Shearer, *The Divorcee*

Director: Lewis Milestone, *All Quiet on the Western Front*

1931 Picture: *Cimarron*

Actor: Lionel Barrymore, *A Free Soul*

Actress: Marie Dressler, *Min and Bill*

Director: Norman Taurog, *Skippy*

1932 Picture: *Grand Hotel*

Actor: Fredric March, *Dr. Jekyll and Mr. Hyde*, and Wallace Beery, *The Champ*

Actress: Helen Hayes, *Sin of Madelon Claudet*

Director: Frank Borzage, *Bad Girl*

Special: Walt Disney, *Mickey Mouse*

1933 Picture: *Cavalcade*

Actor: Charles Laughton, *The Private Life of Henry VIII*

Actress: Katharine Hepburn, *Morning Glory*

Director: Frank Lloyd, *Cavalcade*

1934 Picture: *It Happened One Night*

Actor: Clark Gable, *It Happened One Night*

Actress: Claudette Colbert, *It Happened One Night*

Director: Frank Capra, *It Happened One Night*

1935 Picture: *Mutiny on the Bounty*

Actor: Victor McLaglen, *The Informer*

Actress: Bette Davis, *Dangerous*

Director: John Ford, *The Informer*

1936 Picture: *The Great Ziegfeld*

Actor: Paul Muni, *The Story of Louis Pasteur*

Actress: Luise Rainer, *The Great Ziegfeld*

Supporting Actor: Walter Brennan, *Come and Get It*

Supporting Actress: Gale Sondergaard, *Anthony Adverse*

Director: Frank Capra *Mr. Deeds Goes to Town*

1937 Picture: *The Life of Emile Zola*

Actor: Spencer Tracy, *Captains Courageous*

Actress: Luise Rainer, *The Good Earth*

Supporting Actor: Joseph Schildkraut, *Life of Emil Zola*

Supporting Actress: Alice Brady, *In Old Chicago*

Director: Leo McCarey, *The Awful Truth*

1938 Picture: *You Can't Take It with You*

Actor: Spencer Tracy, *Boys Town*

Actress: Bette Davis, *Jezebel*

Supporting Actor: Walter Brennan, *Kentucky*

Supporting Actress: Fay Bainter, *Jezebel*

Director: Frank Capra, *You Can't Take It With You*

1939 Picture: Gone With the Wind

Actor: Robert Donat, *Goodbye Mr. Chips*

Actress: Vivien Leigh, *Gone With the Wind*

Supporting Actor: Thomas Mitchell, *Stage Coach*

Supporting Actress: Hattie McDaniel, *Gone With the Wind*

Director: Victor Fleming, *Gone With the Wind*

1940 Picture: *Rebecca*

Actor: James Stewart, *The Philadelphia Story*

Actress: Ginger Rogers, *Kitty Foyle*

Supporting Actor: Walter Brennan, *The Westerner*

Supporting Actress: Jane Darwell, *The Grapes of Wrath*

Director: John Ford, *The Grapes of Wrath*

1941 Picture: *How Green Was My Valley*

Actor: Gary Cooper, *Sergeant York*

Actress: Joan Fontaine, *Suspicion*

Supporting Actor: Donald Crisp, *How Green Was My Valley*

Supporting Actress: Mary Astor, *The Great Lie*

Director: John Ford, *How Green Was My Valley*

1942 Picture: *Mrs. Miniver*

Actor: James Cagney, *Yankee Doodle Dandy*

Actress: Greer Garson, *Mrs. Miniver*

Supporting Actor: Van Heflin, *Johnny Eager*

Supporting Actress: Teresa Wright, *Mrs. Miniver*

Director: William Wyler, *Mrs. Miniver*

1943 Picture: *Casablanca*

Actor: Paul Lukas, W*atch on the Rhine*

Actress: Jennifer Jones, *The Song of Bernadette*

Supporting Actor: Charles Coburn, *The More the Merrier*

Supporting Actress: Katina Paxinou, *For Whom the Bell Tolls*

Director: Michael Curtiz, *Casablanca*

1944 Picture: *Going My Way*

Actor: Bing Crosby, *Going My Way*

Actress: Ingrid Bergman, *Gaslight*

Supporting Actor: Barry Fitzgerald, *Going My Way*

Supporting Actress: Ethel Barrymore, *None But the Lonely Heart*

Director: Leo McCarey, *Going My Way*

1945 Picture: *The Lost Weekend*

Actor: Ray Milland, *The Lost Weekend*

Actress: Joan Crawford, *Mildred Pierce*

Supporting Actor: James Dunn, *A Tree Grows in Brooklyn*

Supporting Actress: Anne Revere, *National Velvet*

Director: Billy Wilder, *The Lost Weekend*

1946 Picture: *The Best Years of Our Lives*

Actor: Fredric March, *The Best Years of Our Lives*

Actress: Olivia De Havilland, *To Each His Own*

Supporting Actor: Harold Russell, *The Best Years of Our Lives*

Supporting Actress: Anne Baxter, *The Razor's Edge*

Director: William Wyler, *The Best Years of Our Lives*

1947 Picture: *Gentleman's Agreement*

Actor: Ronald Colman, *A Double Life*

Actress: Loretta Young, *The Farmer's Daughter*

Supporting Actor: Edmund Gwenn, *Miracle on 34th Street*

Supporting Actress: Celeste Holm, *Gentleman's Agreement*

Director: Elia Kazan, *Gentleman's Agreement*

1948 Picture: *Hamlet*

Actor: Laurence Olivier, *Hamlet*

Actress: Jane Wyman, *Johnny Belinda*

Supporting Actor: Walter Huston, *Treasure of Sierra Madre*

Supporting Actress: Claire Trevor, *Key Largo*

Director: John Huston, *Treasure of Sierra Madre*

1949 Picture: *All the King's Men*

Actor: Broderick Crawford, *All the King's Men*

Actress: Olivia de Havilland, *The Heiress*

Supporting Actor: Dean Jagger, *Twelve O'Clock High*

Supporting Actress: Mercedes McCambridge, *All the King's Men*

Director: Joseph L. Mankiewicz, *Letter to Three Wives*

1950 Picture: *All About Eve*

Actor: Jose Ferrer, *Cyrano de Bergerac*

Actress: Judy Holliday, *Born Yesterday*

Supporting Actor: George Sanders, *All About Eve*

Supporting Actress: Josephine Hull, *Harvey*

Director: Joseph L. Mankiewicz, *All About Eve*

1951 Picture: *An American in Paris*

Actor: Humphrey Bogart, *The African Queen*

Actress: Vivien Leigh, *A Streetcar Named Desire*

Supporting Actor: Karl Malden, *A Streetcar Named Desire*

Supporting Actress: Kim Hunter, *A Streetcar Named Desire*

Director: George Stevens, *A Place in the Sun*

1952 Picture: *The Greatest Show on Earth*

Actor: Gary Cooper, *High Noon*

Actress: Shirley Booth, *Come Back, Little Sheba*

Supporting Actor: Anthony Quinn, *Viva Zapata!*

Supporting Actress: Gloria Grahame, *The Bad and the Beautiful*

Director: John Ford, *The Quiet Man*

1953 Picture: *From Here to Eternity*

Actor: William Holden, *Stalag 17*

Actress: Audrey Hepburn, *Roman Holiday*

Supporting Actor: Frank Sinatra, *From Here to Eternity*

Supporting Actress: Donna Reed, *From Here to Eternity*

Director: Fred Zinnemann, *From Here to Eternity*

1954 Picture: *On the Waterfront*

Actor: Marlon Brando, *On the Waterfront*

Actress: Grace Kelly, *The Country Girl*

Supporting Actor: Edmond O'Brien, *The Barefoot Contessa*

Supporting Actress: Eva Marie Saint, *On the Waterfront*

Director: Elia Kazan, *On the Waterfront*

1955 Picture: *Marty*

Actor: Ernest Borgnine, *Marty*

Actress: Anna Magnani, *The Rose Tattoo*

Supporting Actor: Jack Lemmon, *Mister Roberts*

Supporting Actress: Jo Van Fleet, *East of Eden*

Director: Delbert Mann, *Marty*

1956 Picture: *Around the World in 80 Days*

Actor: Yul Brynner, *The King and I*

Actress: Ingrid Bergman, *Anastasia*

Supporting Actor: Anthony Quinn, *Lust for Life*

Supporting Actress: Dorothy Malone, *Written on the Wind*

Director: George Stevens, *Giant*

1957 Picture: *The Bridge on the River Kwai*

Actor: Alec Guinness, *The Bridge on the River Kwai*

Actress: Joanne Woodward, *The Three Faces of Eve*

Supporting Actor: Red Buttons, *Sayonara*

Supporting Actress: Miyoshi Umeki, *Sayonara*

Director: David Lean, *The Bridge on the River Kwai*

1958 Picture: *Gigi*

Actor: David Niven, *Separate Tables*

Actress: Susan Hayward, *I Want to Live*

Supporting Actor: Burl Ives, *The Big Country*

Supporting Actress: Wendy Hiller, *Separate Tables*

Director: Vincente Minnelli, *Gigi*

1959 Picture: *Ben-Hur*

Actor: Charlton Heston, *Ben-Hur*

Actress: Simone Signoret, *Room at the Top*

Supporting Actor: Hugh Griffith, *Ben-Hur*

Supporting Actress: Shelley Winters, *Diary of Anne Frank*

Director: William Wyler, *Ben-Hur*

1960 Picture: *The Apartment*

Actor: Burt Lancaster, *Elmer Gantry*

Actress: Elizabeth Taylor, *Butterfield 8*

Supporting Actor: Peter Ustinov, *Spartacus*

Supporting Actress: Shirley Jones, *Elmer Gantry*

Director: Billy Wilder, *The Apartment*

1961 Picture: *West Side Story*

Actor: Maximilian Schell, *Judgment at Nuremberg*

Actress: Sophia Loren, *Two Women*

Supporting Actor: George Chakiris, *West Side Story*

Supporting Actress: Rita Moreno, *West Side Story*

Director: Jerome Robbins and Robert Wise, *West Side Story*

1962   Picture: *Lawrence of Arabia*

Actor: Gregory Peck, *To Kill a Mockingbird*

Actress: Anne Bancroft, *The Miracle Worker*

Supporting Actor: Ed Begley, *Sweet Bird of Youth*

Supporting Actress: Patty Duke, *The Miracle Worker*

Director: David Lean, *Lawrence of Arabia*

1963   Picture: *Tom Jones*

Actor: Sidney Poitier, *Lilies of the Field*

Actress: Patricia Neal, *Hud*

Supporting Actor: Melvyn Douglas, *Hud*

Supporting Actress: Margaret Rutherford, *The V.I.P.s*

Director: Tony Richardson, *Tom Jones*

1964   Picture: *My Fair Lady*

Actor: Rex Harrison, *My Fair Lady*

Actress: Julie Andrews, *Mary Poppins*

Supporting Actor: Peter Ustinov, *Topkapi*

Supporting Actress: Lila Kedrova, *Zorba the Greek*

Director: George Cukor, *My Fair Lady*

1965   Picture: *The Sound of Music*

Actor: Lee Marvin, *Cat Ballou*

Actress: Julie Christie, *Darling*

Supporting Actor: Martin Balsam, *A Thousand Clowns*

Supporting Actress: Shelley Winters, *A Patch of Blue*

Director: Robert Wise, *The Sound of Music*

1966   Picture: *A Man for All Seasons*

Actor: Paul Scofield, *A Man for All Seasons*

Actress: Elizabeth Taylor, *Who's Afraid of Virginia Woolf?*

Supporting Actor: Walter Matthau, *The Fortune Cookie*

Supporting Actress: Sandy Dennis, *Who's Afraid of Virginia Woolf?*

Director: Fred Zinnemann, *A Man for All Seasons*

1967   Picture: *In the Heat of the Night*

Actor: Rod Steiger, *In the Heat of the Night*

Actress: Katharine Hepburn, *Guess Who's Coming to Dinner*

Supporting Actor: George Kennedy, *Cool Hand Luke*

Supporting Actress: Estelle Parsons, *Bonnie and Clyde*

Director: Mike Nichols, *The Graduate*

1968   Picture: *Oliver!*

Actor: Cliff Robertson, *Charly*

Actress: Katharine Hepburn, *The Lion in Winter*; Barbra Streisand, *Funny Girl* (tie)

Supporting Actor: Jack Albertson, *The Subject Was Roses*

Supporting Actress: Ruth Gordon, *Rosemary's Baby*

Director: Sir Carol Reed, *Oliver!*

1969 Picture: *Midnight Cowboy*

Actor: John Wayne, *True Grit*

Actress: Maggie Smith, *The Prime of Miss Jean Brodie*

Supporting Actor: Gig Young, *They Shoot Horses, Don't They?*

Supporting Actress: Goldie Hawn, *Cactus Flower*

Director: John Schlesinger, *Midnight Cowboy*

1970 Picture: *Patton*

Actor: George C. Scott, *Patton* (refused)

Actress: Glenda Jackson, *Women in Love*

Supporting Actor: John Mills, *Ryan's Daughter*

Supporting Actress: Helen Hayes, *Airport*

Director: Franklin Schaffner, *Patton*

1971 Picture: *The French Connection*

Actor: Gene Hackman, *The French Connection*

Actress: Jane Fonda, *Klute*

Supporting Actor: Ben Johnson, *The Last Picture Show*

Supporting Actress: Cloris Leachman, *The Last Picture Show*

Director: William Friedkin, *The French Connection*

1972 Picture: *The Godfather*

Actor: Marlon Brando, *The Godfather* (refused)

Actress: Liza Minnelli, *Cabaret*

Supporting Actor: Joel Grey, *Cabaret*

Supporting Actress: Eileen Heckart, *Butterflies Are Free*

Director: Bob Fosse, *Cabaret*

1973 Picture: *The Sting*

Actor: Jack Lemmon, *Save the Tiger*

Actress: Glenda Jackson, *A Touch of Class*

Supporting Actor: John Houseman, *The Paper Chase*

Supporting Actress: Tatum O'Neal, *Paper Moon*

Director: George Roy Hill, *The Sting*

1974 Picture: *The Godfather, Part II*

Actor: Art Carney, *Harry and Tonto*

Actress: Ellen Burstyn, *Alice Doesn't Live Here Anymore*

Supporting Actor: Robert DeNiro, *The Godfather, Part II*

Supporting Actress: Ingrid Bergman, *Murder on the Orient Express*

Director: Francis Ford Coppola, *The Godfather, Part II*

1975 Picture: *One Flew Over the Cuckoo's Nest*

Actor: Jack Nicholson, *One Flew Over the Cuckoo's Nest*

Actress: Louise Fletcher, *One Flew Over the Cuckoo's Nest*

Supporting Actor: George Burns, *The Sunshine Boys*

Supporting Actress: Lee Grant, *Shampoo*

Director: Milos Forman, *One Flew Over the Cuckoo's Nest*

1976   Picture: *Rocky*

Actor: Peter Finch, *Network*

Actress: Faye Dunaway, *Network*

Supporting Actor: Jason Robards, *All the President's Men*

Supporting Actress: Beatrice Straight, *Network*

Director: John G. Avildsen, *Rocky*

1977   Picture: *Annie Hall*

Actor: Richard Dreyfuss, *The Goodbye Girl*

Actress: Diane Keaton, *Annie Hall*

Supporting Actor: Jason Robards, *Julia*

Supporting Actress: Vanessa Redgrave, *Julia*

Director: Woody Allen, *Annie Hall*

1978   Picture: *The Deer Hunter*

Actor: Jon Voight, *Coming Home*

Actress: Jane Fonda, *Coming Home*

Supporting Actor: Christopher Walken, *The Deer Hunter*

Supporting Actress: Maggie Smith, *California Suite*

Director: Michael Cimino, *The Deer Hunter*

1979   Picture: *Kramer vs. Kramer*

Actor: Dustin Hoffman, *Kramer vs. Kramer*

Actress: Sally Field, *Norma Rae*

Supporting Actor: Melvyn Douglas, *Being There*

Supporting Actress: Meryl Streep, *Kramer vs. Kramer*

Director: Robert Benton, *Kramer vs. Kramer*

1980   Picture: *Ordinary People*

Actor: Robert DeNiro, *Raging Bull*

Actress: Sissy Spacek, *Coal Miner's Daughter*

Supporting Actor: Timothy Hutton, *Ordinary People*

Supporting Actress: Mary Steenburgen, *Melvin & Howard*

Director: Robert Redford, *Ordinary People*

1981   Picture: *Chariots of Fire*

Actor: Henry Fonda, *On Golden Pond*

Actress: Katharine Hepburn, *On Golden Pond*

Supporting Actor: John Gielgud, *Arthur*

Supporting Actress: Maureen Stapleton, *Reds*

Director: Warren Beatty, *Reds*

1982   Picture: *Gandhi*

Actor: Ben Kingsley, *Gandhi*

Actress: Meryl Streep, *Sophie's Choice*

Supporting Actor: Louis Gossett Jr., *An Officer and a Gentleman*

Supporting Actress: Jessica Lange, *Tootsie*

Director: Richard Attenborough, *Gandhi*

1983   Picture: *Terms of Endearment*

Actor: Robert Duvall, *Tender Mercies*

Actress: Shirley MacLaine, *Terms of Endearment*

Supporting Actor: Jack Nicholson, *Terms of Endearment*

Supporting Actress: Linda Hunt, *The Year of Living Dangerously*

Director: James L. Brooks, *Terms of Endearment*

1984 Picture: *Amadeus*

Actor: F. Murray Abraham, *Amadeus*

Actress: Sally Field, *Places in the Heart*

Supporting Actor: Haing S. Ngor, *The Killing Fields*

Supporting Actress: Peggy Ashcroft, *A Passage to India*

Director: Milos Forman, *Amadeus*

1985 Picture: *Out of Africa*

Actor: William Hurt, *Kiss of the Spider Woman*

Actress: Geraldine Page, *The Trip to Bountiful*

Supporting Actor: Don Ameche, *Cocoon*

Supporting Actress: Anjelica Huston, *Prizzi's Honor*

Director: Sydney Pollack, *Out of Africa*

1986 Picture: *Platoon*

Actor: Paul Newman, *The Color of Money*

Actress: Marlee Matlin, *Children of a Lesser God*

Supporting Actor: Michael Caine, *Hannah and Her Sisters*

Supporting Actress: Dianne Wiest, *Hannah and Her Sisters*

Director: Oliver Stone, *Platoon*

1987 Picture: *The Last Emperor*

Actor: Michael Douglas, *Wall Street*

Actress: Cher, *Moonstruck*

Supporting Actor: Sean Connery, *The Untouchables*

Supporting Actress: Olympia Dukakis, *Moonstruck*

Director: Bernardo Bertolucci, *The Last Emperor*

1988 Picture: *Rain Man*

Actor: Dustin Hoffman, *Rain Man*

Actress: Jodie Foster, *The Accused*

Supporting Actor: Kevin Kline, *A Fish Called Wanda*

Supporting Actress: Geena Davis, *The Accidental Tourist*

Director: Barry Levinson, *Rain Man*

1989 Picture: *Driving Miss Daisy*

Actor: Daniel Day-Lewis, *My Left Foot*

Actress: Jessica Tandy, *Driving Miss Daisy*

Supporting Actor: Denzel Washington, *Glory*

Supporting Actress: Brenda Fricker, *My Left Foot*

Director: Oliver Stone, *Born on the Fourth of July*

1990   Picture: *Dances With Wolves*

Actor: Jeremy Irons, *Reversal of Fortune*

Actress: Kathy Bates, *Misery*

Supporting Actor: Joe Pesci, *Goodfellas*

Supporting Actress: Whoopi Goldberg, *Ghost*

Director: Kevin Costner, *Dances With Wolves*

1991   Picture: *The Silence of the Lambs*

Actor: Anthony Hopkins, *The Silence of the Lambs*

Actress: Jodie Foster, *The Silence of the Lambs*

Supporting Actor: Jack Palance, *City Slickers*

Supporting Actress: Mercedes Ruehl, *The Fisher King*

Director: Jonathan Demme, *The Silence of the Lambs*

1992   Picture: *Unforgiven*

Actor: Al Pacino, *Scent of a Woman*

Actress: Emma Thompson, *Howards End*

Supporting Actor: Gene Hackman, *Unforgiven*

Supporting Actress: Marisa Tomei, *My Cousin Vinny*

Director: Clint Eastwood, *Unforgiven*

1993   Picture: *Schindler's List*

Actor: Tom Hanks, *Philadelphia*

Actress: Holly Hunter, *The Piano*

Supporting Actor: Tommy Lee Jones, *The Fugitive*

Supporting Actress: Anna Paquin, *The Piano*

Director: Steven Spielberg, *Schindler's List*

1994   Picture: *Forrest Gump*

Actor: Tom Hanks, *Forrest Gump*

Actress: Jessica Lange, *Blue Sky*

Supporting Actor: Martin Landau, *Ed Wood*

Supporting Actress: Dianne Weist, *Bullets over Broadway*

Director: Robert Zemeckis, *Forrest Gump*

1995   Picture: *Braveheart*

Actor: Nicholas Cage, *Leaving Las Vegas*

Actress: Susan Sarandon, *Dead Man Walking*

Supporting Actor: Kevin Spacey, *The Usual Suspects*

Supporting Actress: Mira Sorvino, *Mighty Aphrodite*

Director: Mel Gibson, *Braveheart*

1996   Picture: *The English Patient*

Actor: Geoffrey Rush, *Shine*

Actress: Frances McDormand, *Fargo*

Supporting Actor: Cuba Gooding Jr., *Jerry Maguire*

Supporting Actress: Juliette Binoche, *The English Patient*

Director: Anthony Minghella, *The English Patient*

1997   Picture: *Titanic*

Actor: Jack Nicholson, *As Good As It Gets*

Actress: Helen Hunt, *As Good As It Gets*

Supporting Actor: Robin Williams, *Good Will Hunting*

Supporting Actress: Kim Basinger, *L.A. Confidential*

Director: James Cameron, *Titanic*

1998 Picture: *Shakespeare in Love*

Actor: Roberto Benigni, *Life Is Beautiful*

Actress: Gwyneth Paltrow, *Shakespeare in Love*

Supporting Actor: James Coburn, *Affliction*

Supporting Actress: Judi Dench, *Shakespeare in Love*

Director: Steven Spielberg, *Saving Private Ryan*

Tony Awards

The criterion for selection as a recipient of the Antoinette Perry (Tony) Awards is "distinguished achievement in the theatre," not the "best." On occasion, this principle has meant that in certain years more than one winner in each category has been selection.

Dramatic

1947 Play: no award

Actor: Jose Ferrer, *Cyrano de Bergerac*; Frederic March, *Years Ago* (tie)

Actress: Ingrid Bergman, *Joan of Lorraine*; Helen Hayes, *Happy Birthday* (tie)

1948 Play: *Mister Roberts*

Actor: Henry Fonda, *Mister Roberts*; Paul Kelly, *Command Decision*; Basil Rathbone, *The Heiress* (tie)

Actress: Judith Anderson, *Medea*; Katharine Cornell, *Antony and Cleopatra*; Jessica Tandy, *A Streetcar Named Desire* (tie)

1949 Play: *Death of a Salesman*

Actor: Rex Harrison, *Anne of the Thousand Days*

Actress: Martita Hunt, *The Madwoman of Chaillot*

1950 Play: *The Cocktail Party, Come Back, Little Sheba*

Actor: Sidney Blackmer, *Come Back, Little Sheba*

Actress: Shirley Booth, *Come Back, Little Sheba*

1951 Play: *The Rose Tattoo*

Actor: Claude Rains, *Darkness at Noon*

Actress: Uta Hagen, *The Country Girl*

1952 Play: *The Fourposter*

Actor: Jose Ferrer, *The Shrike*

Actress: Julie Harris, *I Am a Camera*

1953 Play: *The Crucible*

Actor: Tom Ewell, *The Seven Year Itch*

Actress: Shirley Booth, *Time of the Cuckoo*

1954 Play: *The Teahouse of the August Moon*

Actor: David Wayne, *The Teahouse of the August Moon*

Actress: Audrey Hepburn, *Ondine*

1955 Play: *The Desperate Hours*

Actor: Alfred Lunt, *Quadrille*

Actress: Nancy Kelly, *The Bad Seed*

1956 Play: *The Diary of Anne Frank*

Actor: Paul Muni, *Inherit the Wind*

Actress: Julie Harris, *The Lark*

1957 Play: *Long Day's Journey into Night*

Actor: Frederic March, *Long Day's Journey into Night*

Actress: Margaret Leighton, *Separate Tables*

1958 Play: *Sunrise at Campobello*

Actor: Ralph Bellamy, *Sunrise at Campobello*

Actress: Helen Hayes, *Time Remembered*

1959 Play: *J.B.*

Actor: Jason Robards, *The Disenchanted*

Actress: Gertrude Berg, *A Majority of One*

1960 Play: *The Miracle Worker*

Actor: Melvyn Douglas, *The Best Man*

Actress: Anne Bancroft, *The Miracle Worker*

1961 Play: *Becket*

Actor: Zero Mostel, *Rhinoceros*

Actress: Joan Plowright, *A Taste of Honey*

1962 Play: *A Man for All Seasons*

Actor: Paul Scofield, *A Man for All Seasons*

Actress: Margaret Leighton, *Night of the Iguana*

1963 Play: *Who's Afraid of Virginia Woolf*

Actor: Arthur Hill, *Who's Afraid of Virginia Woolf*

Actress: Uta Hagen, *Who's Afraid of Virginia Woolf*

1964 Play: *Luther*

Actor: Alec Guinness, *Dylan*

Actress: Sandy Dennis, *Any Wednesday*

1965 Play: *The Subject Was Roses*

Actor: Walter Matthau, *The Odd Couple*

Actress: Irene Worth, *Tiny Alice*

1966 Play: *Marat/Sade*

Actor: Hal Holbrook, *Mark Twain Tonight!*

Actress: Rosemary Harris, *The Lion in Winter*

1967 Play: *The Homecoming*

Actor: Paul Rogers, *The Homecoming*

Actress: Beryl Reid, *The Killing of Sister George*

1968 Play: *Rosencrantz and Guildenstern Are Dead*

Actor: Martin Balsam, *You Know I Can't Hear You When the Water's Running*

Actress: Zoe Caldwell, *The Prime of Miss Jean Brodie*

1969 Play: *The Great White Hope*

Actor: James Earl Jones, *The Great White Hope*

Actress: Julie Harris, *Forty Carats*

1970 Play: *Borstal Boy*

Actor: Fritz Weaver, *Child's Play*

Actress: Tammy Grimes, *Private Lives*

1971 Play: *Sleuth*

Actor: Brian Bedford, *The School for Wives*

Actress: Maureen Stapleton, *Gingerbread Lady*

1972   Play: *Sticks and Bones*

Actor: Cliff Gorman, *Lenny*

Actress: Sada Thompson, *Twigs*

1973   Play: *That Championship Season*

Actor: Alan Bates, *Butley*

Actress: Julie Harris, *The Last of Mrs. Lincoln*

1974   Play: *The River Niger*

Actor: Michael Moriarty, *Find Your Way Home*

Actress: Colleen Dewhurst, *A Moon for the Misbegotten*

1975   Play: *Equus*

Actor: John Kani, *Sizwe Banzi Is Dead*; Winston Ntshona, *The Island* (tie)

Actress: Ellen Burstyn, *Same Time, Next Year*

1976   Play: *Travesties*

Actor: John Wood, *Travesties*

Actress: Irene Worth, *Sweet Bird of Youth*

1977   Play: *The Shadow Box*

Actor: Al Pacino, *The Basic Training of Pavlo Hummel*

Actress: Julie Harris, *The Belle of Amherst*

1978   Play: *Da*

Actor: Barnard Hughes, *Da*

Actress: Jessica Tandy, *The Gin Game*

1979   Play: *The Elephant Man*

Actor: Tom Conti, *Whose Life Is It Anyway?*

Actress: Carole Shelly, *The Elephant Man*; Constance Cummings, *Wings* (tie)

1980   Play: *Children of a Lesser God*

Actor: John Rubinstein, *Children of a Lesser God*

Actress: Phyllis Frelich, *Children of a Lesser God*

1981   Play: *Amadeus*

Actor: Ian McKellen, *Amadeus*

Actress: Jane Lapotaire, *Piaf*

1982   Play: *The Life and Adventures of Nicholas Nickleby*

Actor: Roger Rees, *The Life and Adventures of Nicholas Nickleby*

Actress: Zoe Caldwell, *Medea*

1983   Play: *Torch Song Trilogy*

Actor: Harvey Fierstein, *Torch Song Trilogy*

Actress: Jessica Tandy, *Foxfire*

1984   Play: *The Real Thing*

Actor: Jeremy Irons, *The Real Thing*

Actress: Glenn Close, *The Real Thing*

1985   Play: *Biloxi Blues*

Actor: Derek Jacobi, *Much Ado About Nothing*

Actress: Stockard Channing, *Joe Egg*

1986   Play: *I'm Not Rappaport*

Actor: Judd Hirsch, *I'm Not Rappaport*

Actress: Lily Tomlin, *The Search for Signs of Intelligent Life in the Universe*

1987   Play: *Fences*

Actor: James Earl Jones, *Fences*

Actress: Linda Lavin, *Broadway Bound*

1988   Play: *M. Butterfly*

Actor: Ron Silver, *Speed-The-Plow*

Actress: Joan Allen, *Burn This*

1989   Play: *The Heidi Chronicles*

Actor: Philip Bosco, *Lend Me a Tenor*

Actress: Pauline Collins, *Shirley Valentine*

1990   Play: *The Grapes of Wrath*

Actor: Robert Morse, *Tru*

Actress: Maggie Smith, *Lettice and Lovage*

1991   Play: *Lost in Yonkers*

Actor: Nigel Hawthorne, *Shadowlands*

Actress: Mercedes Ruehl, *Lost in Yonkers*

1992   Play: *Dancing at Lughnasa*

Actor: Judd Hirsch, *Conversations with My Father*

Actress: Glenn Close, *Death and the Maiden*

1993   Play: *Angels in America: Millennium Approaches*

Actor: Ron Leibman, *Angels in America: Millennium Approaches*

Actress: Madeline Kahn, *The Sisters Rosenswieg*

1994   Play: *Angels in America: Perestroika*

Actor: Stephen Spinella, *Angels in America: Perestroika*

Actress: Diana Rigg, *Medea*

1995   Play: *Love! Valour! Compassion!*

Actor: Ralph Fiennes, *Hamlet*

Actress: Cherry Jones, *The Heiress*

1996   Play: *Master Class*

Actor: George Grizzard, *A Delicate Balance*

Actress: Zoe Caldwell, *Master Class*

1997   Play: *Last Night of Ballyhoo*

Actor: Christopher Plummer, *Barrymore*

Actress: Janet McTeer, *A Doll's House*

1998   Play: *Art*

Actor: Anthony LaPaglia, *A View from the Bridge*

Actress: Marie Mullen, *The Beauty Queen of Leenane*

1999   Play: *Side Man*

Actor: Brian Dennehy, *Death of a Salesman*

Actress: Judi Dench, *Amy's View*

Musicals

1947   No awards

1948   Play: No award

Actor: Paul Hartman, *Angel in the Wings*

Actress: Grace Hartman, *Angel in the Wings*

1949   Play: *Kiss Me Kate*

Actor: Ray Bolger, *Where's Charley*

Actress: Nanette Fabray, *Love Life*

1950 Play: *South Pacific*

Actor: Ezio Pinza, *South Pacific*

Actress: Mary Martin, *South Pacific*

1951 Play: *Guys and Dolls*

Actor: Robert Alda, *Guys and Dolls*

Actress: Ethel Merman, *Call Me Madam*

1952 Play: *The King and I*

Actor: Phil Silvers, *Top Banana*

Actress: Gertrude Lawrence, *The King and I*

1953 Play: *Wonderful Town*

Actor: Thomas Mitchell, *Hazel Flagg*

Actress: Rosalind Russell, *Wonderful Town*

1954 Play: *Kismet*

Actor: Alfred Drake, *Kismet*

Actress: Dolores Gray, *Carnival in Flanders*

1955 Play: *The Pajama Game*

Actor: Walter Slezak, *Fanny*

Actress: Mary Martin, *Peter Pan*

1956 Play: *Damn Yankees*

Actor: Ray Walston, *Damn Yankees*

Actress: Gwen Verdon, *Damn Yankees*

1957 Play: *My Fair Lady*

Actor: Rex Harrison, *My Fair Lady*

Actress: Judy Holliday, *Bells Are Ringing*

1958 Play: *The Music Man*

Actor: Robert Preston, *The Music Man*

Actress: Thelma Ritter and Gwen Verdon, *New Girl in Town* (tie)

1959 Play: *Redhead*

Actor: Richard Kiley, *Redhead*

Actress: Gwen Verdon, *Redhead*

1960 Play: *Fiorello*; *The Sound of Music* (tie)

Actor: Jackie Gleason, *Take Me Along*

Actress: Mary Martin, *The Sound of Music*

1961 Play: *Bye, Bye, Birdie*

Actor: Richard Burton, *Camelot*

Actress: Elizabeth Seal, *Irma la Douce*

1962 Play: *How to Succeed in Business Without Really Trying*

Actor: Robert Morse, *How to Succeed in Business Without Really Trying*

Actress: Anna Maria Alberghetti, *Carnival*; Diahann Carroll, *No Strings* (tie)

1963 Play: *A Funny Thing Happened on the Way to the Forum*

Actor: Zero Mostel, *A Funny Thing Happened on the Way to the Forum*

Actress: Viven Leigh, *Tovarich*

1964 Play: *Hello, Dolly!*

Actor: Bert Lahr, *Foxy*

Actress: Carol Channing, *Hello, Dolly!*

1965 Play: *Fiddler on the Roof*

Actor: Zero Mostel, *Fiddler on the Roof*

Actress: Liza Minnelli, *Flora, the Red Menace*

1966 Play: *Man of La Mancha*

Actor: Richard Kiley, *Man of La Mancha*

Actress: Angela Lansbury, *Mame*

1967 Play: *Cabaret*

Actor: Robert Preston, *I Do! I Do!*

Actress: Barbara Harris, *The Apple Tree*

1968 Play: *Hallelujah, Baby!*

Actor: Robert Goulet, *The Happy Time*

Actress: Patricia Routledge, *Darling of the Day*; Leslie Uggams, *Hallelujah, Baby!* (tie)

1969 Play: *1776*

Actor: Jerry Orbach, *Promises, Promises*

Actress: Angela Lansbury, *Dear World*

1970 Play: *Applause*

Actor: Cleavon Little, *Purlie*

Actress: Lauren Bacall, *Applause*

1971 Play: *Company*

Actor: Hal Linden, *The Rothchilds*

Actress: Helen Gallagher, *No, No Nannette* (revival)

1972 Play: *Two Gentlemen of Verona*

Actor: Phil Silvers, *A Funny Thing Happened on the Way to the Forum* (revival)

Actress: Alexis Smith, *Follies*

1973 Play: *A Little Night Music*

Actor: Ben Vereen, *Pippin*

Actress: Glynis Johns, *A Little Night Music*

1974 Play: *Raisin*

Actor: Christopher Plummer, *Cyrano*

Actress: Virginia Capers, *Raisin*

1975 Play: *The Wiz*

Actor: John Cullum, *Shenandoah*

Actress: Angela Lansbury, *Gypsy* (revival)

1976 Play: *A Chorus Line*

Actor: George Rose, *My Fair Lady* (revival)

Actress: Donna McKechnie, *A Chorus Line*

1977 Play: *Annie*

Actor: Barry Bostwick, *The Robber Bridegroom*

Actress: Dorothy Loudon, *Annie*

1978 Play: *Ain't Misbehavin*

Actor: John Cullum, *On the Twentieth Century*

Actress: Liza Minnelli, *The Act*

1979 Play: *Sweeney Todd*

Actor: Len Cariou, *Sweeney Todd*

Actress: Angela Lansbury, *Sweeney Todd*

1980 Play: *Evita*

Actor: Jim Dale, *Barnum*

Actress: Patti LuPone, *Evita*

1981 Play: *42nd Street*

Actor: Kevin Kline, *The Pirates of Penzance*

Actress: Lauren Bacall, *Woman of the Year*

1982 Play: *Nine*

Actor: Ben Harney, *Dreamgirls*

Actress: Jennifer Holliday, *Dreamgirls*

1983 Play: *Cats*

Actor: Tommy Tune, *My One and Only*

Actress: Natalia Makarova, *On Your Toes*

1984 Play: *La Cage Aux Folles*

Actor: George Hearn, *La Cage Aux Folles*

Actress: Chita Rivera, *The Rink*

1985 Play: *Big River*

Actor: no award

Actress: no award

1986 Play: *The Mystery of Edwin Drood*

Actor: George Rose, *The Mystery of Edwin Drood*

Actress: Bernadette Peters, *Song and Dance*

1987 Play: *Les Misérables*

Actor: Robert Lindsay, *Me and My Girl*

Actress: Maryann Plunkett, *Me and My Girl*

1988 Play: *The Phantom of the Opera*

Actor: Michael Crawford, *The Phantom of the Opera*

Actress: Joanna Gleason, *Into the Woods*

1989 Play: *Jerome Robbins' Broadway*

Actor: Jason Alexander, *Jerome Robbins' Broadway*

Actress: Ruth Brown, *Black and Blue*

1990 Play: *City of Angels*

Actor: James Naughton, *City of Angels*

Actress: Tyne Daly, *Gypsy* (revival)

1991 Play: *The Will Rogers Follies*

Actor: Jonathan Pryce, *Miss Saigon*

Actress: Lea Salonga, *Miss Saigon*

1992 Play: *Crazy for You*

Actor: Gregory Hines, *Jelly's Last Jam*

Actress: Faith Prince, *Guys and Dolls* (revival)

1993 Play: *Kiss of the Spider Woman*

Actor: Brent Carver, *Kiss of the Spider Woman*

Actress: Chita Rivera, *Kiss of the Spider Woman*

1994 Play: *Passion*

Actor: Boyd Gaines, *She Loves Me* (revival)

Actress: Donna Murphy, *Passion*

1995 Play: *Sunset Boulevard*

Actor: Matthew Broderick, *How to Succeed in Business Without Really Trying* (revival)

Actress: Glenn Close, *Sunset Boulevard*

1996 Play: Rent

Actor: Nathan Lane, *A Funny Thing Happened on the Way to the Forum* (revival)

Actress: Donna Murphy, *The King and I* (revival)

1997 Play: *Titanic*

Actor: James Naughton, *Chicago* (revival)

Actress: Bebe Neuwirth, *Chicago* (revival)

1998 Play: *Lion King*

Actor: Alan Cumming, *Cabaret* (revival)

Actress: Natasha Richardson, *Cabaret* (revival)

1999 Play: *Fosse*

Actor: Martin Short, *Little Me* (revival)

Actress: Bernadette Peters, *Annie Get Your Gun* (revival)

Emmy Awards

Before 1956, and in 1957, and from 1959–1960 to 1965–1966, acting awards were given without differentiating between comedy or drama. In 1964, awards were given for acting, as indicated below.

1951 Comedy: *Red Skelton Show* (CBS)

Drama: *Studio One* (CBS)

Variety Show: *Your Show of Shows* (NBC)

Actor: Sid Caesar (NBC)

Actress: Imogene Coca (NBC)

1952 Comedy: *I Love Lucy* (CBS)

Drama: *Robert Montgomery Presents* (NBC)

Variety Shows: *Your Show of Shows* (NBC)

Actor: Thomas Mitchell

Actress: Helen Hayes

1953 Comedy: *I Love Lucy* (CBS)

Drama: *The U.S. Steel Hour* (ABC)

Variety Show: *Omnibus* (CBS)

Actor: Donald O'Connor, *Colgate Comedy* (NBC)

Actress: Eve Arden, *Our Miss Brooks* (CBS)

1954 Comedy: *Make Room for Daddy* (ABC)

Drama: *The U.S. Steel Hour* (ABC)

Variety Show: *Disneyland* (ABC)

Actor: Danny Thomas, *Make Room for Daddy* (ABC)

Actress: Loretta Young, *The Loretta Young Show* (NBC)

1955 Comedy: *The Phil Silvers Show* (CBS)

Drama: *Producers' Showcase* (NBC)

Variety Show: *The Ed Sullivan Show* (CBS)

Actor: Phil Silvers, *The Phil Silvers Show* (CBS)

Actress: Lucille Ball, *I Love Lucy* (CBS)

1956 Comedy: *The Phil Silvers Show* (CBS)

Drama: *Requiem for a Heavyweight* (CBS)

Variety Show: *Caesar's Hour* (NBC)

Actor Comedy: Sid Caesar, *Caesar's Hour* (NBC)

Actress Comedy: Nanette Fabray, *Caesar's Hour* (NBC)

Actor Drama: Robert Young, *Father Knows Best* (NBC)

Actress Drama: Loretta Young, *Loretta Young Show* (NBC)

1957   Comedy: *Phil Silvers Show* (CBS)

Drama: *Gunsmoke* (CBS)

Variety Show: *The Dinah Shore Show* (NBC)

Actor: Robert Young, *Father Knows Best* (NBC)

Actress: Jane Wyatt, *Father Knows Best* (NBC)

1958–1959   Comedy: *Jack Benny Show* (CBS)

Drama: *Playhouse 90* (CBS) (over an hour)

Alcoa-Goodyear Theatre (NBC) (under an hour)

Variety Show: *The Dinah Shore Chevy Show* (NBC)

Actor Comedy: Jack Benny, *Jack Benny Show* (CBS)

Actress Comedy: Jane Wyatt, *Father Knows Best* (NBC)

Actor Drama: Raymond Burr, *Perry Mason* (CBS)

Actress Drama: Loretta Young, *Loretta Young Show* (NBC)

1959–1960   Comedy: *Art Carney Special* (NBC)

Drama: *Playhouse 90* (CBS)

Variety Show: *The Fabulous '50s* (CBS)

Actor: Robert Stack, *The Untouchables* (ABC)

Actress: Jane Wyatt, *Father Knows Best* (NBC)

1960–1961   Comedy: *Jack Benny Show* (CBS)

Drama: *Macbeth*, *Hallmark Hall of Fame* (NBC)

Variety Show: *Astaire Time* (NBC)

Actor: Raymond Burr, *Perry Mason* (CBS)

Actress: Barbara Stanwyck, *Barbara Stanwyck Show* (NBC)

1961–1962   Comedy: *Bob Newhart Show* (CBS)

Drama: *The Defenders* (CBS)

Actor: E.G. Marshall, *The Defenders* (CBS)

Actress: Shirley Booth, *Hazel* (NBC)

1962–1963   Comedy: *Dick Van Dyke Show* (CBS)

Drama: *The Defenders* (CBS)

Variety Show: *The Andy Williams Show* (NBC)

Actor: E.G. Marshall, *The Defenders* (CBS)

Actress: Shirley Booth, *Hazel* (NBC)

1963–1964   Comedy: *Dick Van Dyke Show* (CBS)

Drama: *The Defenders* (CBS)

Variety Show: *The Danny Kaye Show* (CBS)

Actor: Dick Van Dyke, *Dick Van Dyke Show* (CBS)

Actress: Mary Tyler Moore, *Dick Van Dyke Show* (CBS)

1964–1965   Acting: Dick Van Dyke, *Dick Van Dyke Show* (CBS)

Acting: Lynn Fontanne and Alfred Lunt, *Hallmark Hall of Fame* (NBC)

Variety Show: *My Name Is Barbra* (CBS)

1965–1966   Comedy: *Dick Van Dyke Show* (CBS)

Drama: *The Fugitive* (ABC)

Variety Show: *The Andy Williams Show* (NBC)

Actor Comedy: Dick Van Dyke, *Dick Van Dyke Show* (CBS)

Actress: Mary Tyler Moore, *Dick Van Dyke Show* (CBS)

Actor Drama: Bill Cosby, *I Spy* (NBC)

Actress Drama: Barbara Stanwyck, *The Big Valley* (ABC)

1966–1967   Comedy: *The Monkees* (NBC)

Drama: *Mission: Impossible* (CBS)

Variety Show: *The Andy Williams Show* (NBC)

Actor Comedy: Don Adams, *Get Smart* (NBC)

Actress Comedy: Lucille Ball, *The Lucy Show* (CBS)

Actor Drama: Bill Cosby, *I Spy* (NBC)

Actress Drama: Barbara Bain, *Mission: Impossible* (CBS)

1967–1968   Comedy: *Get Smart* (NBC)

Drama: *Mission: Impossible* (CBS)

Variety Show: *Rowan & Martin's Laugh-In* (NBC)

Actor Comedy: Don Adams, *Get Smart* (NBC)

Actress Comedy: Lucille Ball, *The Lucy Show* (CBS)

Actor Drama: Bill Cosby, *I Spy* (NBC)

Actress Drama: Barbara Bain, *Mission: Impossible* (CBS)

1968–1969   Comedy: *Get Smart* NBC)

Drama: *NET Playhouse* (NET)

Variety Show: *Rowan & Martin's Laugh-In* (NBC)

Actor Comedy: Don Adams, *Get Smart* (NBC)

Actress Comedy: Hope Lange, *The Ghost and Mrs. Muir* (NBC)

Actor Drama: Carl Betz, *Judd for the Defense* (ABC)

Actress Drama: Barbara Bain, *Mission: Impossible* (CBS)

1969–1970   Comedy: *My World & Welcome to It* (NBC)

Drama: *Marcus Welby, MD* (ABC)

Variety Show: *The David Frost Show* (syndicated)

Actor Comedy: William Windom, *My World & Welcome to It* (NBC)

Actress Comedy: Hope Lange, *The Ghost and Mrs. Muir* (NBC)

Actor Drama: Robert Young, *Marcus Welby MD* (ABC)

Actress Drama: Susan Hampshire, *Forsyte Saga* (NET)

1970–1971   Comedy: *All in the Family* (CBS)

Drama: "The Senator" (segment), *The Bold Ones* (NBC)

Variety Show: *The Flip Wilson Show* (NBC)

Actor Comedy: Jack Klugman, *Odd Couple* (ABC)

Actress Comedy: Jean Stapleton, *All in the Family* (CBS)

Actor Drama: Hal Holbrook "The Senator" (segment), *The Bold Ones* (NBC)

Actress Drama: Susan Hampshire, *The First Churchills* (PBS)

1971–1972 Comedy: *All in the Family* (CBS)

Drama: "Elizabeth R," *Masterpiece Theatre* (PBS)

Music: *The Carol Burnett Show* (CBS)

Talk: *The Dick Cavett Show* (ABC)

Actor Comedy: Carroll O'Connor, *All in the Family* (CBS)

Actress Comedy: Jean Stapleton, *All in the Family* (CBS)

Actor Drama: Peter Falk, *Columbo* (NBC)

Actress Drama: Glenda Jackson, "Elizabeth R," *Masterpiece Theatre* (PBS)

1972–1973 Comedy: *All in the Family* (CBS)

Drama: *The Waltons* (CBS)

Variety Show: *The Julie Andrews Hour* (ABC)

Actor Comedy: Jack Klugman, *Odd Couple* (ABC)

Actress Comedy: Jean Stapleton, *All in the Family* (CBS)

Actor Drama: Richard Thomas, *The Waltons* (CBS)

Actress Drama: Michael Learned, *The Waltons* (CBS)

1973–1974 Comedy: *M*A*S*H* (CBS)

Drama: "Upstairs, Downstairs," *Masterpiece Theatre* (PBS)

Variety Show: *The Carol Burnett Show*

Actor Comedy: Alan Alda, *M*A*S*H* (CBS)

Actress Comedy: Mary Tyler Moore, *Mary Tyler Moore Show* (CBS)

Actor Drama: Telly Savalas, *Kojak* (CBS)

Actress Drama: Michael Learned, *The Waltons* (CBS)

1974–1975 Comedy: *The Mary Tyler Show* (CBS)

Drama: "Upstairs, Downstairs," *Masterpiece Theatre* (PBS)

Variety Show: *The Carol Burnett Show*

Actor Comedy: Tony Randall, *Odd Couple* (ABC)

Actress Comedy: Valerie Harper, *Rhoda* (CBS)

Actor Drama: Robert Blake, *Baretta* (ABC)

Actress Drama: Jean Marsh, "Upstairs, Downstairs," *Masterpiece Theatre* (PBS)

1975–1976 Comedy: *The Mary Tyler Moore Show* (CBS)

Drama: *Police Story* (NBC)

Variety: *NBC's Saturday Night* (NBC)

Actor Comedy: Jack Albertson, *Chico & the Man* (NBC)

Actress Comedy: Mary Tyler Moore, *Mary Tyler Moore Show* (CBS)

Actor Drama: Peter Falk, *Columbo* (NBC)

Actress Drama: Michael Learned, *The Waltons* (CBS)

1976–1977   Comedy: *The Mary Tyler Moore Show* (CBS)

Drama: "Upstairs, Downstairs," *Masterpiece Theatre* (PBS)

Variety Show: *Van Dyke & Company* (NBC)

Actor Comedy: Carroll O'Connor, *All in the Family* (CBS)

Actress Comedy: Beatrice Arthur, *Maude* (CBS)

Actor Drama: James Garner, *Rockford Files* (NBC)

Actress Drama: Lindsay Wagner, *Bionic Woman* (ABC)

1977–1978   Comedy: *All in the Family* (CBS)

Drama: *Rockford Files* (NBC)

Variety Show: *The Muppet Show* (syndicated)

Actor Comedy: Carroll O'Connor, *All in the Family* (CBS)

Actress Comedy: Jean Stapleton, *All in the Family* (CBS)

Actor : Edward Asner, *Lou Grant* (CBS)

Actress Drama: Sada Thompson, *Family* (ABC)

1978–1979   Comedy: *Taxi* (ABC)

Drama: *Lou Grant* (CBS)

Variety Show: "Steve & Eydie Celebrate Irving Berlin" (NBC)

Actor Comedy: Carroll O'Connor, *All in the Family* (CBS)

Actress Comedy: Ruth Gordon, *Taxi* (ABC)

Actor Drama: Ron Leibman, *Kaz* (CBS)

Actress Drama: Mariette Hartley, *Incredible Hulk* (CBS)

1979–1980   Comedy: *Taxi* (ABC)

Drama: *Lou Grant* (CBS)

Variety Show: "BM Presents Baryshnikov on Broadway" (ABC)

Actor Comedy: Richard Mulligan, *Soap* (ABC)

Actress Comedy: Cathryn Damon, *Soap* (ABC)

Actor Drama: Edward Asner, *Lou Grant* (CBS)

Actress Drama: Barbara Bel Geddes, *Dallas* (CBS)

1980–1981   Comedy: *Taxi* (ABC)

Drama: *Hill Street Blues* (NBC)

Variety Show: "Lily: Sold Out" (CBS)

Actor Comedy: Judd Hirsch, *Taxi* (ABC)

Actress Comedy: Isabel Sanford, *The Jeffersons* (CBS)

Actor Drama: Daniel Travanti, *Hill Street Blues* (NBC)

Actress Drama: Barbara Babcock, *Hill Street Blues* (NBC)

1981–1982   Comedy: *Barney Miller* (ABC)

Drama: *Hill Street Blues* (NBC)

Variety Show: "Night of 100 Stars" (ABC)

Comedy-Actor: Alan Alda, *M*A*S*H* (CBS)

Comedy: Actress: Carol Kane, *Taxi* (ABC)

Actor Drama: Daniel Travanti, *Hill Street Blues* (NBC)

Actress Drama: Michael Learned, *Nurse* (CBS)

1982–1983 Comedy: *Cheers* (NBC)

Drama: *Hill Street Blues* (NBC)

Variety Show: "Motown 25: Yesterday, Today, Forever" (NBC)

Actor Comedy: Judd Hirsch, *Taxi* (NBC)

Actress Comedy: Shelley Long, *Cheers* (NBC)

Actor Drama: Ed Flanders, *St. Elsewhere* (NBC)

Actress Drama: Tyne Daly, *Cagney & Lacey* (CBS)

1983–1984 Comedy: *Cheers* (NBC)

Drama: *Hill Street Blues* (NBC)

Variety Show: "The 6th Annual Kennedy Center Honors" (CBS)

Actor Comedy: John Ritter, *Three's Company* (ABC)

Actress Comedy: Jane Curtin, *Kate & Allie* (CBS)

Actor Drama: Tom Selleck, *Magnum P.I.* (CBS)

Actress Drama: Tyne Daly, *Cagney & Lacey* (CBS)

1984–1985 Comedy: *Cosby Show* (NBC)

Drama: *Cagney & Lacey* (CBS)

Variety Show: "Motown Returns to the Apollo" (NBC)

Actor Comedy: Robert Guillaume, *Benson* (ABC)

Actress Comedy: Jane Curtin, *Kate & Allie* (CBS)

Actor Drama: William Daniels, *St. Elsewhere* (NBC)

Actress Drama: Tyne Daly, *Cagney & Lacey* (CBS)

1985–1986 Comedy: *The Golden Girls* (NBC)

Drama: *Cagney & Lacey* (CBS)

Variety Show: "The Kennedy Center Honors" (CBS)

Actor Comedy: Michael J. Fox, *Family Ties* (NBC)

Actress Comedy: Betty White, *The Golden Girls* (NBC)

Actor Drama: William Daniels, *St. Elsewhere* (NBC)

Actress Drama: Sharon Gless, *Cagney & Lacey* (CBS)

1986–1987 Comedy: *The Golden Girls* (NBC)

Drama: *L.A. Law* (NBC)

Variety Show: "The 1987 Tony Awards" (CBS)

Actor Comedy: Michael J. Fox, *Family Ties* (NBC)

Actress Comedy: Rue McClanahan, *The Golden Girls* (NBC)

Actor Drama: Bruce Willis, *Moonlighting* (ABC)

Actress Drama: Sharon Gless, *Cagney & Lacey* (CBS)

1987–1988 Comedy: *The Wonder Years* (ABC)

Drama: *thirtysomething* (ABC)

Variety Show: "Irving Berlin's 100th Birthday Celebration" (CBS)

Actor Comedy: Michael J. Fox, *Family Ties* (NBC)

Actress Comedy: Beatrice Arthur, *The Golden Girls* (NBC)

Actor Drama: Richard Kiley, *A Year in the Life* (NBC)

Actress Drama: Tyne Daly, *Cagney & Lacey* (CBS)

1988–1989 Comedy: *Cheers* (NBC)

Drama: *L.A. Law* (NBC)

Variety Show: *The Tracey Ullman Show* (Fox)

Actor Comedy: Richard Mulligan, *Empty Nest* (NBC)

Actress Comedy: Candice Bergen, *Murphy Brown* (CBS)

Actor Drama: Carroll O'Connor, *In the Heat of the Night* (NBC)

Actress Drama: Dana Delany, *China Beach* (ABC)

1989–1990 Comedy: *Murphy Brown* (CBS)

Drama: *L.A. Law* (NBC)

Variety Show: *In Living Color* (FOX)

Actor Comedy: Ted Danson, *Cheers* (NBC)

Actress Drama: Candice Bergen, *Murphy Brown* (CBS)

Actor Drama: Peter Falk, *Columbo* (ABC)

Actress Drama: Patricia Wettig, *thirtysomething* (ABC)

1990–1991 Comedy: Cheers (NBC)

Drama: *L.A. Law* (NBC)

Variety Show: "The 63rd Annual Academy Awards" (ABC)

Actor Comedy: Burt Reynolds, *Evening Shade* (CBS)

Actress Comedy: Kirstie Alley, *Cheers* (NBC)

Actor Drama: James Earl Jones, *Gabriel's Fire* (ABC)

Actress Drama: Patricia Wettig, *thirtysomething* (ABC)

1991–1992 Comedy: *Murphy Brown* (CBS)

Drama: *Northern Exposure* (CBS)

Variety Show: *The Tonight Show starring Johnny Carson* (NBC)

Actor Comedy: Craig T. Nelson, *Coach* (ABC)

Actress Comedy: Candice Bergen, *Murphy Brown* (CBS)

Actor Drama: Christopher Lloyd, *Avonlea* (Disney)

Actress Drama: Dana Delany, *China Beach* (ABC)

1992–1993 Comedy: *Seinfeld* (NBC)

Drama: *Picket Fences* (CBS)

Variety Show: *Saturday Night Live* (NBC)

Actor Comedy: Ted Danson, *Cheers* (NBC

Actress Comedy: Roseanne Arnold, *Roseanne* (ABC)

Actor Drama: Tom Skerritt, *Picket Fences* (CBS)

Actress Drama: Kathy Baker, *Picket Fences* (CBS)

1993–1994 Comedy: *Frasier* (NBC)

Drama: *Picket Fences* (CBS)

Variety Show: *Late Show with David Letterman* (CBS)

Actor Comedy: Kelsey Grammer, *Frasier* (NBC)

Actress Comedy: Candice Bergen, *Murphy Brown* (CBS)

Actor Drama: Dennis Franz, *NYPD Blue* (ABC)

Actress Drama: Sela Ward, *Sisters* (NBC)

1994–1995 Comedy: *Frasier* (NBC)

Drama: *NYPD Blue* (ABC)

Variety Show: *The Tonight Show with Jay Leno* (NBC)

Actor Comedy: Kelsey Grammer, *Frasier* (NBC)

Actress Comedy: Candice Bergen, *Murphy Brown* (CBS)

Actor Drama: Mandy Patinkin, *Chicago Hope* (CBS)

Actress Drama: Kathy Baker, *Picket Fences* (CBS)

1995–1996 Comedy: *Frasier* (NBC)

Drama: *E.R.* (NBC)

Variety Show: *Dennis Miller Live* (HBO)

Actor Comedy: John Lithgow, *Third Rock from the Sun* (NBC)

Actress Comedy: Helen Hunt, *Mad About You* (NBC)

Actor Drama: Dennis Franz, *NYPD Blue* (ABC)

Actress Drama: Kathy Baker, *Picket Fences* (CBS)

1996–1997 Comedy: *Frasier* (NBC)

Drama: *Law & Order* (NBC)

Variety Show: "Tracey Takes On . . ." (HBO)

Actor Comedy: John Lithgow, *Third Rock from the Sun* (NBC)

Actress Comedy: Helen Hunt, *Mad About You* (NBC)

Actor Drama: Dennis Franz, *NYPD Blue* (ABC)

Actress Drama: Gillian Anderson, *The X-Files* (FOX)

1997–1998 Comedy: *Frasier* (NBC)

Drama: *The Practice* (ABC)

Actor Comedy: Kelsey Grammer, *Frasier* (NBC)

Actress Comedy: Helen Hunt, *Mad About You* (NBC)

Actor Drama: Andre Braugher, *Homicide: Life on the Street* (NBC)

Actress Drama: Christine Lahti, *Chicago Hope* (CBS)

1998–1999 Comedy: *Ally McBeal* (FOX)

Drama: *The Practice* (ABC)

Actor Comedy: John Lithgow, *Third Rock from the Sun* (NBC)

Actress Comedy: Helen Hunt, *Mad About You* (NBC)

Actor Comedy: Dennis Franz, *NYPD Blue* (ABC)

Actress Drama: Edie Falco, *The Sopranos* (HBO)

Grammy Awards (Recording Arts and Sciences)

1958   Record: Domenico Modugno, "Nel Blu Di-pinto Di Blu (Volare)"

Album: Henry Mancini, *The Music From Peter Gunn*

1959   Record: Bobby Darin, "Mack the Knife"

Album: Frank Sinatra, *Come Dance With Me*

1960   Record: Percy Faith, "Theme From a Summer Place"

Album: Bob Newhart, *Button Down Mind*

1961   Record: Henry Mancini, "Moon River"

Album: Judy Garland, *Judy at Carnegie Hall*

1962   Record: Tony Bennett, "I Left My Heart in San Francisco"

Album: Vaughn Meader, *The First Family*

1963   Record: Henry Mancini, "The Days of Wine and Roses"

Album: *The Barbra Streisand Album*

1964   Record: Stan Getz and Astrud Gilberto, "The Girl From Ipanema"

Album: Stan Getz and Astrud Gilberto, *Getz/Gilberto*

1965   Record: Herb Alpert, "A Taste of Honey"

Album: Frank Sinatra, *September of My Years*

1966   Record: Frank Sinatra, "Strangers in the Night"

Album: Frank Sinatra, *A Man and His Music*

1967   Record: 5th Dimension, "Up, Up and Away"

Album: The Beatles, *Sgt. Pepper's Lonely Hearts Club Band*

1968   Record: Simon & Garfunkel, "Mrs. Robinson"

Album: Glen Campbell, *By the Time I Get to Phoenix*

1969   Record: 5th Dimension, "Aquarius/Let the Sunshine In"

Album: Blood, Sweat and Tears, *Blood, Sweat and Tears*

1970   Record: Simon & Garfunkel, "Bridge over Troubled Water"

Album: Simon & Garfunkel, *Bridge over Troubled Water*

1971   Record: Carole King, "It's Too Late"

Album: Carole King, *Tapestry*

1972   Record: Roberta Flack, "The First Time Ever I Saw Your Face"

Album: *The Concert for Bangladesh*

1973   Record: Roberta Flack, "Killing Me Softly With His Song"

Album: Stevie Wonder, *Innervisions*

1974   Record: Olivia Newton-John, "I Honestly Love You"

Album: Stevie Wonder, *Fulfillingness' First Finale*

1975 Record: Captain & Tennille, "Love Will Keep Us Together"

Album: Paul Simon, *Still Crazy After All These Years*

1976 Record: George Benson, "This Masquerade"

Album: Stevie Wonder, *Songs in the Key of Life*

1977 Record: Eagles, "Hotel California"

Album: Fleetwood Mac, *Rumours*

1978 Record: Billy Joel, "Just the Way You Are"

Album: Bee Gees, *Saturday Night Fever*

1979 Record: The Doobie Brothers, "What a Fool Believes"

Album: Billy Joel, *52nd Street*

1980 Record: Christopher Cross, "Sailing"

Album: Christopher Cross, *Christopher Cross*

1981 Record: Kim Carnes, "Bette Davis Eyes"

Album: John Lennon and Yoko Ono, *Double Fantasy*

1982 Record: Toto, "Rosanna"

Album: Toto, *Toto IV*

1983 Record: Michael Jackson, "Beat It"

Album: Michael Jackson, *Thriller*

1984 Record: Tina Turner, "What's Love Got to Do With It"

Album: Lionel Richie, *Can't Slow Down*

1985 Record: USA for Africa, "We Are the World"

Album: Phil Collins, *No Jacket Required*

1986 Record: Steve Winwood, "Higher Love"

Album: Paul Simon, *Graceland*

1987 Record: Paul Simon, "Graceland"

Album: U2, *The Joshua Tree*

1988 Record: Bobby McFerrin, "Don't Worry, Be Happy"

Album: George Michael, *Faith*

1989 Record: Bette Midler, "Wind Beneath My Wings"

Album: Bonnie Raitt, *Nick of Time*

1990 Record: Phil Collins, "Another Day in Paradise"

Album: Quincy Jones, *Back on the Block*

1991 Record: Natalie Cole, with Nat "King" Cole, "Unforgettable"

Album: Natalie Cole, with Nat "King" Cole, *Unforgettable*

1992 Record: Eric Clapton, "Tears in Heaven"

Album: Eric Clapton, *Unplugged*

1993 Record: Whitney Houston, "I Will Always Love You"

Album: Whitney Houston, *The Bodyguard*

1994 Record: Sheryl Crow, "All I Wanna Do"

Album: Tony Bennett, *MTV Unplugged*

1995 Record: Seal, "Kiss from a Rose"

Album: Alanis Morissette, *Jagged Little Pill*

1996 Record: Eric Clapton, "Change the World"

Album: Celine Dion, *Falling into You*

1997 Record: Shawn Colvin, "Sunny Came Home"

Album: Bob Dylan, *Time Out of Mind*

1998 Record: Celine Dion, "My Heart Will Go On"

Album: Lauryn Hill, *The Miseducation of Lauryn Hill*

Miss America Winners

1921 Margaret Gorman, Washington, D.C.

1922–1923 Mary Campbell, Columbus, Ohio

1924 Ruth Malcolmson, Philadelphia, Pennsylvania

1925 Fay Lamphier, Oakland, California

1926 Norma Smallwood, Tulsa, Oklahoma

1927 Lois Delander, Joliet, Illinois

1933 Marion Bergeron, West Haven, Connecticut

1935 Henrietta Leaver, Pittsburgh, Pennsylvania

1936 Rose Coyle, Philadelphia, Pennsylvania

1937 Bette Cooper, Bertrand Island, New Jersey

1938 Marilyn Meseke, Marion, Ohio

1939 Patricia Donnelly, Detroit, Michigan

1940 Frances Marie Burke, Philadelphia, Pennsylvania

1941 Rosemary LaPlanche, Los Angeles, California

1942 Jo-Caroll Dennison, Tyler, Texas

1943 Jean Bartel, Los Angeles, California

1944 Venus Ramey, Washington, D.C.

1945 Bess Myerson, New York City, New York

1946 Marilyn Buferd, Los Angeles, California

1947 Barbara Walker, Memphis, Tennessee

1948 BeBe Shopp, Hopkins, Minnesota

1949 Jacque Mercer, Litchfield, Arizona

1951 Yolande Betbeze, Mobile, Alabama

1952 Colleen Kay Hutchins, Salt Lake City, Utah

1953 Neva Jane Langley, Macon, Georgia

1954 Evelyn Margaret Ay, Ephrata, Pennsylvania

1955 Lee Meriwether, San Francisco, California

1956 Sharon Ritchie, Denver, Colorado

1957 Marian McKnight, Manning, South Carolina

1958 Marilyn Van Derbur, Denver, Colorado

1959 Mary Ann Mobley, Brandon, Mississippi

1960 Lynda Lee Mead, Natchez, Mississippi

1961 Nancy Fleming, Montague, Michigan

1962 Maria Fletcher, Asheville, North Carolina

1963 Jacquelyn Mayer, Sandusky, Ohio

1964 Donna Axum, El Dorado, Arkansas

1965 Vonda Kay Van Dyke, Phoenix, Arizona

1966 Deborah Irene Bryant, Overland Park, Kansas

1967 Jane Anne Jayroe, Laverne, Oklahoma

1968 Debra Dene Barnes, Moran, Kansas

1969 Judith Anne Ford, Belvidere, Illinois

1970 Pamela Anne Eldred, Birmingham, Michigan

1971 Phyllis Ann George, Denton, Texas

1972 Laurie Lea Schaefer, Columbus, Ohio

1973	Terry Anne Meeuwsen, DePere, Wisconsin
1974	Rebecca Ann King, Denver, Colorado
1975	Shirley Cothran, Fort Worth, Texas
1976	Tawney Elaine Godin, Yonkers, New York
1977	Dorothy Kathleen Benham, Edina, Minnesota
1978	Susan Perkins, Columbus, Ohio
1979	Kylene Barker, Galax, Virginia
1980	Cheryl Prewitt, Ackerman, Mississippi
1981	Susan Powell, Elk City, Oklahoma
1982	Elizabeth Ward, Russellville, Arkansas
1983	Debra Maffett, Anaheim, California
1984	Vanessa Williams, Milwood, New York (Resigned July 23, 1984)
	Suzette Charles, Mays Landing, New Jersey
1985	Sharlene Wells, Salt Lake City, Utah
1986	Susan Akin, Meridian, Mississippi
1987	Kellye Cash, Memphis, Tennessee
1988	Kaye Lani Rae Rafko, Monroe, Michigan
1989	Gretchen Carlson, Anoka, Minnesota
1990	Debbye Turner, Columbia, Missouri
1991	Marjorie Vincent, Oak Park, Illlinois
1992	Carolyn Suzanne Sapp, Honolulu, Hawaii
1993	Leanza Cornett, Jacksonville, Florida
1994	Kimberly Aiken, Columbia, South Carolina
1995	Heather Whitestone, Birmingham, Alabama
1996	Shawntel Smith, Muldrow, Oklahoma
1997	Tara Dawn Holland, Overland Park, Kansas
1998	Kate Shindle, Evanston, Illinois
1999	Nicole Johnson, Roanoke, Virginia

(Sources: *World Book*, *World Almanac*, *NYT Almanac*, and *Book of Chronologies*)

FIRST AND FAMOUS TELEVISION DATES

Both as a baby boomer raised on television-watching, and a professional researcher at NBC for 15 years, the history of broadcasting holds a particular fascination for me. Here we trace broadcasting back to the days of theoretical research on the existence of radio waves, through the development of radio programming, and on into the television era—glomming together science, technology, and pop culture in a single chronology.

1864	James Clerk Maxwell theorized existence of radio waves traveling at speed of light.
1880s	German physicist Heinrich Hertz confirmed Maxwell's theory.
1895	Guglielmo Marconi became first person to send radio signals trough air.
1906	Lee De Forest invented the vacuum tube, permitting transmission of voice and music over air waves.
	Reginald A. Fressenden first to transmit human voice via radio.
1909	First sea rescue involving transmission of distress signals by radio: after collision with another vessel at sea, S.S. *Republic* radioed call for help.
1910	First daily radio broadcasts began by Charles Herrold School of Radio Broadcasting in San Jose, California (now operating as KCBS, San Francisco).

1916 David Sarnoff first proposed mass production of radio receivers for home use.

1918 Edwin H. Armstrong invented superheterodyne circuit, improving radio receivers.

1919 Woodrow Wilson first U.S. president to make radio broadcast; spoke from a ship to soldiers aboard other ships.

1920 August 20 – Station WWJ in Detroit first commercial radio station began broadcasting.

November 2 – Station KDKA in Pittsburgh broadcast 1920 presidential election results; generally considered first professional broadcast.

1921 Federal government issued first license to broadcast regularly to station WBZ in Springfield, Massachusetts.

1922 WJZ in New York City and WGY in Schnectady, New York, broadcast World Series; first network (or chain) broadcasting. First radio commercial broadcast over WEAF in New York.

1925–1950 Golden Age of Radio; medium became dominant source of family entertainment in America.

1926 National Broadcasting Company formed first national network.

First public demonstration of television by British inventor J.L. Baird

1927 Radio Act established Federal Radio Commission to regulate broadcasting.

1928 Baird demonstrated color television for first time.

Radio programs *The Voice of Firestone*, featuring live music, and *Amos 'n' Andy* premiered.

1930 Philo T. Farnsworth developed cathode-ray tube, later used in television viewing screens.

Vladimir Zworykin invented image orthicon tube, used in television cameras.

RCA's experimental television station WZRBX began operation.

1933–1945 Franklin D. Roosevelt first president to use radio as effective means to communicate directly to the American public and mobilize support for government policies. First "Fireside Chat" broadcast March 12, 1933.

1933 Edwin Armstrong developed and patented FM (frequency modulation) broadcasting.

1934 Communications Act of 1934 established Federal Communications Commission to regulate broadcasting.

1937 Radio news coverage of *Hindenberg* disaster first radio program broadcast coast-to-coast.

1938 First live televised coverage of news event: NBC mobile unit turned camera on raging fire in Queens, New York.

Radio broadcast of Orson Welles' production of H.G. Wells' *War of the Worlds*, about fictional Martian invasion of New Jersey, caused large-scale panic among naive listeners.

1939 NBC began first regular television broadcasting.

1939 Franklin D. Roosevelt became first president to be televised (during New York World's Fair opening ceremonies).

First television sports broadcast: Princeton vs. Columbia baseball game.

CBS and Dumont first began their television broadcasting.

1940 First color broadcast by CBS.

First political convention broadcast: Republican party.

First opera broadcast: excerpts of *Pagliacci*.

First televised basketball game: University of Pittsburgh vs. Fordham.

First televised hockey game: New York Rangers vs. Montreal Canadiens.

1941 CBS and NBC stations in New York received first commercial licenses.

First commercial featured face of Bulova clock.

First simulcast: *Truth or Consequences* broadcast on television and radio.

Ninety-minute documentary on CBS reported Japanese attack on Pearl Harbor.

First musical comedy written for TV, *Boys from Boise*, sponsored by *Esquire* magazine.

1943 NBC forced to divest itself of one of its two radio networks. Divested network becomes ABC.

1945 President Harry Truman made first presidential network telecast at Navy Day ceremonies in New York's Central Park.

First telecast of Army-Navy football game.

1946 NBC staged first television network broadcast, feeding programs from New York City to Schenectady and Philadelphia.

First television soap opera debuted: *Faraway Hill.*

With wartime restrictions lifted, television industry began rapid growth.

Ted Mack's *Original Amateur Hour*, Ed Sullivan's *Toast of the Town,* and *Arthur Godfrey's Talent Scouts*, premiered.

Boxing great Joe Louis knocked out Billy Conn in televised bout at Yankee Stadium.

1947 First State of the Union telecast

President Harry Truman spoke before Congressional joint session.

First telecast of World Series.

Bell Labs scientists invented the transistor.

Meet the Press, television's longest running series began broadcasting on NBC. *Kraft Television Theater* debuted with live drama; *Howdy Doody* premiered.

1948 First full-length opera presentation on television *Othello* broadcast from the Met.

First Rose Bowl telecast.

Foreign broadcasts begun by Voice of America. Arturo Toscanini conducted NBC Symphony. Milton Berle's *Texaco Star Theater*, Ted Mack's *Original Amateur Hour*, *Lone Ranger*, and *Television Playhouse*, premiered.

1949 Rating system to determine most popular shows established.

First African American to have own television show: pianist Bob Howard.

First Emmy Awards presented. *Kukla Fran and Ollie* and Sid Caesar and Imogene Coca's *Admiral Broadway Review* (later renamed *Your Show of Shows*) debuted.

1950 First Community Antenna Television (cable TV) system began operation. Jackie Gleason originated *The Honeymooners*, as comedy sketches on *Cavalcade of Stars. What's My Line, Beat the Clock*, Groucho Marx's *You Bet Your Life*, and *Beulah* (starring Ethel Waters) premiered. Garry Moore began daily afternoon show.

1951 First regularly scheduled news documentary series premiered: Edward R. Murrow's *See It Now* on CBS. *Amos and Andy* moved from radio to television. *I Love Lucy* and *Cisco Kid* premiered.

First transcontinental television broadcast presented.

Senator Estes Kefauver (D – Tenn.) presided over televised hearings probing crime in America.

1952 First morning news magazine show premiered: *The Today Show* hosted by Dave Garroway on NBC.

Congress began first investigation into effects of TV violence on viewers.

Atomic bomb tests in Nevada broadcast on TV. *Dragnet, Ernie Kovacs Show, Grand Old Opry, My Little Margie,* and *Ozzie and Harriet* premiered.

Congress launched first probe of impact of TV violence on viewers.

September 23 – Republican vice presidential candidate Richard M. Nixon delivered his "Checkers Speech," disavowing wrongdoing in "slush fund" controversy.

1953 First televised Presidential Inauguration: Dwight D. Eisenhower.

First Oscar ceremonies telecast.

Coronation of Queen Elizabeth II of England covered by television news organizations.

Edward R. Murrow's *Person to Person* and Walter Cronkite's *You Are There* programs premiered on CBS. *Marty* broadcast on *Television Playhouse; Red Skelton Show* premiered.

1954 First color television meeting government standards marketed by RCA.

First color network broadcast: NBC telecast "Tournament of Roses Parade."

Army-McCarthy hearings broadcast on TV.

March 9 – Edward R. Murrow reported blistering expose on Senator Joseph McCarthy (R – Wis.), who was later censured by the Senate.

Steve Allen became host on NBC's *The Tonight Show. Lassie, Disneyland, Father Knows Best,* and *Medic* premiered. Bert Parks emceed "Miss America Pageant" for first time

1955 First big-money quiz shows broadcast on network TV: *64,000 Question* premiered.

First recorded presidential news conference (Eisenhower) broadcast.

Wyatt Earp and *Romper Room* debuted. *Gunsmoke* became number-one rated entertainment program.

March 7 – *Peter Pan,* starring Mary Martin, aired on NBC.

1956 *Huntley-Brinkley Report* debuted on NBC. *As the World Turns* and *The Price is Right* aired for first time. Elvis Presley appeared on *Ed Sullivan Show.*

October 11 – *Requiem for a Heavyweight* broadcast live on *Playhouse 90.*

1957 Pocket-sized transistor radio first marketed by Sony. Jack Paar took over as *Tonight Show* host. *American Bandstand, Perry Mason, Leave It to Beaver,* and *Bachelor Father* premiered.

1958 Rigged quiz show scandal broke; premieres of *The Untouchables, Sea Hunt, Bat Masterson,* and *Peter Gunn* aired.

1959 *Bonanza* debuted as first hour-long show broadcast in color.

Sony brought out first transistorized television set. Rigged quiz show scandal shook faith in television. Reference to Nazi gas chambers edited from Playhouse 90's broadcast of "Judgment at Nuremberg" under pressure from sponsor Gas Industry of America.

1960 February 11 – Miffed that NBC censors had bleeped previous show's monologue, *Tonight Show* host Jack Paar quit and walked out during next show's opening monologue. He was back one month later.

September 24 – Final episode of *Howdy Doody*; Clarabell, the clown, spoke for first and only time—to say "Good-bye, kids."

September 26 – John F. Kennedy and Richard M. Nixon engaged in first ever televised presidential debate.

November 25 – Edward R. Murrow's *Harvest of Shame* documentary reported plight of migrant farm workers.

Flintstones, first primetime animated series, *My Three Sons*, *Sing Along With Mitch*, *Andy Griffith Show*, and *Route 66* debuted.

1961 January 25 – First live broadcast of presidential news conference: John F. Kennedy.

First radio communication with man in space (Soviet cosmonaut Yuri Gagarin).

May 5 – Alan Shepard's first American space flight covered by television news.

FCC Chairman Newton Minow coined phrase "vast wasteland" to describe television programming.

Dick Van Dyke Show and *Mr. Ed* (the talking horse) debuted.

1962 First American orbital flight by John Glenn covered by television news. Johnny Carson took over as *Tonight Show* host; *The Virginian* and *McHale's Navy* premiered.

1963 First use of instant replay (Army-Navy game).

First live pictures from space.

May 3 – Network news programs carried pictures of fire hoses and police dogs used to brutally attack civil rights demonstrators in Birmingham, Alabama.

August 28 – Television news covered Martin Luther King Jr.'s "I Have A Dream" speech during March on Washington.

November 22–25 – Networks devoted continuing coverage of President Kennedy's assassination.

November 24 – Jack Ruby shot and killed presumed Kennedy-assassin Lee Harvey Oswald as millions watched on television.

November 25 – Millions watched funeral of John F. Kennedy, including farewell salute by John, Jr.

Premieres of *The Fugitive* and *My Favorite Martian*.

1964 First public demonstration of stationary (geosynchronous) satellite to broadcast television pictures.

NBC correspondent John Chancellor was arrested and escorted off the floor during coverage of Republican convention in San Francisco that nominated Barry Goldwater and booed liberal Republicans like Nelson Rockefeller.

February 9 – Beatles appeared for first time on American television on *The Ed Sullivan Show*.

Addams Family, *The Munsters*, *Bewitched*, and *Gilligan's Island* debuted.

1965 First African-American actor to star in dramatic series: Bill Cosby in *I Spy*.

Premieres of *Get Smart*, *I Dream of Jeannie*, and *Green Acres* were broadcast.

March 7 – TV cameras covered brutal police beatings of voting rights marchers in Bloody Sunday demonstration in Selma, Alabama.

1966 *Amos and Andy* withdrawn from syndication because of complaints of racial stereotyping; *Batman, The Monkees,* and *Star Trek* debuted.

1967 First anti-smoking commercials broadcast. First Super Bowl game played and broadcast. Premieres of *The Flying Nun, Ironside,* and *Smothers Brothers' Comedy Hour.*

August 29 – Final episode of *The Fugitive* saw Dr. Richard Kimble exonerated.

1968 First *Columbo* mystery starring Peter Falk aired. *Mod Squad, Rowan and Martin's Laugh-In,* and *Hawaii Five-0* debuted. Viewers and sponsors objected to segment on NBC special in which white singer Petula Clark touched African-American guest Harry Belafonte's arm.

March 31 – During 40-minute speech on Vietnam war, President Lyndon B. Johnson made surprise announcement he would not seek re-election.

April 4 – TV news carried extensive coverage of aftermath of Martin Luther King Jr. assassination, ensuing rioting in major cities, and funeral.

June 6 – TV cameras captured footage of Robert F. Kennedy's assassination in Los Angeles.

August 28 – During live TV coverage, anti-war demonstrators chanted "The whole world is watching," as Chicago law enforcement agents engaged in what government commission later concluded a "police riot."

September 24 – *60 Minutes* premiered on CBS News.

October 16 – American sprinters Tommie Smith and John Carlos gave black militant clenched-fist salute during playing of "The Star-Spangled Banner" during medal ceremony at Mexico City Olympics.

1969 *Merv Griffin* and *Sesame Street* broadcast for first time. CBS cancelled establishment-bash-ing hit show, *The Smothers Brothers' Comedy Hour* after Nixon administration threatened crackdown on network permissiveness.

July 20 – Network news carried live pictures of Neil Armstrong as he became first man to walk on the moon.

July 25 – Senator Edward M. Kennedy (D – Mass.) delivered television address explaining his explanation and apology for tragic events at Chappaquiddick (car accident involving death of Mary Jo Kopechne).

1970 Premieres of *Mary Tyler Moore Show* and *The Odd Couple.* Cigarette advertising is banned from television.

May 4 – Extensive television coverage of killing of four anti-war students by National Guard troops at Kent State University and ensuing national protests.

1971 *All in the Family* premiered on CBS.

1972 First successful cable network began broadcasting: HBO. *M*A*S*H, Sanford and Son,* and *The Waltons* debuted. Hundreds of angry letters sent to CBS after *Maude* episode in which Beatrice Arthur's character underwent an abortion.

September 5 – Palestinian terrorist attack disrupted Munich Olympic Games, killing two Israeli athletes, taking nine others hostage. All hostages died in firefight with German police. ABC Sports provided live coverage.

1973 Premieres of *Kojak* and *The Police Story* aired. CBS dropped sitcom about mixed-marriage couple, *Bridget Loves Bernie,* starring Meredith Baxter and David Birney, after criticism from Jewish and other religious organizations.

March 19 – TV news broadcast pictures of American POWs returning home from Vietnam.

July 16 – During live coverage of Senate Watergate hearings, Nixon administration official Alexander Butterfield revealed existence of White House taping system.

1974 *Happy Days*, *Police Woman*, *Little House on the Prairie*, and *Rockford Files* premiered.

April 2 – Streaker disrupted Oscars broadcast.

April 8 – TV cameras covered Atlanta Braves' Hank Aaron as he hit home-run 715 to break Babe Ruth's long-standing record.

August 8 – In televised address to the nation, President Richard M. Nixon, beleaguered by Watergate Scandal, announced his resignation; the next morning viewers witnessed his departure from White House.

1975 *Saturday Night Live* debuted.

1976 First woman to co-anchor nightly network newscast: Barbara Walters.

Rich Man, Poor Man became first mini-series; *Alice* and *Charlie's Angels* premiered. Seeking to avoid portrayal of fatherless African-American family, the National Black Media Coalition unsuccessfully pressured producer Norman Lear to replace John Amos when he quit father role in CBS' *Good Times*.

1977 Premieres of *Soap*, *Lou Grant* and *Love Boat* aired. Controversy erupted over Billy Crystal's portrayal of homosexual on ABC's *Soap*. Approximately 32,000 protest letters flooded network offices.

January 23 – *Roots*, a mini-series telecast over eight consecutive nights, became most-watched television drama in history.

March 19 – Final episode of *Mary Tyler Moore Show*.

1978 First African-American network news anchor: Max Robinson. *Dallas*, *Fantasy Island*, *Taxi*, and *Mork and Mindy* premiered. National Federation for Decency's criticism of ABC's "jiggle shows"—*Three's Company* and

Charlie's Angels—led Sears to pull ads off the shows.

1979 First time cameras turned on in House of Representatives; C-SPAN began gavel-to-gavel proceedings coverage. *Nightline* began broadcasting on ABC.

1980 Closed-captioning technology introduced to aid deaf viewers. Bert Parks fired as Miss America emcee; fall season premieres delayed by actors' strike; *Magnum, P.I.* premiered. Cable News Network (CNN) was launched by Atlanta-based Turner Broadcasting.

February 22 – United States hockey team defeated Soviet Union at Winter Olympics on ABC.

March 21 – In biggest cliffhanger in U.S. history, J.R. Ewing was shot and apparently killed in season-ending episode of *Dallas*. Viewers had to wait until next season to find out Kristin shot J.R., but he wasn't killed, just wounded.

1981 MTV debuted on cable television.

Hill Street Blues debuted on NBC.

March 6 – Walter Cronkite retired as *CBS Evening News* anchor after 19 years.

July 29 – Three-quarters of billion people worldwide watched live coverage of Prince Charles and Lady Diana's wedding.

November 16–17 – *General Hospital*'s Luke and Laura got married.

1982 Bryant Gumbel began 15-year stint as *Today Show* anchor at NBC. *Cagney and Lacy*, *Cheers*, *Late Night with David Letterman*, and *St. Elsewhere* debuted. Under pressure from viewers and corporate supporters, PBS deleted segment depicting high school students smoking marijuana from *Middletown* documentary.

February 28 – Final episode of *M*A*S*H*.

September 29 – Sam and Diane kissed for first time on *Cheers*.

1983 *A-Team* and *Scarecrow and Mrs. King* premiered.

January – Wendy's restaurant chain's "Where's the Beef?" commercial began airing for first time.

1984 *Miami Vice* and *Cosby Show* premiered.

August 3 – Mary Lou Retton scored a perfect 10.0 in vault event to win gold medal in all-around gymnastics at Los Angeles Olympics as millions watched on TV.

1985 *Moonlighting* premiered. First corporate take-over of major U.S. television network (Capital Cities Communications acquired ABC).

July 13 – Live-Aid rock concert raised funds for African famine victims.

1986 Fox network began broadcasting as nation's fourth commercial TV network, competing with ABC, CBS, and NBC. Embarrassed Geraldo Rivera discovered only trash in Al Capone's hidden vault in live broadcast. *Designing Women* and *L.A. Law* premiered. Capital Cities merged with ABC. General Electric Co. completed acquisition of RCA, giving it control over RCA's subsidiary NBC television network.

January 28 – Millions watched live coverage of space shuttle *Challenger* launch, which exploded 73 seconds after liftoff, killing all seven crew members.

1987 *Married with Children* and *thirtysomething* debuted.

March 31 – Maddie Hayes and David Addison characters on *Moonlighting* finally made love.

April 6 – Interviewed by Ted Koppel on *Nightline*, Los Angeles Dodgers' executive Al Campanis said African-Americans were not fit to be managers or executives in professional baseball; Dodgers fired him almost immediately.

September 11 – An angry Dan Rather stormed off set of a truncated *CBS Evening News*, leaving six minutes of empty air time.

1988 *Roseanne* and *Murphy Brown* debuted. CBS cut 3-$\frac{1}{2}$ second scene showing Mighty Mouse sniffing crushed flowers after Christian Fundamentalists charged scene advocated cocaine snorting.

January 25 – During live *CBS Evening News* interview with Dan Rather, then-Vice President George Bush and Dan Rather got into an angry exchange.

1989 Dick Clark retired as host of *American Bandstand* after 33 years. Limited high-definition television (HDTV) broadcasts began in Japan. Michigan housewife Terry Rakolta organized unsuccessful boycott against *Married . . . With Children* on Fox-TV.

June 5 – During military crackdown at Beijing's Tiananmen Square, TV news cameras broadcast dramatic footage of a single pro-democracy demonstrator blocking a column of tanks.

1991 January 17 – Network news broadcasts carried live coverage of the bombing of Baghdad during Operation Desert Storm.

March 4 – Networks began broadcasting amateur footage of ruthless beating on March 3 of African-American motorist Rodney King by four Los Angeles police officers.

October 11 – Clarence Thomas denied charges of sexual harassment made by law professor Anita Hill during televised coverage of Supreme Court confirmation hearings.

1992 May 21 – Bette Midler sang tribute to Johnny Carson on Carson's farewell broadcast on *Tonight Show*. Vice President Dan Quayle criticized CBS's *Murphy Brown*, starring Candice Bergen, for favorable depiction of a decision to bear child out-of-wedlock.

December 9 – Network news cameras created circus atmosphere as American troops landed in Somalia during famine rescue operation.

1993 *NYPD* Blue debuted on ABC.

April 19 – Networks provided live news coverage of fire at Waco, Texas, confrontation between FBI and Branch Davidian cultists; more than 80 cultists killed.

1994 FCC adopted revised "must carry rules" governing retransmission of over-the-air television stations on cable system operators.

June 17 – Live coverage of O. J. Simpson's white Bronco car chase even disrupted NBC's basketball playoff broadcast.

1995 September 6 – TV cameras captured Baltimore Orioles' star Cal Ripken Jr. as he broke Lou Gehrig's record for playing most consecutive baseball games. Westinghouse acquired CBS.

October 3 – News cameras provided live coverage of "not guilty" verdict in O.J. Simpson murder trial.

1996 Networks adopted system to rate shows to warn parents about violent and sexual content in programs. Disney acquired ABC television network. Time Warner merged with Turner Broadcasting Co. A joint venture by NBC and Microsoft launched MSNBC as a cable competitor to CNN. Rupert Murdoch's Fox News Channel also joined the all-news, all-the-time cable competition. Congress adopted Telecommunications Act of 1996.

1998 Television sports broadcasts covered the dramatic Sammy Sosa/Mark McGwire race to break Roger Maris' single season homerun record.

1999 *Sopranos* debuted on HBO. Television networks carried live coverage of millennium New Year's Eve celebrations around the world.

(Sources: *World Almanac*, *World Book*, *TV Guide*, NBC broadcast history files, *Encyclopedia of Television*, and *Facts on File*)

MILESTONES IN SPACE EXPLORATION

October 4, 1957 Soviets launched *Sputnik 1*, first satellite to orbit Earth.

October 1, 1958 National Aeronautics and Space Administration (NASA) established.

January 31, 1958 First US. satellite, *Explorer*, launched from Cape Canaveral, Florida; led to discovery of Van Allen radiation belt.

April 12, 1961 Cosmonaut Yuri A. Gagarin became first man in orbital flight, aboard *Vostok I*.

May 5, 1961 Alan Shepard Jr. became first American in sub-orbital flight, aboard *Mercury III*.

May 25, 1961 President John F. Kennedy proclaimed U.S. goal to land man on moon and return safely to Earth by end of decade.

July 21, 1961 Astronaut Virgil I. Grissom rescued as space capsule sank after splashdown.

August 6–7, 1961 Cosmonaut Gherman S. Titov took first space flight longer than 24 hours.

February 20, 1962 First American orbital flight; John Glenn completed three revolutions.

August 27, 1962 *Mariner 2* space probe launched; passed within 22,000 miles of Venus December 14, 1962.

June 16–19, 1963 Cosmonaut Valentina V. Tereshkove became first woman in space.

March 18, 1965 Cosmonaut Aleksei A. Leonov made first space walk.

March 23, 1965 Astronauts Virgil Grissom and John Young aboard first manned spacecraft to alter orbital path.

June 3–7, 1965 Edward White became first American to walk in space.

June 28, 1965 NASA selected six scientist-astronauts; first non-military astronauts.

December 4, 1965 Frank Borman and James Lovell, aboard *Gemini VII*, executed first rendezvous with target in space.

May 30, 1966 *Surveyor I* made first soft landing on moon (unmanned); sent back 11,240 photos.

January 27, 1967 Flash fire in *Apollo I* spacecraft on launch pad killed astronauts Grissom, White, and Roger B. Chaffee.

April 17, 1967 *Surveyor 3* space probe launched; scooped and tested lunar soil.

April 23, 1967 Cosmonaut Vladimir M. Komarov killed when *Soyuz I* crashed on re-entry.

December 21–27, 1968 Borman, Lovell, and William Anders completed first manned moon orbit, aboard *Apollo 8*.

July 20, 1969 Astronauts Neil Armstrong and Buzz Aldrin first humans to set foot on moon; Michael Collins remained aboard *Apollo 11* command module.

November 14–24, 1969 Second moon mission; Charles Conrad Jr. and Alan L. Bean landed on moon.

January 31–February 9, 1971 Third moon landing by Shepard and Edgar Mitchell.

July 26–August 7, 1971 David Scott and James Irwin made fourth moon landing.

November 13, 1971 *Mariner 9* became first spacecraft to orbit Mars (launched May 30, 1971).

March 2, 1972 *Pioneer 10* launched for first fly-by of Jupiter.

April 16–27, 1972 John Young and Charles Duke Jr. in fifth lunar landing.

December 7, 1972 Eugene Cernan and Jack Schmitt in sixth lunar landing on *Apollo 17* mission.

May 14, 1973 First U.S. space station, *Skylab*, damaged on launch but successfully placed in orbit—eventually visited by three astronaut missions—re-entered atmosphere and disintegrated over Australia June 1979.

July 17, 1975 In first international space rendezvous, astronauts Thomas Stafford, Vance Brand, and Deke Slayton aboard *Apollo* command module successfully docked with Soviet *Souz* spacecraft, joining cosmonauts Alexi Leonov and Valeriy Kubasov.

July 20, 1976 *Viking I* first probe to land on Mars.

January 16, 1978 NASA selected 35 new astronauts, including first women and African Americans; group included Ellison Onizuka, Judith Resnik, Ronald McNair, and Francis (Dick) Scobee—all of whom would later die in *Challenger* disaster in January 1986.

April 12, 1981 First space shuttle launch; John Young and Robert Crippen in command.

July 22, 1982 NASA task force discussed sending "citizen" into space.

June 1983 *Pioneer 10*, launched in 1972, became first probe to leave solar system.

June 18, 1983 Sally Ride became first American woman in space.

August 30, 1983 Guion Bluford first African American in space.

February 8, 1984 Bruce McCandless, wearing jet backpack, became first person to walk in space untethered.

August 27, 1984 President Ronald Reagan authorized selection of "a teacher" as first citizen space passenger.

January 28, 1986 *Challenger* shuttle exploded 73 seconds after liftoff killing crew of seven, including teacher Christa McAuliffe.

February 11, 1988 President Reagan unveiled new space policy with enhanced role for private industry, space station goal for NASA.

September 29, 1988 NASA resumed space shuttle missions with *Discovery* launch.

October 18, 1989 *Galileo* space probe launched; encountered Jupiter December 7, 1995.

April 24, 1990 *Discovery* space shuttle crew mission began; crew launched Hubble Space Telescope.

September 12, 1992 *Endeavor* space shuttle crew included Mae Carol Jemison, first African-American woman in space, and Mark Lee and N. Jan Davis, the first married couple to travel together in space.

April 8, 1993 Space shuttle *Discovery* crew included Ellen Ochoa, first Hispanic-American woman in space.

December 2, 1993 Launch date for *Endeavor* space shuttle mission to repair Hubble Space Telescope.

February 3, 1994 Sergei K. Kirkalev became first Russian to fly on American space shuttle mission.

February 3–11, 1995 *Discovery* shuttle rendezvoused with Russian space station, *Mir*.

March 22, 1995 Cosmonaut Valery Polyakov returned to Earth after record 439 days in space.

June 20–July 7, 1996 *Columbia* space shuttle flew longest-duration shuttle mission.

September 26, 1996 Shannon W. Lucid returned to Earth, after setting U.S. and women's individual record for duration in space: 188 days.

October 29–November 7, 1998 Senator John Glenn, age 77, returned to space aboard space shuttle *Discovery*, becoming oldest person to fly in space.

December 4–15, 1998 First assembly operations began for international space station during space shuttle *Endeavor* mission. Space station scheduled for completion in 2004.

July 23–27, 1998 Eileen M. Collins became first woman to command space shuttle mission.

(Sources: *NYT Almanac*, *World Almanac*, *World Book*, and *NBC News Space Book*)

SPORTS CHAMPIONSHIPS

Baseball

Pennant Winners

Until 1968, the pennant winner was the team with the best won-lost record. From 1969–1993 the pennant winner was the winner of a playoff series between East and West division leaders. From 1994 to the present, pennant winners were decided by the outcome of a three-division playoff (East, West, and Central) in both American and National Leagues. Thus, since 1969, pennant winner did not necessarily have the league's best won-lost record.

NATIONAL LEAGUE

Year	Winner	Won	Lost	Pct.
1901	Pittsburgh	90	49	0.647
1902	Pittsburgh	103	36	0.741
1903	Pittsburgh	91	49	0.650

Year	Winner	Won	Lost	Pct.	Year	Winner	Won	Lost	Pct.
1904	New York	106	47	0.693	1928	St. Louis	95	59	0.617
1905	New York	105	48	0.686	1929	Chicago	98	54	0.645
1906	Chicago	116	36	0.763	1930	St. Louis	92	62	0.597
1907	Chicago	107	45	0.704	1931	St. Louis	101	53	0.656
1908	Chicago	99	55	0.643	1932	Chicago	90	64	0.584
1909	Pittsburgh	110	42	0.724	1933	New York	91	61	0.599
1910	Chicago	104	50	0.675	1934	St. Louis	95	58	0.621
1911	New York	99	54	0.647	1935	Chicago	100	54	0.649
1912	New York	103	48	0.682	1936	New York	91	62	0.597
1913	New York	101	51	0.664	1937	New York	95	57	0.625
1914	Boston	94	59	0.614	1938	Chicago	89	63	0.586
1915	Philadelphia	90	62	0.592	1939	Cincinnati	97	57	0.630
1916	Brooklyn	94	60	0.610	1940	Cincinnati	100	53	0.654
1917	New York	98	56	0.636	1941	Brooklyn	100	0.5	0.649
1918	Chicago	84	45	0.651	1942	St. Louis	106	48	0.688
1919	Cincinnati	96	44	0.686	1943	St. Louis	105	49	0.682
1920	Brooklyn	93	60	0.604	1944	St. Louis	105	49	0.682
1921	New York	94	56	0.614	1945	Chicago	98	56	0.636
1922	New York	93	61	0.604	1946	St. Louis	98	58	0.628
1923	New York	95	58	0.621	1947	Brooklyn	94	60	0.610
1924	New York	93	60	0.608	1948	Boston	91	62	0.595
1925	Pittsburgh	95	58	0.621	1949	Brooklyn	97	57	0.630
1926	St. Louis	89	65	0.578	1950	Philadelphia	91	63	0.591
1927	Pittsburgh	94	60	0.610	1951	New York	98	59	0.624

Year	Winner	Won	Lost	Pct.	Year	Winner	Won	Lost	Pct.
1952	Brooklyn	96	57	0.627	1976	Cincinnati	102	60	0.630
1953	Brooklyn	105	49	0.682	1977	Los Angeles	98	64	0.605
1954	New York	97	57	0.630	1978	Los Angeles	95	67	0.586
1955	Brooklyn	98	55	0.641	1979	Pittsburgh	98	64	0.605
1956	Brooklyn	93	61	0.604	1980	Philadelphia	91	71	0.562
1957	Milwaukee	95	59	0.617	1981[1]	Los Angeles	36	21	0.632
1958	Milwaukee	92	62	0.597	1982	St. Louis	92	70	0.568
1959	Los Angeles	88	68	0.564	1983	Philadelphia	90	72	0.556
1960	Pittsburgh	95	59	0.617	1984	San Diego	92	70	0.568
1961	Cincinnati	93	61	0.604	1985	St. Louis	101	61	0.623
1962	San Francisco	103	62	0.624	1986	N.Y. Mets	108	54	0.667
1963	Los Angeles	99	63	0.611	1987	St. Louis	95	67	0.586
1964	St. Louis	93	69	0.574	1988	Los Angeles	94	67	0.584
1965	Los Angeles	97	65	0.599	1989	San Francisco	92	70	0.568
1966	Los Angeles	95	67	0.586	1990	Cincinnati	91	71	0.562
1967	St. Louis	101	60	0.627	1991	Atlanta	94	68	0.580
1968	St. Louis	97	65	0.599	1992	Atlanta	98	64	0.605
1969	N.Y. Mets	100	62	0.617	1993	Philadelphia	97	65	0.599
1970	Cincinnati	102	60	0.630	1994[2]				
1971	Pittsburgh	97	65	0.599	1995	Atlanta	90	54	0.625
1972	Cincinnati	95	59	0. 617					
1973	N.Y. Mets	82	79	0.509					
1974	Los Angeles	102	60	0.630					
1975	Cincinnati	108	54	0.667					

1. Because of a 49-day strike in the middle of the season, players and management agreed to a special playoff format pitting divisional leaders of each "half" of the interrupted season against each other. Los Angeles led the Western Division in the first half of the season and won NL playoffs.
2. Due to labor stoppage in August, no playoffs were held to decide pennant winners.

Year	Winner	Won	Lost	Pct.
1996	Atlanta	96	66	0.593
1997	Florida	92	70	0.568
1998	San Diego	97	64	0.602
1999	Atlanta	103	59	0.636

AMERICAN LEAGUE

Year	Winner	Won	Lost	Pct.
1901	Chicago	83	53	0.610
1902	Philadelphia	83	53	0.610
1903	Boston	91	47	0.659
1904	Boston	95	59	0.617
1905	Philadelphia	92	56	0.622
1906	Chicago	93	58	0.616
1907	Detroit	92	58	0.613
1908	Detroit	90	63	0.588
1909	Detroit	98	54	0.645
1910	Philadelphia	102	48	0.680
1911	Philadelphia	101	50	0.669
1912	Boston	105	47	0.691
1913	Philadelphia	96	57	0.627
1914	Philadelphia	99	53	0.651
1915	Boston	101	50	0.669
1916	Boston	91	63	0.591
1917	Chicago	100	54	0.649

Year	Winner	Won	Lost	Pct.
1918	Boston	75	51	0.595
1919	Chicago	88	52	0.629
1920	Cleveland	98	56	0.636
1921	New York	98	55	0.641
1922	New York	94	60	0.610
1923	New York	98	54	0.645
1924	Washington	92	62	0.597
1925	Washington	96	55	0.636
1926	New York	91	63	0.591
1927	New York	110	44	0.714
1928	New York	101	53	0.656
1929	Philadelphia	104	46	0.693
1930	Philadelphia	102	52	0.662
1931	Philadelphia	107	45	0.704
1932	New York	107	47	0.695
1933	Washington	99	53	0.651
1934	Detroit	101	53	0.656
1935	Detroit	93	58	0.616
1936	New York	102	51	0.667
1937	New York	102	52	0.662
1938	New York	99	53	0.651
1939	New York	106	45	0.702
1940	Detroit	90	64	0.584
1941	New York	101	53	0.656

Year	Winner	Won	Lost	Pct.	Year	Winner	Won	Lost	Pct.
1942	New York	103	51	0.669	1966	Baltimore	97	63	0.606
1943	New York	98	56	0.663	1967	Boston	92	70	0.568
1944	St. Louis	89	65	0.578	1968	Detroit	103	59	0.636
1945	Detroit	88	65	0.575	1969	Baltimore	109	53	0.673
1946	Boston	104	50	0.675	1970	Baltimore	108	54	0.667
1947	New York	97	57	0.630	1971	Baltimore	101	57	0.639
1948	Cleveland	97	58	0.626	1972	Oakland	93	62	0.600
1949	New York	97	57	0.630	1973	Oakland	94	68	0.580
1950	New York	98	56	0.636	1973	Oakland	90	72	0.556
1951	New York	98	56	0.636	1975	Boston	95	65	0.594
1952	New York	95	59	0.617	1976	New York	97	62	0.610
1953	New York	99	52	0.656	1977	New York	100	62	0.617
1954	Cleveland	111	43	0.721	1978	New York	100	63	0.613
1955	New York	96	58	0.623	1979	Baltimore	102	57	0.642
1956	New York	97	57	0.630	1980	Kansas City	97	65	0.599
1957	New York	98	56	0.636	1981[1]	New York	34	22	0.607
1958	New York	92	62	0.597	1982	Milwaukee	95	67	0.586
1959	Chicago	94	60	0.610	1983	Baltimore	98	64	0.605
1960	New York	97	57	0.630	1984	Detroit	104	58	0.642
1961	New York	109	53	0.673	1985	Kansas City	91	71	0.562
1962	New York	96	66	0.593	1986	Boston	95	66	0.590
1963	New York	104	57	0.646					
1964	New York	99	63	0.611					
1965	Minnesota	102	60	0.630					

1. Because of a 49-strike in the middle of the season, players and management agreed to a special playoff format pitting divisional leaders of each "half" of the interrupted season against each other. New York led the Eastern Division in the first half of the season and won the AL play-offs.

1987	Minnesota	85	77	0.525
1989	Oakland	99	63	0.611
1990	Oakland	103	59	0.636
1991	Minnesota	95	67	0.586
1992	Toronto	96	66	0.593
1993	Toronto	95	67	0.586
1994[2]				
1995	Cleveland	100	44	0.694
1996	New York	92	70	0.568
1997	Cleveland	86	75	0.534
1998	New York	114	48	0.704
1999	New York	98	64	0.605

2. Due to labor stoppage in August, no playoffs were held to decide pennant winners.

World Series

1903 Boston AL 5, Pittsburgh NL 3

1904 No series

1905 New York NL 4, Philadelphia AL 1

1906 Chicago AL 4, Chicago NL 2

1907 Chicago NL 4, Detroit AL 0, 1 tie (called due to darkness)

1908 Chicago NL 4, Detroit AL 1

1909 Pittsburgh NL 4, Detroit AL 3

1910 Philadelphia AL 4, Chicago NL 1

1911 Philadelphia AL 4, New York NL 2

1912 Boston AL 4, New York NL 3, 1 tie (called due to darkness)

1913 Philadelphia AL 4, New York NL 1

1914 Boston NL 4, Philadelphia AL 0

1915 Boston AL 4, Philadelphia NL 1

1916 Boston AL 4, Brooklyn NL 1

1917 Chicago AL 4, New York NL 2

1918 Boston AL 4, Chicago NL 2

1919 Cincinnati NL 5, Chicago AL 3[1]

1920 Cleveland AL 5, Brooklyn NL 2

1921 New York NL 5, New York AL 3

1922 New York NL 4, New York AL 0, 1 tie

1923 New York AL 4, New York NL 2

1924 Washington AL 4, New York NL 3

1925 Pittsburgh NL 4, Washington AL 3

1926 St. Louis NL 4, New York AL 3

1927 New York AL 4, Pittsburgh NL 0

1928 New York AL 4, St. Louis NL 0

1929 Philadelphia AL 4, Chicago NL 1

1930 Philadelphia AL 4, St. Louis NL 2

1931 St. Louis NL 4, Philadelphia AL 3

1932 New York AL 4, Chicago NL 0

1933 New York NL 4, Washington AL 1

1934 St. Louis NL 4, Detroit AL 3

1935 Detroit AL 4, Chicago NL 2

1. Results invalidated after eight Chicago White Sox players revealed to have thrown games.

1936	New York AL 4, New York NL 2		1961	New York AL 4, Cincinnati NL 1
1937	New York AL 4, New York NL 1		1962	New York AL 4, San Francisco NL 3
1938	New York AL 4, Chicago NL 0		1963	Los Angeles NL 4, New York AL 0
1939	New York AL 4, Cincinnati NL 0		1964	St. Louis NL 4, New York AL 3
1940	Cincinnati NL 4, Detroit AL 3		1965	Los Angeles NL 4, Minnesota AL 3
1941	New York AL 4, Brooklyn NL 1		1966	Baltimore AL 4, Los Angeles NL 0
1942	St. Louis NL 4, New York AL 1		1967	St. Louis NL 4, Boston AL 3
1943	New York AL 4, St. Louis NL 1		1968	Detroit AL 4, St. Louis NL 3
1944	St. Louis NL 4, St. Louis AL 2		1969	New York NL 4, Baltimore AL 1
1945	Detroit AL 4, Chicago NL 3		1970	Baltimore AL 4, Cincinnati NL 1
1946	St. Louis NL 4, Boston AL 3		1971	Pittsburgh NL 4, Baltimore AL 3
1947	New York AL 4, Brooklyn NL 3		1972	Oakland AL 4, Cincinnati NL 3
1948	Cleveland AL 4, Boston NL 2		1973	Oakland AL 4, New York NL 3
1949	New York AL 4, Brooklyn NL 1		1974	Oakland AL 4, Los Angeles NL 1
1950	New York AL 4, Philadelphia NL 0		1975	Cincinnati NL 4, Boston AL 3
1951	New York AL 4, New York NL 2		1976	Cincinnati NL 4, New York AL 0
1952	New York AL 4, Brooklyn NL 3		1977	New York AL 4, Los Angeles NL 2
1953	New York AL 4, Brooklyn NL 2		1978	New York AL 4, Los Angeles NL 2
1954	New York NL 4, Cleveland AL 0		1979	Pittsburgh NL 4, Baltimore AL 3
1955	Brooklyn NL 4, New York AL 3		1980	Philadelphia NL 4, Kansas City AL
1956	New York AL 4, Brooklyn NL 3		1981	Los Angeles NL 4, New York AL 2
1957	Milwaukee NL 4, New York AL 3		1982	St. Louis NL 4, Milwaukee AL 3
1958	New York AL 4, Milwaukee NL 3		1983	Baltimore AL 4, Philadelphia NL 1
1959	Los Angeles NL 4, Chicago AL 2		1984	Detroit AL 4, San Diego NL 1
1960	Pittsburgh NL 4, New York AL 3		1985	Kansas City AL 4, St. Louis NL 3

1986	New York NL 4, Boston AL 3
1987	Minnesota AL 4, St. Louis NL 3
1988	Los Angeles NL 4, Oakland AL 1
1989	Oakland AL 4, San Francisco NL 0
1990	Cincinnati NL 4, Oakland AL 0
1991	Minnesota AL 4, Atlanta NL 3
1992	Toronto AL 4, Atlanta NL 2
1993	Toronto AL 4, Philadelphia NL 2
1994	No series due to labor dispute
1995	Atlanta NL 4, Cleveland AL 2
1996	New York AL 4, Atlanta NL 2
1997	Florida NL 4, Cleveland AL 3
1998	New York AL 4, San Diego NL 0
1999	New York AL 4, Atlanta, NL 0

MVP National League

(Selected by Baseball Writers Association)

Year	Player, team
1931	Frank Frisch, St. Louis
1932	Chuck Klein, Philadelphia
1933	Carl Hubbell, New York
1934	Dizzy Dean, St. Louis
1935	Gabby Hartnett, Chicago
1936	Carl Hubbell, New York
1937	Joe Medwick, St. Louis
1938	Ernie Lombardi, Cincinnati

Year	Player, team
1939	Bucky Walters, Cincinnati
1940	Frank McCormick, Cincinnati
1941	Dolph Camilli, Brooklyn
1942	Mort Cooper, St. Louis
1943	Stan Musial, St. Louis
1944	Martin Marion, St. Louis
1945	Phil Cavarretta, Chicago
1946	Stan Musial, St. Louis
1947	Bob Elliott, Boston
1948	Stan Musial, St. Louis
1949	Jackie Robinson, Brooklyn
1950	Jim Konstanty, Philadelphia
1951	Roy Campanella, Brooklyn
1952	Hank Sauer, Chicago
1953	Roy Campanella, Brooklyn
1954	Willie Mays, New York
1955	Roy Campanella, Brooklyn
1956	Don Newcombe, Brooklyn
1957	Hank Aaron, Milwaukee
1958	Ernie Banks, Chicago
1959	Ernie Banks, Chicago
1960	Dick Groat, Pittsburgh
1961	Frank Robinson, Cincinnati
1962	Maury Wills, Los Angeles

Year	Player, team		Year	Player, team
1963	Sandy Koufax, Los Angeles		1986	Mike Schmidt, Philadelphia
1964	Ken Boyer, St. Louis		1987	Andre Dawson, Chicago
1965	Willie Mays, San Francisco		1988	Kirk Gibson, Los Angeles
1966	Roberto Clemente, Pittsburgh		1989	Kevin Mitchell, San Francisco
1967	Orlando Cepeda, St. Louis		1990	Barry Bonds, Pittsburgh
1968	Bob Gibson, St. Louis		1991	Terry Pendleton, Atlanta
1969	Willie McCovey, San Francisco		1992	Barry Bonds, Pittsburgh
1970	Johnny Bench, Cincinnati		1993	Barry Bonds, San Francisco
1971	Joe Torre, St. Louis		1994	Jeff Bagwell, Houston
1972	Johnny Bench, Cincinnati		1995	Barry Larkin, Cincinnati
1973	Pete Rose, Cincinnati		1996	Ken Caminiti, San Diego
1974	Steve Garvey, Los Angeles		1997	Larry Walker, Colorado
1975	Joe Morgan, Cincinnati		1998	Sammy Sosa, Chicago
1976	Joe Morgan, Cincinnati		1999	Chipper Jones, Atlanta
1977	George Foster, Cincinnati			

MVP American League

Year	Player, team
1978	Dave Parker, Pittsburgh
1979	Willie Stargell, Pittsburgh
	Keith Hernandez, St. Louis (tie)
1980	Mike Schmidt, Philadelphia
1981	Mike Schmidt, Philadelphia
1982	Dale Murphy, Atlanta
1983	Dale Murphy, Atlanta
1984	Ryne Sandberg, Chicago
1985	Willie McGee, St. Louis

Year	Player, team
1931	Lefty Grove, Philadelphia
1932	Jimmie Foxx, Philadelphia
1933	Jimmie Foxx, Philadelphia
1934	Mickey Cochrane, Detroit
1935	Hank Greenberg, Detroit
1936	Lou Gehrig, New York
1937	Charley Gehringer, Detroit
1938	Jimmie Foxx, Boston
1939	Joe DiMaggio, New York

Year	Player, team	Year	Player, team
1940	Hank Greenberg, Detroit	1964	Brooks Robinson, Baltimore
1941	Joe DiMaggio, New York	1965	Zoilo Versalles, Minnesota
1942	Joe Gordon, New York	1966	Frank Robinson, Baltimore
1943	Spud Chandler, New York	1967	Carl Yastrzemski, Boston
1944	Hal Newhouser, Detroit	1968	Denny McLain, Detroit
1945	Hal Newhouser, Detroit	1969	Harmon Killebrew, Minnesota
1946	Ted Williams, Boston	1970	John (Boog) Powell, Baltimore
1947	Joe DiMaggio, New York	1971	Vida Blue, Oakland
1948	Lou Boudreau, Cleveland	1972	Dick Allen, Chicago
1949	Ted Williams, Boston	1973	Reggie Jackson, Oakland
1950	Phil Rizzuto, New York	1974	Jeff Burroughs, Texas
1951	Yogi Berra, New York	1975	Fred Lynn, Boston
1952	Bobby Shantz, Philadelphia	1976	Thurman Munson, New York
1953	Al Rosen, Cleveland	1977	Rod Carew, Minnesota
1954	Yogi Berra, New York	1978	Jim Rice, Boston
1955	Yogi Berra, New York	1979	Don Baylor, California
1956	Mickey Mantle, New York	1980	George Brett, Kansas City
1957	Mickey Mantle, New York	1981	Rollie Fingers, Milwaukee
1958	Jackie Jensen, Boston	1982	Robin Yount, Milwaukee
1959	Nellie Fox, Chicago	1983	Cal Ripken Jr., Baltimore
1960	Roger Maris, New York	1984	Willie Hernandez, Detroit
1961	Roger Maris, New York	1985	Don Mattingly, New York
1962	Mickey Mantle, New York	1986	Roger Clemens, Boston
1963	Elston Howard, New York	1987	George Bell, Toronto

Year	Player, team
1988	Jose Canseco, Oakland
1989	Robin Yount, Milwaukee
1990	Rickey Henderson, Oakland
1991	Cal Ripken Jr., Baltimore
1992	Dennis Eckersley, Oakland
1993	Frank Thomas, Chicago
1994	Frank Thomas, Chicago
1995	Mo Vaughn, Boston
1996	Juan Gonzalez, Texas
1997	Ken Griffey Jr., Seattle
1998	Juan Gonzalez, Texas
1999	Ivan Rodriguez, Texas

Basketball

National Basketball Association (NBA) Championships

Year	Winner	Runner-up
1947	Philadelphia	Chicago
1948	Baltimore	Philadelphia
1949	Minneapolis	Washington
1950	Minneapolis	Syracuse
1951	Rochester	New York
1952	Minneapolis	New York
1953	Minneapolis	New York
1954	Minneapolis	Syracuse

Year	Winner	Runner-up
1955	Syracuse	Ft. Wayne
1956	Philadelphia	Ft. Wayne
1957	Boston	St. Louis
1958	St. Louis	Boston
1959	Boston	Minneapolis
1960	Boston	St. Louis
1961	Boston	St. Louis
1962	Boston	Los Angeles
1963	Boston	Los Angeles
1964	Boston	San Francisco
1965	Boston	Los Angeles
1966	Boston	Los Angeles
1967	Philadelphia	San Francisco
1968	Boston	Los Angeles
1969	Boston	Los Angeles
1970	New York	Los Angeles
1971	Milwaukee	Baltimore
1972	Los Angeles	New York
1973	New York	Los Angeles
1974	Boston	Milwaukee
1975	Golden State	Washington
1976	Boston	Phoenix
1977	Portland	Philadelphia
1978	Washington	Seattle

Year	Winner	Runner-up
1979	Seattle	Washington
1980	Los Angeles	Philadelphia
1981	Boston	Houston
1982	Los Angeles	Philadelphia
1983	Philadelphia	Los Angeles
1984	Boston	Los Angeles
1985	L.A. Lakers	Boston
1986	Boston	Houston
1987	LA. Lakers	Boston
1988	L.A. Lakers	Detroit
1989	Detroit	L.A. Lakers
1990	Detroit	Portland
1991	Chicago	LA. Lakers
1992	Chicago	Portland
1993	Chicago	Phoenix
1994	Houston	New York
1995	Houston	Orlando
1996	Chicago	Seattle
1997	Chicago	Utah
1998	Chicago	Utah
1999	San Antonio	New York

NBA Most Valuable Player

1956	Bob Pettit, St. Louis	
1957	Bob Cousy, Boston	
1958	Bill Russell, Boston	
1959	Bob Pettit, St. Louis	
1960	Wilt Chamberlain, Philadelphia Warriors	
1961	Bill Russell, Boston	
1962	Bill Russell, Boston	
1963	Bill Russell, Boston	
1964	Oscar Robertson, Cincinnati	
1965	Bill Russell, Boston	
1966	Wilt Chamberlain, Philadelphia '76ers	
1967	Wilt Chamberlain, Philadelphia '76ers	
1968	Wilt Chamberlain, Philadelphia '76ers	
1969	Wes Unseld, Baltimore	
1970	Willis Reed, New York	
1971	Lew Alcindor (Kareem Abdul-Jabbar), Milwaukee	
1972	Kareem Abdul-Jabbar, Milwaukee	
1973	Dave Cowens, Boston	
1974	Kareem Abdul-Jabbar, Milwaukee	
1975	Bob McAdoo, Buffalo	
1976	Kareem Abdul-Jabbar, Los Angeles Lakers	
1977	Kareem Abdul-Jabbar, Los Angeles Lakers	
1978	Bill Walton, Portland	
1979	Moses Malone, Houston	
1980	Kareem Abdul-Jabbar, Los Angeles Lakers	
1981	Julius Erving, Philadelphia '76ers	
1982	Moses Malone, Houston	

1983	Moses Malone, Philadelphia '76ers
1984	Larry Bird, Boston
1985	Larry Bird, Boston
1986	Larry Bird, Boston
1987	Magic Johnson, Los Angeles Lakers
1988	Michael Jordan, Chicago
1989	Magic Johnson, Los Angeles Lakers
1990	Magic Johnson, Los Angeles Lakers
1991	Michael Jordan, Chicago
1992	Michael Jordan, Chicago
1993	Charles Barkley, Phoenix Suns
1994	Hakeem Olajuwon, Houston
1995	David Robinson, San Antonio
1996	Michael Jordan, Chicago
1997	Karl Malone, Utah
1998	Michael Jordan, Chicago

Women's Professional Basketball

WNBA Championship

1997	Houston Comets 1,	New York Liberty 0
1998	Houston Comets 2,	Phoenix Mercury 1
1999	Houston Comets 2,	New York Liberty 1

Football

National Football League (NFL) Champions

Year	Playoffs
1933	Chicago Bears 23, New York 21
1934	New York 30, Chicago Bears 13
1935	Detroit 26, New York 7
1936	Green Bay 21, Boston 6
1937	Washington 28, Chicago Bears 21
1938	New York 23, Green Bay 17
1939	Green Bay 27, New York 0
1940	Chicago Bears 73, Washington 0
1941	Chicago Bears 37, New York 9
1942	Washington 14, Chicago Bears 6
1943	Chicago Bears, 41, Washington 21
1944	Green Bay 14, New York 7
1945	Cleveland 15, Washington 14
1946	Chicago Bears 24, New York 14
1947	Chicago Cardinals 28, Philadelphia 21
1948	Philadelphia 7, Chicago Cardinals 0
1949	Philadelphia 14, Los Angeles 0
1950	Cleveland 30, Los Angeles 28
1951	Los Angeles 24, Cleveland 17
1952	Detroit 17, Cleveland 7
1953	Detroit 17, Cleveland 16

Year	Playoffs
1954	Cleveland 56, Detroit 10
1955	Cleveland 38, Los Angeles 14
1956	New York 47, Chicago Bears 7
1957	Detroit 59, Cleveland 14
1958	Baltimore 23, New York 17
1959	Baltimore 31, New York 16
1960	Philadelphia 17, Green Bay 13
1961	Green Bay 37, New York 0
1962	Green Bay 16, New York 7
1963	Chicago 14, New York 10
1964	Cleveland 27, Baltimore 0
1965	Green Bay 23, Cleveland 12
1966	Green Bay 34, Dallas 27

NFL Superbowl Champions

No.	Year	Winner/Loser
I	**1967**	Green Bay Packers, 35 Kansas City Chiefs, 10
II	**1968**	Green Bay Packers, 33 Oakland Raiders, 14
III	**1969**	New York Jets, 16 Baltimore Colts, 7
IV	**1970**	Kansas City Chiefs, 23 Minnesota Vikings, 7
V	**1971**	Baltimore Colts, 16 Dallas Cowboys, 13
VI	**1972**	Dallas Cowboys, 24 Miami Dolphins, 3

No.	Year	Winner/Loser
VII	**1973**	Miami Dolphins, 14 Washington Redskins, 7
VIII	**1974**	Miami Dolphins, 24 Minnesota Vikings, 7
IX	**1975**	Pittsburgh Steelers, 16 Minnesota Vikings, 6
X	**1976**	Pittsburgh Steelers, 21 Dallas Cowboys, 17
XI	**1977**	Oakland Raiders, 32 Minnesota Vikings, 14
XII	**1978**	Dallas Cowboys, 27 Denver Broncos, 10
XIII	**1979**	Pittsburgh Steelers, 36 Dallas Cowboys, 31
XIV	**1980**	Pittsburgh Steelers, 31 Los Angeles Rams, 19
XV	**1981**	Oakland Raiders, 27 Philadelphia Eagles, 10
XVI	**1982**	San Francisco 49ers, 26 Cincinnati Bengals, 21
XVII	**1983**	Washington Redskins, 27 Miami Dolphins, 17
XVIII	**1984**	Los Angeles Raiders, 38 Washington Redskins, 9
XIX	**1985**	San Francisco 49ers, 28 Miami Dolphins, 16
XX	**1986**	Chicago Bears, 46 New England Patriots, 10
XXI	**1987**	Now York Giants, 39 Denver Broncos, 20
XXII	**1988**	Washington Redskins, 42 Denver Broncos, 10

XXIII	1989	San Francisco 49ers, 20
		Cincinnati Bengals, 16
XXIV	1990	San Francisco 49ers, 55
		Denver Broncos, 10
XV	1991	New York Giants, 20
		Buffalo Bills, 19
XXVI	1992	Washington Redskins, 37
		Buffalo Bills, 24
XXVII	1993	Dallas Cowboys, 52
		Buffalo Bills, 17
XXVIII	1994	Dallas Cowboys, 30
		Buffalo Bills, 13
XXIX	1995	San Francisco 49ers, 49
		San Diego Chargers, 26
XXX	1996	Dallas Cowboys, 27
		Pittsburgh Steelers, 17
XXXI	1997	Green Bay Packers, 35
		New England Patriots, 21
XXXII	1998	Denver Broncos, 31
		Green Bay Packers, 24
XXXIII	1999	Denver Broncos, 34
		Atlanta Falcons, 19

NFL Player of the Year

1957	Jim Brown, Cleveland
1958	Jim Brown, Cleveland
1959	Johnny Unitas, Baltimore
1960	Norm Van Brocklin, Philadelphia
1961	Paul Hornung, Green Bay
1962	Y.A. Tittle, New York Giants
1963	Y.A. Tittle, New York Giants

1964	Johnny Unitas, Baltimore
1965	Jim Brown, Cleveland
1966	Bart Starr, Green Bay
1967	Johnny Unitas, Baltimore
1968	Earl Morrall, Baltimore
1969	Roman Gabriel, Los Angeles Rams
1970	NFC[1] John Brodie, San Francisco
	AFC George Blanda, Oakland
1971	NFC Roger Staubach, Dallas
	AFC Bob Griese, Miami
1972	NFC Larry Brown, Washington
	AFC Earl Morrall, Miami
1973	NFC John Hadl, Los Angeles Rams
	AFC O.J. Simpson, Buffalo
1974	NFC Chuck Foreman, Minnesota
	AFC Ken Stabler, Oakland
1975	NFC Fran Tarkenton, Minnesota
	AFC O.J. Simpson, Buffalo
1976	NFC Walter Payton, Chicago
	AFC Ken Stabler, Oakland
1977	NFC Walter Payton, Chicago
	AFC Craig Morton, Denver

---

1. From 1970 to 1979, *The Sporting News* selected Player of the Year for each NFL Conference, and then resumed practice of a single selection for the entire league in 1980.

1978	NFC Archie Manning, New Orleans
	AFC Earl Campbell, Houston
1979	NFC Ottis Anderson, St. Louis
	AFC Dan Fouts, San Diego
1980	Brian Sipe, Cleveland
1981	Ken Anderson, Cincinnati
1982	Mark Moseley, Washington
1983	Eric Dickerson, Los Angeles Rams
1984	Dan Marino, Miami
1985	Marcus Allen, Los Angeles Raiders
1986	Lawrence Taylor, New York Giants
1987	Jerry Rice, San Francisco
1988	Boomer Esiason, Cincinnati
1989	Joe Montana, San Francisco
1990	Jerry Rice, San Francisco
1991	Thurman Thomas, Buffalo
1992	Steve Young, San Francisco
1993	Emmitt Smith, Dallas
1994	Steve Young, San Francisco
1995	Brett Favre, Green Bay
1996	Brett Favre, Green Bay
1997	Brett Favre, Green Bay
1998	Barry Sanders, Detroit

American Football League (AFC) Championships

1960	Houston 24, Los Angeles 16
1961	Houston 10, San Diego 3
1962	Dallas 20, Houston 17 (two overtimes)
1963	San Diego 51, Boston 10
1964	Buffalo 20, San Diego 7
1965	Buffalo 23, San Diego 0
1966	Kansas City 31, Buffalo 7
1967	Oakland 40, Houston 7
1968	New York 27, Oakland 23
1969	Kansas City 17, Oakland 7

Golf

U.S. Open Championship

1895	Horace Rawlins
1896	James Foulis
1897	Joe Lloyd
1898	Fred Herd
1899	Willie Smith
1900	Harry Vardo
1901	Willie Anderson
1902	Laurie Auchterlonie
1903	Willie Anderson

1904	Willie Anderson	1928	John Farrell
1905	Willie Anderson	1929	Bobby Jones*
1906	Alex Smith	1930	Bobby Jones*
1907	Alex Ross	1931	William Burke
1908	Fred McLeod	1932	Gene Sarazen
1909	George Sargent	1933	John Goodman*
1910	Alex Smith	1934	Olin Dutra
1911	John McDermott	1935	Sam Parks Jr.
1912	John McDermott	1936	Tony Manero
1913	Francis Ouimet*	1937	Ralph Guldahl
1914	Walter Hagen	1938	Ralph Guldahl
1915	Jerome Travers*	1939	Byron Nelson
1916	Chick Evans*	1940	Lawson Little
1917	No Championship	1941	Craig Wood
1918	No Championship	1942	No Championship
1919	Walter Hagen	1943	No Championship
1920	Edward Ray	1944	No Championship
1921	Jim Barnes	1945	No Championship
1922	Gene Sarazen	1946	Lloyd Mangrum
1923	Bobby Jones*	1947	L. Worsham
1924	Cyril Walker	1948	Ben Hogan
1925	Willie MacFarlane	1949	Cary Middlecoff
1926	Bobby Jones*	1950	Ben Hogan
1927	Tommy Armour	1951	Ben Hogan
		1952	Julius Boros

* Amateur

1953	Ben Hogan

1954	Ed Furgol	1979	Hale Irwin
1955	Jack Fleck	1980	Jack Nicklaus
1956	Cary Middlecoff	1981	David Graham
1957	Dick Mayer	1982	Tom Watson
1958	Tommy Bolt	1983	Larry Nelson
1959	Billy Casper	1984	Fuzzy Zoeller
1960	Arnold Palmer	1985	Andy North
1961	Gene Littler	1986	Ray Floyd
1962	Jack Nicklaus	1987	Scott Simpson
1963	Julius Boros	1988	Curtis Strange
1964	Ken Venturi	1989	Curtis Strange
1965	Gary Player	1990	Hale Irwin
1966	Billy Casper	1991	Payne Stewart
1967	Jack Nicklaus	1992	Tom Kite
1968	Lee Trevino	1993	Lee Janzen
1969	Orville Moody	1994	Ernie Els
1970	Tony Jacklin	1995	Corey Pavin
1971	Lee Trevino	1996	Steve Jones
1972	Jack Nicklaus	1997	Ernie Els
1973	Johnny Miller	1998	Lee Janzen
1974	Hale Irwin		
1975	Lou Graham		
1976	Jerry Pate		
1977	Hubert Green		
1978	Andy North		

PGA Championship

1916	James M. Barnes
1917	No Championship
1918	No Championship
1919	James M. Barnes

1920	Jock Hutchison	**1945**	Byron Nelson
1921	Walter Hagen	**1946**	Ben Hogan
1922	Gene Sarazen	**1947**	Jim Ferrier
1923	Gene Sarazen	**1948**	Ben Hogan
1924	Walter Hagen	**1949**	Sam Snead
1925	Walter Hagen	**1950**	Chandler Harper
1926	Walter Hagen	**1951**	Sam Snead
1927	Walter Hagen	**1952**	James Turnesa
1928	Leo Diegel	**1953**	Walter Burkemo
1929	Leo Diegel	**1954**	Melvin Harbert
1930	Tommy Armour	**1955**	Doug Ford
1931	Tom Creavy	**1956**	Jack Burke Jr.
1932	Olin Dutra	**1957**	Lionel Hebert
1933	Gene Sarazen	**1958**	Dow Finsterwald
1934	Paul Runyan	**1959**	Bob Rosburg
1935	Johnny Revolta	**1960**	Jay Hebert
1936	Denny Shute	**1961**	Jerry Barber
1937	Denny Shute	**1962**	Gary Player
1938	Paul Runyan	**1963**	Jack Nicklaus
1939	Henry Picard	**1964**	Bob Nichols
1940	Byron Nelson	**1965**	Dave Marr
1941	Victor Ghezzi	**1966**	Al Geiberger
1942	Sam Snead	**1967**	Don January
1943	No Championship	**1968**	Julius Boros
1944	Bob Hamilton	**1969**	Ray Floyd

1970	Dave Stockton	1995	Steve Elkington
1971	Jack Nicklaus	1996	Mark Brooks
1972	Gary Player	1997	Davis Love III
1973	Jack Nicklaus	1998	Vijay Singh

1974	Lee Trevino

The Masters Champions

1975	Jack Nicklaus	1934	Horton Smith
1976	Dave Stockton	1935	Gene Sarazen
1977	Lanny Wadkins	1936	Horton Smith
1978	John Mahaffey	1937	Byron Nelson
1979	David Graham	1938	Henry Picard
1980	Jack Nicklaus	1939	Ralph Guldahl
1981	Larry Nelson	1940	Jimmy Demaret
1982	Ray Floyd	1941	Craig Wood
1983	Hal Sutton	1942	Byron Nelson
1984	Lee Trevino	1943	No Championship
1985	Hubert Green	1944	No Championship
1986	Bob Tway	1945	No Championship
1987	Larry Nelson	1946	Herman Keiser
1988	Jeff Sluman	1947	Jimmy Demaret
1989	Payne Stewart	1948	Claude Harman
1990	Wayne Grady	1949	Sam Snead
1991	John Daly	1950	Jimmy Demaret
1992	Nick Price	1951	Ben Hogan
1993	Paul Azinger	1952	Sam Snead
1994	Nick Price	1953	Ben Hogan

1954	Sam Snead		1979	Fuzzy Zoeller
1955	Cary Middlecoff		1980	Seve Ballesteros
1956	Jack Burke Jr.		1981	Tom Watson
1957	Doug Ford		1982	Craig Stadler
1958	Arnold Palmer		1983	Seve Ballesteros
1959	Art Wall Jr.		1984	Ben Crenshaw
1960	Arnold Palmer		1985	Bernhard Langer
1961	Gary Player		1986	Jack Nicklaus
1962	Arnold Palmer		1987	Larry Mize
1963	Jack Nicklaus		1988	Sandy Lyle
1964	Arnold Palmer		1989	Nick Faldo
1965	Jack Nicklaus		1990	Nick Faldo
1966	Jack Nicklaus		1991	Ian Woosnam
1967	Gay Brewer Jr.		1992	Fred Couples
1968	Bob Goalby		1993	Bernhard Langer
1969	George Archer		1994	Jose Maria Olazabal
1970	Billy Casper		1995	Ben Crenshaw
1971	Charles Coody		1996	Nick Faldo
1972	Jack Nicklaus		1997	Tiger Woods
1973	Tommy Aaron		1998	Mark O'Meara

U.S. Women's Open Championship

1974	Gary Player		1946	Patty Berg
1975	Jack Nicklaus		1947	Betty Jameson
1976	Ray Floyd		1948	Babe Zaharias
1977	Tom Watson			
1978	Gary Player			

1949	Louise Suggs	1975	Sandra Palmer
1950	Babe Zaharias	1976	JoAnne Carner
1951	Betsy Rawls	1977	Hollis Stacy
1952	Louise Suggs	1978	Hollis Stacy
1953	Betsy Rawls	1979	Jerilyn Britz
1954	Babe Zaharias	1980	Amy Alcott
1955	Fay Crocker	1981	Pat Bradley
1956	Kathy Cornelius	1982	Janet Anderson
1957	Betsy Rawls	1983	Jan Stephenson
1958	Mickey Wright	1984	Hollis Stacy
1959	Mickey Wright	1985	Kathy Baker
1960	Betsy Rawls	1986	Jane Geddes
1961	Mickey Wright	1987	Laura Davies
1962	Murle Lindstrom	1988	Liselotte Neumann
1963	Mary Mills	1989	Betsy King
1964	Mickey Wright	1990	Betsy King
1965	Carol Mann	1991	Meg Mallon
1966	Sandra Spuzich	1992	Patty Sheehan
1967	Catherine LaCoste	1993	Lauri Merten
1968	Susie Maxwell Berning	1994	Patty Sheehan
1969	Donna Caponi	1995	Annika Sorenstam
1970	Donna Caponi	1996	Annika Sorenstam
1971	JoAnne Carner	1997	Alison Nicholas
1972	Susie Maxwell Berning	1998	Se Ri Pak
1973	Susie Maxwell Berning		
1974	Sandra Haynie		

Year	Champion	Final Opponent

Hockey

National Hockey League (NHL) Stanley Cup Champions

Year	Champion	Final Opponent
1927	Ottawa	Boston
1928	New York Rangers	Montreal
1929	Boston	New York Rangers
1930	Montreal	Boston
1931	Montreal	Chicago
1932	Toronto	New York Rangers
1933	New York Rangers	Toronto
1934	Chicago	Detroit
1935	Montreal	Toronto
1936	Detroit	Toronto
1937	Detroit	New York Rangers
1938	Chicago	Toronto
1939	Boston	Toronto
1940	New York Rangers	Toronto
1941	Boston	Detroit
1942	Toronto	Detroit
1943	Detroit	Boston
1944	Montreal	Chicago
1945	Toronto	Detroit
1946	Montreal	Boston
1947	Toronto	Montreal
1948	Toronto	Detroit
1949	Toronto	Detroit
1950	Detroit	New York Rangers
1951	Toronto	Montreal
1952	Detroit	Montreal
1953	Montreal	Boston
1954	Detroit	Montreal
1955	Detroit	Montreal
1956	Montreal	Detroit
1957	Montreal	Boston
1958	Montreal	Boston
1959	Montreal	Toronto
1960	Montreal	Toronto
1961	Chicago	Detroit
1962	Toronto	Chicago
1963	Toronto	Detroit
1964	Toronto	Detroit
1965	Montreal	Chicago
1966	Montreal	Detroit
1967	Toronto	Montreal
1968	Montreal	St. Louis
1969	Montreal	St. Louis
1970	Boston	St. Louis

Year	Champion	Final Opponent
1971	Montreal	Chicago
1972	Boston	New York Rangers
1973	Montreal	Chicago
1974	Philadelphia	Boston
1975	Philadelphia	Buffalo
1976	Montreal	Philadelphia
1977	Montreal	Boston
1978	Montreal	Boston
1979	Montreal	New York Rangers
1980	New York Islanders	Philadelphia
1981	New York Islanders	Minnesota
1982	New York Islanders	Vancouver
1983	New York Islanders	Edmonton
1984	Edmonton	New York Islanders
1985	Edmonton	Philadelphia
1986	Montreal	Calgary
1987	Edmonton	Philadelphia
1988	Edmonton	Boston
1989	Calgary	Montreal
1990	Edmonton	Boston
1991	Pittsburgh	Minnesota
1992	Pittsburgh	Chicago
1993	Montreal	Los Angeles
1994	New York Rangers	Vancouver

Year	Champion	Final Opponent
1995	New Jersey	Detroit
1996	Colorado	Florida
1997	Detroit	Philadelphia
1998	Detroit	Washington
1999	Dallas	Buffalo

Hart Memorial Trophy (MVP for the NHL)

1927	Herb Gardiner, Montreal
1928	Howie Morenz, Montreal
1929	Roy Worters, New York Americans
1930	Nels Stewart, Montreal Maroons
1931	Howie Morenz, Montreal
1932	Howie Morenz, Montreal
1933	Eddie Shore, Boston
1934	Aurel Joliet, Montreal
1935	Eddie Shore, Boston
1936	Eddie Shore, Boston
1937	Babe Siebert, Montreal
1938	Eddie Shore, Boston
1939	Toe Blake, Montreal
1940	Ebbie Goodfellow, Detroit
1941	Bill Cowley, Boston
1942	Tom Anderson, New York Americans
1943	Bill Cowley, Boston
1944	Babe Pratt, Toronto

1945	Elmer Loch, Montreal	1970	Bobby Orr, Boston
1946	Max Bentley, Chicago	1971	Bobby Orr, Boston
1947	Maurice Richard, Montreal	1972	Bobby Orr, Boston
1948	Buddy O'Connor, New York Rangers	1973	Bobby Clarke, Philadelphia
1949	Sid Abel, Detroit	1974	Phil Esposito, Boston
1950	Chuck Rayner, New York Rangers	1975	Bobby Clarke, Philadelphia
1951	Milt Schmidt, Boston	1976	Bobby Clarke. Philadelphia
1952	Gordie Howe, Detroit	1977	Guy Lafleur, Montreal
1953	Gordie Howe, Detroit	1978	Guy Lafleur, Montreal
1954	A.J. Rollins, Chicago	1979	Bryan Trottier, New York Islanders
1955	Ted Kennedy, Toronto	1980	Wayne Gretzky, Edmonton
1956	Jean Beliveau, Montreal	1991	Wayne Gretzky, Edmonton
1957	Gordie Howe, Detroit	1982	Wayne Gretzky, Edmonton
1958	Gordie Howe, Detroit	1983	Wayne Gretzky, Edmonton
1959	Andy Bathgate, New York Rangers	1984	Wayne Gretzky, Edmonton
1960	Gordie Howe, Detroit	1985	Wayne Gretzky, Edmonton
1961	Bernie Geoffrion, Montreal	1986	Wayne Gretzky, Edmonton
1962	Jacques Plante, Montreal	1987	Wayne Gretzky, Edmonton
1963	Gordie Howe, Detroit	1988	Mario Lemieux, Pittsburgh
1964	Jean Beliveau, Montreal	1989	Wayne Gretzky, Los Angeles
1965	Bobby Hull, Chicago	1990	Mark Messier, Edmonton
1966	Bobby Hull, Chicago	1991	Brett Hull, St. Louis
1967	Stan Mikita, Chicago	1992	Mark Messier, New York Rangers
1968	Stan Mikita, Chicago	1993	Mario Lemieux, Pittsburgh
1969	Phil Esposito, Boston	1994	Sergei Fedorov, Detroit

1995	Eric Lindros, Philadelphia
1996	Mario Lemieux, Pittsburgh
1997	Dominik Hasek, Buffalo
1998	Dominik Hasek, Buffalo
1999	Jaromir Jagr, Pittsburgh

Horse Racing

Triple Crown Winners

The following horses have won the Kentucky Derby, the Preakness, and the Belmont Stakes.

1919	Sir Barton
1930	Gallant Fox
1935	Omaha
1937	War Admiral
1941	Whirlaway
1943	Count Fleet
1946	Assault
1948	Citation
1973	Secretariat
1977	Seattle Slew
1978	Affirmed

Kentucky Derby Winners

1875	Aristides
1876	Vagrant
1877	Baden Baden
1878	Day Star
1879	Lord Murphy
1880	Fonso
1881	Hindoo
1882	Apollo
1883	Leonatus
1884	Buchanan
1885	Joe Cotton
1886	Ben Ali
1887	Montrose
1888	Macbeth II
1889	Spokane
1890	Riley
1891	Kingman
1892	Azra
1893	Lookout
1894	Chant
1895	Halma
1896	Ben Brush
1897	Typhoon II
1898	Plaudit
1899	Manuel
1900	Lieut. Gibson
1901	His Eminence
1902	Alan-a-Dale

1903	Judge Himes	**1928**	Reigh Count
1904	Elwood	**1929**	Clyde Van Dusen
1905	Agile	**1930**	Gallant Fox
1906	Sir Huon	**1931**	Twenty Grand
1907	Pink Star	**1932**	Burgoo King
1908	Stone Street	**1933**	Brokers Tip
1909	Wintergreen	**1934**	Cavalcade
1910	Donau	**1935**	Omaha
1911	Meridian	**1936**	Bold Venture
1912	Worth	**1937**	War Admiral
1913	Donerall	**1938**	Lawrin
1914	Old Rosebud	**1939**	Johnston
1915	Regret	**1940**	Gallahadion
1916	George Smith	**1941**	Whirlaway
1917	Omar Khayyam	**1942**	Shut Out
1918	Exterminator	**1943**	Count Fleet
1919	Sir Barton	**1944**	Pensive
1920	Paul Jones	**1945**	Hoop, Jr.
1921	Behave Yourself	**1946**	Assault
1922	Morvich	**1947**	Jet Pilot
1923	Zev	**1948**	Citation
1924	Black Gold	**1949**	Ponder
1925	Flying Ebony	**1950**	Middleground
1926	Bubbling Over	**1951**	Count Turf
1927	Whiskery	**1952**	Hill Gail

1953	Dark Star	**1976**	Bold Forbes
1954	Determine	**1977**	Seattle Slew
1955	Swaps	**1978**	Affirmed
1956	Needles	**1979**	Spectacular Bid
1957	Iron Liege	**1980**	Genuine Risk
1958	Tim Tam	**1981**	Pleasant Colony
1959	Tomy Lee	**1982**	Gato del Sol
1960	Venetian Way	**1983**	Sunny's Halo
1961	Carry Back	**1984**	Swale
1962	Decidedly	**1985**	Spend a Buck
1963	Chateaugay	**1986**	Ferdinand
1964	Northern Dancer	**1987**	Alysheba
1965	Lucky Debonair	**1988**	Winning Colors
1966	Kauai King	**1989**	Sunday Silence
1967	Proud Clarion	**1990**	Unbridled
1968	Dancer's Image / Forward Pass[1]	**1991**	Strike the Gold
1969	Majestic Prince	**1992**	Lil E. Tee
1970	Dust Commander	**1993**	Sea Hero
1971	Canonero II	**1994**	Go for Gin
1972	Riva Ridge	**1995**	Thunder Gulch
1973	Secretariat	**1996**	Grindstone
1974	Cannonade	**1997**	Silver Charm
1975	Foolish Pleasure	**1998**	Real Quiet
		1999	Charismatic

1. Dancer's Image was disqualified from purse money because a pain-killing drug was used; Forward Pass received first-place money.

Preakness Stakes Winners

1873	Survivor
1874	Culpepper
1875	Tom Ochiltree
1876	Shirley
1877	Cloverbrook
1878	Duke of Magenta
1879	Harold
1880	Grenada
1881	Saunterer
1882	Vanguard
1883	Jacobus
1884	Knight of Ellerslie
1885	Tecumseh
1886	The Bard
1887	Dunboyne
1888	Refund
1889	Buddhist
1890	Montague
1891–1893	Race Not Run
1894	Assignee
1895	Belmar
1896	Margrave
1897	Paul Kauver
1898	Sly Fox

1899	Half Time
1900	Hindus
1901	The Parader
1902	Old England
1903	Flocarline
1904	Bryn Mawr
1905	Cairngorm
1906	Whimsical
1907	Don Enrique
1908	Royal Tourist
1909	Effendi
1910	Layminister
1911	Watervale
1912	Colonel Holloway
1913	Buskin
1914	Holiday
1915	Rhine Maiden
1916	Damrosch
1917	Kalitan
1918	War Cloud
	Jack Hare, Jr. (tie)
1919	Sir Barton
1920	Man o' War
1921	Broomspun
1922	Pillory

1923	Vigil	1948	Citation
1924	Nellie Morse	1949	Capot
1925	Coventry	1950	Hill Prince
1926	Display	1951	Bold
1927	Bostonian	1952	Blue Man
1928	Victorian	1953	Native Dancer
1929	Dr. Freeland	1954	Hasty Road
1930	Gallant Fox	1955	Nashua
1931	Mate	1956	Fabius
1932	Burgoo King	1957	Bold Ruler
1933	Head Play	1958	Tim Tam
1934	High Quest	1959	Royal Orbit
1935	Omaha	1960	Bally Ache
1936	Bold Venture	1961	Carry Back
1937	War Admiral	1962	Greek Money
1938	Dauber	1963	Candy Spots
1939	Challedon	1964	Northern Dancer
1940	Bimelech	1965	Tom Rolfe
1941	Whirlaway	1966	Kauai King
1942	Alsab	1967	Damascus
1943	Count Fleet	1968	Forward Pass
1944	Pensive	1969	Majestic Prince
1945	Polynesian	1970	Personality
1946	Assault	1971	Canonero II
1947	Faultless	1972	Bee Bee Bee

1973	Secretariat		1998	Real Quiet
1974	Little Current		1999	Charismatic
1975	Master Derby			
1976	Elocutionist			

Belmont Stakes

1977	Seattle Slew		1867	Ruthless
1978	Affirmed		1868	General Duke
1979	Spectacular Bid		1869	Fenian
1980	Codex		1870	Kingfisher
1981	Pleasant Colony		1871	Harry Bassett
1982	Aloma's Ruler		1872	Joe Daniels
1983	Deputed Testamony		1873	Springbok
1984	Gate Dancer		1874	Saxon
1985	Tank's Prospect		1875	Calvin
1986	Snow Chief		1876	Algerine
1987	Alysheba		1877	Cloverbrook
1988	Risen Star		1878	Duke of Magenta
1989	Sunday Silence		1879	Spendthrift
1990	Summer Squall		1880	Grenada
1991	Hansel		1881	Saunterer
1992	Pine Bluff		1882	Forester
1993	Prairie Bayou		1883	George Kinney
1994	Tabasco Cat		1884	Panique
1995	Timber Country		1885	Tyrant
1996	Louis Quatorze		1886	Inspector B
1997	Silver Charm		1887	Hanover
			1888	Sir Dixon

1889	Eric	1915	The Finn
1890	Burlington	1916	Friar Rock
1891	Foxford	1917	Hourless
1892	Patron	1918	Johren
1893	Comanche	1919	Sir Barton
1894	Henry of Navarre	1920	Man o' War
1895	Belmar	1921	Grey Lag
1896	Hastings	1922	Pillory
1897	Scottish Chieftain	1923	Zev
1898	Bowling Brook	1924	Mad Play
1899	Jean Bereaud	1925	American Flag
1900	Ildrim	1926	Crusader
1901	Commando	1927	Chance Shot
1902	Masterman	1928	Vito
1903	Africander	1929	Blue Larkspur
1904	Delhi	1930	Gallant Fox
1905	Tanya	1931	Twenty Grand
1906	Burgomaster	1932	Faireno
1907	Peter Pan	1933	Hurryoff
1908	Colin	1934	Peace Chance
1909	Joe Madden	1935	Omaha
1910	Sweep	1936	Granville
1911–1912	Race Not Run	1937	War Admiral
1913	Prince Eugene	1938	Pasteurized
1914	Luke McLuke	1939	Johnstown

1940	Bimelech	1965	Hail to All
1941	Whirlaway	1966	Amberoid
1942	Shut Out	1967	Damascus
1943	Count Fleet	1968	Stage Door Johnny
1944	Bounding Home	1969	Arts and Letters
1945	Pavot	1970	High Echelon
1946	Assault	1971	Pass Catcher
1947	Phalanx	1972	Riva Ridge
1948	Citation	1973	Secretariat
1949	Capot	1974	Little Current
1950	Middleground	1975	Avatar
1951	Counterpoint	1976	Bold Forbes
1952	One Count	1977	Seattle Slew
1953	Native Dancer	1978	Affirmed
1954	High Gun	1979	Coastal
1955	Nashua	1980	Temperence Hill
1956	Needles	1981	Summing
1957	Gallant Man	1982	Conquistador Cielo
1958	Cavan	1983	Caveat
1959	Sword Dancer	1984	Swale
1960	Celtic Ash	1985	Creme Fraiche
1961	Sherluck	1986	Danzig Connection
1962	Jaipur	1987	Bet Twice
1963	Chateaugay	1988	Risen Star
1964	Quadrangle	1989	Easy Goer

Year	Champion
1990	Go and Go
1991	Hansel
1992	A.P. Indy
1993	Colonial Affair
1994	Tabasco Cat
1995	Thunder Gulch
1996	Editor's Note
1997	Touch Gold
1998	Victory Gallop
1999	Lemon Drop Kid

Tennis

U.S. Open Tennis Championship

MEN'S SINGLES

Year	Champion
1920	Bill Tilden
1921	Bill Tilden
1922	Bill Tilden
1923	Bill Tilden
1924	Bill Tilden
1925	Bill Tilden
1926	Rene Lacoste
1927	Rene Lacoste
1928	Henri Cochet
1929	Bill Tilden

Year	Champion
1930	John Doeg
1931	H. Ellsworth Vines
1932	H. Ellsworth Vines
1933	Fred Perry
1934	Fred Perry
1935	Wilmer Allison
1936	Fred Perry
1937	Don Budge
1938	Don Budge
1939	Bobby Riggs
1940	Don McNeill
1941	Bobby Riggs
1942	Frederick Schroeder Jr.
1943	Joseph Hunt
1944	Frank Parker
1945	Frank Parker
1946	Jack Kramer
1947	Jack Kramer
1948	Pancho Gonzales
1949	Pancho Gonzales
1950	Arthur Larsen
1951	Frank Sedgman
1952	Frank Sedgman
1953	Tony Trabert

Year	Champion	Year	Champion
1954	E. Victor Seixas Jr.	1977	Guillermo Vilas
1955	Tony Trabert	1978	Jimmy Connors
1956	Ken Rosewall	1979	John McEnroe
1957	Malcolm Anderson	1980	John McEnroe
1958	Ashley Cooper	1981	John McEnroe
1959	Neale A. Fraser	1982	Jimmy Connors
1960	Neale A. Fraser	1983	Jimmy Connors
1961	Roy Emerson	1984	John McEnroe
1962	Rod Laver	1985	Ivan Lendl
1963	Rafael Osuna	1986	Ivan Lendl
1964	Roy Emerson	1987	Ivan Lendl
1965	Manuel Santana	1988	Mats Wilander
1966	Fred Stolle	1989	Boris Becker
1967	John Newcombe	1990	Pete Sampras
1968	Arthur Ashe	1991	Stefan Edberg
1969	Rod Laver	1992	Stefan Edberg
1970	Ken Rosewall	1993	Pete Sampras
1971	Stan Smith	1994	Andre Agassi
1972	Ilie Nastase	1995	Pete Sampras
1973	John Newcombe	1996	Pete Sampras
1974	Jimmy Connors	1997	Patrick Rafter
1975	Manuel Orantes	1998	Patrick Rafter
1976	Jimmy Connors	1999	Andre Agassi

WOMEN'S SINGLES

Year	Champion
1920	Molla B. Mallory
1921	Molla B. Mallory
1922	Molla B. Mallory
1923	Helen Wills
1924	Molla B. Mallory
1925	Helen Willis
1926	Molla B. Mallory
1927	Helen Wills
1928	Helen Wills
1929	Helen Wills
1930	Betty Nuthall
1931	Helen Wills Moody
1932	Helen Jacobs
1933	Helen Jacobs
1934	Helen Jacobs
1935	Helen Jacobs
1936	Alice Marble
1937	Anita Lizana
1938	Alice Marble
1939	Alice Marble
1940	Alice Marble
1941	Sarah Palfrey Cooke
1942	Pauline Betz

Year	Champion
1943	Pauline Betz
1944	Pauline Betz
1945	Sarah Palfrey Cooke
1946	Pauline Betz
1947	Louise Brough
1948	Margaret Osborne duPont
1949	Margaret Osborne duPont
1950	Margaret Osborne duPont
1951	Maureen Connolly
1952	Maureen Connolly
1953	Maureen Connolly
1954	Doris Hart
1955	Doris Hart
1956	Shirley Fry
1957	Althea Gibson
1958	Althea Gibson
1959	Maria Bueno
1960	Darlene Hard
1961	Darlene Hard
1962	Margaret Smith
1963	Maria Bueno
1964	Maria Bueno
1965	Margaret Smith
1966	Maria Bueno

Year	Champion		Year	Champion
1967	Billie Jean King		**1984**	Martina Navratilova
1968	Virginia Wade		**1985**	Hana Mandlikova
1969	Margaret Smith Court		**1986**	Martina Navratilova
1970	Margaret Smith Court		**1987**	Martina Navratilova
1971	Billie Jean King		**1988**	Steffi Graf
1972	Billie Jean King		**1989**	Steffi Graf
1973	Margaret Smith Court		**1990**	Gabriela Sabatini
1974	Billie Jean King		**1991**	Monica Seles
1975	Chris Evert		**1992**	Monica Seles
1976	Chris Evert		**1993**	Steffi Graf
1977	Chris Evert		**1994**	Arantxa Sanchez Vicario
1978	Chris Evert		**1995**	Steffi Graf
1979	Tracy Austin		**1996**	Steffi Graf
1980	Chris Evert Lloyd		**1997**	Martina Hingis
1981	Tracy Austin		**1998**	Lindsay Davenport
1982	Chris Evert Lloyd		**1999**	Serena Williams
1983	Martina Navratilova			

Bibliography

The Alyson Almanac: The Fact Book of the Lesbian and Gay Community. 3rd ed. 1993. Boston: Alyson Publications.

Anderson, James, and David Zarefsky, eds. 1989. *American Voices: Significant Speeches in American History.* White Plains, NY: Longman.

Banks, James A. 1991. *Teaching Strategies for Ethnic Studies.* 5th ed. Boston: Allyn and Bacon.

Carruth, Gorton. 1970. *The Encyclopedia of American Facts and Dates.* New York: Thomas Y. Crowell Company.

Clarke, James W. 1982. *American Assassins: the Darker Side of Politics.* Princeton, NJ: Princeton University Press.

DeGregorio, William A. 1984. *The Complete Book of U.S. Presidents.* New York: Dembner Books.

Diller, Daniel. 1997. *The Presidents, First Ladies, and Vice Presidents: White House Biographies, 1789–1997.* Washington, D.C.: Congressional Quarterly.

Educational Research Council of America. Social Science Staff. 1993. *Explorers and Discoverers of the World.* Detroit: Gale Research.

Encyclopedia Americana. 1996. Danbury, CT: Grolier Incorporated.

The Encyclopedia of American Facts and Dates. 5th ed. 1971. New York: Thomas Y. Crowell.

Encyclopedia of the American Constitution. 1986. New York: Free Press.

Encyclopedia of the Vietnam War. 1996. New York: Charles Scribner's Sons.

The European Powers in the First World War: An Encyclopedia. 1996. New York: Garland.

Facts About the States. 1993. New York: H.W. Wilson.

Frazier, Thomas, ed. 1996. *The Many Sides of America: 1945 to the Present.* Fort Worth, TX: Harcourt Brace College Publishers.

Gall, Susan, ed. 1995. *Asian-American Almanac: A Reference Work on Asians in the United States.* Detroit: Gale Research.

The Gay Almanac. 1996. New York: Berkley Books.

Goralski, Robert. 1981. *World War II Almanac, 1931–1945: A Political and Military Record.* New York: Putnam.

Graff, Henry F., ed. 1996. *The Presidents: A Reference History.* 2nd ed. New York: Charles Scribner's Sons.

Gribetz, Judah. 1993. *The Timetables of Jewish History: A Chronology of the Most Important People and Events in Jewish History.* New York: Simon & Schuster.

Grun, Bernard. 1979. *The Timetables of History.* New York: Simon & Schuster.

The Hispanic-American Almanac: A Reference Work on Hispanics in the United States. 1993. Detroit: Gale Research.

Hoyt, Edwin Palmer. 1987. *America's Wars and Military Excursions.* New York: McGraw-Hill.

The Inaugural Story, 1789–1969. 1969. New York: American Heritage Pub. Co.

Kane, Joseph Nathan. 1981. *Facts about the Presidents: A Compilation of Biographical and Historical Information.* New York: H.W. Wilson Company.

Kane, Joseph Nathan, Janet Podell, and Steven Anzovin. 1993. *Facts About the States.* New York: H.W. Wilson Co.

Kohn, Goerge C.1986. *Dictionary of Wars.* New York: Facts on File.

The Korean War: An Encyclopedia. 1995. New York: Garland Publishing, Inc.

Lentz, Harris M.1988. *Assassinations and Executions: An Encyclopedia of Political Violence, 1865–1986.* Jefferson, NC: McFarland & Company.

The Lesbian Almanac. 1996. New York: Berkley Books.

Lieberman, Jethro K. 1992. *The Evolving Constitution: How the Supreme Court Has Ruled on Issues from Abortion to Zoning.* New York: Random House.

McDonald, Forrest 1982. *A Constitutional History of the United States.* New York: F. Watts.

NBC News/Rand McNally World Atlas & Almanac. 1989, 1990, 1991, and 1992. Skokie, IL: Rand McNally.

The Negro Almanac: A Reference Work on the African-American. 5th ed. 1989. Detroit: Gale Research.

New York Times Almanac. 1998. New York: Penguin Group Penguin Putnam.

The Oxford Companion to World War II. 1995. Oxford: Oxford University Press.

Paddock, Lisa. 1996. *Facts About the Supreme Court of the United States.* New York: H. W. Wilson Company.

Pope, Stephen. 1995. *The Dictionary of the First World War.* New York: St. Martin's Press.

Presidential Elections, 1789–1992. 1995. Washington, D.C.: Congressional Quarterly.

The Presidents Speak: The Inaugural Addresses of the American Presidents from Washington to *Clinton*. 1994. New York: H. Holt and Co.

A Reference Guide to the United States Supreme Court. 1985. New York: Facts on File.

Shafritz, Jay M. 1991. *Almanac of Modern Terrorism*. New York: Facts on File.

Smith, Jessie Carney, ed. 1994. *Black Firsts: 2,000 Years of Extraordinary Achievement*. Detroit: Gale Research.

Smith, Page. 1978. *The Constitution: A Documentary and Narrative History*. Norwalk, CT: The Easton Press.

Southwick, Leslie. 1984. *Presidential Also-Rans and Running Mates, 1788–1980*. Jefferson, NC: McFarland & Co.

Straub, Deborah Gillan. 1995. *Voices of Multicultural America: Notable Speeches Delivered by African, Asian, Hispanic, and Native Americans, 1790–1995*. New York: Gale Research.

Summers, Harry G. 1985. *Vietnam War Almanac*. New York: Facts on File.

Torricelli, Robert G., ed. 1999. *In Our Own Words: Extraordinary Speeches of the American Century*. New York: Kodansha International.

Trager, James. 1994. *The Peoples Chronology: A Year-by-Year Record of Human Events from Prehistory to the Present*. New York: Henry Holt and Co.

Urdang, Laurence, ed. 1981. *The Timetables of American History*. New York: Simon & Schuster.

Vile, John R. 1996. *Encyclopedia of Constitutional Amendments, Proposed Amendments, and Amending Issues, 1789-1995*. Santa Barbara, CA: ABC-CLIO.

Wetterau, Bruce. 1990. *New York Public Library Book of Chronologies*. New York: Prentice Hall Press.

World Almanac & Book of Facts. 1998 and 1999. Mahwah, NJ: World Almanac Books.

World Book Encyclopedia. 1996. Chicago: World Book, Inc.

Young, Peter, ed. 1981. *The World Almanac Book of World War II*. New York: World Almanac Publications.

Periodicals Consulted

Facts on File
The New York Times
TV Guide, July 29, 1996
The Washington Post
National Intelligence (Washington, D.C., March 1813)

Subject Index

C

Homestead Act, 4
homosexuality (see Gay Americans)
horse-racing
    Belmont Stakes, 266–269
    Kentucky Derby winners, 261–263
    Preakness Stakes winners, 264–266
    Triple Crown winners, 261
hurricanes
    general chronology155–156
    Hurricane Agnes, 52
    Hurricane Andrew, 44
    Hurricane Audrey, 74
    Hurricane Betsy, 50
    Hurricane Bob, 51
    Hurricane Frederick, 56

I

Idaho, 45–46
Illinois, 46–47
immigration
    Asian immigration, 28
    Chinese Exclusion Act of 1882, 29
    Cubans, 43
    European immigration in 19th century, 24–25
    Haitians, 43
    Irish Potato Famine & immigration, 4
    Japanese, (Gentlemen's Agreement), 5
    Jews, 25–26
    Johnson Act, 25
    quotas imposed, 6
income tax (see taxation)
Indian Removal Act, 19
Indiana, 47
inventions
    cotton gin, 3
    electric light, 5, 61
    ice box, 51
    motion picture camera, 5
    nylon, 43
    phonograph, 5
    reaping machine, 4, 46
    steamboat, 63
    steam engine (coal fed), 52
    steel plow, 46
    telegraph, 4, 52
    telephone, 4
Iowa, 47–48
Iranian Hostage Crisis, 10
Irish Potato Famine, 4, 24
iron-ore, 55

J

Japanese Americans
    internment camps, 7, 45

Jews
    anti-semitism, 26
    first Jewish senator, 25, 43
    first synagogue, 2
    immigration, 25
    Jewish Defense League, 26
    Jewish Theological Seminary, 26
Jim Crow, 21, 49

K

Kansas, 48–49
Kellogg-Briand Treaty, 6
Kentucky, 49–50
King ranch, 74
Know-Nothing Party, 24
Korean War, 8, 144–145
Kosovo War, 12–13
Ku Klux Klan, 50

L

labor unions
    AFL and CIO merger, 8
    American Federation of Labor founded, 5
    Congress of Industrial Organizations founded, 7
    Knights of Labor, 46
    Matewan Massacre, 78
    Mother Jones, 78
    restrictions, under Taft-Hartley Act, 8
    Teamsters, 8, 55
    United Auto Workers (UAW), 54
    United Mine Workers, 78
    Western Federation of Miners, 45
Lewis and Clark expedition, 3, 58, 58, 72
libraries, 71
Lincoln-Douglas Debates, 4
Little Big Horn, Battle of , 5
lotteries —see gambling
Louisiana, 50
Louisiana Purchase, 18, 58, 65, 72, 78
Love Canal, 64

M

Maine, 51
Marines, U.S., 130–131
Maryland, 2, 51–52, 69
Massachusetts, 52–53
Mayflower Compact, 2
Mayo Clinic, 55
McCaughey septuplets
McCoy-Hatfield feud, 50
McDonalds (hamburger restaurant), 47
medicare, 9
Mexican War, 4, 73, 136–137
Mexico, 1, 73

Nuclear Freeze demonstration at UN, 11
SALT I Treaty, 10
SALT II Treaty, 10
Treaty of Guadalupe Hidalgo, 27
Treaty of Paris, 3
Treaty of Portsmouth, 5
Treaty of Versailles, 6, 101, 141
tunnels
    Holland Tunnel, 61

U

underground railway, 21
unemployment
    Coxey's Army, 5
    worst since Great Depression, 11
uranium, 62, 75
U.S. Steel, 5
Utah, 74–75

V

Vermont, 75–76
vice presidents, 123–124
Vietnam War
    draft evaders pardoned, 10
    general chronology, 145–149
    Gulf of Tonkin Resolution, 9, 106, 146
    My Lai Massacre, 9
    Pentagon Papers published, 10
    Vietnamization, 9
Vinland, 1

Virginia, 2, 76–77
Virginia House of Burgesses, 2
volcanoes, 68, 77

W

Walt Disney World, 43
War of 1812, 135
War on Poverty, 9
Wars
    general chronology, 134
    see also specific wars
Washington (state), 77–78
Washington, D.C., 79–80
Watergate scandal, 10, 107
West Point, U.S. Military Academy at, 3, 63
West Virginia, 77–78
Weyerhaeuser Corporation, 77
Wisconsin, 78
women in the military, 134
women's rights movement, 63, 70
women's suffrage, 4, 45, 49, 68, 79
Woodstock, 9
workmen's compensation, 52
World War I, 139–141
World War II, 141–144
world's fairs, 57, 64, 73, 77
Wyoming, 4, 79

Z

zoot suits, 27

Name Index

Braugher, Andre, 222
Braun, Carol Moseley, 47
Brazil, Jeff, 169
Breathed, Berke, 177
Breckinridge, John C., 124
Breen, Stephen P., 177
Brennan, Walter, 199
Breslin, Jimmy, 170
Brett, George, 245
Brewer, Gay, Jr., 255
Bridger, Jim, 74, 79
Brier, Royce, 167
Brink, Carol Ryrie, 194
Brinkley, Joel, 172
Britz, Jerilyn, 257
Broder, David S., 169
Broderick, Matthew, 214
Brodie, John, 250
Bromfield, Louis, 181
Brooke, Edward W., 197
Brooks, Gwendolyn, 189
Brooks, James L., 206
Brooks, Mark, 255
Brooks, Milton, 177
Brooks, Van Wyck, 185
Brough, Louise, 271
Brown, Caro, 168
Brown, Jim, 250
Brown, John, 4, 33, 48, 78
Brown, Larry, 250
Brown, Lee, 74
Brown, Marcia, 195–96
Brown, Ruth, 214
Browne, Malcolm W., 172
Bruce, Robert V., 186
Bruce, William Cabell, 187
Brule, Etienne, 53
Bruzelius, Nils, 169
Bryan, William Jennings, 33, 59, 123
Bryant, Deborah Irene, 225
Brynner, Yul, 202
Buchanan, Edna, 169
Buchanan, James, 75, 95–96, 115, 120
Buchwald, Art, 170
Buck, Paul Herman, 185
Buck, Pearl S., 181
Budge, Don, 269
Bueno, Maria, 271
Buferd, Marilyn, 225
Buley, R. Carlyle, 185
Bullard, F. Lauriston, 174
Bunche, Ralph J., 197
Bunker, Earl L., 177
Burck, Jacob, 176

Burger, Warren E., 55
Burke, Frances Marie, 225
Burke, Jack, Jr., 254, 255
Burke, William, 252
Burkemo, Walter, 254
Burleigh, Harry T., 196
Burns, George, 205
Burns, James McGregor, 186
Burns, John F., 173
Burr, Aaron, 61, 122
Burr, Raymond, 216
Burroughs, Jeff, 245
Burrows, Abe, 183
Burrows, Edwin G., 186
Burstyn, Ellen, 204, 210
Burton, Richard, 212
Burton, Virginia Lee, 195
Bush, George H.W., 11, 34, 51, 75,
    110–111, 119, 122–124
Bush, George W., 13
Butler, Robert N., 191
Butler, Robert Olen, 182
Butterfield, Alexander, 232
Buttons, Red, 202
Buxton, Frank, 174
Byars, Betsy, 194

C

Cabot, John, 1, 51–52
Cabrillo, Juan Rodriguez, 40
Caen, Herb, 179
Caesar, Sid, 218, 228
Cage, Nicholas, 207
Cagney, James, 200
Cahn, Robert, 171
Caine, Michael, 206
Caldwell, Nathan G., 171
Caldwell, William A., 169
Caldwell, Zoe, 209, 210, 211
Calhoun, John C, 33, 71, 124.
Calley, William, 9
Callum, John, 213
Callvert, Ronald G., 174
Calvert, Cecilius, 51
Cameron, James, 208
Camilli, Dolph, 243
Caminiti, Ken, 244
Camp, John, 179
Campanella, Roy, 243
Campbell, Benjamin Nighthorse, 42
Campbell, Earl, 251
Campbell, Glen, 223
Campbell, Mary, 225
Campbell, Robert, 170

Canseco, Jose, 246
Capers, Robert S., 180
Capers, Virginia, 213
Capone, Alphonse, 6
Capra, Frank, 199
Captain & Tennile, 223
Cardoza, Norman F., 175
Carew, Rod, 245
Carey, Pete, 173
Cariou, Len, 213
Carlson, Gretchen, 226
Carner, JoAnne, 257
Carnes, Kim, 224
Carney, Art, 204
Caro, Robert A., 188
Carollo, Russell, 171
Carpenter, Teresa, 179
Carraway, Hattie W., 40
Carson, Johnny, 230, 233
Carson, Kit, 61
Carter, Elliot, 192
Carter, Hodding, 174
Carter, Jimmy, 10, 44, 108–109, 119,
    122, 123
Carter, Kevin, 179
Carter, Ovie, 172
Cartier, Jacques, 1
Carvalho, George de, 167
Carver, Brent, 214
Carver, George W., 196
Casey, Ron, 175
Cash, Kellye, 226
Casper, Billy, 253, 255
Cass, Lewis, 123
Castro, Fidel, 27, 28
Cather, Willa, 181
Cato, 21
Catton, Bruce, 185
Cavarretta, Phil, 243
Cavazos, Lauro F., 28
Cavelier, Rene-Robert, 47, 49, 50, 56,
    58, 65–66, 71
Cepeda, Orlando, 244
Cermak, Anton J., 7, 43, 127
Cernan, Eugene, 235
Chaffee, Roger B., 235
Chakiris, George, 202
Chamberlain, Wilt, 247
Chambers, Lenoir, 174
Champlain, Samuel de, 75
Chancellor, John, 230, 232
Chandler, Alfred D. Jr., 186
Chandler, Spud, 245
Chaney, James, 9, 22, 56

Hughes, Langston, 30, 197
Hughes, R. John, 172
Hull, Jennifer, 201
Humes, Edward, 180
Humphrey, Hubert, 55, 121, 123, 124
Hunt, Guy, 39
Hunt, Helen, 207, 222, 223
Hunt, Henry A., 197
Hunt, Irene, 194
Hunt, Joseph, 269
Hunt, Linda, 206
Hunt, Martita, 208
Hunter, Holly, 207
Hunter, Kim, 201
Hurt, William, 206
Husa, Karel, 192
Huston, Anjelica, 206
Huston, John, 201
Huston, Margo, 168
Huston, Walter, 201
Hutchins, Coleen Kay, 225
Hutchison, Jock, 254
Hutton, Timothy, 205
Huxtable, Ada Louise, 169
Hylton, Thomas J., 175
Hyman, Trina Schart, 196

I

Inge, William, 183
Ingrassia, Paul, 180
Irons, Jeremy, 207, 210
Irwin, Hale, 253
Ison, Chris, 169
Issac, Rhys L., 186
Ives, Burl, 202
Ives, Charles E., 192

J

Jackson, Andrew, 3, 38, 50, 72, 92, 114, 122, 127
Jackson, Glenda, 204, 218
Jackson, Harold, 175
Jackson, Helen Hunt, 19
Jackson, Jesse, 10, 23, 26, 34, 198
Jackson, Jimmie Lee, 23
Jackson, Maynard, Jr., 44
Jackson, Michael, 224
Jackson, Reggie, 245
Jackson, Robert H., 177
Jacobi, Derek, 210
Jacobs, Helen, 271
Jaffe, Louis Isaac, 174
Jagger, Dean, 201
James, Henry, 187

James, Howard, 171
James, Jesse, 57
James, Marquis, 187
James, Sheryl, 180
James, Will, 193
Jameson, Betty, 256
Jamieson, Francis A., 167
Jannings, Emil, 198
January, Don, 254
Janzen, Lee, 253
Jaspin, Elliot G., 168
Jaworski, Leon, 10
Jayroe, Jane Anne, 225
Jefferson, Margo, 170
Jefferson, Thomas, 3, 33, 76, 90, 112–113, 122
Jemison, Mae Carol, 236
Jensen, Jackie, 245
Joel, Billy, 224
Johns, Glynis, 213
Johnson, Andrew, 4, 73, 96–97, 115, 122, 124–125
Johnson, Ben, 204
Johnson, Haynes, 171
Johnson, James W., 197
Johnson, John H., 197
Johnson, Josephine W., 181
Johnson, Lyndon B., 9, 34, 76, 96–97, 118, 124, 231
Johnson, Magic, 248
Johnson, Malcolm, 167
Johnson, Mordecai W., 197
Johnson, Nicole, 226
Johnston, Alva, 167
Joio, Norman Dello, 192
Joliet, Louis, 2, 40, 46, 78
Jolson, Al, 6
Jones, Alex S., 180
Jones, Bill T., 32
Jones, Bobby, 252
Jones, Cherry, 211
Jones, Chipper, 244
Jones, Elizabeth Orton, 195
Jones, Howard Mumford, 191
Jones, James Earl, 209, 211, 221
Jones, Jennifer, 200
Jones, Jennifer, 200
Jones, "Mother" Mary, 78
Jones, Quincy, 224
Jones, Russell, 172
Jones, Shirley, 202
Jones, Tommy Lee, 207
Jones, William Hugh, 168
Jordan, Barbara, 198

Jordan, Michael, 248
Julian, Dr. Percy L., 197
Jusserand, J.J., 184
Just, Ernest E., 196
Justice, Donald, 190

K

Kahane, Meir, 26, 128
Kahn, Madeline, 211
Kakutani, Michiko, 170
Kamin, Blair, 170
Kamm, Henry, 172
Kammen, Michael, 186
Kane, Carol, 219
Kani, John, 210
Kann, Peter R., 172
Kantor, MacKinlay, 181
Kaplan, John, 179
Kaplan, Justin, 188
Karmin, Monroe, 171
Karnow, Stanley, 186
Kase, Max, 179
Kaufman, George S., 183
Kazan, Elia, 201, 202
Keats, Ezra Jack, 195
Kedrova, Lila, 203
Keeler, Bob, 180
Kefauver, Estes, 229
Keiser, Herman, 255
Keith, Damon, 198
Keith, Harold, 194
Keller, Bill, 173
Kelly, Eric P., 193
Kelly, George, 183
Kelly, Grace, 201
Kelly, Nancy, 209
Kelly, Paul, 208
Kelly, Thomas J. III, 178
Kempton, Murray, 170
Kennan, George F., 185, 188
Kennedy, Carolyn Bessette, 53
Kennedy, Edward M., 9, 231
Kennedy, George, 203
Kennedy, Joey, 175
Kennedy, John F., 9, 34, 53, 74, 78, 105–106, 118, 127, 188
Kennedy, John F., Jr., 53
Kennedy, Robert F., 9, 41
Kennedy, William, 182
Kennerly, Dave, 178
Kerby, Philip, 175
Kernis, Aaron Jay, 193
Kerr, Walter, 169
Kerry, Bob, 59

Wilder, Billy, 200, 202
Wilder, L. Douglas, 77, 198
Wilder, Thornton, 181, 183
Wilford, John Noble, 171
Wilkerson, Isabel, 180
Wilkins, Roy, 197
Wilkinson, Signe, 177
Will, George F., 169
Willard, Nancy, 194
Wille, Lois, 175
Williams, Clarence, 179, 180
Williams, G. Mennen, 54
Williams, Jesse Lynch, 182
Williams, Paul R., 197
Williams, Robin, 208
Williams, Roger, 2. 33, 70
Williams, Serena, 272
Williams, T. Harry, 188
Williams, Ted, 245
Williams, Tennessee, 183
Williams, Vanessa, 226
Williams, Wayne B., 44
Williams, William Carlos, 190
Williams, William T.B., 197
Williamson, Michael, 191
Willkie, Wendell, 123
Wills, Garry, 191
Wills, Helen, 271
Wills, Maury, 243
Wilson, August, 184
Wilson, Edward O., 191
Wilson, Forrest, 187
Wilson, Henry, 124
Wilson, Lanford, 184
Wilson, Margaret, 181
Wilson, Pete, 41
Wilson, Richard, 170
Wilson, Woodrow, 6, 33, 61, 100–101, 117, 121, 227

Windom, Willliam, 217
Winslow, Ola Elizabeth, 187
Winters, Shelley, 202, 203
Winwood, Steve, 224
Wise, Robert, 203
Wisniewski, David, 196
Woestendiek, John, 169
Wofford, Harris, 70
Wojciechowska, Maja, 194
Wolfe, Linny Marsh, 187
Wolfert, Ira, 172
Woltman, Frederick, 167
Wonder, Stevie, 223, 224
Wood, Craig, 252, 255
Wood, Gordon S., 186
Woods, Tiger, 256
Woodson, Carter G., 197
Woodward, C. Vann, 186
Woodward, Joanne, 202
Woosnam, Ian, 256
Worsham, L., 252
Worth, Irene, 209
Wouk, Herman, 181
Wright, Charles, 190
Wright, Don, 176
Wright, James, 190
Wright, Louis T., 197
Wright, Mickey, 257
Wright, Orville, 5, 65, 67
Wright, Richard, 197
Wright, Teresa, 200
Wright, Wilbur, 5, 65, 67
Wu Dunn, Sheryl, 173
Wuorinen, Charles W., 192
Wurdemann, Audrey, 189
Wyatt, Jane, 216
Wyler, William, 200, 202
Wyman, Jane, 201

Y

Yamasaki, Taro M., 178
Yardley, Jonathan, 170
Yastrzemski, Carl, 245
Yates, Elizabeth, 194
Yergan, Max, 197
Yergin, Daniel, 191
Yoder, Edwin M., 175
York, Michael M., 169
York, Robert, 176
Young, Andrew, 198
Young, Brigham, 46. 74
Young, Charles, 196
Young, Coleman A., 54, 198
Young, Ed, 196
Young, Gig, 205
Young, John, 235
Young, Loretta, 200, 215, 216
Young, Robert, 215, 216, 217
Young, Steve, 251
Yount, Robin, 245, 246
Yulee, David Levy, 25

Z

Zaharias, Babe, 256, 257
Zangara, Guiseppe , 7
Zaturenska, Marya, 189
Zelinsky, Paul O., 196
Zemach, Margot, 196
Zemeckis, Robert, 207
Zemlianichenko, Alexander, 179
Zenger, John Peter, 2, 62
Zindel, Paul, 184
Zinnemann, Fred, 201, 203
Zoeller, Fuzzy, 256
Zucchino, David, 180
Zwilich, Ellen T., 193
Zworykin, Vladimir, 227

About the Author

Jerry Bornstein worked for fifteen years at NBC News as an archivist and senior researcher in the NBC News Reference Library. He researched and wrote a number of background books for internal use by NBC News journalists and the *NBC News/Rand McNally World News Atlas* (1989-1992). He is the author of seven other books on topics ranging from police brutality to neo-nazism to the Berlin Wall. He has also worked as a freelance journalist, with articles published in the *New York Daily News* magazine section, *The Progressive*, and *Harper's Weekly*. He currently works as an assistant professor on the Newman Library faculty at Baruch College, the City University of New York, where he serves as liaison to the Journalism Program and the School of Public Affairs. In the Journalism Program, Prof. Bornstein teaches electronic research courses for undergraduate and graduate students. He is the author of a recent study on ethical dilemmas confronted by librarians in the news media.